Things Were Different
In Royce's Day

Things Were Different In Royce's Day

Royce S. Pitkin as Progressive Educator:
A Perspective From Goddard College, 1950 - 1967

Forest K. Davis

Adamant Press
Adamant, Vermont USA
1996

Library of Congress Cataloging-in-Publication Data

Davis, Forest K., 1918-
    Things were different in Royce's day : Royce S. Pitkin as
progressive educator, a perspective from Goddard College, 1950-1967
/ Forest K. Davis.
        p.   cm.
    Includes bibliographical references and index.
    ISBN 0-912362-17-0
    1. Pitkin, Royce S. 2. Goddard College--Presidents--Biography.
3. Progressive education--Vermont--History.   I. Pitkin, Royce S.
II. Title.
LD2001.G4517P583   1996
378.743'4--dc20   96-5973
                                                            CIP

Dustjacket design: The Laughing Bear Associates, Inc., Montpelier, Vermont 05602
Dustjacket drawing: Edward Epstein, Montpelier, VT 05602
Typography by Accura Printing, Barre, Vermont 05641
Printed by L. Brown & Sons, Barre, Vermont 05641

Published by Adamant Press, Box 7, Adamant, Vermont 05640 USA

ACKNOWLEDGMENTS AND APPRECIATIONS

Grateful acknowledgment is made to the Vermont Historical Society for the use of the archive on Royce S. Pitkin held by its Library, to the Librarians for a great many courtesies, and to William E. Osgood, for his extensive work in cataloguing the collection over a considerable period of time. Mrs. Helen Pitkin, who deposited the papers with VHS some years ago, has been much interested in studies made of her late husband; students of his life and work are immeasurably in her debt. Our thanks go also to her and to members of her family.

An address made by the author on the occasion of the opening of the papers for use at VHS Library in May, 1994 was condensed by the editors of the April 1995 issue of Vermont History NEWS, a small periodical of the Society, for reasons of space. The full text of this brief piece, slightly revised, reappears here as the Introduction immediately following.

– Forest K. Davis
August lst, 1995

CONTENTS

PART ONE

The Things That Were Different

INTRODUCTION

Royce S. Pitkin's Goddard College, the Plainfield institution of the years 1938-1969, grew in new and distinctive forms. Some have endured; some have appeared in other colleges and universities, modified or not; some are at risk of being forgotten. Some of his educational methods are also at risk of being forgotten.

The purpose of education, Tim often said, is to establish the conditions for learning. Students have to learn by themselves. Learning enables change. Change was what interested Tim most. It was as if individual originalities produced imbalance in the social matrix. Learning should be encouraged as movement toward balance. Balance is relative; individual initiative and originality figure in the mix. Change is necessary for society to realize new possibilities.

Tim lived at the center of a vortex. Around him things happened all the time. People think of him as a disciple of John Dewey. Dewey's writings were read and discussed in his classes. But the teacher of whom Tim spoke most frequently was William Heard Kilpatrick, Dewey's colleague at Teachers College, with whom Tim had pursued some graduate studies. Kilpatrick wrote some things. Mostly he talked. Tim, who also wrote some things, mostly talked as well. From the beginning he worked in the discussion format with groups of interested persons. He would do this all his life. It was his mode of expression. In the Junior College years at the Goddard Seminary campus in Barre (1935-1938) he brought together the Vermonters who helped with ideas and plans for the college and the move to Greatwood Farm in Plainfield.

He had arrived at Goddard Seminary with a social philosophy of how education worked best. He would develop and refine it year by year. It entailed a social metaphysics, a position on what was really real. He would not have been captivated by this description; he might have been amused by it. His emphasis would always be on the social realities of what worked best in the educational dimension. This meant, what worked at Goddard College.

Goddard became an experimental college; it was his greatest aim for it – trying new ways in education, working out new methods, forms and programs. In the end it was his great achievement.

If it was in the nature of Tim's thought and practice to work with other people, who were his associates? The Goddard faculty met weekly in his living rooms, looking out on Vermont scenes of field and wood, parts of which would later become the second campus. The discussions were intense, centering on issues which needed solutions - major learning experiences for participants. Tim was a great hand to work off opposing viewpoints against each other, achieving resolutions through dialogue, compromise or voted choice. Students were a major source of learning. Tim was part of the learning process. He made choices and took sides. He conducted many an argumentative session in community meetings with students who were determined to know best and do better. Sometimes the discussions were political. He could take an unpopular side and come out ahead by keeping the questions open until everyone else went to sleep. He did not believe in letting go of crucial issues. Solutions were forthcoming partly from his inherent force and partly from strategic endurance.

He did not always have to win. He tried hard to win; no doubt he did win most of the time. But he was willing to strive over the issues. He was willing to try things of which he profoundly disapproved. He would bounce down the corridor from his office in the silo, singing a 19th century hymn in a melodious baritone, stop at a door where some of us were – pausing suddenly in his music, a scowl spreading over his face – and say with emphasis, "Oh, about (such-and-such), you understand that I am *not happy about this.* – But you can try it. We will see later how it works." And he would be off again down the stairs, hymn resuming, leaving us speechless and wondering how we had escaped the judgment. Royce never fired anyone in the heat of conflict. Rather, he contested the issues and made something useful come of them. But we all understood that at the end of contract periods there would be performance evaluations. Nothing was permanent at Goddard unless it was the process among persons by which realities emerged from possibility.

He was gracious in his learning. We have all heard him say how much he learned from colleagues, – about India from Thomas Yahkub, about education from George Beecher, about counselling from Robert Mattuck, about writing from Wilfrid Hamlin, about college admissions from John Hall, – from students about every last thing. Yet at times it seemed that he knew more about our several jobs than we did. If Goddard was a learning situation – and it surely was – it could also be difficult. Sooner or later we all learned that the process of learning was hard work.

Goddard was not the end of anything. It was the beginning. The impacts Tim made upon the world only began there. They were felt nearby and far away, by resonance, by direct transfer, by adaptation. He was a moving force in the founding of educational networks and consortia among colleges and universities in Vermont and across the country, always in the interest of educational progress and change. He was totally uninterested in ceremonies. He wanted to talk about education. He did that. Wherever he went, his presence was felt. He believed in the metaphysics of the dialectic. He gave it a new force and a new reality at home and overseas.

Notice a distinctive element in the dialectical force which Royce exerted. There was a sharp difference in the way he conducted an exchange. In his discussion method the purpose was to produce change. He might be gentle or he might be rough. His aim was to make a difference. It was not necessary to involve everyone in the process. Effective discussion had a price. Feelings of participants could be hurt. People could be left out. Not everyone had a say. The discussion was to lead to an objective, an effect, a difference, perhaps to a new beginning. It was supposed to do this. The intention was to get somewhere. The price was to be paid.

The history of Royce Pitkin's educational ideas and their applications might be told in terms of the college at Greatwood Farm, with its amazing dimensions of outreach domestic and foreign. It might be told in terms of the networks and consortia. It might be told in the perspectives expressed by his students. Do we suppose that his impact was principally on higher education? It should be remembered that several generations of Goddard students went out to teach in kindergartens and elementary schools and in high schools of differing kinds. Tim often spoke with deep respect of the accomplishments of teachers in high schools. He felt that they had harder jobs and heavier responsibilities by far than did college teachers. His students who did these things only took him at his word.

Eventually his ideas and their consequences would bespeak the major currents of educational thought and practice at all levels and in several cultures. His work would begin to redefine the liberal arts, shifting their centers of gravity by a little. The understanding we have of education is different today from what it would have been without his long labors and his great force. If Goddard College was Royce Pitkin's educational thought writ large, so was the web of relationships he built among people in the interest of genuine education. He could and did cut educational nonsense to the bone. Perhaps his greatest gift to those who followed him was to make it possible for them to perceive the contrasts in educational thought and application, between what was nonsense and what was genuine. If there is a central theme he taught, it is not that he changed the face of education in our time – although he did that. It is that by becoming able to perceive contrasts and take sides we may be able to change its face again in times to come.

PREFACE

Statement of the Study

This study is an effort to identify what Royce Pitkin did in his 31 years at Goddard College, - even more to the point, how he did it. It takes as its major focus his ideas, how he thought about education and what he did about it, how he thought about people and what he did about them. It is an individual approach, necessary, perhaps to one person's understanding of the little college at Greatwood Farm that marked so profoundly the lives of a generation of colleagues on the faculty and staff and of some seven — nearly eight — college generations of students and graduates.

Be clear that had Tim Pitkin been doing the study, this is not how he would have gone about it. He was an intensely practical person; he did not start with ideas. Ideas had their place, and they served him in ways that enabled and assisted in what he wanted to do. Trial and error in the hypothetical stages of undertakings would have been such a way. He also had a philosophy of his own, though he did not spend much time on its details, and more immediately, sets of assumptions of the kind that become reflective systems. He was not philosophically restricted except as he restricted his own forays into the realm of idea-systems, in the interest of attending closely and constantly to what he really wanted to do. The metaphor which comes to mind here is of a formidable figure off about his daily business unmindful of a wake of trailing sparks. That was more or less what Royce expected of ideas. They were useful enough in their place, and they made their contribution, but their job was to keep up with him, not his to keep up with them.

It is not really possible to separate Tim Pitkin from Goddard College, at least not from this perspective. As soon as he arrived at the Seminary in Barre, Vermont in 1935 he started to think about it; from that point on it evolved. He had been thinking before about a junior college, perhaps one for women; he had been headmaster at the New London, N. H. high school, in close proximity to the New London private school for women, so he had reason to think about it. It would in time become the Colby-Sawyer College known today in New London. Of course Tim was thinking about such a school in Vermont. Goddard became that school, that opportunity. It became it because he took hold of it and shook it. He had attended Goddard Seminary himself in years past as a secondary or high school student. So had other members of his family; so had other people he knew. There was nothing unfamiliar about it. As soon as he was ready with a junior college idea for Vermont he showed up, knocking on doors in Barre to talk with the trustees. That was where it started. But even this was not the real beginning. He had been engaged already in New London in the types of small-group meetings and discussions of social issues with local citizens that were to become his trademark. One can see well enough how it all began.

We have long thought that there should be a series of books about Royce and about Goddard. Each of us who worked with him had and still has an individual view of him and of it. Any of us could easily write a book about both. This one is ours — one that came to mind in the small hours as such things commonly do. It has been said often enough that a book is only an extension of an individual position; a series of books would be then only an extended discussion. Some things have been written about Goddard and about Royce Pitkin, to be sure. Ann Giles Benson and Frank Adams have produced *To Know For Real: Royce S. Pitkin and Goddard College* (1987), an oral history cast in Tim's words for the most part, based on notes and on extended personal interviews with him. It has an autobiographical flavor, although it is not an autobiography. Neither is it quite a history, although it has history in it. It has biographical material in it as well, though it is not a biography. At present there is no history as such of Goddard, just as there is no biography as such of Royce Pitkin. The latter was attempted once but never came off. The former is in process even now; it is to be hoped that it will come off properly. As soon as it is done someone else should write another, and so on. Books are parts of the social dialectic. We need a lot of them for anything that matters.

The period at Goddard from which the perspective of this study derives is 1950-1967. These were the years we were at the College. Notice that the perspective referred to is not that *on* these 17 years. These were the years *from* which the perspective derives. We shall feel free to write about the earlier years, even the later years — though surely less of the latter, knowing, as we do, much less about them. It is a conceptual matter, something to be aware of but by which in the nature of things one is not limited.

A case could be made that 1950-1967 were the great years of the College. Royce was at his prime in those years; circumstances began to move his way in that period. The point need not be labored; it could be debated. It will be helpful to review aspects of Goddard history well before that time, and we shall. But notice several cautions.

The plan of the study is to cast it in parallel lines, fitting the lines to the major strains of thought and practice reflected in what Royce did in and through Goddard College. The awkwardness of having to work one's way

several times through the thirty years of his leadership (thirty-one if his retirement year with its world travel is to be counted - a gift of the Trustees in
his honor) is hardly to be denied. A straight history of "Goddard", hereinafter
often to be referred to as "the College", would be more likely to find its approach in a single chronology, perhaps selecting a succession of outstanding
periods of its development for examination, reserving the divisions for content
internal to each period. Here the repetition would lie in the themes in which
Royce and others worked rather than in the time-sequences. No one approach is clearly superior to another. Reasonably, future writers about Royce
Pitkin and about Goddard might devise approaches different from either of
these. Royce would have said the same.

Further, it may appear from this undertaking that there never was anyone
else on campus except Royce Pitkin during the period of his presidency, simply because the present method does not call for a study of his colleagues and
associates. This is a risk we shall have to take. It will lessen somewhat in the
late 1950s and following when the several divisions of the College were set up
and parts of the reports began to be written by division heads. The intent of
this effort is to identify what Royce did and what he thought. Other books
can surely be usefully written about different aspects of this great time in the
history of the College. It gave rise to many things, some of them associated
with particular persons, some a consequence of certain configurations of time,
place and circumstance. For the moment what is proposed as the focus of this
study is sufficient. It may even help to enable a succession of differing approaches. Royce is sure to have been open to just such an interpretation. He
was fully taken up with his own concerns, but he was very much aware of the
variant approaches and interpretations of persons other than himself. He greatly liked to contest the issues as he and his associates conceived of them; he had
an enormous respect for persons who disagreed with him, or those whose efforts differed from his. He might not always have said so, especially in the
midst of a discussion in which he had an interest. It might not have been pol-
itic. It was, however, central to his educational philosophy and to its vectors.
It lay at the root of his regard for students, and of his pursuit of educational
methods and policies which assured them of the central place in educational
thought and practice. It was a fundamental principle of all his work and
thought. Without its leavening resonance his mode of educational dialectic
would have been far different from its reality.

Certain aspects of Goddard operations with which Royce was heavily concerned we shall pass over - budgets and finance, for example, for reasons of
lack of competence. Other students of the College will have to deal with
them. As we find things which Tim wrote which bear on the educational
ideas and practices which constitute the central focus of the present study, we
will draw them in. Clearly this will lead to a substantial appendix section, designated later on as Part Two.

Notice that this study, as initially conceived, does not have as one of its objectives the definitive settling of every question with which it deals. Certainly

we have our opinions about some of them; when this is the case, we will state them for what they are worth. It is to be expected that other students of these times, this institution, and this central figure will have varied perspectives on people, elements and processes having roles here. They are by all means entitled to them. We shall read of them with interest. A thing we shall do often is suggest additional topics for study and research, directional as well as substantive, items that may be merely unclear at the present time with available sources, or for that matter, wholly unknown. Tim's involvement in the Institute for Individualized Education at SUNY-Empire State College was not only new to us, as it turned up in the archive, but led to recollections by former colleagues of still other involvements at Empire State of which we had never heard. One can not know when new and unexpected dimensions will turn up to confound the student who may have thought he had a fair grasp of a topic, only to discover lacunae of which he was not aware.

It remains to note a point of significance to the present effort. In the course of this study we shall refer to President Pitkin sometimes as Royce and sometimes as Tim. We do this on purpose; it is not a mistake or an oversight. In his adult years a great many people used 'Tim' as his name, no doubt because he told them to. It was nearly universal. He used it himself as a signature for personal notes and in exchanges on the College campus and among friends and relatives. When he had a document to sign, he signed it Royce S. Pitkin. He knew what his name was. In the Pitkin archive there is a notebook he constructed in the 4th grade with his name on it in his own hand, in just those formal terms. The probability is that he knew quite well the formidable nature of his impact in social situations. It was a disarming characteristic that any student on the Goddard campus could knock on his door and address him as an equal, by a nickname. Philosophically, he also believed in it. No doubt it helped him enormously all his life that he did what he did with his name.

He was a towering figure. He was also a person of modest height who thought himself the equal of every other person. It follows mathematically that every other person in a certain sense was his equal. It would not trouble him that we might speak of him now in one sense, now in another. – "I know the faculty hates me," he said once, in a wry moment, referring to the fact that faculty members had wills of their own and were obliged to contend with him for the room to move which often his determination denied them in the interest of focusing the institution on a central task. Of course he knew very well that the faculty did not hate him: they were very fond of him, though sometimes too gruff to say so. He has been gone some few years now. The time seems hardly a breath. As a personality he is as alive as ever he was.

This study reaches for the reasons. We may find them in the dialectic.

I

APPEARANCE OF THE MAJOR PROBLEMS

P rogressive has not always been a welcome term in education. Most recently it has applied to a period from early to mid-20th century in
which John Dewey and colleagues were working at Columbia University's Teachers College. A number of strands reached out from there to become what passes for a "movement" in a variety of institutions or parts of
them. Movement, too, has not always been a welcome term in education.
The reason for the negativity in these connections is probably the implication
that everything may not be perfect in education, and that some persons with
different ideas want to introduce change and move from things as they have
been to things as they might be – presumably better. To some, the implied
judgment is understandably unwelcome.

Years ago a paragraph was often quoted in histories of educational thought,
which purported to come from one of the early church fathers. It reflected
the concern of the teacher for gathering and holding the interest of students
during the teaching processes of fifteen hundred years ago (or so). Someone
even in a church setting and even so long ago somehow became aware of the
need for securing the attention of students in order to encourage learning. It is
possible that new things in education have indeed surfaced from time to time,
perhaps as a result of efforts by thoughtful and good teachers somewhat ac-
cidentally in local educational situations, although few records were kept of
them and little of permanent value was set aside as a consequence to help other teachers and learners in comparable circumstances later on.

If the ideas being taught in a particular time are thought to be more important than the people who are learning, and if the assumption is that the
formulations and descriptions of the nature of things are satisfactory in their
current forms, then perhaps the essence of the educational process will be held
to be transmission of traditional views, and there will not be much new

1

movement, culturally speaking, in most fields to bring about change in ideas and practices. Technological change, which may seem to occur more nearly by itself, may have an impact on the field of ideas; it may not be certain whether this is the effect of direct influence, whether the process is analogical, or even whether there is any connection at all between technology and reflective or general ideas.

Certain conditions in 1935 seem now to have been relatively restricted. More likely, they had not then developed beyond early stages. *Societal communications* probably occurred in islands of approximately common concern. Some of these islands were geographic, as in cities and parts of cities; some were educational, as in colleges and universities, some of which were within cities and others in rural areas. Innumerable variations applied as to sizes of islands, degrees of intensity as to common concerns, and placements with respect to settings. It is interesting to speculate on relative gains in communication in the millennium since the Middle Ages. Certain group configurations serving as grounds for communicational enablement might not have changed greatly, though they would have multiplied notably in numbers of instances. Societies were very much larger in 1935, for example, than they would have been in 935. There would simply have been more cases, more islands, more talk. When Royce Pitkin arrived in Barre nobody would have noticed him until he stepped onto their porches and rang their bells. There were telephones; he could have called them up. But he had explorational concerns; he wanted to speak with them personally. It was more effective - faster, more efficient, and allowed a focus more to the point. Did they think a junior college for women (girls, they were called) was a promising idea for the development of Goddard Seminary? Yes, they did. They would have been interested in almost any suggestion for helping their elderly school to reach for a new role in the city, in a time when competition between older private secondary schools and newly arriving public high schools was rising. The competition among these two groups of institutions, which occurred generally in New England and perhaps on the eastern seaboard, probably reflected a growth change in the relative sizes of social groups involved. It was one of those millennial consequences.

Calling on the trustees about the new junior college was certainly a very old form of initiating social communication, far older than a thousand years. Adventurous persons in 935 and long before would have known exactly what was going on as Tim approached the trustees of Goddard for the first time, centuries later.

He did not at once become head of Goddard Seminary. He became head of a junior college for women in the same place and in the same institution. After a while the principal of the Seminary (high school section) left, and he inherited that section as well. If faculty meetings included the entire Seminary group, the indications are that early faculty discussions did not reach anywhere near the sophistication and intensity levels which were common in faculty meetings in Plainfield later on. Something significant happened there.

Developing the new junior college for women confronted Royce with most of the major problems with which he would contend for the rest of his professional life, and if the truth were known, into his retirement. The story goes that after he retired, in a season when the College was in one of its financially dry periods, he conjured up $25,000 from personal insurance sources and loaned it to Goddard to get it out of one of its innumerable financial holes. He had always been interested in the potential of new kinds of insurance for educational support. Not much is known about this; it would be of interest to know if he inquired at all into the reasons for the dry spell, or if he gave anyone advice as to the problem. Most likely not; he had been in plenty of financial holes himself over the years; he would have had only sympathy for the difficulty, and he had an amazing restraint with persons who were in trouble. He probably just saw to it that the College got the money.[1]

Besides communications, then, *financial support* grew into one of the largest problem-areas in Tim's life. The period of heavy government aid to educational institutions in America lay ahead; indeed, Royce would have something original to do with shaping possibilities for governmental aid to education in the mid-century decades.

His attitude toward financial shortages appeared early in his management experience with educational institutions. Before the College was actually founded and moved to Plainfield, while he and it were still in Barre, he noted among the minutes and reports for the junior college a term which became representative of his approach to the condition of financial adversity: "perplexing". It was always a perplexing problem. Where were the needed funds to come from? Whom could he approach for the support? Educational bills - salaries, food costs, board and room overhead for students, building repairs, new residential space construction, program expenses - the myriad burdens that landed on the desk of the central administrator, constituted a perplexing problem. Progressive education theorists have long drawn flak for making everything that has to be done into a "problem". The term refers simply to a configuration of needed tasks. It is a useful handle and earns its way in common usage. The need to raise money was always present in the history of the College. The president in the last analysis had to do it. He was the one who spoke for the institution. Only the larger, well-supported universities could afford to assign to second-level staffers the responsibilities of speaking for the institution.

From the one term which Tim used so often to describe the difficulties of fund-raising we begin to see the approach he took to face down what might otherwise have been a fearsome recurrent condition, the insufficient supply of money. "Perplexing": notice what this did for him as he faced almost alone the dreaded burden of not having enough funds. It transformed an agonizing

---

[1] This story comes from John Hall, longtime staffer at Goddard and SUNY-Empire State College in a variety of posts, and president of Goddard in the late 1970s. The chances are that he had the best of reasons to know about it.

situation into a very ordinary "problem", something an administrator could simply address in the normal course as one more of the difficulties for which a solution needed to be found as soon as he could conveniently get around to it. If he needed to go grocery shopping first, or talk to someone who wanted to see him, or do some other needed thing, that would work most of the time. He could see to the fund-raising when time permitted. It was just another problem to work on. We don't really know of course whether he actually taught himself how not to worry. We may – and do – think he did. It would be difficult otherwise to account for his ability to work with a large number of different questions all of which required solutions in the reasonable future. Worry can kill administrators; he would surely have needed to defend himself against its ravages. From long association we think he acquired the ability to cope with very difficult problems but to have a good time doing enjoyable things even while he managed them.

Problems in *admissions* confronted Royce Pitkin from his earliest times with the junior college in Barre; they would always be a major concern as the years went by with the four-year college in its Plainfield phases. Just when it appeared that the new junior college in Barre was ready to roll, with faculty on hand and at least some facilities, he discovered an embarrassing fact: there were very few students. This came to notice, fortunately, in the spring of the year in which the institution expected to open. He had a few months to do something about it. It would prove entirely typical of his attitude toward crises that he jumped in personally with the staffers responsible and joined them in the activities which promised the best results. They all, Tim included, visited schools, followed up lists of various kinds, sent out publicity materials, and interviewed potential students and sources of students. When the dust settled weeks later there were some students - not any vast number, perhaps - but students. The new junior college could and did open.

It is embarrassing even now to remember the years in Plainfield when it appeared there would be too few students to make up a respectable class. One spring day in the early-1950s, probably soon after he had returned from a trip away on college business, he called in at the Admissions office to see how the fall enrolment was going. He never let the field of admissions go very long without checking. It had been a "problem" too long to be neglected. In those days Goddard was not a member of the New England Association of Colleges and Secondary Schools - which is to say, in practical terms, it was not accredited. The New England Association claimed it did not accredit; it just admitted or declined to admit various institutions which applied for membership. It declined to admit Goddard to membership twice before acceding to the request in 1959. The College "came of age" that year; it was 21 years old in its four-year format, and it was admitted to the Association. It was accredited. Everyone knew that admission to membership amounted to accreditation; the Association knew; the College knew; the public knew. A celebration was held on campus.

All that was later. In the early-1950s when Royce called in to see how many admissions the College had, it turned out there were just 17. Now that is the sort of thing that could cause an earthquake. Precisely why was this? Had we been on enough field trips to talk to schools? Had we interviewed enough young people? Talked to enough sources? After all, there were things one could and should do when there were not enough students. They had all been done before; people knew what most of them were. What plans did we have for doing them? The chances are quite good that a number of them got under way rather suddenly. The enrolment, we seem to recall, did rise a bit, perhaps to 23. The year lingered in memory for a long time as one of under-achievement in the field of admissions.

There were years when the entering classes were not much larger than that, though that was probably a record. It happened even after 1959; admissions improved, but the problem lingered. There were years even then when Royce joined in the admissions effort by combining trips west and south so that admissions visits and interviews could be done even while he was making educational addresses in others of his roles as an educational leader. He might approve arrangements for several staffers at once to go on field trips. A certain amount of field work was investment in the future, undertaken to keep channels of communication open and field acquaintanceships operative with schools and community sources of students. There would come a bizarre time in the history of the College when admissions efforts were stopped; the process was turned over to students, who felt no burdens for keeping channels open for future years. They conducted interviews and made the immediate admissions decisions, and that was the end of it. Enrolments plummeted. But that was after Royce retired. We never heard what he thought about it. It would be like him never to say. The College could see later how it worked.

Royce's *faculty and student dialectic* does not appear in the records quite as early in his work with the development of the College as did the cluster of survival problems - communications, financial support, and admissions. In a way it belongs in *societal communications* as a phase of social exchange in the broadest sense. It was however a special case; the very nature of the College as an educational institution in the experimental category depended upon it. At once it carried forward and shaped the formation of Goddard; it was indispensable to what became of the College over a 30-year period. More than any other one thing, it was the creation of Royce Pitkin. The other major problems of the College were general problems; all colleges had them. They had to be solved or there was no college. The question with respect to them here is, how were they solved? What did Royce do with them? The *social dialectic* however was quite another thing. It was something that Tim did all by himself. It was his unique contribution to the life of the institution without which it would have been a different and a lesser place.

Of course it was never called a dialectic. It was sometimes called discussion, or discussion method. It was all written up in the educational literature of the progressive movement. As an approach it was familiar enough. A great many people did it, in a variety of ways. Royce would never have admitted there was anything unusual in what he did in discussion. He was always trying to emulate his own teachers, like William Heard Kilpatrick, who, he frequently said, had no peer in the field of discussion. In this retrospective contemplation, however, we enter a dissent from Royce's perspective. He was entitled to his view; it was his own; he believed in it. Nevertheless, in our view, and from a distance, what happened on the Goddard campus over a 30-year period was something qualitatively different from the run of even very good discussion modes of interchange. It had a kind of determined genius about it. Part of its shimmering quality lay in its unrelieved level of sustained discourse, on innumerable themes and topics, semester after semester, year after year, in the course of which innumerable "problems" were addressed. Part of it, therefore, was what he did, case by case and day by day, and part was the entity of his doing it, in a stretch of professional life 30 years long, during all of which his address to the mode and the energy he accorded it, never ceased.

It was indeed a great and remarkable thing that he did. Few if any of us who were on campus during those years understood the nature of his achievement at the time. As for Royce himself, he would never have given it the time of day. He would have brushed it off. He saw it in a different perspective: there were problems to solve, and this was how one went about solving them.

Faculty meetings were only one locus; community meetings were another; student meetings of all sorts, counseling encounters, committee meetings, administrative sessions, were still others. The thing has to be seen as a unity, to be grasped.

It is interesting to keep in mind what has been noted before, that social exchange seen as an enabling mode was relatively slower to appear in his professional life and work than were the handlings of the several practical problems of institutional survival. There will be opportunity to see this as the successive stages of the College unfold.

Lastly, there was *educational outreach*. The College even from its early days worked to dissolve the boundaries that commonly stand between campus and community. It reached out, and it went out. It invited the community in. The patterns of association widened, became numerous, complex. It can be seen in the President's Reports which form the backbone of his on-going history of the College. These are his distinctive accounts of events and trends in the history of Goddard. From time to time they become repositories for passages of educational philosophy appearing in the midst of reports of action programs. He would undertake to describe the programs and either in the course of doing so or as a setting for doing so, would provide the reflective rationales for them. In one of these, that for December 31st, 1965, when the College was entering on its first year as a two-campus institution, he re-stated the philosophy of the College as if for students and faculty to have in mind as they moved into a new and unprecedented phase. This single report, ostensibly written to the Trustees as perhaps most or all of the Quarterly and Annual Reports were, might in his mind have been intended for a more general reading audience. No one seems to remember, however, that the Reports were ever generally distributed. We shall reprint the 1965 Report (textual section), along with similar Reports from various periods, chiefly by himself, less often partially by staffers, at the time or in retrospect, to illustrate what Tim saw happening with programs and ideas interwoven to form the substance of a college.[2]

Stylistically, the president's reports are revealing of Tim's major interests as an educational leader. Very often he started with the outreach factors, how they played out and how they promised for the future. The future was always with him. He could endure hardship and despair as long as there was hope of an 'improved' future to come. Where local programmatic interests were involved, notice that so far as the residential college was concerned it was always the experimental programs which were of primary interest to him. Experimental aspects included the off-campus, non- or low-residency lines of programmatic development; they also marked the on-campus, residential programs. They may have developed most markedly in later years; wherever they were, they were clearly where his mind came down most times out of a hundred. There is some discussion to be pursued in connection with the category of "experimental" programs; we will return to it in the later treatment of George Beecher's section of the Goddard educational programs.

There is one more small problem in this early review of Tim's intellectual and programmatic roots: he often said, when accounting for his outreach toward the Danish folk high school movement, that it stemmed from a book he read while in his graduate doctoral program at Teachers College, Columbia University. Edgar W. Knight, Kenan professor of education at the University of North Carolina, was visiting professor again at Teachers College the year Tim was doing his doctoral residency there; he had taken a course with him earlier during his Master's degree studies. Knight had recently returned from Denmark and had written *Among the Danes*, a book in which Tim became much interested.[3]

Tim's way of describing how this happened was to say that he had been greatly "influenced" by Edgar Knight and by Knight's book about the Danes.

---

[2] Cf. Part Two (10). Tim wrote three quarterly reports and one annual report each year, respectively on September 30th, December 31st, and March 31st, with the annual reports being dated (after 1940) on June 30th. These reports are all available in the Royce S. Pitkin archive at the Vermont Historical Society in Montpelier, where Mrs. Helen Pitkin deposited them some years ago, and presumably in the archives of Goddard College in Plainfield, Vt. These accounts are based on the VHS materials in the first instance, the College copies being in reserve.

[3] Ann Giles Benson and Frank Adams tell this story in Tim's words in the Goddard book, *To Know for Real: Royce S. Pitkin and Goddard College*, Adamant, 1987. The Benson and Adams volume is a very engaging piece of writing on Royce and on Goddard. It not only has a great deal of indispensable material; it also captures remarkably the flavor of Tim's conversational style. Ann Giles Benson, daughter of H. Harry Giles, distinguished psychologist and educator of New York University and leader of many conferences in Goddard's winter programs, was a graduate of the residential undergraduate program at Goddard and eventually became a Methodist clergyperson in the Carolinas. Frank Adams began professional life as a journalist in the South, graduated from the adult studies program at Goddard, took other graduate studies and degrees, administered and taught at Goddard, and became an educator in the industrial cooperative movement. At this time he resided in the Boston area. He has published several books on social movements and their leaders: e.g., *Unearthing Seeds of Fire: The Idea of Highlander,* (with Myles Horton), Winston-Salem, 1975.

The concept of "influence" among people seems to us to fall short of any useful mark. The idea of "resonance" seems far more appropriate to illumine the process of transmission of ideas, as from teacher to student, or from student to teacher. The difference is encompassed in the idea of readiness of the learner to "hear" what is being said or to "see into" what is being written. Along these lines, it has to be granted that we do not know why the idea of educational outreach appealed to Tim when offered by Edgar Knight and by his book. The fact is, Tim remained interested in Danish folk education for the rest of his life. Three faculty members of the Danish folk high schools were appointed to teach at Goddard at intervals in the 1950s and '60s, and Tim himself eventually became involved in Scandinavian affairs and cultures and in their educational programs. In his later years, both when active and when "retired", he attended conferences on international adult education held in Europe, visiting Denmark himself more than once. As late as 1983 his interest in Grundtvig was as active as it had ever been.[4]

What the student of Royce Pitkin's work and ideas is left with is a conceptualization of individual development and growth much more complex and realistic than is envisioned by the misleading terms "influenced" or "influenced by". The concept of resonance presupposes a tendency or a decision on the part of the individual to move and respond in a certain direction, in a certain way. It involves something the individual does, as distinct from something done by someone else to an individual. This small problem can come up again for consideration in these pages if there is any need for it.

---

[4] Cf. *Grundtvig's Ideas in North America: Influences and Parallels.* Copenhagen, Det Danske Selskab, 1983. Pp.133 & ff. "An informal Comparison of the Educational Concepts of Grundtvig and Dewey." -Royce S. Pitkin.

II

Societal Communication

The first of the fundamental dimensions in which Royce Pitkin began to give expression to his individual vectors appears here. Recall that he had grown up on the family farm in Marshfield, Vermont, with all that that implies. Already the steps he had taken to move into larger social relations were numerous, shared with large elements in American and New England society. So far, there was nothing unusual. He had lived and gone to graduate school in New York City and New Haven. He had taught and administered in public schools in Woodsville, N.H. and Wallingford, Vermont before going to New London, N.H. This too was typical enough of persons starting teaching careers in Vermont or New England. Career placements aside for the moment, in which certain amounts of mobility were common for the times, conceptual awareness of islands of communication or lack of it in the 1930s may have been another story.

In broad terms, New England towns were still made up of ethnic groups which existed, often, within themselves and had little to do with groups outside their irregular borders. These were some of the cultural borders which Tim would strive all his life to break down by educational means. The young people in these areas would meet each other in schools. That was perhaps as much mutual encounter as there would be until years later. Even the churches tended to be mutually exclusive by reason of language and tradition. Tim was not a speaker of European languages any more than any other member of his Marshfield community. But something was different in his awareness of the need for intercultural exchange. He would go to some lengths in the 1950s to develop language experience and intercultural awareness through the Comparative Cultures program at Goddard. These efforts dealt for the most part with French and Spanish, making use of cultural residencies in Quebec and Puerto Rico, respectively, during non-resident winter work terms in January and February seasons. It is interesting to reflect now, after the passage of years, how the New England Association pounded at him and refused Goddard membership essentially because it did not have language programs which looked like theirs. The Comparative Cultures program was better than other language programs because of its social and cultural studies components carried on along with the language study components, for double credit or more. Never mind: stamp on the little upstart college; it does not look like us, so it must be a bad and a poor place. Fortunately that would go on only a decade or so before the educational snobbery was undone by the irresistible march of cultural change. Later in these pages we shall consider what happens to programs and groups in point of age and weariness and boredom. We need to know why there may not be any programs like Comparative Cultures in operation today.

In the 1930s colleges and businesses and other social institutions seemingly talked to each other rather little, except in line with their own special activities such as admissions to college or buying and selling goods. At Goddard that would all change. It was an uphill struggle, but it would change. After 1959 when the slow-minded higher educational community decided that it could no longer avoid speaking politely to Goddard, Royce initiated a series of consortial networks all of which were concerned with development in a variety of ways, finance, educational programs, educational studies. Membership was specialized; the colleges which had the potential for thinking in new ways were invited to join. We shall see later what some of these organizations were and what they did. The point now is to see that this was a significant new dimension for societal communication. The mode would spread in all directions.

The business community was another instance. Businesses and industries did not hobnob with colleges in the 1930s. Consider only two of the ranges in which the College worked with commercial enterprises. Tim had a distinct advantage over other college presidents in Vermont. He came off a Vermont farm. People knew who he was, and they were not afraid of him. He was one of them. He talked like them, wrote like them; in some ways he thought like them. One of the first adult education groups that appeared at Goddard once it entered its Plainfield phases was the Vermont Labor and Farm School. Tim had already discovered that citizens of communities in many occupations would come to discussion groups on campus to talk about problems which beset them. They were ready to consider new ideas, especially practical ones. It was called learning. For a while Goddard had the reputation of being scary, radical, un-Vermontlike. This was generalized nonsense. The Vermont Labor and Farm School registrants rolled off their farms and from their unions onto the campus in full-conference numbers regularly each January, blizzards or no, for the better part of twenty years. A staff office had to be assigned to make arrangements for them. We shall see later what they did and what they studied. They were something to see, – weathered, browned by sun and wind, leathery-faced and rough of hands from long years on the machines, hard-bitten, often, by rough experiences not only with the elements but with un-yielding social forces. These were the people who came to the Labor and Farm School – to talk about things like economics, government, community organization and development. These were people who could recognize a problem when they saw one; they were ready to face anything or anyone in order to get a handle on something that might be of help to them.

Then there was the Canadian-American Seminar for Management. This began from an idea of one of the Goddard trustees, so Tim said, who had had experience in the developmental and commercial sides of adult education. The idea was that middle-management persons from both Canadian and American firms, firms that were interested in the development of Canadian-American relations, closer and more intense relations, might conjoin in a con-ference setting to consider business, industrial and cultural dimensions and reaches of their and similar enterprises. The format which developed often in-cluded two to three days of conference meetings on the Goddard campus, with interspersed bus trips or air trips into Canada or to Washington, D.C., where the governmental networks of both countries enabled meeting with leadership figures for the study of issues central to the conference theme of that year. Tim was on a first-name basis with both Vermont senators in those years (George Aiken, Ralph Flanders); they could and did help significantly with appointments around the federal establishment. The Seminar could see about anyone it wanted to. Appointments in Canada proved handleable by di-rect approach; Canadian federal and provincial officials were eminently reach-able. They would invite the Seminar in to meet with the Ministers in charge of departments and would spend whatever time-periods were helpful to con-sider an issue seriously. The Ministers would come to the Plainfield campus now and then to meet with Seminar participants. Goddard was not teaching business and industrial subjects in the 1960s, but it proved possible to draw on faculty sources for social science topics and on outside consultants for tech-nical business and financial topics. The Seminars ran for a number of years without competition; eventually other universities began to see the values in the program. The University of Vermont and one or two institutions in the northern mid-west started similar programs. Goddard retired from the field with what grace it could muster, the point for educational purposes having been made.[5]

The idea of community became central for an area of Goddard adult and undergraduate studies in the 1950s and 1960s. It was not a new idea, entirely. On the strictly theoretical side, Josiah Royce, one of the distinguished Har-vard philosophers of the period of the First World War, is the reflective think-er whose name is associated with this field, along with the philosophy of

---

[5] Vermont faculty made careers out of their version of the Seminar. We ran into some of them twenty years later on the Board of the Center for Northern Studies in Wolcott, Vt., an institute specializing in sci-entific, cultural and international studies of the Arctic region. By this time there had been a change in the climate of business and industrial activities. The program appeared to be in a decline. See later reviews of the problem of programmatic age in educational settings: something in this needs study.

values. That was two generations before Goddard turned its attention to this area.[6] The Goddard format took as its focus community development, not only in the theoretical dimension but also in the practical. This was typical of the Goddard conception of social studies. Real communities would be dealt with; students would work in the communities as parts of their studies; elements of communities would be welcomed on campus. Faculty and students alike would become elements in the life of the communities being studied. The objective would of course in part be added knowledge of the communities, added learning by both students and community members, and social change – for the better. The communities would understand themselves better as a consequence of studies in which they themselves had taken part. Their awarenesses of themselves and of their community lives would enlarge; their self-confidence in facing their futures would gain ground. They would know better what they could do in concert if they wished, and how they might go about doing it.

Socio-cultural change is very complex and moves like an avalanche across the social landscape. Goddard was not responsible all by itself for the avalanche. It made use of the avalanche in a time of complex and irresistible change. It no doubt affected that change, no doubt helped to shape it especially in the fields of education in which it primarily worked. In some part it spent its developing years adjusting to social change. Its patterns began to show reliably in the midst of seeming chaos. Its students grew to relative maturity by grasping and grappling with change. They learned how to communicate across group borders, how to work with people to define a problem of common interest, how to work with it, how to define and achieve objectives. We used to reflect in our days of being closer to the non-resident work terms than we were later, that Goddard students who had had two or three work terms of experience had a nearly infallible ability to go anywhere in the country or abroad, get jobs when they needed to, support themselves, and manage very well as long as they needed to. It was something they learned how to do over periods of time. Some students, humanly speaking, were probably better at it than others. The patterns of study and development became recognizable, however. This was the College that Royce Pitkin built. It is of prime importance to know how he did it.

The instances of societal communication referred to under this heading are a selection. The Goddard enterprise, in all of its programs and most of its efforts, was shot through with this mode of expression and interchange. It may

---

[6] In the 1930s when we were still in college in Cambridge, one of our stamping grounds was the young people's group which met in the First Parish (Unitarian) in Cambridge, across Massachusetts Avenue from Harvard Yard. One autumn evening a new face showed in the group. We asked him his name: – "Josiah Royce," he said, without a flicker. The famous philosopher had of course died in California some twenty years before. We stared. The young man was amused. He had expected to create a small sensation, and he did. Eventually he explained that he was Royce's grandson. After a year or two, he decided that he did not like Harvard, grandfather or no; he packed up and went back to California where he had come from.

be helpful in going through succeeding headings to make one's own references back to this rubric. It will find further expression in many of them; it will indeed include many of them.

III

THE PERPLEXING PROBLEM

If financial support was a problem perplexing to Tim, it was more threatening to his associates on the staff. His staffers could not, after all, raise much in the way of funds for the College. They were more often frightened by the prospects. Some of them took flight and went off to other posts. He used to keep everyone informed about financial conditions, as part of what he had thought was the proper democratic stance, but he learned to be careful about doing this. Explaining to some of us in the early 1950s why he did not want to say much about some financial hazards that were operative at the time, he was fairly direct about it. "The staff can't stand it," he observed; they might get scared and depart. On occasion when funds were short he would pay the staff and faculty, and quietly refrain from paying himself. Apparently he could sidestep a fair number of hazards by such means. It serves to show the closeness to the hazard line that he could resort to this and the staff never find out the true state of affairs.[7]

---

[7]Notice that Tim referred to faculty and administrative staff alike as "staff". He was unreservedly opposed to the sanctity of administrative positions, often regarded as above teaching positions. He went to considerable lengths to shake out common academic functions by naming them in unorthodox ways. When John Hall was named administrative head of College fund-raising and later of the College Business Office he became the Provost. Tim also appointed a great number of Directors. This might have appeared odd, because one observed that the people so appointed rarely ended up directing anything. They were never expected to direct anything. His point was that it was an unfamiliar title in academic circles. That had distinct advantages in academic management. It was important to keep the staff cut down to size. He intensely disliked the title of Dean; the College eventually agreed to take one on, but the staff all knew he detested the idea. We must say that when, years later, we had occasion to become reacquainted with staff positions at Goddard, and found we could count a total of seven {7} deans on the staff, all at the same time, we acquired a new respect for his reluctance to have even one. Later he appointed several other deans - much later. Tim would call all faculty and staff "staff"; he never referred to either as "staffers". That was a staff term, and came later. He was quite willing to use the term "faculty", and often did. Here his fundamental idea was that there should be no distinction between teachers and administrators. He loved to reassign administrators to teaching responsibilities, and often did so. The New England Association visiting teams had a very hard time with all this, much to Royce's mischievous delight.

It is worth noting, in connection with the problem of finding financial support, that the original Goddard Seminary in Barre was a Universalist sponsored institution. This made a difference in the future of the new four-year college. It did not, as it turned out, make a financial difference. It made an Admissions difference. The Universalists did not in those days have any funds to disburse for an indigent college. It was all they could do to keep their own heads above water. There was one thing the new little junior college for women could do; it could make up lists of Universalist churches and Universalist clergy and church members to whom materials could be sent inviting contributions. The college staff did that. Some gifts came in. They are carefully listed in the president's filed reports, name by name and gift by gift. Royce would always do that, down to his last day as president. In those early days the gifts were very small, – of the order of five dollars or so per gift. Of course money was worth more in the 1930s than it would be years later. However, this range of gift would not have been such as to guarantee continuance, even then. It also has to be remembered that the Universalists and the graduates and former students of the Seminary had mixed feelings about the College's move to Plainfield and its corporate change to a four-year institution. These feelings would endure for a number of years. Not every potential donor wanted to give the College support. Still, the basic relationships between the College and the Universalist Convention and the churches were reasonably stable and reasonably friendly. Tim had served as leader of the Sunday School in the Barre Universalist church, a comparatively strong local institution with an extensive history in Vermont. He would eventually become president of the Convention, an association of Universalist churches, for a term. The clergy rather generally understood what Goddard was about, educationally. They would send their own children to be students in Plainfield, and did so quite often. Less often students from Universalist settings would be referred by clergy for admissions consideration, especially if there was need for scholarship or tuition adjustment assistance from the College. That was quite all right with Tim. He believed in tuition adjustment for needy students, and would see that they got it. Many a good student from these sources went through Goddard and did well there and afterward.

The name Goddard was a family name which appeared also in the endowments of Tufts University in Medford, Massachusetts. Funds had been left in trust for both institutions. Tufts apparently had them. When the name of Green Mountain Central Institute, the original name of Goddard Seminary dating from its founding in 1863, was changed to Goddard Seminary, it was because of funds received from this family source. Tufts recognized some obligation in respect of the funds when Goddard had moved to Plainfield and there were corporate changes ensuing; it assumed the obligation of supplying an annual lectureship at Goddard for a number of years. Eventually Royce told the staff that he had had a letter from Tufts that the funds would no longer support the undertaking and that the lectureship was being discontinued.

He rather regretted it; it had been a pleasant and interesting affair for its lifetime, and no doubt added something to the intellectual ambience at the College.

The Unitarian connection was a little different. Here there was no historical stemline to nurture. Unitarian ministers who held churches in Vermont were often friendly; one, Rev. Skillman Myers of the Burlington church, had been a faculty member and taught at Goddard for a number of years. Rev. Dayton Yoder of the Montpelier church was supportive, and remained so even after leaving Montpelier for churches elsewhere. He served on a field committee for the College from posts in western churches for a number of years, and his family sent a student to Goddard every so often. Nancy Yoder, a student and graduate, later served for a time as Assistant Director of Admissions on the Goddard staff. A family member showed up as late as 1994-95 in the Montpelier Unitarian church and made a point of looking people up and reviving old associations. She was bright and forthright in the prime of life and was clearly glad to be around Vermont again if only briefly, and to encounter some of the old Goddard crowd. Unitarian connections tended to be of this friendly associational nature. They were based on liberal social views on both sides, and an acceptance and understanding of the educational and social principles and practices of the College.

The problem of indigent schools and colleges was not uncommon in the Unitarian denomination. Proctor Academy in Andover, N.H. was a case in point. It was an old private high school which had difficult periods. It was not as old or well established as some others; probably the public thought it could tell a desirable school by looking at its buildings while driving by on the road. Every so often the Unitarian headquarters in Boston would hear that it was in danger of closing from lack of operating funds. There would be anxious periods before the sources of funds made up their minds what to do. They did not like to bail out indigent schools or colleges. It is no real detraction from the values of an educational institution if it has financially dry periods. People don't always understand this, especially if the plant looks old and rundown or even just atypical. The Proctor Academy buildings today have clearly moved into the twenty-first century. Goddard's buildings were built in the first instance for farming. They looked it. Now, of course, they have been remodelled and adapted. One has to look in the faculty advertisements to find its agricultural motifs among the architectural logos.

There may be occasion later to refer to the differences between the Universalists and the Unitarians where higher education was concerned. There were differences. On the whole the Universalists understood more and did better. The Unitarians had more money but were less inclined to give it away. Goddard never got any funds at all from central Unitarian sources. Universalist funds underlay Goddard Seminary in its Barre period; those resources were built into the new four-year college in Plainfield and helped to send it on its way. Beyond this the Universalists could not readily go, due to financial limitations.

The first fifteen years of the Plainfield phases must have been financially a very tight squeeze for Goddard. Tim learned a good deal about how to get loans from banks; he had friends who were in the main not educators and not especially liberal socially, who were in prominent places in banks. Tim had gone to school and college with them; they were all Vermonters together; they knew each other personally. Judicious loans were made when requested; in times of need Tim had people he could talk to about money. There were always campaigns for funds. The results are all listed. They did not bring in large sums in this period. When Royce was re-figuring the balance between students and residential space and it became necessary to remodel another agricultural building as a college residence he usually had to ask someone for a loan. The entire range of sums being passed back and forth in those years was relatively small. Tim usually got his loans. He may not always have known how he was going to pay them back, but that was a problem for the future. He used to remark that it was a good thing that the College was not required to know in September, when the school year opened, how it was going to finish the year in June. There were not many years, he said, when he could have supplied the answer. In plain language, most academic years at Goddard began without sufficient assured income to complete them. Think what that meant: he had to work all year long to raise funds sufficient to pay the bills due in the spring. The existence of the College for an indeterminate number of years depended on the President's sheer nerve. Without that, there would have been no college. He lived constantly on the brink of a precipice. Most of the time most of the staff never knew it.

Major remodelling of Goddard agricultural buildings with federal assistance began in the mid-to-late 1940s. The names of the agencies supplying the building funds, or parts of the funds, may not be familiar to us today. Frequently the funds came from several sources – some federal, some private. One of the seemingly original things that Royce did was to apply for funds from agencies which might not have suspected that part of their mission in life was to support higher education. Perhaps he was turned down by a few; eventually some grants were received and the remodelling began to go forward. 1947 was such a year. It was the beginning of a long road.

Private gifts to the College in its first full decade appear to have risen from low levels in the late 1930s in the range of a few hundred dollars to a few thousand dollars. Probably these reflected in both cases the abilities and the readinesses of parents of students to make contributions over and above tuition, room and board. Numbers of small gifts were still received. Raising the sights of potential contributors may have been a slow process. Tim used to remark on how long it took him to realize that certain persons actually could make substantial contributions.

The late 1940s were years of a large influx of students, among them veterans of World War II. Many did not have large family resources, but they needed places to go to college. Veterans had the G.I. Bill, and Goddard did what it could with tuition adjustment; veterans who came to Goddard made up disproportionately large percentages of the habitually small entering classes, accounting for the post-war rise in admissions.

Tuition adjustment was a very interesting socio-financial process. Tim had thought about it for years. It had a central place in his theory and practice of college admissions and financial aid. As a theory it was a bit intricate. A good many colleges and universities had endowments; Goddard at that time and for long years after, had no endowments. Endowment income for institutions which had it was often applied to operational costs. Tim thought it should be applied to tuition adjustment, replacing funds which needy students might not have. Operational support was of as much use to well-to-do students as to needy students. He argued that wealthy students could pay the extra freight, operational costs included, while needy students could not. The trick would be to raise the general tuition level across the board to place wealthy students in the position of having to pay a proper proportion of operational costs, and apply relatively larger aid funds to students needing more assistance with college expenses. It was part of his conceptualization of democratic methods applied to college operations. In the early 1950s he set about doing this. The proposal wound its way through the usual discussional stages and was duly set in motion. At some point Tim made inquiries at a number of other colleges to see how they felt about it. Some of them had endowments. There was a general howl of protest; nobody else would entertain an idea like that. For once, Tim was shaken. He began to have doubts about the wisdom of his own proposal, even to reconsider it. It was too late. It had been cast in print, incorporated in College policy, and sent out to families of entering students. There was nothing to be done except wait and see what happened. The policy was an outstanding success. No doubt with some relief, he remarked in later reports that he was glad it had been done.

Once upon a time, probably in the early 1950s, Tim was due to leave on a college trip and had not had time to review the tuition adjustment assignments. He asked two or three of us to do the reviews and make sure that the assignments were on good grounds so that students needing less assistance would be encouraged to carry their share of the costs. Innocently enough, we did that; we took $10,000 out of the assignments for that semester, thinking all the while what a good, careful job we were doing for the College. When Tim returned and found what we had done he did not say a word to any of us. Indirectly we heard, however, that he had sharply disagreed with our decisions. His intention had been not to place added burdens on students who could ill afford it. The ideal solution would have been to find additional assistance funds somewhere else. Alas, it took some of us another forty years to figure out his complete theory of tuition assistance.

For the first fifteen years, from 1938 to 1953, the financial predicaments of the college were more or less a succession of crises. It will be apparent later that the crises did not cease in 1953. But beginning in 1953 or shortly thereafter, there began to be signs of a weather-change. It is interesting to reflect on what these signs meant. They meant that Royce was beginning to encounter a different set of persons. He was beginning to meet the main players in certain foundations concerned with education. He had of course applied for grants before; the moves had in general not been very successful. But a great deal depends on the people one knows. Nowadays these acquaintanceships are sometimes called "business friendships". What they mean is that the relationships are founded on functions rather than on personal friendships in the first instance. They may become personal friendships. Whether they do or not, they result in genuine acquaintanceships with genuine groundworks in substantive content. In the case of the content, both sides need the acquaintanceship. A college needs funds for a certain program. A foundation needs a place to put its funds in accordance with its aims and stated interests. A foundation needs to give away money – but in accordance with the requirements of its founders. Not all foundations are focused on education; one does not apply to these for educational grants. It happened that the Ford Foundation was interested in education.

The grants from Ford to Goddard began in lower ranges than was the case later. This probably reflected a beginning acquaintanceship between Royce and the Foundation representatives for program purposes. About this time there begin to be, in the President's Reports to the Trustees, references to the Vermont Youth Study. This was a sociological program to investigate social conditions among Vermont young people. It was designed as part academic study on campus and part field study in Vermont communities, especially small communities, involving participation by students in the class who spent time in the study communities gathering data, becoming to some degrees familiar with and partial members of those villages or towns. The pattern of student participation in studies being conducted off campus became very familiar at Goddard. It was one of the ways in which Tim put his stamp on academic work at the College; its applications might vary; faculty persons teaching and learning in this category of study varied. Fields of study expressing the study patterns would be quite different. Funding opportunities in such studies were, so to speak, one-to-one. There was always at least one such opening for applications to be made to one or more foundations to help with the expenses. Sometimes there were several such opportunities under the same heading. Staff members, following Royce's lead, would develop aspects of a study in ways that led to further projects, and incidentally to additional possibilities for support requests. The Vermont Youth Study was headed in its first years by Dr. Jerome Himelhoch, an academic sociologist with an excellent reputation and credentials, who found it congenial to have students assisting him in the field as well as in classes. He was also good with foundations. It all worked out well enough. The supporting foundation was always advised of the progress of the study, as part of the on-going accountability. The Foundation supporting this study was Ford; the range of the initial grant was around $37,000 over two years, with opportunity for renewal as needed. Typically, such a project would go on for several years with declining amounts of support as the studies proceeded, and as they eventually moved into their final evaluation phases.

Evaluation was current and continuing throughout the studies. This was an indispensable part of Tim's design for such studies. He always wanted to know what the results were, what implications had shown up, and what conclusions had been reached. He did not just ask the project faculty for the implications. He set up faculty discussions around the projects, set aside time for periodic reports to the faculty, and saw to it that faculty discussion time was adequate for results and implications. We shall see this pattern repeating itself constantly in the experimentation sections of this account. Tim himself and the faculty generally would have ample opportunity to examine the substance, processes and implications of research and experimentation projects. Hours and hours of faculty time went into them. Notice that a "report" was not just a report. It was invariably an opportunity for discussion, being so designed.

This is beginning to sound as if Royce simply applied for grants, got them, and carried out the projects for which the funds were intended. There were many occasions when the grants were declined. The pattern which Tim developed at such times was equally typical and equally persistent. He would come into a faculty meeting or into a committee or council meeting and report what had happened. Immediately he would raise the question of how the study, or a part of the study, or an altered version of the original study proposal, could still be carried out. Discussion would ensue. An approach would emerge. A viable project, perhaps changed or reduced, would be formulated. He would look around the room as if he had never before that moment thought of the possibility of a staff member's taking on the direction and teaching involved in the project, and forthwith would light upon someone to do just that. Many a project was carried out in this way in the early Goddard years. The staff members usually liked the ideas generated in this way. It was part of the ambient excitement of the institution that few ever objected to the added workload. People on staff became adept at making adjustments in the interest of getting more things done in the same or in added hours. We cannot remember an instance when any staffer was reluctant to move in these respects. Perhaps there were some instances; if so, they are lost in the mists of antiquity.

Over periods of time the foundation staffs became used to the small college president from Vermont who was always applying for funds to do something educational that was different, and had the added advantage of being sensible and comprehensible. Under such circumstances probably the foundation people hunt around for one of their staff members who is familiar enough with a proposed field to judge effectively what is happening with projects generally in the point of origin. Gradually they shake things out, to ascertain that a proposal is or is not within their scope. Probably they also need to see how the proposer wears.

Gradually, one assumes, Royce grew on people. They got to think of him first, perhaps, as a Vermonter with ideas, and with a certain twang about him, and then as a granite type who had conviction and endurance, who knew what he wanted to do, and who stayed the course. In 1959 the six-year study called the Experiment in Curriculum Organization was funded. Ford had decided that Royce could be trusted, and that his "experiments" were worth continuing on an enlarged scale. Under the later sections of this account we shall need to return to the study in Curriculum Organization. In this section on college support, the point is that that support had now moved into a new phase. From this time on the College would command ranges of support approximately twice the size of any support it had received before from private sources.

Having more substantial sums coming in did not mean in the long run any fundamental change in the needs of the College to work hard to find operating funds. Tim explained this often enough in his reports to the College Trustees. What he was getting were funds for project support, special program enablement. Now that he had the support he had to find staff to do the various jobs, arrange the project in appropriate ways, and relate the new project to existing operations of the institution. He could pay the new staff out of the grant funds, and pay certain expenses which the project itself incurred. No other college costs could be paid from the grant. The other costs went on as usual.

Gains to the College from such a grant were of course enormous. It was just that they were not strictly in the financial dimension. New faculty came on, with all that that implied. Tim usually was able to have a foundation-based staffer teach an on-campus course in his academic field, carry some counselees and some advisees as a full-load faculty person normally would, and at the same time carry out the plan for the grant-project at the proper full scale level. Part of this would comprise the academic class aspect and part the field-study aspect. The proportional time-burdens would be of the order of 1/3 normal faculty activities and 2/3 grant project activities – some of which were of course teaching and some research dimension. Potential faculty appointees were charmed at the idea of supported field studies. The value to students was outstanding. Very good students often signed up to participate in such projects, and ended by becoming even better students with excellent graduate study prospects and eventual career appointments.

When a grant project involved an institutional self-study, as the Curriculum Organization study did, the new support could perhaps be assigned in part to cover the time of certain participating and administering faculty; however, allowances had to be made for reductions in normal faculty activities in the interest of attending to the project program; when this was done, support amounts assigned to and away from those faculty participants had to reflect their time commitments in those dimensions.

Private financial gifts to the College had already begun to go up from the first-decade levels when the foundation grants commenced. This was the result of a long and gradual rise in the sense of obligation which the College trustees felt. Royce was commonly very direct with the Trustees as he reported the need for funds for some project or some construction. It is easy to see now as one reads the files that he was in point of fact putting enormous pressure on trustees to contribute funds. Unfortunately not a great many of them had large sums to give away. Tim's theory was that trustees should support an institution for which they held legal responsibility. One of their prime duties was to give money, or arrange for other people with larger resources to give money. He was clear about this; he used to remark it now and then in comments to staffers about financial matters. We do not know what he said to the trustees in verbal exchanges, but he would surely not have been so direct. The quarterly and annual reports, however, were direct. If the trustees read them they knew what he meant. It was not that he told them to give money; he would never have done such a thing. It would have been contrary to a democratic approach to a problem. People had to decide these matters for themselves. No one else could decide for them. He simply stated the needs of the College simply and directly. The result would have been, in certain circumstances, a formidable pressure to do whatever could be done. Tim would have been entirely aware of this.

An intermediate stage in private support began to be felt in the later phase of the first fifteen-year period. It came from parents and the friends of parents who shared fund-raising causes with others in the same region. The Philadelphia region was most helpful in this respect. For a number of years a benefit performance of some outstanding kind would be held, such as a theatre evening with the great French mime, Marcel Marceau, at which the institution benefitting would be defined as Goddard College. The College might receive something of the order of $15,000 for this event. In later years the amounts were reduced to about a tenth of that. Royce was equally grateful on both levels. Money was money, and always hard to come by. Once there was one of the endless campaigns for money and some students took up a collection on campus. From one source they received fifty-nine cents. It was duly reported to Tim and sent to the General Fund. The entry can be read to this day in the annals of the financial campaigns. Desperate as he might be for funds, Royce never overlooked small gifts. He really and genuinely appreciated them. He was very well aware of what the smallest gift might mean to the giver. There is something in the New Testament about just such genuine appreciation.

Contributions then went up in series of average levels over a thirty-year period somewhat in the following order: $5.00, $50.00, $500., $5,000, $15,000, $50,000, $125,000, and $250,000. This took the College into the 1960s. The $50,000 gift range began somewhat before the building of the Village for Learning, Royce's name for the 11-12 residential houses which went up between Greatwood Drive and the President's house. He was bound to build relatively small houses, for capacities of only 12 or 14 students. Numbers planned for in the houses changed slightly as ideas were changed, but that was the range. The first house built was Pratt House; it was begun early, before the other houses were funded by a relatively large loan from a government agency. Eliot D. Pratt of New Milford, Conn. was chairman of the Goddard Board of Trustees. It was he who made possible the first house. Royce was profoundly grateful for his having done it. It started the new phase of college expansion when Tim had thought there would be further delays. Eliot Pratt was a shy, soft-spoken person, disabled in his later years, who undertook much philanthropy of which few people ever heard. He was responsible for a revolving student loan fund at Goddard of the order of $8,500 at a time when loan funds for students were at a very low ebb. But this was moderate compared to other contributions he made. They grew from small contributions over some years, to regular gifts in five figures. If one keeps doing something like that, it makes a difference. Eliot kept on doing it, - not every week, but nearly every month. His period of involvement in the College ran from 1949-50 to the late 1960s when his increasing disability due to Parkinson's disease began to make it impossible for him to carry on active participation in his many interests. He had many and distinctive interests – pottery and ceramics, farming his Connecticut estate, cattle interests, many social and philanthropic interests to which there are only vague references. There were apt to be research components in things he undertook. He would carry on the research personally in many areas. He had been asked to join the Goddard Board of Trustees in 1942, and had declined on grounds of too many interests; he also did not wish to take on another philanthropic cause at that time, being already committed to active participation in the workcamp movement. It is clear enough that there is a shadowy connection between this interest of Eliot's, and the later Camp Winooski, a summer project at Goddard which flourished in the 1950s, its format being off-campus work in communities surrounding Goddard in Plainfield. It is only the bare truth to say that Eliot Deming Pratt of New Milford, Conn. and New York City probably saved Goddard between five and fifteen times a year for nearly eighteen years in the 1950s and 1960s. A study could be made of this. It is an instance of a creative socio-educational thrust being expressed through the medium of philanthropic contributions.

Another of Eliot Pratt's interests was *Current* Magazine, a digest of social material from other magazines on public affairs of the day; eventually he placed it in the hands of a new corporation, Goddard Publications, Inc., and it came to live on campus for a time. It came on hard times and was given away after two or three years to a foundation in Washington, D.C. He became a prime mover in the commitment of the College to build a library and learning center to stand in the woods between the two existing campuses. It was begun in 1968. It is with good reason that the Library/Learning Center bears his name today. He did a great deal to help the College on its way, at a time when others were not rushing to its relief. In doing this, he gave expression to certain rooted convictions and interests of his own.

The final category of financial assistance in the expansion of the College came from the government, and accounts for the last and highest in the series of averages. This figure ($250,000) is an estimate and a symbol, rather than exact in detail. Some years before there had been loans ($80,000 or so) involved in the Haybarn Theatre remodelling; Tim tried mortgages, insurance

loans, private funds, and government funds. Government funding was normally in the form of loans; income from student room fees was commonly
tied up so that the loans could be repaid properly. The College did not have
any freedom in its management. Government agencies were involved in the
Village for Learning on Greatwood Campus, in the Library/Learning Center,
and in the residence construction on Northwood Campus. There were public
laws in force in the federal government to enable residential and central services construction on college campuses; a good many colleges did the same
thing that Goddard was doing – up to a point. Royce's originality in this situation was again a typical combination of new ideas and sheer persistence.
The new ideas centered in part around the design of a small residence, for the
proposed dozen or fourteen students each; this was unheard-of. The federal
granting agencies, which were willing to support a request from Goddard for
housing, demurred at the financial inefficiency of the proposal. For, say, 125
or so students, they would be glad to approve a square or rectangular standard
brick residence hall to encompass such a number. It would have one central
heating plant for all occupants, and so forth. It would be efficient, a better use
of federal funds. If he absolutely insisted on his small individual houses they
might reluctantly go along, but he could at least put brick around them so
they would look like college residences.

One can imagine how that response would set with Tim. One might suppose he would have blown the federals out of the water. Unlikely; his typical
behavior under such circumstances would have been to go to work to educate
them to the facts of group behavior and the realities of educationally sound
residential life. As for brick walls, he could not afford them. Wooden houses
were it. He might not have felt he needed to convince them that he was correct in every detail, because of course other colleges were applying for the
square or rectangular brick residences and would be very glad just to get
them, let alone cut them down to smaller size. Tim might well have been
content to convince them that he believed what he said and had no intention
of building anything like a conventional dormitory. They could make their
peace with it. If they didn't there was clearly going to be more trouble. They
read the writing on the walls and made their peace with it. Royce got his residences the way he wanted them. Of course he did. What did they expect?
He had been at this college-building business then for twenty-five years.
Everything about Goddard except the fullness of financing had come out the
way he wanted it. He had had a good deal of practice at it. And he never sac-
rificed what he believed were sound educational principles to expediency.
Construction began forthwith on the Village for Learning. The houses were
of wood.

There was less delay between the expansion of Greatwood Campus and the
building of Northwood Campus than one might expect; there was less delay
between that and the construction of the Pratt Library and Learning Center
also than one might expect. The times were right. Tim knew a ready situation
when he saw one. The drive to build the second campus soon began and was

unrelenting. It was designed in a different way from the Greatwood Village for Learning residences, the intention being to have it develop in individual ways, not in the same ways as Greatwood. This, too, happened as planned. An elaborate water system was designed and installed to supply the needs of both campuses; in accordance with sound policy in community relations provisions were made to enable the College and the village of Plainfield to exchange water in case of need. This was the shape of Goddard until the troubles of a later college generation came home to roost. It operated for a number of years with a two-campus situation, the Library, drama, and service buildings being between them to provide necessary services in an "efficient" manner.

It is clear that there was little distance between the two-campus situation and the addition of the third campus. There were signs that the third campus was coming. It did not come. What happened to it? There seems never to have been any announcement that it was not coming. If we ever find one we will write it down. There had to be a financial component among the variables in the problem.[8]

In his Quarterly Report for March 1966 Tim wrote an observation which could stand as a grim warning to future leaders of Goddard College. Goddard was then four times what its size had been in 1959. There was more money around, clearly. But consider these conditions, he wrote: a 10% overrun with a budget range of $100,000 was $10,000 − a manageable deficit range which could be handled by way of loans or gifts over a period of a few years. A 10% overrun with a budget range of $1,500,000 would be $150,000, a deficit size "crippling in the short run, devastating in the longer run." Royce's point was, for the annual budget level to go up ten times, creates a fundamentally different set of operating conditions. As the years passed, who besides Royce would know this?

It is probably time to move to consideration of the third major problem of Royce Pitkin's long presidency, − admissions and enrolment. Tim retired in 1969; we would be unwise to go beyond that point, knowing as we have said far less about it. He left the college in that year with a full enrolment and a substantial amount in the treasury. The existing components of the College were in balance. That is a thing to note. He was very pleased, it is said, to leave the institution in such good shape for the arrival of the new president,

---

[8]If Royce had come up severely short of funds to complete the third campus plan the chances are fairly good that he would have done just what appears to have happened: nothing. This would have been because he would not have wished to preclude the possibility of building it should the funds for it have been found. It is curious that there is not more indication of this in the records but the theory appears reasonable. John Hall thinks that the first realization of the critical shortage of construction funds was earlier − when the bids were opened for the second campus, and Tim realized that he could not build even the community center for Northwood. It would have been a realistic judgment. The Center was not built. The maintenance shop, also in the central design, was renamed the Northwood Community Center and dining hall, and was used in place of the intended building. John thinks that the plans for Westwood Campus began to fade from that moment. For a qualification of this theory, see also Notes [13] & [15].

Gerald Witherspoon. What happened to the balance and to the students and resources had perhaps best be the concern of historians who can deal with the more than ordinarily obstreperous decade of the 1970s.

IV

THE OTHER LEARNERS

Here we snap back again to the early days of Goddard to run an impressionist eye over the history of the admissions situation. Reading the files of the Barre years at this late date is to encounter a foreign country. It may have been similar for Royce himself, at least to a degree. He too was a new arrival then; but that was normal. He had held several positions before, and had been a new arrival in each of them. There would not have been anything remarkable in the Barre experience in this respect. What may have happened in Barre is that he began to feel acutely the appropriateness of creating his own institution. As it turned out, this meant finding his own staff and faculty and finding his own students. The reader senses that he was not entirely comfortable with the staff and faculty he found. It was not remarkable if this was so. They had been installed at Goddard Seminary for varying lengths of time; they had their ways of working and their own views of what they were doing. There might have been some discomfort all around. Some of the faculty and staff went with him to Plainfield when the transition was made. None of them lasted very long. Those were pioneering and uncertain years; staff could hardly be criticized if their endurance proved to be short-lived. Royce himself may have been more abrasive in the early period than he was later when he came to understand better the implications of his own theory of education. Some of them, adminstratively speaking, may have found him a new experience.

Anne Squire, a painter and art teacher with a specialty in wood engraving, was probably the most likely candidate for continuance at the College in its Plainfield phases. Unfortunately, she became ill with a rare combination of diseases the conflicting treatments of which left her living for many years on a knife-edge. She survived into old age by imposing on herself a firm and courageous regimen in which she relied on a severe diet on one hand and on the other slept for years, summer and winter, in a little cabin built beside her

Plainfield house. Her name for it was Windy. It was something of an institution in Plainfield in those years. She had a small apartment in her house
and processed solemnly and goodnaturedly to and from it morning and night.
She supplemented her retirement income by renting the rest of the house to
successive new faculty and staff arrivals at the College. She was enormously
interested in her associations with people over the years, and talked endlessly
about them with her series of renters. She had relatives in various parts of
Vermont and occasionally went to visit them. But where she wanted to be
was in her little Plainfield home. In a way she continued as an unofficial and
unpaid member of the College community, operating as an informal teacher
of new members of the staff and their families. There was a wood furnace in
her cellar by which the house was heated. We had almost forgotten how
much we learned about splitting wood down there, in the process actively
ruining one of her axes by using it as a wedge. Later we became quite proficient with wedges. She was very sympathetic to and supportive of the College, and was probably one of the social originals of the College community.
Her paintings and wood engravings survive today on numerous walls of her
friends' houses.

Students are the proper and necessary focus of admissions; Tim was firmly
centered on them as an indispensable element in an educational institution.
He always had to have staff assistance to carry out the tasks of the admissions
office, a part of which was to search for students. But he commonly did a lot
of admissions work himself. This began in Barre, as we have seen, and it continued in Plainfield. His supervision of the admissions office and staff was constant, his impact on it considerable. Admissions and Records were normally
yoked as complementary functions. The same person was normally in charge,
more or less, of both operations. Royce was really in charge, of course.

Records were, in plain language, the bane of his existence. He disliked
them intensely. He was aware that there had to be records for education to do
a fair job for the students. What he resented was anything which tended to
force compliance from teachers and students, and which defeated the view of
education as a living process in which teachers and students took first and
equal part. Every so often Royce bit off more than he could chew. He had a
sense of humor, and we have occasionally wondered how he felt when he realized that one of his staff had bested him at his own game. He used to preach
to us now and then about how we should never traffick with all that canard
about translating Goddard evaluations into the educational coin of the realm
in order to get students into graduate school or into something else they
wanted to get into, which required a recognizable transcript of record. Most
of us who were ever in charge of Records upheld the Goddard standard fairly
well until it came to the crunch when a student was going to pass or fail
somewhere else because of something we said in the record. Then we found a
way to get the student where it was desirable to go, mostly without doing the
Goddard culture any harm. Tim did some of it himself, usually by letter. We
have had to do it now and then over the years, most recently in 1993-94.

One Goddard Records officer totally refused to do this. Tim had always said, speaking of graduate schools, – don't give in to them; if we give them what they want how will they ever learn the right way of doing things? – The Records officer was convinced, and forthwith never gave out anything but Goddard evaluations. No translations, no comparisons – no nothing. The students could flail and thrash; it availed them naught. Here was a staffer who believed what Tim said and went him one better. Some of us, from remote quarters of the country, watched with interest.

Admissions in the 1940s were slow until the postwar boom created a rise in the enrolment profile. When rises like this occurred, as they did every few years for different reasons, the College was thrown off balance. It would see a larger entering class coming and would have to re-figure its residential space capacities to know where it was going to put them. Over the years a number of stopgap building purchases were made, as for example of a house in the Meadow which was acquired on a shortterm basis, used as a residence for a semester or two, and then re-sold to free the funds invested in it. The Plainfield Inn, a rambling, rickety structure overlooking the bridge intersection at the bend in School Street, was made available once or twice in this way. This had been a hotel in one of its private ownership periods; senior citizens around Plainfield liked to tell of older days when expeditions used to visit local picnic or resort locations around the village, coming by train or carriage and staying at the Inn for a while. We once bought an old trunk at an auction somewhere in Calais because it looked interesting; it turned out to have nothing at all in it except, under a loose board in the bottom, the Guest Book of the Plainfield Inn covering a stretch of years. We took it to the Calais Room of the Kent Tavern Museum, and suppose that this volume is still in the Calais collections or in the Vermont Historical Society, which owned the Museum for a number of years. The problem with the Plainfield Inn was, who was going to buy it when the College wanted to sell it again? It was an odd building, with lots of floors and lots of rooms on all of them; it was not adapted to just any use. There had to be some good reason why anyone would want it. For periods of time it would stand vacant because no good reason had occurred to anyone for buying it. When we came to Plainfield for a first interview in 1950 we got off the train at the woodsy Plainfield station and walked to the Inn, thinking it was still a hotel. It was early morning. No one was around. We found a chair in the Lobby and felt at home waiting for the day to start. Doors began to slam; chaps came and went in various states of dishabille, processing hither and yon, slamming doors again and disappearing. Greetings were exchanged. No one minded having visitors. No one looked twice to see who it was or to inquire what people were doing sitting around before breakfast in the big front rooms. After a while it dawned on us that there was something unusual about all this. It turned out that this was one of the periods when it was a men's residence for the College. It hadn't been an inn for years. The College was at the other end of the village. The people we were seeing were very likely the graduating seniors of the wave of World War II veterans who were completing their college studies as Grade 16 students that year. They had to walk back and to for meals in the College Dining Room three times a day if they wanted to eat - and they usually did. It was our introduction to the College. The impression conveyed was of a self-sufficient community in which a good deal could happen without anyone's paying it any mind. On the whole we remembered the episode at the Inn more clearly in later years than we did the interviews which followed it, except for Tim's amusement when he found out where we had been.

Admissions were clearly the central concern of the Admissions and Records responsibility. In Tim's concept of a living college, Admissions had the advantage of being a living process. Records had only the disadvantage of being inert. We were never quite sure they were as inert as Royce thought. There is after all something potentially creative about a piece of paper with writing on it. Somewhere in the later reaches of this study we shall encounter a totally fascinating discussional issue involving records which convulsed the Greatwood faculty in the year 1968-69, which may point up aspects of Royce's distinctive view of records as part of educational administration. Probably this will come up in the last section on the Experimental Programs administered by George Beecher, who was at the root of the discussion.

The enrolment range for the opening semester of Goddard in 1938 was 47, 25 of these having come over from the Seminary/Junior College; 22 new students had showed up over the summer. It apparently dropped the second year, to 25. In the third year, enrolment was up to 63. In 1943 it was listed at 48. The first graduation of four-year students took place that year: there were two graduates, Evalyn Bates and Peter Liveright. From this point on the Senior College would show commonly in the files. Before that the graduates had been two-year people. Things were clearly choppy in those first years. By 1946, as we have seen, the veterans began to show, and the enrolment profile showed an expected rise. The College planned for it, which meant that Tim planned for it. He bought the Plainfield Inn in 1948 for $8,500 from Mr. and Mrs. Harold Weed of Weed Farm in neighboring East Montpelier; it would certainly be interesting to know what they had thought they were going to do with it. So it became a college residence for men. In 1946 enrolment was 69; by 1948 it was 125. Remarks were made about turbulence on the college campus.

In this period Tim began to advise the trustees in his reports and no doubt in other ways that it was time to consider providing for an enrolment of 250, doubling the capacity of the College. Not much seemed to happen. Probably this meant that he had not yet found the funds to finish remaining space in the agricultural buildings on campus. One wonders where the figure of 250 came from. It would become a key figure in the design of the two-campus operation of some 15 years into the future; it would have been a factor in the design of the missing third campus, ghostly Westwood, had that been built.

There was indeed discussion of 250 as perhaps an ideal size of the smaller units being proposed in the Goddard plan for a multi-campus college. It was a dozen or so years later; Greatwood Campus had actually reached about 300 students. There occurred a more than ordinarily difficult semester, referring to internal human relations problems between students and faculty on campus. Tim remarked in his Reports that he had become unable to relate as well to students as he had when the campus population had been 250. He knew more students in absolute numbers, he said, but over-all knew far fewer out of the total number. The implication was that if a second campus was to be built it might be far pleasanter and more manageable all around if the number on each campus fell back to 250. As the outcome of a discussion or a speculation that made good sense; one might think one understood the dilemma and the reasons for Tim's approach to it. It would have been an understandable outcome of experience with group-behaviors of two sizes.

In this first instance, however, that does not stack up. When he first proposed to increase the campus population from 125 to 250, the College had never had 250 students. The chances are that the suggestion was a practical one the implication of which was that college management would be easier and more nearly solvent if the campus population were doubled. There is always a deceptive element in such a conclusion: as college populations rise in numbers service costs, faculty and financial aid costs also rise, so that the financial advantages of more income from students are diminished. It is a very tricky matter whether growth in size brings advantage or disadvantage. By this time the College was accredited and added numbers were showing up with less effort. More faculty had had to be added. It had all happened relatively rapidly. There had been very little time for the seasoning of personnel at all levels and in all categories, students included. That was one characteristic of all those strenuous years when the College had been unaccredited and had been struggling with financial and developmental problems of all sorts. People were seasoned. There was not much in the way of difficulty which had not happened enough times to make it familiar. People of all ages were used to each other and fond of each other (relatively), and could generally speaking take time to work things out.

What might have happened if Royce had reached for the figure of 200 rather than 250? By normal extension each campus population would have been 200, and the three-campus population 600 instead of the projected 750. As it turned out the two-campus College would have had 400 students instead of 500. It is a very interesting question, one which the old Goddard hands will no doubt debate among themselves. Hindsight is no virtue and no wisdom. None of us who were on campus in those days can claim either wisdom or virtue in respect of decisions which might have been different. Royce did what he thought was best. Angels, as the saying goes, can do no more.

The 1950s were a good decade on the Goddard campus. It had of course begun in 1948 when the first refusal to admit Goddard to the New England Association had been encountered. This had the effect of focusing educational activities on the work at hand, rather than on the showy aspects of material success. Royce's reports centered quarter after quarter and year after year on outreach activities, as we shall see later. The College grew slowly. It had the time to age a bit, to become seasoned. Not being accredited gave it leisure for sound and slow development. It must be admitted that no one noticed on campus any marked leisure; everyone was busy enough for several persons all the time. In retrospect it seems relatively quiet and peaceful. No doubt this is partly a retrospective illusion. Accreditation and material growth would come soon enough, bringing with them the turbulence of the 1960s and degrees of social upheaval that might well have been dreaded.

In the early 1950s the Universalists and Unitarians appear again in the Goddard narrative. They may not have given the College any money after the initial send-off, but they did send students. It was quite interesting. Each year mailings were sent to lists of both denominational groups; they would not amalgamate into one denomination until 1961, so they were conceptually separate. The liberal wings of both groups knew what Goddard was about. Of the two groups, probably the Universalists were the most genuinely liberal in the social sense. But college choice was an individual family matter: it would depend on what an individual family thought best to do. As a general thing in those days, year after year, 15-18% of the entering classes came from these sources. It was quite reliable as a category, with only minor variations. It probably derived in the main from social conviction; the Universalists were traditionally strong in that category, the Unitarians only relatively so. Their liberalism centered in theology, not a prime area in college considerations. The Unitarians were educationally traditional and conservative; they seemed not to have absorbed progressive educational thought from their much-honored association with the noted religious education leaders of the 1940s and following, Sophia L. Fahs of Union Theological Seminary in New York and Ernest Kuebler, the administrative head in the Religious Education Department at Unitarian headquarters in Boston. However, the Unitarians did send students to Goddard, again, like the Universalists, largely from social conviction and largely on an individual family basis. Church leadership was not involved, except as individual families among leaders supported choices made by their young people to come to the College as students.

By 1957 the enrolment on campus was 93. The New England Association visited again that year, and declined again to invite Goddard to join its membership. In 1959 they would come yet another time, and would admit Goddard to membership only after a reluctant visiting committee had voted two to one against a positive report, only to be overturned among the Committees and on the floor of the Association by the daring sleight of hand of President William C. Fels of Bennington College. Goddard had worked hard for where it had landed. It had learned and taught much; it had a right to its brief celebration. Robert M. Mattuck, senior member of the faculty and longtime Senior Counselor on Greatwood Campus, had taken the call from Royce at the Association meeting in southern New England; when he turned from the telephone and spoke to the dining room full of people, in his enduring British accents, ["Goddard is accredited!"], the room roared with one voice. It was a rare moment. The College may never have earned another like it.

So we come to 1960, the opening of a new decade. This was going to be different. It surely was.

Enrolment in 1960 is listed at 156. There had been 13 Senior Division graduates (with the Bachelor of Arts degree), 32 graduates from the Junior Division. The Junior College had been dropped as a divisional concept somewhere along the line, as the conceptualization of the four-year college had become firmer. Tim had believed in the notion of the junior college; numbers of students would always prefer to leave college at the end of two years, and there should be an institutional way, he thought, to recognize this. Educationally, it was quite all right to go to college, in his view, for just two years. Gradually the notion of a two-year college that was conceptually different had blurred into the idea of a two-year division, and it had replaced the older form. Eventually, the change was recognized, probably just by writing things differently in the student records. We do not remember a formal change. If there was one, probably few of us knew about it.

In 1961 the enrolment is listed at 165 residential students, plus 6 adults – notice this new category – these would have been adults in studies on campus. That is how the far-reaching Adult Degree Program at Goddard began, not as a separate program at all, but simply as adults, probably from the Vermont environs, mostly, came and went to and from classes. Royce had studied this development and watched it closely from its first appearance. There would have been occasional adult students on campus for classes from time to time in past years. Tim would have been pleased to have them, and would have welcomed them as beneficial elements in the student populations, good for the adult students and good for the younger student majorities who would be able to dialogue with older people in classes as a helpful educational and social process. He designated Evalyn Bates, his longtime first assistant in many posts associated with the President's office, to watch this new category. Mentions of adult studies are noted as early as 1958, when the President's Report defined three major categories in the College as the Four-Year College, the Division of Educational Experimentation, and the Division of Adult Education and Community Services, of which Evalyn Bates was head.[9]

Enrolment in 1962 stood at 188 in both semesters; the figure was often not steady, as there were changes in student plans between terms; 205 different persons were students that year. Royce always gave the various figures precisely, though we do not always present the details here. He liked figures, often using them to make a telling point. One always has to read his writing

---

[9]A. R. Elliott, Jr., the Jack Elliott whom we all knew from his early years as Business Manager, College Controller, and sometime faculty member in Economics and Business-related studies, had served first as Director of Adult Education when he had only just arrived on staff in 1948; in his various Business Office posts he had seen the College through very dry times from the early 1950s on, wearing himself down as one anxious period succeeded another. Later Jack retired due to illness, became a noted goldsmith and artistic jeweler, and maintained a jewelry and crafts supply business for quite some time. He had well earned his years of relative quiet and peace. Royce Pitkin, Richard Hathaway and other friends spoke at his memorial service in 1980.

with care; he mostly meant exactly what he said and not something else which might have been mistaken for it.

The formal proposal for the new Adult Degree Program, involving brief periodic residencies between longer periods of off-campus independent study, appears first in the President's Quarterly Report for March 1962. This as we shall see hereafter, became one of the thriving and most widespread of the Goddard program inventions. It certainly became a factor in the total enrolment situation throughout this period.

Enrolments kept climbing through this period, not rapidly, but steadily. Mercifully, our term as Director of Admissions had only lasted a few years in the early 1950s. That was probably the reason for the improvement; we never over-estimated our achievements as an Admissions person.[10]

Records were a different matter. There was that element of creativity about pen and paper. Tim could never understand how anyone could endure records work, but he was glad enough to get it done so he didn't raise much commotion about it most of the time. Part of his interest was in fixing things so he would not have to do the records work himself. Actually, we didn't last more than a year or two longer in the Records Office than had been the case with Admissions, though we cannot remember why right now.[11]

The new houses in the Village for Learning were being built in 1963. Their capacity would be 176. Enrolment in that year is listed at 244. Adult education enrolment was due to jump soon, Royce noted. Space for adult students at times of year when the planned study cycles would bring them to campus had to be ready. Tim had all these factors and variables constantly in mind. The first Adult Degree Program study cycle began in August 1963,

---

[10]Tim liked sending his admissions representatives to visit schools and school administrators whom he knew personally. He had a very wide acquaintance among them. He was faintly mischievous about it, never really explaining anything. We would have only the vaguest idea of the connections. So we would show up in all innocence and literally anything might happen. One day we duly appeared in the office of the headmaster of a distinguished private school and undertook to talk about whatever occurred to us as of interest about Goddard. "Where did you go to college?" he interrupted. We told him. "Well," he said, with the friendliest of smiles, "I suppose you understand that we don't really want to see you here; we want to see a graduate of Goddard." Quite possibly Tim got the point even better than we did. See Note [11] below.

[11]John Hall succeeded us in every job we held at the College for quite a number of years. He was very goodnatured about it most of the time, but after a while he became plaintive. In later years we would spend time wondering how it happened. As of retirement days on trips around Vermont we had never managed to figure it out. It was just one of those odd things which seemed to happen at the College without anyone's intending it. But then an idea occurred to us: we undoubtedly went home and told Royce what the headmaster had said. Tim might not have said much to us, but perhaps after a while he fixed it. There might have been a very good reason why John Hall ended up in the Admissions Office at Goddard, with that vast reputation he got as an Admissions person at both Goddard and SUNY/Empire State College. . . . John Hall graduated from Goddard with the 1950 class, after a wartime career in the Merchant Marine and the Navy. He had been trained in the unlikely skills of underwater demolition, and had sailed just about everywhere that mattered, apparently without ever demolishing anything. Royce got him a job in the Cooperative movement in Ohio along with Reed Rexford, another graduate and later Vermont State Commissioner of Agriculture in the Hoff administration. John joined the College staff in 1954, and the rest is history. Tim liked to appoint graduates of the College to posts on the College staff. He did it often over the years. See Note [10] above.

with 16 students. These were different adults from the local residents who had come on and off campus for years taking classes and occasionally graduating. In this format they could come from anywhere, stay through the short residency and go home to resume their jobs and lives while pursuing study independently. The program was dynamite, though that may not have been obvious yet. The format would spread to dozens, hundreds, of colleges everywhere. In another twenty years, after many College vicissitudes, the Adult Degree format would carry the entire College, old residential programs included, and the same phenomenon would be seen in other institutions. People would want to study in this way; it might be the wave of the future in American higher education. Tim was apprehensive: well before the larger numbers of adult students began to appear on campus he saw what might happen. The College had to be ready. Recognizing that the College administration could not turn the adult degree program efforts on and off seasonally, due to needs for preparation in matters of space, faculty and services, he set up a division which would be at least partially concerned with managing this burgeoning program. There was already a Division of Adult Education and Community Services. When the Adult Degree Program began to expand noticeably and its implications became clear the Program was given its own decanal head, Wilfrid G. Hamlin.[12]

Enrolment in 1964 was 314, up 35% from the previous year. Eliot Pratt made another gift to the College to start off the new campus. The David Batchelder gifts to the Haybarn Theater were recorded; David had been a student in 1956-58, and had died since. He had been fond of Goddard and had enjoyed his time there; when his illness grew upon him he lost neither his courage nor his optimism, but figured out things he could do for the College even while confined to the hospital. He gave funds to build a needed lighting booth and storage room in the Theater, a favorite interest of his in student days; after his death the College received in his name a magnificent grand piano, given by his parents.

Notice that Cate Farm in East Montpelier, next to the Goddard campus on the west, was bought in this year from Gerald and Elsie Ibey for $25,000. This appears in the Quarterly Report for March 1964.[13]

---

[12] Along with Helen Pitkin, Evalyn Bates, Robert Mattuck, George Beecher, Thomas Yahkub, A. R. Elliott, Jr., and a very few others, Wilfrid Hamlin was and is one of that great group of Goddard originals, the last of whom arrived on staff in 1948, who have been marked by the College and have in their turns put their marks on it. Wilfrid, alone among them, still labors in the vineyard, active as ever, full of educational ideas. He attended Antioch and Black Mountain Colleges in earlier years, and graduated from Wayne State University. He later took advanced degrees from alternative educational programs. At Goddard he taught in many fields of literature, drama, educational philosophy, and writing. Above all he was a writer, serving as College Editor most of his professional life.

In lighter vein, Wilfrid and his twin brother Talbot looked so much alike that it was difficult to tell them apart. When travelers from the College were going where his brother lived, Will sometimes warned them not to mind if they thought they saw him on the street and he walked by without speaking; it would not be he; it would be Talbot. Curiously enough, this happened to us once, probably in Boston. We were walking on the street and suddenly here came Will Hamlin, as it appeared, walking by without speaking. Sure enough, it was not Wilfrid. It was Talbot.

The two campuses began to operate as separate entities in 1965. North-wood was late in coming on line; adjustments had had to be made so that Northwood students could be an entity from the beginning even if the new campus was not habitable on time that September. They were in Marshfield for a term, and some shared space on Greatwood into the spring of 1966. Eventually it opened, and even the later students moved in. Alan Walker, the new Dean of Northwood, had been on leave for two years following his participation in the complex of community studies, to carry out a project for the American Friends Service Committee in South America. He was, if we remember, more or less called home to pick up the new campus responsibilities. Enrolment on Northwood built up gradually; its style was very different from Greatwood's, as it was intended to be. It was not that anyone set out - then or later – to make it different. The idea was to let it evolve as it would, and see what happened.

Enrolment noted in the March 1966 Quarterly Report was 411, – 279 on Greatwood, 132 on Northwood – which was very new and still developing its separate population. The Adult Degree Program, distinctive now and on the near side of its initial roll, registered 122 students. Off-campus adult students in commuting campus operations seem to have been 22 on Greatwood, none yet on Northwood. The geographic origins of the two groups of adult students do not appear here: Tim probably listed them. He was interested in things like that. And such data did describe significant aspects of the situation. What he would have found was very likely that the 22 adults in regular classes were from the Vermont environs, while the enrolment in the Adult Degree Program was beginning to come from everywhere across the country; this program (ADP) operated in successive cycles of alternating short residencies on campus and periods of independent study at students' homes and on their usual jobs. The format would become general in colleges and universities adopting the program in future years. It was not general in this period. The potential of the program was to imply fundamental changes in large sections of American higher education.

Notice how things were falling into place within Royce's conception of the College. Two campuses were built and working. The normal on-campus residential program had shown that it could absorb visiting adult students from surrounding communities within commuting distance with advantages to all participating groups. The Adult Degree Program, a new concept of educational organization, was beginning to enlarge irresistibly, drawing students

---

[13] As of March, 1964, then, Royce was still hammer and tongs after building the third campus; otherwise he would not have spent $25,000 to buy the land for it. The bids for the second campus would have had to be opened at about this time as well. We might need to enter a demurrer to John Hall's theory as to when Tim's plans for the Westwood campus began to fade. They may just never have faded that much. He may still have wanted and intended to build it. One of the gifts from Eliot Pratt in this period was applied to the purchase of the land for Westwood. Tim wrote Eliot about it with engaging enthusiasm. See Note [8] above, Note [15] and Note 67 in Part Two, for the President's Report of June 30th, 1969.

from wherever, operating cyclically on an individual and independent study base. Among Royce's figures is still another category, also off-campus students, with 18 on Greatwood and 5 on Northwood; these are in the 411, but not the commuting adults nor the Adult Degree Program students. Thus the grand total for this semester was 563. The off-campus students here were probably adult students matriculated for a degree, as distinct from visiting adult commuters who may have come in simply for a course they happened to want. Royce was heavy on distinctions like that.[14] For a still later judgment on the problem of the third campus, see Note.[15]

By June 1966, enrolment stood over-all at 662, the largest in Goddard's history. By December 1968 it was 883; by June 1969, Royce's final year report, it was 1,021. In some of these reports he would take a side-long look at various indicators of college size, by addressing it in different categories, such as numbers of graduating students, or numbers and types of buildings used, comparing several years over a stretch of time. We will not try to follow him around in all these convolutions. Even in the occasional figures listed here it is clear that the College in his last presidential years was growing at a furious rate. The forward direction appeared to be set. Certain sections of his reports, written latterly by Dean Alan Walker on Northwood and by Dean Ernest Cassara on Greatwood, speak of turbulence and social unrest on both campuses. This was clearly a puzzle: how was it to be handled in a set of circumstances wherein the prime governing principles had long been established as democratic? The College depended on its students, for whom it existed, to provide the substance of self-government − and the students would not gov-

---

[14]In this period the College was not yet out of the financial woods, even with all the students and all the programs. Royce and colleagues were still constantly looking for ways to acquire grant or fund resources, or both. Support was still coming from Eliot Pratt and other trustee and trustee-related donors in this period. When some new expense loomed, − Tim would write to Eliot and say, as if he had never thought of him before as a potential donor, − "Do you know where we can get hold of some money [for such-and-such]?" − Unless he was temporarily pinched for funds by his range of charitable contributions, Eliot Pratt would send the money. If the College received other gifts of any size, as $1,000 or more, Tim would write to Eliot and let him know. They both kept track of funds coming in. One objective was to relieve Eliot of the financial burdens he carried with respect to the College; another was to stay up with efforts to broaden the base of financial contributions to the College. Tim kept Eliot informed about all sorts of events and trends at Goddard. His letters to Eliot are one of the useful sources of information about many details of campus life and work of a programmatic and social nature, other than financial. He would talk to Eliot about things which did not appear in the periodic formal reports, because often they were simply passing the time of day. Eliot's letters were mostly brief and hand-written, yet they often contained homely references to family or other events, or to his own other study or work or research interests. Eliot Pratt and Royce Pitkin were friends.

[15]When reading source files one has to behave variously with different types of material. With correspondence one has to turn every page and look at every paragraph. In April 1971 Royce wrote a short note to a college official from New Jersey otherwise unknown to him who had written to inquire into Tim's view of "cluster colleges". Without applying the term to Goddard, Tim summarized his experience and intention with respect to the two-campus operation. They had been designed to develop programmatically each in its own way, he said, within the general educational philosophy and policy of the College. His successor as president did not favor the multi-campus organization and so had discontinued it. − So now we know: Gerald Witherspoon derailed Westwood campus, along with the two-campus operation.

ern. This is necessarily the question with which we approach the next great problem-area, the fourth among five in which Royce spent his enormous energies over a professional life at Goddard – in all its applicable phases – of 34 years.

V

THE ROYCEAN DIALECTIC

E very so often out of the mists of time there emerges the memory of
something Tim said which had struck us at its moment of origin, and in
some way had stayed strong in recollection. We would be exchanging notes
on some question, in an off-hand circumstance; he would move from the case
in hand to the realm of the general idea, and would let go a conclusion of a
general nature. Because it was so much his nature to concentrate on the particular case, the general idea stood out in figurative relief. – "You can't get far
without the faculty," – was all he said. We had been speaking about some faculty configuration or other around some issue. What he said was a surprise: it
might not have occurred to us up to that point that there was doubt about his
being able to count on faculty cooperation. There was pulling and hauling often enough in the faculty, over campus issues; that was the nature of genuine
discussion of questions. In the end a policy always emerged which drew everyone in and along in a common effort. That this process might have limits
was a faintly startling idea; we would not have been aware that Royce would
acknowledge the possibility of limits. It was not that he would or would not;
it was that we would not have anticipated the issue.

The ambience at Goddard in all these years partook of social democracy. It
was an assumption, articulated perhaps only occasionally but very generally
understood and taken the rest of the time for granted. Part of the problem of
reduced or non-existent cooperation may lie precisely here. The assumption
was clear enough; there was no real objection to it, – no attempt to under-
mine it or to implement anything different. In the early years of the College
the impression we have is that there was relative responsibility on the part of
students. The numbers of on-campus people were of course much smaller
than was the case later. This may have been a large factor in the differences
between early times and later times. In a small-group which included both

faculty and students the effort required to separate oneself from the majority would have been greater than in a large-group. It would have been less apt to occur. There was horse-opera turbulence, understandably; the Plainfield community would have commented on this from time to time. Philosophical or social detachment lay in the future.

In the midst of this group process, the emphasis of the operating principles of the College, constantly re-stated, was always to encourage individual responsibility. If the students were encouraged to take responsibility and to make their own decisions, - who is to object if they did so? If one of their decisions was to disregard the expectations of the College and the Community, as for example in the performance of work program jobs, who is to be shocked? Here we have the potentiality of conflict. Of course this is a judgment from the 1960s. How did it come to pass?

There is naturally very little evidence from the 1935-38 period as to what Royce did with the faculty and students at the Seminary/Junior College in Barre. At this time he would have been preoccupied with survival, represented in the first three categories of problem-areas, initial communications with his primary groups inside and outside of his institution, financial support, and admissions. He was not yet in full charge of the institution; the secondary school division, the original seminary, was still run by its existing staff. Once in Plainfield the situation could and probably did change. Bear in mind that we had no personal presence in those years, from 1938 to 1950. Opinions on what happened then are hypothetical, based on what must presumably have happened to enable what was found operative in 1950.

Tim was 37 when the College moved to Plainfield and set up shop. That was old enough for him to know quite a lot about what he wanted to do. He had begun to consider questions of what he wanted to do while still in Barre, with the group of advisors and prominent citizens whom he called together to begin the design of a new college. The chances are that he went to work soon and hard with his existing faculty, drawing on both the experience with the Vermont group on the obvious level and on his own graduate study exposures from the 1920s and 1930s. One's guess would be that it took him some time to develop the discussional impact that he came to have. This, together with the hardships common in the early period, may have accounted for the turnover in faculty brought from Barre. Topics of discussion in the first months and years would have helped to form the educational procedures which were fundamental in the operations of the College by 1950.

The early President's Reports first appearing in January 1939 and continuing for several years contain a good many of the nuts and bolts of finance, enrolment, trustee appearances, building notes (the Flynn Building was constructed in 1939-40) and deficit anticipations which might be expected. However, there are also clues that no grass was growing anywhere as the institution began to set its feet where it intended to go. Tim remarks in the first report for the second year that there was the short run – difficult in practical respects – and then there was the long run – new college, new campus, and sound principles of education operating in it. He had confidence that the practical problems would be solved. The second Quarterly Report in 1940 covered the Winter term; here there had been eight winter conferences on a variety of topics with a total conference enrolment of 450.[16] Right off we notice that the College had begun by arriving in full dress at a high rate of speed. This was not so very different from the winter conference format and enrolment level of years later. If the financial situation was worse – and it was – he at least had the conference format and accomplishments to think about. He also thought about finances. His very typical remark was: "It is essential that some action be taken concerning the situation." Already he was speaking firmly to the Trustees, to whom the Reports were always addressed. There is not much evidence that they heard him. The early Boards might not have been fully prepared for Royce Pitkin. But they would learn.

In this march-past we are looking for places where Royce was putting his energies and establishing operational patterns for the institution. Early presidential reports were shorter than they tended to be later. They are, however, succinct. In his April 1941 Report he says there were 14 Winter Conferences in 1941, with a total enrolment of 517. The Non-Resident Work Term was heard from that time; 58 students had worked on 17 different types of jobs. This enduring pattern in college operations accounted for why the College plant was relatively empty in January/February, opening the place for the Winter conferences for groups from outside. We don't know the extent to which Tim himself ran any of the winter conferences in early years. The format later called for outside leaders, often from a field specialty; Dr. H. Harry Giles of New York University, acquired a tremendous reputation for his skills in leading conferences in the Winter series, chiefly Current Educational Issues. By the 1950s and 1960s, an occasional faculty person from Goddard in an appropriately related field would be found in a conference chair. In the middle years and later, Royce rarely or never ran a winter or summer conference. He might confer on setting up a conference, and he was the source of innumerable ideas for new conferences. The Division of Adult Education and Community Services would see to the details and the implementations. It may be useful to look later on at some of the consortial conferences to see what Tim's role was. It is likely that he had more to do with those in direct ways. (Cf. VI).

---

[16]Winter conference enrolment for 1939, the first year, had been 257. If the figures of 450 for the second year and even higher for a year soon to follow, are close to accurate, these were larger than winter conference attendance totals in some later years of the College. The difference might be accounted for by the nature of the conferences, as for example the degrees of specialization in different thematic developments. Certain conferences sustained themselves for numbers of years and grew to be expected winter events by persons in certain professional fields. Notice however that Royce and colleagues working on conference plans did not aim at large populations in these seasonal events. Their objective was to keep the plant in use in off-seasons and to emphasize educationally sound and useful studies. The "conference" format is of course a focus needing study, proceeding as it did on the basis of the Roycean dialectic. (Cf. VI & VII below.)

Readers of the President's Reports for the decade of the 1940s are impressed by how familiar they all sound. With respect to writing itself as writing, Tim hit his favorite format early, and pursued it for the next three decades, refining it as might be warranted. The order of topics would vary from report to report; the general topical headings tend to be reliably present. He would cover the main problem-areas, giving what figures pleased him in various connections; he would pick out educational themes which interested him and would comment on them. In selecting certain of his reports for Part Two we have reached for the ones which tell the most about his educational thought and its expression in various ways through the institution.

A judgment made on the basis of a fair acquaintance with Royce's writings suggests that his best composition is in the Presidential Reports. One document, an address to the Community in 1961, achieves nearly the same level of careful writing. In the Presidential Reports and in the rare occasional document is where his genuine metaphysics and his active expression of social philosophy taken as social process come through in the record. His writing is remarkably precise and exact. It is impossible to paraphrase him. Nothing else one can think of for terms and phrases catches the level of exactness for which he sought and which he could achieve whenever he put his mind to it.

He did not always put his mind to it – which is to say that a good deal of his writing, including most of his articles published in magazines during his professional life prior to retirement, was made up of pieces written for public relations purposes. He needed to describe to the potential public and especially to young people what Goddard was like as a college, what it did in educational process and why and how it did it. A good deal of his composition, especially for speeches – of which he gave a great number in the community outside the College in many locations and at many events around the country – was off-the-cuff. He would warn people who were inviting him to speak at a college commencement where his appearance would be the principal event that there would be no written version of what he would say. He meant by that that he would have no trouble coming up with a topic and its treatment, but he was not going to produce a scholarly piece for them to publish. He didn't have time. If they wanted to keep his remarks they could tape them. That was their problem. There was never any hesitation. They took it for granted that he was coming and the conditions he set were always all right.

In the conceptual formulation of the Roycean dialectic it appears that by far the best of his writings have no part. On the face of it this might appear strange. The fact seems to be that no members of the old staff presently remember that the President's Reports were ever generally distributed. Perhaps such reports rarely are. Philosophically, it fits with the way Royce ordered his expressional life and work that this was his choice. His mode of communication was verbal, discussional. Yet he wrote in those quarterly and annual reports over a thirty-year period a remarkable set of documents which constitute a fascinating history of the College. At intervals he wrote in them statements of his educational philosophy.[17]

The picture of Royce in faculty meeting in memories from the 1950s is distinctive. There would have been a faculty tea served just ahead of the meeting in the dining alcove of the President's House, a stand-around affair with a lot of friendly talk all around. Helen Pitkin was hostess for these teas. The rest of the week she would have been doing anything and everything in the College, teaching classes, working in the library, counselling, taking care of the Manor gardens, taking part in committees. At the Friday afternoon teatimes she was hostess. Tim would be part of the group, involved in group conversations as might occur. Then the faculty would disperse to a circle in the living room; Tim's chair was in the corner where he could see the room and everyone in it. He had the agenda, possibly a small paper in his hand. Sometimes he took notes: not till 1995 did we ever see a note he took, but some of them are in the archive. He had a curious method of numbering paragraphs and sub-paragraphs in decimals, 1.0, 1.1, 1.2, etc. We never knew that before. Actually it went far back in his history with the faculty and with faculty and community conferences. It appears early in conference and meeting records. One might say that he had always done it, but that is only guessing; nor do we know where he got the habit. We had not seen anything like it since the later days of Bloom's Taxonomy at Empire State, one of the educational fads that blew through that place in the 1970s. Taking notes for his own use was the only application Tim made of this system so far as we know. Probably few of us ever knew he did it. It never appears in the definitive Reports.

When the discussion became intense, as it was likely to do from time to time, Tim might hitch forward in his chair to meet the onslaught of opinion, making discussional thrusts at every turn, challenging, probing, glancing around the room to keep track of faculty interests and potential expressions. He was forthrightly involved in every phase of the discussion, actively leading it, occasionally running ahead to keep up but mostly meeting the expressions head-on, turning them over in response, shaking them out, reaching for further questions. At intervals he might essay a tentative summary, as of a proposed policy. The result might go either way, forward into a trial formulation or back into the crucible. There might be several topics to consider; if so, he had the sequence in mind; if there was only one topic of the day, he kept attention on it so there was no wandering afield. His great art in these affairs was to keep the discussion going until a common thread emerged to be wov-

---

[17]As noted earlier, when the pressure was on in the Community over a philosophical or policy matter, it was as if Tim resorted to his Reports to make fundamental statements of position, perhaps expecting that they might serve as points of reference however the issues were resolved. Probably that was not the point: if the issues were to be effectively resolved, they would be resolved by discussional means and not by referring to authoritative positions in writing, not even his own. He did not have much use for authoritative writings. His accounts of the history of the College were just that, even in the philosophical dimension. This is how he expected them to remain. We may see later if there was any modification of his views with respect to educational philosophy. At this point we suspect there may have been.

en into a group position. Usually this happened; it was how institutional policy was worked out. Now and then issues required time in successive meetings to set a policy in motion on which there was general agreement.

It was a tiring process. When closing time came and we trooped out to cars to go home we knew we had been through a demanding affair. Meetings like this occurred on Friday afternoons all fall and spring. There were other conferences on campus, often with students on a community basis. Royce was not necessarily the leader for those; he would be a participant quite as readily. The tail might have wagged the dog a fair share of the time in such matters, but the forms were important; Community Meetings were run by the elected Chairpersons of the community, almost always students. The community meetings were also tiring processes, occurring as they did mostly in evenings after a day's work. A variation on the theme were "meetings of the community", which Royce called rarely when he had something to say to the large-group. These were understood to be different from Community Meetings and were not the vehicle for policy-setting in the governance sense. They were apt to be for reflective or study purposes. There were some pre-semester and post-semester faculty conferences if the issues warranted. In the middle years there were mid-semester conferences which involved both faculty and community.

Royce was chair of the faculty for purposes of meetings and discussions from the opening of the College in 1938 until the opening of the second campus in 1965, the division having the effect of moving faculty chair responsibilities to the deans of Greatwood and Northwood. This was because the conception of the two campuses included the idea that the faculties were separate on them and should each develop in individual ways. Each campus was to have of the order of 250 students; somewhere among the archive notes is the figure in Tim's hand of 260 as the objective of each group; we do not know what this means – perhaps only that Tim was constantly turning over in his mind relevant issues having to do with the operation of the College and that he may have been trying out the figure to see where it led. There were occasional meetings of the total faculty together, called All-College Faculty meetings and for those Royce was Chair. But there were not a great number of those; they were not intended to expand or to take over direction of the campuses and they did not do so. They would have dealt with issues common to both campuses and applicable throughout the institution.

It is very interesting that Royce could do this and stay with it as an operational policy. It must have cost him a good deal to bring it off.[18] But bring it off he did: he never went back on his arrangement, whatever the cost to himself personally.

---

[18]It did indeed cost him something. He is supposed to have said to one of the staff who was around often enough to hear things like this, that after the division into two campuses he no longer knew how to be President. This would have been in the period from 1965 to 1969. Still, he stayed with his arrangement, and he never gave the slightest sign of unease. One really had to admire him for it. He took the consequences of the common policies, and learned new ways just like everyone else.

A potential field of conflict may have been developing in the College as he withdrew himself and his expressional force from direct involvement and participation in campus-level social and political developments. The conflict-potential lay in the relationship between the democratic social philosophy of the College, and Tim's iron conviction that the educational philosophy of the institution, worked out over a professional lifetime of a generation or more, was not to be abandoned by a return to conventionality and not to be super-annuated by a flitting after fashionable willow-the-wisps of innovation for the sake of innovation.[19]

The implied opposition may have developed gradually, without all of its implications being clear. There were a number of upheavals on campus, at intervals of several years. One evidently occurred as early as 1956. We cannot call up its details out of the mists, and Royce rarely noted such things in his Reports. He might refer in a general way to moods and climates on campus in a particular term; one does not recall that he ever made much of a point beyond that. How then do we know of this one?

By devious means, surely, – almost but not quite by accident. A student of that time had been a prisoner in World War II in one of the Nazi concentration camps. He had learned the prison-camp equivalent of "street-ways", and had survived, barely. He had been recommended as a student for Goddard by a social service connection in Boston. In due time he showed up, ready for college. He had had a hard time all by himself over the years; he knew a good thing when he saw it. College was a good thing. Upheavals were not a good thing. They interfered with college studies. Whatever happened in 1956, Steve watched with interest. Apparently there was a community gathering of sorts, in the course of which Royce, who was not, remember, necessarily in charge of the meeting, got up and took a stand; in all probability, he laid down the law. The revolt, if that was what it was, dissipated. Tim could do that. He had the prestige and the presence; if by chance he became irritated and showed anger – a very rare occurrence, but an occasional occurrence nonetheless – he could be literally terrifying. All of this would happen not at all by indirection, but in direct confrontation with students. This was not like anything they had been raised up by the College to expect. Humanly speaking, very humanly speaking, normal persons in such circumstances would think immediately of self-preservation. Whatever happened to cause the reaction and the fright would be very unlikely to be repeated for a while.[20]

With reference to the 1956 incident, the student in question eventually wrote a one-page account of it, and sent it, perhaps sometime later, to the College library. How it got to the Royce Pitkin archive one does not know. The student developed a vast respect for Tim out of the incident, and did

---

[19]Royce spoke a good deal about innovation over the years, like most everyone else in that period. It was not difficult to conclude that he really thought there was something special in it. There was of course something special in it as long as one was aware of the context: innovation with respect to convention was one thing; with respect to the educational philosophy of the College it was quite another. There may be occasion to revisit this issue later.

what he could to preserve a recollection of it. In the end, he wanted also to let people know how highly he regarded what Royce had done for the College and for the community of students who wanted a solid education uninterrupted by upheavals.

If one of these revolts occurred in 1956, and another later by a few years, one should perhaps ask, of what were they symptomatic? Very likely they meant something. If the College philosophy encouraged individual independence and initiative, and if then in a trial incident the students suddenly found themselves up against an immovable object, might there not be trouble? There was at least the potential of a clash. If periodic clashes did occur, need we be surprised? Not being a student at the time, we may have missed some of the student ambience. It may be fair to look for the same quality of confusion on the faculty level. Probably it was present. Suppose that from time to time new movements were made in the faculties the implications of which were, if one looked far enough, to call into question certain provisions of the College educational philosophy. In the period of the two-campus development each of the campus faculties was expected to develop in unique ways – within the general framework of the existing institutional philosophy. How were faculty members to know what was expected of them in the philosophical dimension? The older people on the faculty in point of length of service would have known the answer readily enough. They would have absorbed the College philosophy over years of practice and of dialectic. They were, in short, seasoned. But they might not have known that they were seasoned; it might not have occurred even to the people longest on campus that they should have been more aware of significant dangers of rapid development in the College.

In the 1960s the pace of enlargement took off as the time for opening the second campus approached. Additions to the faculty were common enough, but in small numbers per semester or academic year, carefully controlled by attention to the balance between rising numbers of students, residential space for them, and faculty and other central services which had to be provided. There was iron control of these factors, stemming from Royce's office. The budget was not out of control in this period. The College was always short of money; the financial situation was nearly as scary in the 1960s as it had been in the 1950s. It was scary for different reasons: remember the note that Tim

---

[20]A very funny story dating from the period of 1967-68 has been told in a variety of ways. We were not on campus then, so we don't know which version is accurate. Three flag-poles stood in front of the Flynn Building in that year, from which three flags commonly flew, – the United Nations flag, the Vermont State flag, and properly on its own right according to flag etiquette, the American flag. Some students took a notion that the American flag should not be flown, and they took it down. The UN flag and the Vermont flag could stay, but the American flag had to go. Whether Tim just happened along or whether it was reported where he heard of it, the story is clear that he showed up. All versions agree that he told them to put it back up. Well, they wanted to know, why should they? It was their College and they could take the flag down if they wanted to. No, he is reported on good authority to have replied, they couldn't. Goddard was a public institution and public institutions flew the flag. It was his College, and as long as he was President the American flag would be flown in front of it. If they didn't like it they were free to leave whenever they liked. That was the end of it. The flag went back up and stayed there.

wrote to show what happens in hypothetical situations of 10% shortage when the annual budget was in the range of $100,000 and when it was in the range ten times larger. The dangers of miscalculation in the budget area rose disproportionately in the situation prevalent in the mid-1960s. The time would come in the history of the College when these dangers were ignored. The cost to the College was dreadful. In certain significant respects Goddard may never have fully recovered. But all that was later, after Royce retired.

Faculty additions prior to the two-campus division were of the order of two or three new teachers per year or term, probably varying slightly with changing circumstances. In the crucial year of 1965 when the second campus opened, the number was 13, about four times the normal complement. These would have been divided among the two campuses with the greater number probably going to the new campus, Northwood, or serving as replacements for Greatwood staffers who may have chosen to go to Northwood. It may have been too many new persons all at once. There may not have been the adjustment programs called for by the situation. Orientation was not a common word at Goddard; it smacked unduly of the conventional. But there might have been ways of encouraging development on the part of new people which could have brought about earlier understanding of what would be expected of them. It is hard to tell at this distance; what did happen is none too clear in recollection. It is all too easy to mix it up with ideas on what ought to have happened.

The two campuses were indeed different. They were intended to be, and they were. Dean Alan Walker on Northwood was a lifelong Quaker, expressive of the enormous discipline which marked the tradition of the Friends. This discipline involved a profundity of respect for and restraint toward the opinions of others that might be said to be unknown outside the Quaker context. He had worked for several years at Goddard as leader of the newly developing program in the study of the community, by which was meant the community as exemplified in Vermont small towns and villages. A field component went along with academic study, so that, as in the Vermont Youth Study described elsewhere, students were on- and off-campus for parts of the study, and often became partial members of their study communities. Following this Alan had taken a two-year leave to fulfill another Quaker tradition, that of service to the wider community under the auspices of The American Friends Service Committee. The locus of this was in South America, and Alan was on duty there in the second year when he was called home to take the leadership of Northwood campus faculty and students. It is probably not to the point to regard his religious approach by itself as determinative of the mode and the politics of the second campus. He was simply greatly skilled in the counseling arts and had learned how to encourage people of student and faculty ages to develop individual approaches to whatever problems presented themselves. The community development studies he had led earlier had been notably effective. For whatever reason, Northwood developed in less structured ways than may have been the case on Greatwood Campus.

For reasons of awkwardness we will refrain from describing the characteristics of the deanship on Greatwood, since we were it. There was a commonly perceived attribute of the campus itself which was described as of the nature of structure: there was more structure on Greatwood, so the story went, though it might have been difficult to put a finger on the precise loci where it could be said to have shown itself. Without doubt there were established ways of proceeding on Greatwood, simply because it had been there from the beginning. There was some awareness of the need to separate the Greatwood Deanery from the President's office, and to assist with this the Deanery was physically moved to Greatwood Cottage, where it occupied the large second floor room over the switchboard, surrounded by quiet leafy outlooks. It was a very pleasant office; we always liked it. Students would come in to report on independent studies, and would pace its full length and back repeatedly, talking about whatever they wanted to talk about. Those were among the few lectures ever given at Goddard, unless someone like Perry Miller came to address the Community on a special occasion.

We are not of course sure whether this is accurate, but we tended to think that when the tension grew between faculty and administration it grew first and most markedly on Greatwood. If this was the case, it might have been in part because Northwood people had been handled from the beginning with greater latitude and less expectation of particular outcomes. Possibly Greatwood people might have had more precise notions of what was expected of them. At least, some may have thought so. Bear in mind that there could be different opinions about this.

Another dimension may offer a better explanation. Some may have felt that there was on Greatwood a slightly stronger movement toward the conventional in academic behavior and ideas. Something of the same sort of interest showed itself years later at Empire State College. It was as if it was not quite enough for faculty members to be participants in an experimental educational institution; some may have felt a need to be classical professors in a more traditional sense, and to do what classical academics do. If this was so, it might have appeared more naturally on Greatwood than on Northwood, where expectations were perhaps diverse enough so that the effect was a natural screening out of persons with larger interests in the traditions of academe. At this distance ideas of this sort may be more hypotheses than observations.

After 1965 the Roycean dialectic was inevitably less obvious on both campuses. So much of Tim's presence on campus had been marked by discussional interchange over living educational issues that to have him suddenly define his involvement less by verbal dialogue over the issues than by remoter factors of practical development even if these were demanding, left something of a vacuum. It was probably unavoidable. It wasn't that he was less busy; quite the opposite. He remarks somewhere that the construction of the two campuses largely on federal funds meant a vast increase in the administrative attention which had to be given to federal relations. His associates would have seen to many of the details. The large scale issues undoubtedly still landed on his desk. Indeed, the survival of the institution was wrapped up in many of these larger scale matters. He could not have escaped the new demands on his time.

When one of Tim's friends came down with a disability and was threatened with a period of hospitalization, Tim wrote him to soften the impact. He, too, he said, had had hospitalizations; they weren't so bad. In 1963, and again in 1966, he had had "a heart attack".[21] Nothing much was said about his illnesses on campus. We knew he was out sick, but were led to think he was resting at home. Probably these were just more of the de facto separations we were to get used to. There were no observable consequences on campus. Everything went along as usual.

If the Roycean dialectic became less personal and less immediate on campus in the 1960s its further effects did not. The forces of the dialectic which he had set in motion and established on a repetitional basis kept on working. The conferences were held, summer and winter; classes took place as usual, (though later called 'group studies'), modified only by a rising incidence of independent studies. These were a later educational stage than classes, and were understood to be so, – and subject to being earned by demonstration of student readiness. In some way independent studies were built on the educational foundations achieved in classes, where the dialectic was operative, albeit through persons other than Royce. This meant, of course, that the dialectic was different for different persons and combinations of persons. It was also undoubtedly different for different situations; it could be intense in independent studies as readily as in groups. It was essentially an expressional force, modified by personality considerations and framed for the most part in the posing of questions which gave opportunity for reflection and response – in short, a generative phenomenon. What appears to have happened in this was that over a period of years involving successive generations of students and faculty, people had learned how to understand the nature of this approach to learning and had become proficient in it. They could in the end do it as well in the independent study as in a class or group study.[22]

A fine line was to be drawn between the faculty role in operation of the dialectic and the necessity for staff persons to get out of the way of students and to stay out. In effect, there were two currents constantly flowing at the same time, not in the same direction: the drive of the dialectic in which participants were endlessly challenged in every phase of their common concerns, and fol-

---

[21] It is interesting that he wrote of these events as if they were one and the same. He said he had a heart attack in 1963 and again in 1966, as if they were one. Most people might have spoken of two attacks. He had spent time in hospital in both years. He made it sound as if he had rather liked it. Actually, that would have been quite atypical. What he would have wanted was to get back on campus and get busy. He had to take blood thinners, he went on. He was of course trying to have a palliative effect on the feelings of his threatened colleague. As it turned out, he was not so far from the mark. He did not have future attacks, and can be said to have made a full recovery. Toward the end of his life he became seriously ill, what he had was kidney disease. – "If you have to get a terminal disease," he observed to us many years later, sitting in his living room and making wry comments on problems of senior citizens, "don't get kidney failure. Get something else!" –

lowing upon the recognition of the student's need to paddle his own canoe, the resolve to hold back the challenge and to let the student – when the student was ready – have his head and endure the consequences of choices made. Judgments had continually to be made as to which stage a situation was in, and therefore which policy was appropriate for the circumstance.

The Roycean dialectic was then in the end apparent in many different realizations, according to the faculty and staff people involved and conditioned also by the student initiatives and responses. It was never – unless long ago in its first manifestations – unidirectional. But it had a heavy initial component if it was manifesting itself in a case-instance. Neither was it a single event except in the simplistic assessment of timed events. It was a process. If it were applied or expressed effectively, the questions lingered in mind, as indeed they would have been intended to do.[23]

Beginning in the 1950s and continuing well into the 1960s another of those parallel lines of Roycean expression manifests itself, adding yet another dimension to the several modes in which Tim worked, all at the same time. Thus far we have addressed on-campus components of his many interests. In speaking of his off-campus activities we risk falling over the line into Section VI, where his educational outreach concerns are a central focus. This is again a risk to be taken – helpful because it enables a review of the working of the dialectic in a different context. Immediately confronting the student of Royce's work and thought is of course the question of how one person could do all this. But we wonder about that when addressing only his on-campus concerns. Soon we shall find he had an array of off-campus educational involvements which would – it seems from this distance – have taken up the full time of at least one educational figure, perhaps of several. Remembering the question from the early days in Barre about whether Tim had taught him-

---

[22]Somewhere in earlier writings we have remarked the history of the development of independent study at Goddard. It was introduced first as a senior-level study experience, and gradually moved back in successive time-periods to the third-year students, and then to the second-year people; in the end, selected first-year people could request it and at least in their second semesters on campus expect to try one or so. Independent studies undeniably became fashionable; they were marks of moderate distinction; young people wanted them. If they could not have them for some reason they felt deprived and put upon. What we have always thought happened here to a great extent was that experienced students taught younger students how to pursue independent studies, in successive waves. Independent studies were part of the community ambience. They were, so to speak, in the air. In a manner of speaking, the community taught itself how to do independent studies. The faculty were involved; Royce himself was involved: he taught one class a semester whenever he could manage it - which was most of the time. He taught independent studies, like everyone else. He really liked to teach, like most of the rest of us. And the students were involved. If one is looking to understand this phenomenon, bear in mind what this meant: everywhere a new student looked, older students were doing independent studies. It was a formative and formidable condition in which to be immersed.

[23]There has been reason to remark many times over the years that in a situation like the one at Goddard where the question loomed so large in the nature of the real, there was no more powerful weapon – if one conceived of argumentation and discussion as involving 'weapons' – in the dialectic. Statement was never so strong as a question well-put, then left to do its work. Notice the different conceptualization of the nature of the self required by this realization: in the background of the conception is the figure of the individual student poised to respond, to create a new understanding and a new synthesis in the process of doing so. It is as if the student were waiting for the question, and to respond to it with another form of the question and therefore with another formulation of the real, actual or implied.

self not to worry, about finance when he was being questioned about education, about building space when he was concerned with personnel, about admissions when the central issue may have been his class or an independent
study, or the educational design of a conference, the reflective observer is
forced further toward the conclusion that indeed he must have learned how
to set aside one klatsch of concerns while addressing another. He must have
learned how not to worry.

In the mid-1950s the records tell of his immersion in the adult education
movement. His primary loyalty was to the residential adult education section
of the Adult Education Association of the USA. It is not clear how he first became involved in this; he simply begins to appear in the archives as Chair of
the Residential Adult Education section. What this may mean is that he himself was responsible for the initiation of the section within the AEA, and that
as so often happens once an interest is clear, he was made Chair and left to
run it. He was equal to the task. For a number of years he ricocheted off a
companion group of adult education leaders who shared his commitment to
adult education of the residential variety, doing in an off-campus network
much of what he had done so intensely on-campus.[24]

In the later 1950s Royce was succeeded in the post by Myles Horton,
founder and head of Highlander Folk School in Tennessee. Myles had been a
close associate in the Residential Adult Educational Committee for some
time. He was of course heavily involved in Highlander. Judging by the archive record the thread of events in the R.A.E. section may not have been so
active for a while. But the presumption is that developments continued in that
context. It may have been that Royce's attention moved to an international
focus. There seem not to have been sharp dividing lines between Tim's major
interests in one period and the next, or between the expressional activities of
one period and the next. It is as if they fade in and out in a weaving design, so
that the emphases would change, even while the themes remained operative
to greater or lesser degrees, recoverable or not as might be desirable. The
moving finger would write along for a few years and the focus would be
somewhere else. We shall see this happening.

People on campus, except for his special assistants concerned with these
fields, might know relatively little about what he was doing in a certain field.
He came and went, sometimes reporting developments in faculty meetings if
he thought we should discuss them. About the turn of the 1960s the international residential adult education conferences begin to take center stage.
Recall his early interests in the Danish folk schools: repeatedly this interest
comes to mind in reflections on the residential adult education formats in
America in the 1950s and 1960s. In the record intermittent inquiries came in
about what schools in the United States and Canada were closest to the Danish models. He or his staff would answer. There were not very many instances

---

[24]Evalyn C. Bates, long-time Director of the Division of Adult Education and Community Services at
Goddard, confirmed that this was more or less how it happened. Before the 1950s there had not been such
a section in the AEA.

to list in reply, – Highlander was usually one – perhaps only three or four, or half a dozen, allowing for certain ones no longer operating. There had been cultural efforts to preserve some of them as Scandinavian populations moved to North America. Some were not successful for very long, and were remembered mainly in the context of cultural nostalgia, as such cultural groups often strive to preserve their remembered traditions. The answers were always patient and courteous, but Tim's mind was clearly on future developments. The succession of international residential adult education conferences was beginning.

What of the Roycean dialectic in this context? The applications of it would have been more occasional; the international conferences were generally at two-year intervals. In between, people would have been remembering the one just past and planning for the next to come. The principal medium of communication was of course letters. There were a lot of them; Tim's were models of clarity, as always. The contents were often not profound; conferences took a lot of business to arrange. Once in a while there would be a telegram, but not often. Telephone use was nothing like what it is today, perhaps rare by comparison. Mostly people wrote letters to each other. That is a form of communication, like other forms, if slower than what we know now, and more deliberate. Perhaps it suited the times.

During actual conference sessions Tim would have operated much as he did in on-campus situations. For purposes of the Roycean dialectic the applications would have been at wider intervals, but the form of the dialectic might not have been markedly different. He might have had some of the same problems in conferences that he had at home in the College. He probably did not provide the conferees with a great deal of rest. At the College everyone was used to this; he was a walking dynamo wherever he turned; things happened when he walked into a room. On the other hand, his theory of the residential adult education conference was quite clear: it required an absolute minimum of one overnight and two days with meals; it was a recognition that education was to be of the whole person, and that included sociability and leisure, recreational and cultural activities as well as intellectual labor. During the winter conferences on campus, that famous series of annual events which marked the Vermont seasons of snow and blizzards, the intensity was such that the staff, who had more or less the run of any of them they wished to attend, would invariably select the three major conference landmarks and would emerge from them so tired they could not face many more. It may appear odd to say so, but Royce's lead was enormously energetic in the directions of the multiple activities which marked the nature of the conference motif, including the rest and recreation which were part of the conference format.

The fundamental pattern of the conference format became familiar in the extreme, so much so that people went to some trouble to vary it. A presentation or so might normally come first, in the large-group setting, followed by a meal and a breaking-up into small-groups for discussion purposes; free-time might follow in the late afternoon, with a large-group reporting session to wind up formal sessions. Free time or recreational activity might ensue. Times and minor orders might vary. There were practical reasons for introducing free times. People got tired; the attention factor and the cerebration could be wearing. One left the sessions with a sense of a very rich diet for the most part; boredom was unknown. The sense of personal or individual experience was intense. One consequence was that sometimes facing the talkback session, in which the small-groups reported their tentative results, was a trifle more than the aching mind could bear. Still, as a basic event it had its place and its value, a sense of accomplishment all its own. This pattern could repeat itself either once or twice in three days. A common conclusion was a summing up by the conference presenter, or by a conference chair of the stature of H. Harry Giles, who had few peers at shaking out the essentials of the process.

It should not be supposed that Royce would interpose all the time or dominate the sessions. He did no such thing. He could and did insert trenchant remarks; no remark of his was ever wasted. The dialectic was represented in the conference format by the persons whose presence he had helped arrange, by the level of the discussion, to which he contributed as a participant, and by the tentative outcomes, which were commonly outstanding. This pattern was not in itself unique; it was part of conference formats wherever adult education was pursued. It was the level of the process which stood out. Everything stood out: the participants, the sharp topics – general though they might be in the formulations – the process in which seasoned and experienced personnel expressed their ideas and modified them under pressure from peers.

One has to be careful in characterizing conclusions. In a discussional setting and process conclusions might not be warranted, or achieved. What might be achieved were tentative places to pause for a regrouping, a reconsideration, a temporary policy recommendation; probably not anything close to a conclusion. These were dialectical ganglia glimpsed in the midst of sociocommunicational effort. They might have had no beginning and no end, but they were a solid process between the non-terminals which had its own reality, and provided the basis for relative understanding and for social movement. A ground was left, invariably, for future study through a repetition or continuation of the process, in a future occasion, a year or two years into the future, based on another formulation of the problem – which often Tim would set by reaching for another but related title, enough in itself to start the process again. The succession of conference considerations could and often did go on for years, perhaps with a variety of chairpersons, a partial overlap of conferees but also some new attendees, year by year. An overdrive ambience might suffuse the series of conferences; people would come full of expectations, and leave excited, tired, challenged and changed, anticipating the gathering next intended.

The Roycean dialectic was then Royce's thing, a process on a level which raised an entire array of individually based horizons; but it was a process which Royce shared around in a curious blend of multiple formulations and participations. It was his great achievement, which he could and did give away freely, generating a multiple energy represented in the persons with whom he interacted. In some part he was almost certainly aware of all this; from his earliest days in the winter conferences in Plainfield in the late 1930s he had carefully counted and recorded the numbers of persons touched by participation in those events; he would count them and record the figures all his professional life. It was one simple way to keep track of educational process; behind it was a complex set of reflective assumptions concerning human nature and the educative process about which he might not have been explicit but on the ground of which he found he was well able to proceed.

VI

EDUCATIONAL OUTREACH AND THE
GROWING EDGE

The Division of Educational Experimentation, the last and greatest of the divisions at Goddard beginning in the late 1950s when the divisions were first introduced, was what it was in many respects because of Royce's fundamental interest in what went on in it. Of course the divisions were not really divisions at all; they were not mutually exclusive. They were emphases, – ganglia, perhaps. They might have been called centers. They were called divisions, when they were called anything; as a name it did well enough. Nobody was much interested in demarcations. What it meant was that certain activities were focused in certain ways and attended to in certain ways. There was a rough selection of concerns under certain headings; that would have accounted for most of the phenomena in each of them. The Division of Educational Experimentation had activities centered in each of the other divisions. Its job was to look after those concerns, and to develop new ones. The person in charge of it was George Beecher.[25]

George Beecher was a caution. He had this great reputation as a teacher, but nobody could figure out what he did. He would go into a class and sit

---

[25]The person in charge of all the divisions was in the first instance Royce Pitkin. People understood that. That was how we all wanted it. He had more ideas than we did, and he had them first. When currents get to flowing with a certain momentum a lot of new things happen of the same general classification, perhaps with variations. This tended to be how it was in the divisions. There was remarkably little friction among the various persons primarily concerned. Occasionally Tim would do something suddenly without consulting everybody, and there would be a discussion. Once he did this in the Greatwood context. We can't remember what it was now, and it doesn't matter. We were annoyed and went in to see him. Probably we scowled all the way into the silo. Perhaps we thought we were going to be diplomatic and come at it obliquely. He listened to the point-questions, and after a few minutes developed a mischievous small smile. – "You know," he said, "I think the real problem here is that I interfered with you." – Both of us spent the rest of the appointment time laughing.

down, and sometimes he wouldn't say anything. Classes at Goddard were basically 90 minutes, with variations later usually in the direction of extended length. There was time for quite a lot to happen. In one of George's classes the students might get restless waiting for something to start; after a while someone might start to talk. It often turned out to be an excellent class. In later semesters and later years students often said that his classes were the best ones they had in college. It had something to do with his gift for getting people to take the initiative in the carrying out of a study. George was not only a remarkable teacher; he was also a truly original thinker. Nobody could figure that out either. There appeared to be a certain circularity to the ways he thought about things; if one were trying to follow what he said in a committee or a faculty meeting one frequently ended up back at the beginning. It had something to do with the ways in which he dealt with conceptualizations. He could always tell the difference between what was real and what people thought was real.[26] Anyway, this was the person whose principal administrative responsibility was looking after educational experiments. These experiments were all over the place at Goddard, everywhere one looked; they were on both campuses; they were in adult education and community services; they were off-campus wherever the College had a role to play. Of course they tended to be organized into programs, so they were not quite as complicated to look after as one might think. But they were complicated enough. In effect, in one way or another, everyone ended up on everyone else's staff. It all worked quite well.

Before the setting up of the divisions the College had been relatively self-contained. The winter conferences typically in January and February had begun abruptly in the Winter of 1939; we have had occasion to speak of that. To the student of the College now it is surprising to see it happening so suddenly; the pace never really slowed. The conference enrolments probably went up some, if the numbers of conferences increased, but not very much within each conference. The particular focus of some conferences undoubtedly changed with changing interests. The pattern, however, was set, and it persisted.

One way of looking at things is to regard what might be called the outreach dimension of educational activity at the College as one of two predecessor-stages of the Division of Experimentation. It lasted twenty years or so. Time was taken up in on-campus educational programs and in seasonal conferences all of which had justifications in their own terms; both of these

---

[26]After refusing to publish anything in haste all his professional life George came up with a book, well into his retirement years. Cf. Beecher, *Learning and Self-Governing: Questions on the Future of Democracy in America*. Adamant, 1994. It was pure Beecher. The reader had to ask at every turn, – what assumptions is George making here? What are the implications? Where is he going with the argument? Its role in the larger dialectic of the book culture was to raise impossible questions. What became of them was not necessarily George's prime concern. He dug a lot of holes around for readers to fall into, about the way he did in class discussions. Whether they fell into them or into others was their problem. Its principal emphasis was less on formal education than on learning aspects of public affairs and the relation of individuals to governing, especially individual participation in development and applications of public policy.

categories contributed to the disciplinary matrix for staffers who continued with the College for long or relatively long periods of time. This would have made a difference when the chips were down. The transition to the mode of formal experimentation was made with no difficulty, as one remembers it from a perspective of 30 years. During the earlier decades of concentration on becoming a college in the progressive educational format Tim worked intensely and intensively with the staff in the dialectic which was his trademark. One finds out over time how many other activities he was involved in, in some of these years; the recollection is that he still did not miss many faculty meetings or many chances to interact with staffers and students.

One should not lose sight of the fact that the early years of the College, say the first 20 years, were a time of hard and conscientious work for all hands. It must have been especially laborious for Royce. In the first 20 years he was directly and intensively involved on-campus with faculty and student interactions on innumerable topics and in innumerable areas. In terms of traditional academic concerns in higher education, he was his own dean in the various fields that deans can be involved with, not to mention being president, with all that that entailed, and besides that, an active faculty teacher.[27] This assay of the early Goddard years may stand up fairly well when in the 1960s Royce turned up as a member of the Board of Trustees of Nasson College in Springvale, Maine, not far from Portland. Roger Gay was the president of Nasson at the time. He and Tim were acquainted and on a friendly basis. Tim's nine-year stretch on this board led to a number of archive deposits involving papers on and from Nasson during a period of difficulty when Nasson was struggling with the attempt to form a new, experimental campus pursuing different ways of learning and teaching. Without undertaking anything like a study of the Nasson situation it may be safe to say that the basic difference between Goddard and Nasson was the long period of intense education at Goddard which preceded its move into a more complete experimental mode. There is little or no indication that anything like this occurred at Nasson. Its solution to the problem of experimentation was to found a new campus nearby, put the new programs and new people over there, and enter upon a period of internal conflict and anxiety marked by tension between the campuses and the faculty groups. The outcome was disastrous for Nasson. The archive suggests that the picture at Nasson was not simple, nor the misfortune based in any particular location. Each group was simply very defensive and self-protective; each thought it was the genius of Nasson. It was all very human and very regrettable. Nothing of the sort ever happened at Goddard; nothing like it was ever contemplated on either campus or in any section of

---

[27]A mildly shocking thought in connection with Royce Pitkin, disliking as he did the role and title of dean. We think what it meant was that his idea of academic structure was essentially horizontal: what he really liked was being able to dialogue directly with anyone and everyone, about anything and everything. When he began to have assistants and associates the relationships required compromise. This was difficult, except as dialogue always involves compromise. There is no question but that dialogue does involve compromise; it adds to the perception that the Roycean dialectic was very hard work, especially for Royce himself.

the College. That it did not occur at Goddard had to have been due to the long years of involvement in educational thought and discussion which was Royce's distinctive mode and which we have called the dialectic. The existing campus and faculty were brought constantly along through interactive participation, week by week, semester by semester, year by year. When the time came to divide the College and to build the second campus, in general, whatever the individual shortcomings, everyone was ready; no one was surprised or threatened by anything. Everyone was used to new things, to the nature of change. People argued about facets and aspects of things; that was natural. It did not occur to anyone to object to anything or to try to block anything or go back to any previous stage. At Nasson all these things occurred to somebody at one time or another. The events in Springvale took place in the late 1960s. Tim was a member of that Board from about 1963 to about 1972. Roger Gay resigned the presidency of Nasson about 1968, after 18 years. Tim saw it all. It could not have been an easy process to observe, especially for one committed to facilitating educational change and development. He never said much about it. Probably most of us at Goddard never knew that Royce was a member of the Nasson Board. If some of us knew it, we did not pay it any mind. Events at Nasson must have worried him; he was undoubtedly fond of Roger Gay and would have been eager to help him do well with an experiment and at the same time stay out of trouble. He was also a trustee on the Nasson Board, and would have felt some burdens for its success or failure. It is no part of our purpose here to make any judgments about what happened at Nasson. The Nasson papers in the Royce S. Pitkin archive consist of trustee records and in addition a number of faculty, staff, and student reports, – the kinds of things one would expect to find in a trustee file. If there is something to be learned about Goddard concerns in this experience of Tim's we should not pass it by. Probably there is something to learn. If one were looking for significance in educational change, it might be that a considerable period of breaking-in would be highly desirable as a way of leading up to it. It might be indispensable.

The long period of breaking-in was what Goddard had. Not all the staff survived it. There would be many reasons for making changes, professionally. Some went back to graduate school; some sought other types of work; some dreaded the risks. All this is normal in an academic situation. What we are after here is what happened with Royce. The first point is already amply made. He worked in a number of parallel lines of responsibility. One simply does not know how he did it. That he could do it argues a powerful energy level which did not allow itself to be diverted from central purposes. A second point to note is that his energy input was enormous in all these parallel lines. Perhaps the third point would be that the Roycean dialectic, his ability to dialogue constantly with people in a wide variety of settings, was the enabling factor which made possible the numerous facets of college development. Royce's objective might have been, in long-range terms, the realization and implementation of the small experimental college; it may help to focus on the dialectic as the enabling force which made this possible.[28]

It does not follow that Tim was unaffected by the dialectic in which he engaged. He was indeed affected by it. Where fundamental educational principles were concerned he fought his ship to the death. Where learning was concerned, which was just about everywhere and just about most of the time, he was very willing to learn. As indicated in the Introduction earlier, he was very gracious about his own learning. He was not reluctant to acknowledge areas in which he was originally deficient and in which he had learned new approaches and new content from his colleagues. Robert Mattuck, George Beecher, Thomas Yahkub and Will Hamlin were cases in point. Each of them, he felt, had taught him a great deal about their areas of special competence. The metaphysics of the dialectic would have demanded further acknowledgment beyond this. Its nature was such that for its theory to work in actual cases it would have been necessary for stages of dialogue to be marked at each step by changes in the participants, – small changes, perhaps, but changes nonetheless. Each participant would have emerged from each stage changed by a very little; learning was involved in this process. Over periods of time the locus of the exchange would have moved slightly in response to succeeding stages. Any confusion in this area was probably due to episodes in which fundamental educational principles were at issue. There were moments of this kind, infrequent, but occasional. Here we come to a genuine source of confusion in the development of the College.

The educational principles of the College were on the whole fairly well understood by members of the staff and faculty. After a few years and a good deal of exposure to cases – cases were one of Royce's favorite ways of framing significant discussions – staffers might not have spent a great deal of time worrying about general principles. We commonly took them for granted. Events went on in their normal tracks, in accordance with understood policies. Bringing up general principles was a little like running up the flag. Most of the time one might not have been that dramatic. When matters became close, so to speak, in discussions of educational policy, then the flag might go up; the person who ran it up oftenest was Tim. It was interesting when he did that. We were instantly aware that the discussion had moved into dangerous country. Somebody was ready to nail the colors to the mast. There had to be some quick reviews of things that had just been said to determine what the real issue was. There had to be something that had caused this. If it didn't show up right off, the chances were good that we were going to get told what it was in short order.

---

[28]The point has perhaps been sufficiently made that for Royce discussion was not just casual expression of verbiage. It had responsibilities to discharge. It had to get somewhere, to accomplish something. Neither was it the simple issuance of tongues of flame. Its duty was to be clear, to make distinctions, to move toward greater understanding. It was hard, down-to-earth labor. It is hardly to be assumed that Tim did not enjoy dialogue. He undoubtedly did. He certainly would have been well aware that a great deal of his power to get things done and preferably done in a certain way, lay in his ability to dialogue effectively with many different kinds of people, over long periods of time.

Because these occurrences were so rare, one tended to forget about their possibility. It was not that people forgot about the educational principles; most of us could have recited them on most days of the week if we had had to. Mostly we were concerned with cases. In a socially oriented educational program that simply tends to be the way things run. Policy is after all a short-hand form of general principle applied in practical contexts.

If a staffer was new and hadn't yet been through very much of the dialectic on campus, there was room to get into trouble before acclimatization was accomplished. This sometimes happened. We were a little sorry for the new staffer when that happened; somebody would take the person aside and explain matters. Of course that should have happened during candidates' interviews, and mostly it did. Certainly someone would have tried. But there were occasonal slips. Mostly everyone survived.[29]

The serious slippage that might occur in a situation like Goddard's may have been that of sliding unawares into convention or near-convention. It was unlikely to be personal or open conflict. By and large people at the College faced in the same general direction. They each had original approaches, their own fields, and varied applications in them. They tended to think, perhaps humanly, that their particular approaches were the most promising. But in general, they did tend to face in the same direction. One of the directions was that students stood at the center of the educational operation. As far as it went, this was an accepted stance at Goddard. It was an educational principle in terms of which the College operated; faculty members believed in it. It could, however, be pushed to excess. It might happen this way: there might be at times a tendency to do too much for students. One was not really supposed to do that. There were points at which it was better to let a student have his or her head and try out something even if staffers were convinced it was the wrong thing to do and that the student would suffer for it. That might be painful for staffers and students alike. The converse principle which applied in such a case was that students should make their own choices and endure their consequences. The problem was the location of the line where one general principle gave way to another.

In this category as well is the discussion of the separation of evaluations from records which occurred on Greatwood Campus in 1968-69, during Tim's last year as president. It began about June, 1968, and derived from a proposal by George Beecher that evaluations of student work in classes, by students and teachers, be separated from records and kept separate. Records would consist of a bone-simple attendance record, credit for which followed automatically upon completion of the class term if the student's attendance

---

[29]On one occasion a candidate and his wife were on campus for interviews. A group was standing around on a lawn talking with the spouse about ways of doing things at Goddard, while the candidate was off in one of the interview stages. In an effort to be helpful and explain things handily a remark was passed about how the interview with Tim would be sure to help to define matters so that what was really one thing would be less likely to end up looking like something else. – "Oh, yes," she said, reflectively, she having already met Tim, "I thought there was a little bulldog in there, somewhere." – If there ever was a conclusion to this story we never heard what it was.

was reasonably satisfactory. The discussion became involved, as such discussions have a way of doing, and was referred to the first fall faculty meeting. The discussion in the fall became further involved and was referred along to future meetings in fall and winter. This kept happening until spring came, and all of a sudden it was close to Commencement and Royce's retirement. Something of a formal approval ensued.

We were long gone by that time so we have no personal recollections to help out the archive as to what this was really all about. 1968-69 was also the year when Royce and Helen Pitkin were supposed to be away for several months on a round-the-world cruise presented to them by the Goddard Board of Trustees as a retirement honor. This trip, long anticipated, kept being postponed and shortened because the search committees for Tim's successor had had a hard time and couldn't come up with an appointee in time to be of any help. Finally it was decided that the two intended travelers would go on a shortened 10 - 12 week tour by sea and air, leaving in late January and returning in late April or early May. They did that, and from all accounts they had a deservedly good time, visiting a lot of places and people where they had been before and some which were new. Notice that September 1968 is the only gap in the nearly unbroken sequence of president's reports between 1938 and 1969. If there was a report for that summer quarter it appears not to be in the VHS archive at present.[30]

As the semester was ending Royce became a factor in the records discussion. It was as if he had never heard of it before, and were startled by the implications of it. He notified the Greatwood people that he would be glad to meet with them and talk about it, but obviously could not prior to Commencement because of other pressing problems. In late June he met with the Greatwood faculty, taking the position that the decisional stance they had assumed was contrary to the established Goddard philosophy because in effect it created a pass-fail grading system. His view of this had to be based on a separation of the evaluation component from the records component. As noted before, Tim cordially disliked records and probably wished there did not have to be any. There had to be some to enable students to compile records of studies which they could use in their futures. So the problem was to find the least harmful way of managing them. What Tim had done was create an evaluation system in two parts, one a self-evaluation by the student of his or her own work in a study, and one by the teacher of the student's work in the study, with a mechanism in it which required a small dialogue to take place between the student and teacher regarding that record. Note the appearance

---

[30]Efforts were made to find the finished text of the President's Report for September 30, 1968 at Goddard. The working file for it turned up unexpectedly; it contained the usual fed-in sub-reports from division and program heads as would normally have been expected. It also contained early-draft material for the final report, but no final version. We think the final version probably does exist, in a file of President's Reports kept elsewhere, perhaps mislaid. An institution the principal energy of which addresses the future often finds it difficult to keep track of its past. It requires an investment of staff time and money. All too often, there is neither. Present and future needs are simply too demanding.

of the dialectic here again, in a less formidable, more personal shape, the objective of which was to move the educational experience from one stage to another stage.

The faculty minutes can be read without their contributing significantly to understanding of how the 1968-69 discussions went and what they were really about. The first thing to notice is that the issue was posed by George Beecher. He had, as has been observed, a genuinely solvent mind. He could take an ordinary issue, dissolve it in 15 or 20 minutes, and cook it into something quite different. George was not mischievous; he saw something interesting and he was after it. Royce knew all about George; he knew what he did, and that it was usually worth doing. In this case he would probably have waited to see how it came out. Faculty discussions that went on over a period of time had a way of getting off onto different tracks, of becoming something other than what they had once been; this one went on, according to the archives, a full year. It is probably not reasonable to assume that Tim had never heard of the Greatwood discussions before he paid attention to them in the late spring of 1969. He had been away for three months or so, but that would not account for his being unaware of it. He always knew what was really going on.

This is hypothetical, of course: - what we think happened here was that when the evaluation was separated from the records for what would have been to George Beecher interesting educational reasons the effect in Tim's mind was to let the records component snap away from the evaluation dialectic and emerge from the discussion with a metaphysical standing all its own. It was in effect constructed into a separate system of providing the student with a record of success or failure. It became a grading or marking system, – something Royce had fought against all his professional life. George's interest would have been quite different; he had always been interested in learning for its own sake, wherever possible without any system at all, to speak of; systems only got in the way of real education. He would have been much interested in getting rid of the philosophical or structural baggage. The effects of his proposal on the standing of the remaining baggage, with which, of course, the Records Office would have been stuck, in terms of the proposal to separate, would have been entirely accidental from his standpoint. What would have been his prime interest here would have been the charm of pursuing education, genuine education and genuine learning, without the burdens of the records structure.

The consequence here was that Tim attended the late June meeting to review the issue with the Greatwood faculty. We don't know, of course, what he said or how he said it. Like any good firefighter, he put the fire out. It seemed never to have any steam after that, as an issue. In the archive, reproduced here toward the end of Part Two, appears a letter which he wrote to Dean Ernest Cassara about the arising of the issue, and what and how he felt about that. Then appear the Minutes of the Greatwood Faculty Meeting of June 4, 1969, a 2-page topical outline originally in Tim's hand listing the topics up for discussion in connection with this issue, on June 18th, 1969, and finally a page from the Goddard catalogue of 1968, probably the version in use in 1969, bearing on Evaluation, written – one assumes – by Will Hamlin. A few days later Tim came to the end of his 30, 31, or 34 years as the head of the Goddard operation. It was a pity that he had to deal with the possibility of conventional slippage in the last days of his last month on duty. It might have bothered him, considering the possibility of future problems with future conventions. On the other hand, it may have been accidental, the sort of development which nobody really intended. It was an intricate bit of reasoning and deduction, ratiocination, really, which the faculty of Greatwood and he had had to go through. It was altogether typical of him that he never said much about it. Probably he dealt with it on a case basis, rather than as a problem in philosophical principle. That was sound. The issue of the principle was in it, to be sure. By dealing with it as a case he could cut the total volume of the argument down to a manageable size. People would have emerged from the dialectical exchange far less threatened and with a greater sense of receptivity than would have been so had he fought the convention on a strict ground of fundamental principle. It was perhaps due in some part to a lack of experience in ratiocination in connection with the implications of issues in the reflective dimension.

Here was a proposed experiment that did not work out. Most of the experiments at Goddard did work out. Perspectives on an institution naturally vary from individual to individual. Others may see things differently. Our view of the experimental thread which ran through the history of the College is that the winter conferences and the educational nature of the conference process itself taken as a substantive social entity, on one hand, and the major on-campus educational components which marked the early years of the College before the construction of the second campus, on the other hand, together constituted the woven thread which in time would be recognized as the experimental college which came to be known as Royce's great achievement. Royce never forgot or overlooked the earliest components of Goddard which marked it from the very beginning. He took as much satisfaction in them in his last years as president as he had 30 years previously. We shall see this in the 1968 presidential reports when he made a point of having the Non-Resident Term written up to show its significance in the weave of college programs which had marked the educational design of the institution for so long. The difference in 1968 was only in the fact that it had then its first full-time director. Before that it had always been bracketed with other college programs such as the on-campus work program or the off-campus field services. All of these program characteristics remained fresh in his mind even as the years went by. It was perhaps part of his gift of enormous energy that this was so.

Sometime in the middle years of the College occurred a discussion of the nature of the experiment as applied in the educational process and in social process generally. We remember it, so it must have been before 1967. It was an interesting little gambit. We no longer know where it came from or who was involved; but it was clearly a potential issue, on a small scale. Some of the natural scientists on the faculty might have been involved in the first instance, the definitional stage. After a while it would have picked up other interests. Among the special interests would be any concerned with catching Royce off base.

The issue raised was the impropriety of calling the supposed educational experiments at Goddard by the name "experiment", because they did not have proper controls. In the natural sciences, so the argument ran, experiments worthy of the term had control groups set up and subjected to controlled conditions in order to be sure of the results that could be ascribed to the hypotheses being tested. If one did not have the control groups and if one did not subject them to carefully screened conditions, there would be no scientific way of identifying the effects of the conditions one wished to test. There was no way to set up control groups in a setting in higher education; it would be too expensive; time and personnel, hard enough to come by just for the single situation under examination, would become a mountainous burden if the scientific definition of "experiment" were to be imposed on the socio-educational matrix.

This is of course a very old ground of criticism. It presumes that all social and educational situations require replication of conditions appropriate for natural science experiments. In the field of metaphysics it means that one never knows anything for certain except within the natural science context. Persons subscribing to this position are called positivists. People who assumed this stance in metaphysics had their day at one point in the not-so-distant past; probably there are still some left here and there. Most philosophical positions leave residual outposts and sentinels to stand watch long after the main body of troops associated with a position have retreated into intellectual history. We forget who may have had positivist leanings on the Goddard campuses long ago. Perhaps there were none to speak of.

But it was an interesting argument to start, and somebody started it. Probably there was some small mischief in the effort. If doubt could be introduced into the situation at Goddard, Royce might be embarrassed. That might have made it all worthwhile. Alas for such hopes: – Royce breezed through that one. He was long used to opposition much worse than philosophical disagreement. We would guess he slept better afterward than he had for months, reflecting that if his critics couldn't come up with anything better than that, he and all the Goddard experiments were probably quite well off. Certainly no pauses were introduced into the College experiments.

His position in a discussion of this intellectual gambit probably would have been that the general application of natural science standards in the social science contexts had plenty of problems of its own. Goddard, he would have observed with a certain clarity, was under no obligation to throw up obstacles in its own path on any such rickety ground as this. Besides, it was clear that the College could not afford the luxury of having to raise 100% more funds to keep on its track if it should subscribe to the positivist hypothesis.

A minor comment comes to mind here. A powerful leader in the nature of things may generate opposition, less on particular grounds than just as an exercise. It would be like the legends of the "fastest guns in the West"; if someone seemed to fill the role, someone else was sure to show up to enter a challenge, less on any sound ground than just as an interesting thing to do. One could add that a certain number of persons with fast guns in the West put their best feet forward and lost their shirts with not very much to show for it. Considering everything, the College had remarkably little of that kind of opposition.

It does not follow that the Goddard faculty were easy marks or pushovers. They were not. The emphasis on the development of responsibility and individualism had an effect in the faculty as well as among students. One might describe it as a double-sided coin on one face of which was the cultivation of individualism and creativity and on the other was the equally obvious weight of the learning situation. It was possible to get the two mixed up, but on the whole they stayed straight enough. The effect of this constellation was to make the Roycean dialectic even more forceful than it had been before; it had to be to stay ahead of the rapidly flowing current with its many eddies.

About the turn of the 1950s into the 1960s several experimental programs developed which were in part based off-campus in one or another of the consortia whch Royce had helped to set up, and in part settled on-campus in the participatory involvement of the College. In general these involved self-study programs the energies of which were directed toward analyses and description of student experiential education on campus, which is to say, student development during college, and encouragement of participatory studies in social science offering field components along with academic elements. The consortia were The Council for the Advancement of Small Colleges (CASC), and the Union for Research and Experimentation in Higher Education (UREHE), the latter of which eventually became the Union for Experimenting Colleges and Universities (UECU). They had overlapping institutional memberships, which joined in conducting experimental programs and self-studies. Each had an organization, a Board, and such committees as were called for by whatever they were doing. Each consortium applied for grants for its own program purposes and for staff support. Sooner or later there developed a floating cadre of project administrators, evaluators, and special purpose people, more or less mutually acquainted among themselves, who subsisted and survived on the basis of grants associated with these groups or with parent institutions. It used to be difficult to keep track of them. They were very useful people in that they knew how to do the breadth and depth extensions which were helpful to small institutions which might not have had wide experience in the big world, but who needed just that breadth and depth. They also knew the funding source people in private foundations and in the federal agencies and endowments which were often interested in making grants for what they were doing. What is more, the funding people knew them. Probably there never was a better instance of what can be accomplished through simply knowing people in relevant positions. It worked both ways. Foundation and federal grants people had need of places to make grants as much as recipients had need of grants to do what they needed to do. It led to the formation of a curious group of lightly tethered personnel who floated on agendas of their own for relatively long periods of time. They might be physically stationed on some college or university campus, as a matter of convenience or because they had been on the staff there once and knew the people, who in turn knew them. Their allegiances and titles would relate to the consortial group they were in. Their responsibilities on the local campus might be variable, but were often simply those of campers who were there one day and might be gone the next. It was noticeable that their careers depended in large part on their ability to get grants when they needed them. Eventually some of them might have suffered from the loss or reduction of local connections. It might have been a question of degrees of professional abstraction. Probably there will some day be studies of this group of floating academic professionals, perhaps by curious graduate students to whom they will appear like a new socio-academic phenomenon. It may prove to be only a matter of degrees of independence.

From the institutional standpoint, essentially what was happening here was that small and relatively inexperienced institutions were learning to talk with other institutions about what was worth doing in the educational dimension. This led to their being able to undertake new activities which otherwise might have been very much longer in arriving on scene. Royce was in a key position in that he could and did define his roles in these partially overlapping consortia, to hold a position from which imaginative educational reaches could be suggested at appropriate times to appropriate groups of people, who might then pick them up or apply significant aspects of them as might be helpful. The consortia were not by any means entirely organized around imaginative educational goals. CASC was originally conceived of as a group of small colleges which had desperate financial needs, so that the consortial purpose with which Royce was first confronted was fund-raising. This was, notably, for all Goddard's perpetual need for funds and fund-raising, very far from being Tim's interest in the consortia.

His prime interest was educational change. In the case of CASC the wing in which Tim eventually found his niche and his formative role in the organization was that which was concerned with educational innovation and experimentation. Someone else was always president of the consortium; if it was the flow of the group of institutions to be involved in fundraising as the primary concern, they were free to see to that. He was free to search out interesting and educationally promising projects for the consortia to pursue, with whatever wings of their organizations might have been focused on that future. Watchers of the consortia of those days will see this pattern replicating itself in other consortia with which Tim was concerned. We do not know the precise mechanisms by which this revealing development would occur. It just tended to occur. It was a sound system. It provided opportunities for persons with different interests to follow them up and to work through a consortium toward objectives which fitted their purposes and their philosophies.

Innovation needs to come up somewhere as a prominent piece of educational furniture in the common consortial talk of those days. Tim was only one of many who spent time talking about the virtues of educational innovation. We all heard a good deal about it. It was roughly equivalent in its implications to "the good stuff". The terms 'innovation' and 'innovative' came to be used a good deal in discussions in this period as synonyms for programs which were desirable within an experimental setting. The terminology would show up in project proposals as well as in grant proposals. It became suitable lingo designed to promote something which a proposer wanted to do. This worked all right because of the particular juxtaposition at the time of contents of the experimental movement and the contrasting backgrounds from which these contents emerged. There was indeed a gap between things as they had been done and the ways in which they would be done providing the new proposals were implemented. This happy arrangement would not last indefinitely, and its eventual failure would make a lot of trouble for Tim's successors who were groping for new and interesting things to do to sustain Goddard's leadership among the experimental institutions. The terms 'innovative' and 'innovation' must be kept in mind as carrying with them deceptive risks which could and did introduce hazards into the Goddard context.[31]

The flourishing of the consortia went on for some years and had many in-

---

[31]The alarm bell for this went off in Royce's Marshfield living room on March 1st, 1984. We were always careful about intruding into Tim's retirement, but every so often something would come up to talk about; then one called him up and inquired if he was receiving company. He always was. We forget what we went over for that day, but as usual it doesn't matter because he had something on his mind – and this was it. It was nearly the end of the conversation, because what he said was so startling that there had be an interval for reflection. – It was never the intention at Goddard, he observed, with just the suggestion of a smile, to have innovation established there as the criterion of decision for choosing programs or policies. The criterion was intended to be the fundamental principles which made up the educational philosophy of the College. – We stared. We simply sat and stared. These sorts of Jovian thunderbolts had arrived a few times in the past, for what reasons we cannot recall now, but we had developed a technique for handling them. The trick was to maintain a totally immobile countenance and say nothing; it was not yet time for the Roycean dialectic to be handleable. One had to absorb something first. One might respond inside one's head sooner or later, in whch case the Roycean dialectic was well and happy. But it was clearly going to take some time. We don't know whether our countenance behaved itself on this occasion or not. After all, we had all heard Royce talk for years about innovation in just those terms of acceptable decisional criterion, in just those sets of circumstances. What on earth could he mean? Self-contradiction was surely not his normal stance. Ten years later, almost to the day, we knew what he meant. There was no sudden illumination, – not even an awareness of a reached conclusion. It was all very ordinary, taken as intellectual process. What he intended to leave as an impress was that when the chips were down in the experimental educational setting, what made the difference was the array of fundamental educational principles which had built themselves up over a 30-year period and had become the irreducible groundwork for deciding what was worth doing at the College and what was not. If this conflicted with the values of innovation in any particular case, it was the principles which should call the shots, not the values of innovation taken by themselves. The experience of the College since his retirement in 1969 had refined the perspective which applied to this configuration. In effect, a serious mistake had been made in the history of the College. We shall need to return to this matter later in the Interpretations section (VIII).

teresting consequences, most of them beneficial to their memberships and to the educational programs with which they were concerned. A certain institutional self-consciousness showed itself from time to time among some of them. Running such a consortium was probably a heady business. As long as the grants came freely, as was more nearly the case in those days than it was later, the administrative people had the advantages of functional prominence without the disadvantages of having to labor in the local vineyards. It was a situation marked by a relatively high degree of abstraction from many of the diverting conditions which characterized life on the residential campuses. On the latter, student life conditions were or soon would become increasingly difficult. These were, after all, the 1960s, legendary for the amounts of on-campus noise which students made when things of one sort or another were not to their liking. Some have said, of the student situation in those times, that it was the age of the wide-open mouth. A number of famous photographs taken by the news media attest to this. One of these, taken hard by University Hall in Harvard Yard, is especially memorable in this connection.

In retrospect, what appeared to be operative in the configuration of the consortia and the supporting colleges and universities in those days was a happy juxtaposition, mutually supportive, of institutions of two kinds the differing efforts of which led to many useful experiments in education and to a shift in general ways of operating educational institutions. The consortia supplied leverage for moving the supporting institutions from one way of operating toward new ways. They employed consultants who could come onto campuses and say things which the standing faculties and administrators found it awkward to say. The supporting institutions were the ground on which the consortia worked; without them, nothing would have happened. They had to be interested in new ways of doing things for the consortia to have a chance to work. The consortia had to be invited in. What this all meant was that there had to be people in the supporting institutions and in the consortia who wished to work together to produce better ways of running educational institutions.

Another group, much smaller and more definitive, kept a foot in both camps and enabled the juxtaposition of the two groups of institutions to endure and to move from one useful stage of research and experimentation to another. Royce Pitkin belonged to this group. So did James P. Dixon, the president of Antioch College in this period. There were a very few others. If combinations of these people met and decided something, nothing would ever be quite the same afterward. The leverage and the support – from respective institutions – were simultaneously entailed. Things were sure to happen.

The point here is not so much to detail these institutional consortia as to call attention to the ways in which Tim spent his energy when he was not doing the other things he did. The consortia probably accounted for a fair percentage of his time from the late 1950s to the period of his retirement at the end of the 1960s. His consortial activities during this period were not necessarily all that clear to everyone on the Goddard staff. We were busy too, doing what we were supposed to do. He would be gone a while, and then he would be back. If he thought we should know something he told us. If not, we were often too busy to inquire. A good deal of the mosaic of his energy applications throughout the period when we knew him best have turned out in these recent days to be something of a surprise. We might not have known more than 60% or 65% of what he did in any one year.

In the mid-1960s when the new residences were being built on Greatwood Campus and the new set of buildings constructed on Northwood Campus, probably Tim concentrated more of his efforts at Goddard than had been or would be the case at other times when the home pressures were lower. But it is reasonably clear that whether the staff knew it or not, Royce's roles among the consortia and therefore at large in the American higher educational community of colleges and universities were substantially larger and more pervasive than many of his colleagues were aware.

When retirement came for Royce, this was not the involvement that he relinquished. Probably its forms and energy levels moderated. But these were activities which he could and did carry on for years in his retirement. Here, too, there was a weave, a design, the threads of which moved with varying emphases in and out with respect to each other, reflecting his interests and the different posts he held on Boards of Trustees, commissions, committees, and occasionally in operating consortia.

Royce's memberships on boards and committees of other institutions were notable in his retirement years. They come up appropriately in the outreach-and-growing-edge section because without exception they showed commitment to and judicious assistance with the problems involved in educational statesmanship in the forward-moving dimension. There were, as has been seen, precedents for these involvements even in his most active years at Goddard – as for example with Nasson College. The idea of being on a board of trustees for an institution different from Goddard was far from new. He had been doing it for years, whether his colleagues were well-informed about it or not. It was natural to continue it as long as opportunities for it appeared. They appeared, and often went on for some time as individual involvements.

VII

RETIREMENT DIMENSIONS

Tim had an interesting philosophy of board membership. It reflected his methods of operation when he had been active at Goddard, often in some detail. When he was the chief executive of a college with a board of trustees his idea was that the trustees should, if they accepted responsibility for an institution, either give financial support or, if they did not themselves have funds to give, help arrange for other persons to contribute who were in a position to do so. It did not immediately follow that this happened. It took a while for the earlier trustees to find out what was expected of them. Probably quite a few of the earlier trustees were not in a bracket to make substantial contributions. Eventually they did realize it, very likely when several generations of trustees had come and gone. When Royce himself became more commonly a member of other institutional boards he operated on exactly the same set of principles. He did not have large sums to give, and as we shall see, he became involved in the late 1970s in a life-and-death institutional fundraising campaign for Goddard, as if it had never happened before. He gave what he could, very clearly and precisely, with specific instructions as to how to use it. He was apt to direct the president of the institution that the check was to be assigned to whatever causes the president thought most appropriate. The funds were to be unrestricted otherwise. It was made clear at these points that he was supporting the decisions of the receiving president as to what should be done with his gift. He was likely to give such gifts several times a year. He repeated his instructions each time. It was his way of being clear what he thought the role of a president should be. The records of gifts management at Goddard show that this was indeed how he had behaved when receiving gifts. He did not expect donors to tell him what was to be done with funds, unless the donation had previously been requested by him for a specific purpose.[32]

Some of the Boards Royce served on after his retirement in 1969, apart from Nasson College concerning which note has already been taken, were Trinity College, Burlington, Vermont, of which Sr. Elizabeth Candon was president at the time; Stowe School, Stowe, Vermont, a private preparatory school; Twinfield (Marshfield/Plainfield) Union School District; the Vermont Council on the Humanities and Public Issues; the Vermont Educational Advisory Council of the State Education Dept.; the Scandinavian Seminar, New York City; and of course Goddard itself, which Board he had agreed to join in 1975 at the behest of his current successor at that time, Richard Graham. On all these boards he was active and interested; he worked hard at their tasks, attended meetings, reflected upon issues and took positions. The patterns of his interests show in all of them. He made donations to the schools, colleges and institutes among them, not as a large donor at all, but making small, steady gifts as a matter of principle, always with the proviso that the institution president allocate the checks to where they would be most useful. Where trustee expenses were paid he arranged donations so as to cover the expenses he was being paid.

Tim's rejoining the Goddard community in the role of trustee is a story in itself. When he retired as president he withdrew from contacts with the College except as he might be invited back to address graduations, take part in occasional classes or seminars, or attend some celebration. It was all perfectly friendly; it was simply his way of giving his successors a free hand. He was as strict with it as he had been with the delegation of deanery responsibilities on the two campuses in 1965, and the principle was the same. It was part of his learning to live with change. By 1975 when the issue arose as to whether he should join (not rejoin, for technically he had never been a member as a member before), the College had literally been well out over the abyss in a number of unfortunate episodes; its troubles had been written up in the media; it had been nearly ruined by financial mismanagement; worst of all, educationally it had wandered far afield in its search for its wave of the future. Sooner or later it would be threatened with dismissal from the New England Association. It was altogether typical of him that he never mentioned any of this. There is nothing in the archive about any part of it.

It is a great relief that there are historians at work to whom we can leave the unravelling of the mysteries of this difficult period. History shows no mercy; it will someday all be told. For any who were parts of the great days things have been heard and read about the 1970s which do not belong with wel-

---

[32]Another prerogative of the presidency as Tim defined it was in appointing staff and faculty. He was occasionally very clear about this, often enough so there was no doubt about his position. In practice he consulted with staff about appointments, and shared interviewing widely, as part no doubt of the candidates' professional education, not to mention the staffers'; in the end it was clear that he would make the final decision himself taking into account the advices he had asked for and received. We usually left the silo with a reasonably clear idea of what he would do, but not always. He would also occasionally tell the presidents of colleges whose boards he served on what his view was of this presidential responsibility. Implied was his slant on how it ought to be managed.

come memories. The mind turns away from posing the dreadful question, –
what must Royce have felt and thought? It is a useless question: he would
never, never, have said. But when the question of his joining the Goddard
Board was raised in 1975, in a rare sense, in his own way, he may have said all
that he would ever say about it. Saying nothing, he agreed to go on the
Board. So began to shape itself the last great struggle of his life: the fight to
draw the College back from the edge of disaster yet another time. It would
occupy him more and more intensely in his last years.

Do we suppose that all his energies were taken up by this rescue effort?
When do we ever learn? In the 1970s he continued to do what he had done
all his life in one way or another. He continued to teach. A new klatsch of alternative graduate schools had appeared, to handle graduate students who
were pursuing masters' and doctoral level studies not available in the usual
graduate channels. The Union Graduate School in Cincinnati was one of
these; another was Walden University, which worked out of Florida; there
are probably some we have forgotten. (Still another new one appeared as late
as the 1990s.) These showed minor differences, but essentially what they did
was set up individualized programs of study for masters' and doctoral programs. They needed field faculty as well as core or central staff faculty, and
they needed second readers for final student theses. The central staff faculty
were on the staffs of the graduate study institutions. The rest were drawn in as
needed, often being chosen for certain field competences and with respect to
the needs of students. Royce sat in his Marshfield house; the students came
looking for him. What he was known for was often educational administration; perhaps the greatest number of students wanted him for this area of
study. A few of them were known to him; most seemed to be strangers. It
was not a great burden in terms of time. It did not interfere with his travel
plans and it could be worked into the schedule of meetings to which he constantly went. There were not a great number of them.

He developed an interesting pattern of responding to them which had not
appeared before, although students who took classes or independent studies
with him may have been familiar with it. He would reflect in his written
comments what the student had actually done, express appreciation of accomplishments in a positive way, clearly approve what the student had successfully brought off – and then he would tell the student things which had
not been done and ways in which the study could be or have been improved.
The files do not say what the students did about these comments. Tim had
learned the pattern earlier from colleagues and graduate teachers (cf. Benson
and Adams, *To Know for Real* [1987]).

Another dimension which Tim undertook in his retirement was that of the
single episode or single institution consultancy. He would be asked to visit an
institution and report back, as perhaps to the Vermont State Education Department, or to the inquiring institution itself, concerning some aspect of its
operations or some part of its programs. Commonly these requests came as a
result of his involvement in various Vermont boards and projects. Others

were similar to an institutional Board membership, except that they focused on a restricted program area or a more concentrated nexus of problems. Mercyhurst College in Erie, Pennsylvania was such an episode; he was asked to visit in mid-spring, interview college people intensively for several days, and report back several weeks later at Commencement on what he had found and what he had to suggest for promising changes. This type of challenge he seemed to enjoy a good deal. He would find ways of gathering information which may have surprised his sponsors, but they were always courteous and interested in what he did.

So much has been new in our readings of what Royce did in his retirement that it is surprising to remember or be reminded that two of his retirement dimensions involved institutions where we were or near where we were at the time.

One such instance concerned Wilmington College in Ohio. Tim had met some people from there at a Chicago consortial encounter about 1972 or shortly before, and had been struck by a report the staff had made concerning "Man in Focus", a study program for entering students. This study program was already operating; the Wilmington people were thinking of expanding it for upper classes in Wilmington. There was evidently some discussion about it. In the Spring of 1972 Tim was invited to Wilmington to look at it and to consult on behalf of the Strategies for Change project of UECU, in which Wilmington College participated. We were at Wilberforce University in Wilberforce, Ohio at the time. He sent word he was coming, so we had chances to meet. Our own connection with Wilmington College was through at least one of two consortia operative then in Southwestern Ohio, in which Wilmington and Wilberforce were active, along with Antioch College and a dozen or so other institutions belonging to the Great Lakes Colleges Association (GLCA) to which Antioch also belonged and which it drew into the study. The consortial focus here was the Consortium for Higher Education Religion Studies (CHERS) and its institutional partner, legally necessary for fund-raising purposes, the Consortium for Research and Development (CONRAD). It went by the acronym, CHERS-CONRAD, and was centered at United Theological Seminary, Dayton, for administrative purposes. The other consortium was the Dayton-Miami Valley Consortium (DMVC), the focus of which was on fund-raising for the half-dozen or so member-institutions with respect to the business and industrial community of Greater Dayton. This consortium, regardless of technical involvements on assisting levels, was really run by the several institutional presidents, all of whom were powerful executives who knew exactly what they wanted to do, and invariably did it. We Wilberforce staffers used to like to watch for the dust clouds over Dayton when President Rembert Stokes was on a tear at a meeting of DMVC. We were usually not at the meetings, but in a manner of speaking one had only to look out the windows toward Dayton to know what was going on.[33]

Royce was not involved in CHERS-CONRAD or in DMVC. It was

rather the UREHE/UECU vector, such as Strategies for Change, with which Jack Lindquist was working about this time, which provided the ground on which he met Dean Sterling Olmstead and other faculty and staff people from Wilmington. He conferred around with staff and students at Wilmington; he always had a good time doing that, getting acquainted with new people and seeing and hearing what they were doing educationally. There was a late afternoon or evening session of some kind; the program says we were there, so we probably were. It would have been very like Tim to involve people he knew in the neighborhood in a program of that kind. Typically, we would have been delighted to go and hear what he said about Goddard; we were always looking for fresh news of the place. It happened that that was what Wilmington wanted him to talk about.

Three years later, in 1975, after we had moved to SUNY/Empire State College in New York State, Royce was back again at Wilmington and was again on a program, perhaps one connected with Wilmington's participation in the Strategies for Change project. We do not know whether he was there between the two visits noted in the archive. The 1975 visit most likely had to do with the assessment of results which would have been due about then. Tim was always firm on the need for results – finding out as much as possible about what had happened in an experimental learning program. He was known for it; Wilmington might have encouraged him to be helpful in finding out what had happened in their program. A second reason for his visit to Wilmington may appear in a short talk he gave to a Seminar there on April 10, 1975. This will appear among his writings at the end of Part Two in the present study. He might simply have been invited to come and give this, or it might have been one of several reasons for his trip. This configuration of visits to Wilmington makes up a small problem for the student of Royce's educational thought.

As a problem it fits with implications of more recent awareness of Quaker thought. Wilmington College was a Quaker institution; it was small, off in the country of Southwestern Ohio 15 or 20 miles from the Dayton, Xenia and Wilberforce urban semi-circle, and had no doubt a somewhat traditional and conservative approach to the liberal arts as college studies. It also had an increasing population of socially conscious students; it was thoughtful about them and resolved to develop a studies program to challenge them where they were. If they wished to contribute to the social improvement of American society there ought to be ways in which a Quaker college could be of assistance to them. "Man In Focus" was a first step on this road. They then thought of

---

[33]CHERS-CONRAD did raise some funds; its primary initial funding source was the Danforth Foundation. CONRAD existed to have some place legally appropriate to put funds when necessary to receive them. It was a legal solution to a delicate problem involving institutions some of which were religiously focused. CHERS was primarily a study consortium concerned with the types of institutions, public and private, which might work together on common problems, even if their starting commitments were conceptually different. The implications for church-state cooperation were of considerable interest here. Among various writings on the CHERS-CONRAD phenomenon we unfortunately remember our own most readily. Cf. Davis, Forest K., *Journey Among Mountains*, Adamant, 1974; XIII & XIV.

moving the new studies program gradually upward through the second, third and fourth years. Notice that this vector would be opposite in direction to that by which Goddard had moved its independent studies program downward from Grade 16 students to Grades 15, 14, and 2nd-semester-13 students. Notice, too, that Wilmington, even while it moved to develop studies of the social order, and progressive studies at that, reaffirmed its commitment to liberal arts studies in a philosophical sense. Wilmington further thought it would not require the new social studies program of all its students; it intended to be flexible and offer choices among programs to suit different student frames of mind. This would have been about what Royce found when he first came to Wilmington in 1972, and what defined his 1975 visit.

It was then all well in hand when the innovative consortia showed up on scene. The situation was quite different from that of many small, traditional colleges which encountered the innovative consortia and experienced a radical shaking up as a consequence. This is impressionistic and hypothetical; there is no real evidence for it; Royce never said anything about it; nothing is written by him in the archive about it. Still, an idea persists in mind. It might be so or it might not. In addition to Tim's responsibilities as a consortial advisor and guest, there are a number of interesting questions to account for his interest in the situation. Wilmington was doing things differently. Quakers, Friends, are just plain different from a lot of religious groups. The Quakers at Wilmington were of course Ohio Quakers, not New England Quakers. We make no effort to deal with Quaker differences. Quakers can explain them far better than we. On visits to Wilmington College one sensed some of the differences which apply in many Quaker groups regardless of geography. Quakers appear to be subject to a profound discipline, evolved over centuries of social consciousness and assumption of social responsibility in the midst of criticism and unpopularity. There tends to be an equally profound respect for the opinions of others, irrespective of agreement or disagreement. Quakers have an intense and intensive mutually supportive counseling system for helping colleagues work through problems of principle and the applications of principle in social situations. While visitors to Wilmington College might not have seen visible signs of all this, one might have sensed their consequences.

Notice, too, that Wilmington people were not really asking anybody what they ought to do; they already had a fairly clear idea of what they might do. They were however very interested in what other people, groups and institutions were doing. When Royce went there in 1972 they asked him to speak about Goddard programs. They didn't ask for suggestions of what they should do. They were going to process whatever they heard about from other sources; they were going to think it over, shake it out, talk about it, see what happened inside their heads. It would take time; it always takes time. But there was and is time. It would happen.

Royce was a religious liberal. One thinks of him always as a Universalist; his family had been Universalists. But the fact is that he spoke of himself as a

Universalist Unitarian. He put the terms in that order; that was significant. It was undoubtedly deliberate. He was very precise about things like that. If he had meant Unitarian Universalist he would have said so. From the late 1930s through the mid-to-late 1940s he was very active in the Vermont-Quebec Universalist Convention, the purpose of which was to oversee and assist Universalist churches in those areas. For several years of this time he was the Convention president. He conducted large quantities of business with various trustees and treasurers relating to the settling of wills, handling of inheritances, sales and management of real estate owned by the Convention, and sales of abandoned churches, this being the later stage of the great Universalist decline which had marked the period in Northern New England between, say, 1890 and 1950. He had even taken a hand in the placement of ministers, especially in Vermont. He had been involved in more than one re-formulation of the constitutions and by-laws of the Convention. He had notably insisted upon re-titling the Convention to include Unitarians with Universalists, and he clearly knew exactly why he wanted this done. It had to do with similarities between the two groups. Union of the two groups came about in 1961; he was 20 years ahead of his time in talking about this as precisely as he did in the early 1940s. During those years he was a religious liberal, and he knew why he was that. In later years he might have called himself simply a liberal, but he would have been very clear in mind as to why. He was aware of religious positions, and was comfortable with people who held quite diverse positions in this conceptual and emotional area even while perhaps not holding those positions himself.

At risk of drawing illustrative lines which are not really there, we hazard the guess that when Royce walked onto the Wilmington College campus he thought he was going to understand without much effort the religious phenomena appearing there. What he found may have been at least a partial surprise. He may not have been immediately able to understand it in terms familiar to him in his own experience. That may account for his maintaining the connection with Wilmington so that when 1975 came and he was asked back yet another time, for whatever reasons, he wanted to go. There might have been something there which still issued its challenge to more familiar experiential constructs.

There is a good deal here which we do not know for certain. It may be enough to repeat the obvious, – that Wilmington College was a very interesting institution, that it offered dimensions for study and learning, and that it genuinely appreciated what Tim brought by way of experience in educational experimentation. Wilmington would have understood what he represented, though they would have expected to make their own uses of it. All of this he would come to perceive and in his own turn appreciate. It ought to have been a good match among educators, each side having something to learn and something to give. It appears to have been reasonably close to this.

In these same years Tim was beginning a trustee relationship with Trinity College in Burlington, Vermont, which would run for two Board terms, and continuing a dialogue with Loretto Heights College in Colorado (Sr. Patricia Jean Manion). His experience as invited visitor at Mercyhurst College in Pennsylvania was in 1973. In 1970 he was Commencement speaker at Hartwick College in Oneonta, New York, after a two-month consultancy, following which he had advices to give, and gave with moderate politesse. He was leaving the Board of Trustees at Nasson (1972), and going on the Board at his own home institution (Goddard), in October, 1975.

Interesting aspects of Royce's involvements in the Strategies for Change project, deriving from his membership on its advisory board, appear in Jack Lindquist's book with that title (Berkeley, 1978), for referral to which we are indebted to Arthur Chickering.

In these same years, at periodic intervals, he conducted an intermittent correspondence with a small boy in the Waterbury, Vermont area (Russell Martell) about topics of interest around Vermont history and ways of doing things; Russell had written to him earlier about Tim's book for young people, *Maple Sugar Time* (Brattleboro, Stephen Daye Press, 1934 and succeeding editions), and one thing had led to another; it went on for some years. This was the period too of his serving as graduate level consultant for ten or so masters' and doctoral students at some of the alternative graduate study institutions already mentioned. The reader of the archive on Royce in this time begins to get the same sense of heavy involvement that one seems always to get from him if while considering one topic in a period one glances from side to side and glimpses what else he was doing at the same moment. He would not be the first person whose retirement rivalled his commitments while professionally active. On the level of his normal workload, however, for a retirement to do this might be something to think about with an open mind.

The Center for Individualized Education at the State University of New York/Empire State College (ESC), the second of these two instances, was one of the fingers of outreach and response emerging from the Goddard history in the field of experimental education. Royce Pitkin was a consultant at a National Workshop in the program in March, 1977, in Minneapolis, Minnesota. F. Tom Clark, then of Empire State, was head of this program. There were mentions of two ESC faculty in the Royce S. Pitkin archive as attending the national workshop. We had long since sluiced out a good deal of the recollection about the Center as an entity and as a program so we sounded around to see what our former colleagues remembered about it. John Spissinger, longtime faculty member at the Plattsburgh, N. Y. unit of Empire State, bounced; he remembered quite a lot. In fact he remembered so much it was funny.

There had been a series of local workshops on Individualized Education in our network of units in Central N.Y. State and quite probably in other networks of ESC units around the state; we had both been at our own series, John said, and it had been very helpful in calling attention to such things as the affective component in education (as distinct from the cognitive element which everyone acknowledged). Arthur Chickering, who was also at the Workshop from Empire State, was heavily invested in this component; back at Goddard Robert Mattuck had driven it home year after year in faculty discussions. John Spissinger remembered Royce as circulating around the National Workshop, visiting everything he could get to, and making a brief appearance on a summational program. He was a sort of philosopher-king at the workshop, John observed, lending legitimacy to the theme and its applications among the sessions. The Center for Individualized Education was phased out of Empire State when the supporting grants were exhausted, as so often happens.   Still, it is clear that recollections did endure for some; evidently there were individual impacts among participating faculty.

The record also shows that in 1976 and 1977, and perhaps later, several pamphlets were published by Empire State College which derived from this stream of faculty study and research. Myra Fooden had written a "Field Work Descriptor Guide" (1976); Elizabeth Steltenpohl and Jane Shipton had collaborated on a "Guide to Resources for Life Career Educational Planning" (1977); Carolyn Forrey wrote "Faculty Development at Empire State College: Issues and Priorities" (1977). Probably there were others in later years, just as there were a series of conferences and institutional discussions and reports on topics such as "Competency-Based Learning", "Community Resources", "New Student Populations", "New Faculty Roles", "Admininstrative Concerns:, and "Acceptance and Support." It is hard to tell where the lines of study and development begin and end.

John came up with a filed program of the 1977 Workshop; actually eight or nine members of the ESC faculty and administration were listed as attending it.   Among them were Tom Clark, Director, Pres. James W. Hall, Carolyn (Forrey) Broadaway, Jane Shipton, Riecelle Schecter, John Spissinger, Arthur Chickering, Richard Debus, and Jack Lindquist, who was variously connected with Empire State and with Memphis State, although for Workshop purposes he was from the Center at the University of Michigan where he directed the Kellogg Project on Knowledge Dissemination and Utilization, and who would succeed Victor Loefflath-Ehly in the early 1980s to become the 7th president of Goddard.   John remembered that Dean William R. Dodge of Empire State was also at the Workshop although it does not show on the program. This was entirely likely. Dean Dodge, who had been at Empire State since its inception and at SUNY-Central before that, was an enduring free-lance administrator who went places and took part in programs, on very little notice, particularly ones having to do with his special interests, which often centered around new efforts in higher education for which he was administratively responsible at the State University of New York and more immediately at Empire State in this period. He had a gift for handling different people and new dimensions on the college and university levels. He could understand what they were about and could fit them into established administrative contexts in a way that left everyone getting along with everyone else with a minimum of friction. In the Empire State/SUNY context this was a contribution of very considerable significance. When the history of Empire State is written this will no doubt appear in an appropriate perspective.

He probably decided late to go to the Workshop to see what was going on. Evidently he spent a good deal of time with Tim and Art Chickering while at the Workshop, which suggests that he found what he was looking for. Both of them would have had a good deal in mind about the topic and its areas of concern. If he went around with Tim at all extensively, he would have visited most of what was going on. That was Tim's pattern at conferences: he would go to most of the events and hear most of what was said. Typically he would take notes on a good deal of what he heard.

Dean Dodge remembered another visit Royce made to Empire State College when it was in its early planning stage. We had never heard of this encounter, then or since. No paper record of it shows readily in the archive. It might all have been arranged by telephone.

Empire State College was opened in the fall of 1971; the offices were in Saratoga Springs, New York; the initial unit opened in Albany (Fall, 1971). A preliminary planning year had taken place in 1970-71. Among the planners were James W. Hall, later the president, Arthur W. Chickering, William R. Dodge, and a number of others probably from SUNY-Central in Albany. In the background was Ernest Boyer, who had been at Upland College in California, had been in the consortial conferences and inter-institutional programs of the early days at Goddard and elsewhere, had become an assistant to Sam Gould of Antioch College when the latter became Chancellor of the State University of New York in Albany, and was himself Chancellor thereafter. People at ESC were always convinced that Ernest Boyer was committed to the founding of Empire State College within the State University of New York, and was a major factor in its establishment. Funding for the projects in Individualized Education at the five or six colleges and universities which worked somewhat together and somewhat by themselves in this extended U.S. and Canadian network had been largely provided by the Danforth Foundation; notably, the Center at SUNY/Empire State had received additional special funding support from the Chancellor's Fund for Innovation at SUNY. Ernest Boyer did not often show up in person at events such as conferences and programs of study within SUNY institutions; his shadow was long, however, and not infrequently fell across them in one way or another.

A planning visit by Royce to the infant Empire State would surely have been in the 1970-71 year. Bill Dodge remembers one of the themes that Royce emphasized at the time as that of student-centeredness. There would have been good reason for anxiety concerning it. The State University of New York was a huge institution even then, with 70 or so residential campuses in several classifications. Any way one sliced it, Empire State College was going to be an oddball institution in that context. Royce would have been concerned with a number of educational themes in this connection. Student-centeredness makes sense as one of these. Another would have been size; Royce was invariably concerned to preserve smallness in college organization. It was the principal idea behind the pattern of successive small campuses at Goddard in the 1960s – Greatwood, the original campus at Goddard and the only campus from 1938 to 1965; Northwood, the second campus, extant from 1965 until its reincorporation with Greatwood in the Witherspoon administration, and the ghostly Westwood, distinguished mostly by the fact that it never materialized at all. Royce would have gone to the Empire State planning discussions with the Goddard campus complex and its attendant ideas, whatever their condition at the time, vividly in mind. He would not have had an active role at Goddard at this time, however; it would have been in the midst of his strictly-hands-off period. At present we have to remember that not much is known about this planning conference or about Tim's involvement in it. It is another of those tantalizing topics which awaits discovery and further study. Materials about it probably do still exist in various dusty files, and perhaps in personal recollections of participants.

It may be useful to repeat here a caution advanced before in these pages. The purpose of this account is to concentrate on the educational involvements and activities of Royce Pitkin, in as wide a range as can be discovered. One of the hazards of doing this is to make it appear that there was no one else on various scenes except Tim. It is a risk we need to take simply because it is the focus of this study, but it is not so. When the history of Empire State College is written, by Richard Bonnabeau, Empire State College Historian and Archivist, and by his colleagues and assigns, notice will of course be taken of the wide range of sources of ideas and practices which fed into the unusual institutional context which became Empire State College within the framework of the State University of New York. No doubt everyone understands this well enough. The heritage of Antioch College has not been properly assessed here, for example, it not being a central focus of this book. It would have been an active element in the formation of Empire State College as a stream of thought and practice deriving from the historical association of SUNY Chancellor Ernest Boyer with his predecessor as chancellor, Sam Gould, former president of Antioch. Among a wide variety of strands, this will need study in the course of time. In the C.I.E. context referred to here, for instance, several figures appear in advisory capacities just as Royce did. Among them were Stephen E. Brooks, then of the Philadelphia Urban Semester Society for Field Experience Education, later of Teachers College, Columbia, and Minnesota, who became a prolific writer on various aspects of Adult Education, and on the Eduard C. Lindeman role in it; King V. Cheek, at that time president of the Union for Experimenting Colleges and Universities, Yellow Springs, Ohio, later head of leading southern educational institutions; Robert E. L. Strider, longtime head of Colby College (Maine) where there was a center for coordinated studies which was so to speak in the family of educational experiments in this field; and Malcolm S. Knowles, first executive director of the Adult Education Association of the USA, also connected with the Eduard C. Lindeman strain, an enduring second-generation authority in fields of adult education. All of these persons, and many others, were sources for Empire State's Center for Individualized Education; some had connections with Tim Pitkin, and some did not. The point is simply that where influences and lines of intellectual descent are concerned, ramifications and extensions can become numerous and complex.

Dated late in August, 1969, in the summer of Tim's retirement year, a 24-page typed paper signed by him was handed to Vermont Education Commissioner Harvey Scribner. It was entitled something like "A Vermont Secondary School Program".[34]

It stands by itself in the file, so we do not know what if anything was done about it. Harvey Scribner was considered one of the imaginative heads to serve the Vermont State Dept. of Education in recent years. What did follow was a series of involvements in public education, extending into the 1970s. Most of them have already been noted. What may be useful for present purposes is simply to call attention to them in a retirement decade when it would be reasonable for most people to look for some time to rest. It does not appear that Royce ever rested. It was not that he ever went around looking tired; it was just that he never seemed to be tired. It was as if he never needed rest. We don't suppose that was literally true. It just seems that way.

To an observer of the period from 1975 to about 1980 for Royce it appears that this must have been a depressing and difficult time for him. We have to remember that this may simply not have been true in his case. In some respects it may appear that he was back in harness in this half-decade. When he went onto the Goddard Board of Trustees at the invitation of Richard Graham he must have known something about the predicament the College was in. He would have known it was short of funds; the question was, did he know how short? It is not part of our task here to uncover all the details of this. What we know from his own files is simply that he continued imperturbably on his way, seeing to concerns he had, fielding the concerns of others. He wrote a lot of letters on behalf of persons who asked him for references for job interests, in several cases over and over again. His correspondence never seemed to diminish. He was unfailingly courteous in all his relationships with other people. Most of his correspondents wanted something. He never failed to respond. If he could help them he did. The point to note here is how much time this correspondence took. He had not had any secretarial assistance since Evalyn Bates had moved to Hartwick College in 1970, and the Field Studies Centers office was moved from the Plainfield Inn to the central UREHE/UECU office in Yellow Springs. His letters were typed at home with casual carbons.

Tim had spent some part of 1969-70 following his retirement as Coordinator of Field Studies Centers for that consortium. It was an interesting (and unsalaried) job and he clearly enjoyed it. He also was very deft in han-

---

[34]It is interesting to remember that 28 years before, under date of October 3, 1941, Royce had sent around the Vermont and Quebec Universalist Unitarian Convention a single-sheet mimeographed proposal entitled "A Program for Liberals of Vermont and Quebec". He was already president of the Convention at that time, and would remain so for another four or five years. The file does not show whether anything came of this. It simply shows how Royce tended to think. It may be helpful to run this brief piece among his Selected Writings in Part Two of this study of his thought and practice.

dling some awkward situations involving student placements overseas.[35] He did not plan to keep the Coordinator's post very long; it was in a formative stage, which was probably its attraction. He was interested in formative stages. He would later undertake a six-month placement of a similar sort as Executive Director of the Vermont Council on the Humanities (and Public Affairs) during its initial planning phase, which is to say, its formative period. Again he had no plans to continue in the post, though it took longer to find a permanent appointee than had been anticipated. Victor Swenson was appointed to the post in January 1975. Royce remained on the Council for several years, taking an active part in proposal assessment and the grants process. An interesting aspect of this (also unsalaried) responsibility was how it came to be concerned with Humanities *and Public Affairs*. This appeared to make a fundamental difference in the work of the Council for a number of years. It is not clear how the definitional expansion occurred.

Philosophically, of course, Royce was very well prepared for his responsibilities as a trustee of Goddard College when he went on the Board in October/November, 1975. One might have said he was a cocked gun waiting to go off. He knew exactly what a trustee ought in his judgment to do by way of support for the institution of which he was a trustee. He also knew where to draw the line. It might have seemed like olden days to him when in succeeding years he was deep into his last campaign to raise crucial funds for the College. He had done it all so many times before. College presidents indeed had to raise funds; who else was to do it? He had many times made it clear that he thought trustees should give funds or raise funds in accordance with their abilities. Figuring out what to do about Goddard's serious financial needs in the late 1970s was not going to be any mystery, though it might prove more than ordinarily difficult.

It is an interesting story to read, twenty years later. Essentially he did it by returning to the people he knew from earlier times, who had given support to the College often enough when it was indispensable to its survival that this should be done. Eliot Pratt had been gone nearly a decade, but a number of

---

[35]One of these involved a student from a west coast college who had contracted to work and study at Mitraniketan near Trivandrum, India. It was a rural placement requiring community service as many of the Center programs did. Mitraniketan was run by a magnetic young Indian teacher who had captured the imagination of Arthur E. Morgan, long-retired president of Antioch College and builder of the Tennessee Valley Authority electrical generating plants in New Deal/FDR days. Tim had known about the center for some years and was interested in it. The actual designation of Mitraniketan as a Field Study Center had probably involved Arthur Morgan and Sam Baskin, president of UREHE/UECU with its headquarters in Yellow Springs; it is hard not to imagine that Arthur Morgan would have been very direct with the people at UREHE when it was first being considered. He spent a lot of time on the Antioch campus even at his then advanced age, and was thought to be something of a tartar. Anyway, the student from California went there along with some Goddard/Northwood students from Vermont, and immediately decided that he could work out a more interesting placement for himself in a nearby city. Forthwith he moved to the city and requested his money back. A considerable correspondence ensued. Knowing Royce as one did, and being certain the student was eventually going to see the error of his ways, it was a liberal education to watch the scenario work itself out. It took about two months. Tim never raised his voice; he simply pointed out the consequences. Half a world away, everybody eventually got in line.

the old support group were left. He wrote detailed personal and persuading letters. The addressees were an educated group; they knew Tim and trusted him; they had heard he was back in the situation (it is difficult not to say, back on the Board), and that gave them confidence. A number of them came through handsomely for the College campaigns between 1975 and 1980. Tim had had some words with the Business Office over his retirement stipend; he had long since requested that his stipend be cut in half; the College did that; it lasted several months, and then the original level was restored, by whom does not show in the record. Tim was not consulted about it. Then the crisis got worse: Tim sharply instructed the Business Office to cease and desist totally in the matter of the stipend, pending a time when the financial situation should be safely recovered. It appears this time to have been done. Had it not, he would have been placed in an impossible position with respect to the fund-raising. His fund-raising with the major givers was only part of the effort he made. The rest was made up of his personal donations. These went up by factors of five to ten in this period. Sometimes they were matching gifts, in which case he himself saw to the matching funds search. In the second category it was not unusual for the totals per year to reach into five figures. In the first category, it commonly reached into six. It appears to have been an amazing performance. In the end it was not enough to enable the College, at least as it was then being run, to avoid a threatening catastrophe. It is not clear that Royce took any part in College management in these years. It would have been contrary to his principles of trusteeship to have done so. The record does not show any such participation. We of course have no conversational records covering exchanges with College persons; the presumption has to be at this stage that he delivered the funds and expected the College to do the best it could with them. There is a great deal here that we do not know and make no effort to discover, the focus of our search being Royce's way of thinking – which for him included his way of acting. Thought and action for him were very closely linked, being even differing ends of a single continuum. Thus far in this study, this is the conclusion we reach. There is no reason to change the conclusion at this point. As far as can be stated now, factual points beyond these are for the more general historians to unravel.

Eventually there would be a move to sell off for financial reasons certain programs developed by the College, accompanied by reductions in faculty. Concerning the proposed reductions in faculty and staff Tim made no comments; this may mean that he understood the necessity for them. He after all had had to reduce faculty himself in times past when the wolf was at the door. It is a common enough circumstance in college and university administration. Selling off College-designed and -created programs which were in themselves profitable in practical terms and educationally sound besides, was quite another matter. On this issue Royce would leave the Board (May, 1981) and once again separate himself from the College, at least in a formal sense. It must have entailed a certain agony.

On that occasion Robert Mattuck wrote him one of those letters by which he sometimes let someone know that he understood what was involved in a situation. The College had not been what it should have been for the past ten years, he said, ... but it was better to face the future positively than to commiserate. Six days later Tim replied that there had been missed options which the Board didn't consider .... Then he repeated what he had said several times before, in other circumstances, affirming his appreciation for what Robert had meant in the history of the College: – "...you introduced me to an aspect of student development that I had missed in my earlier encounters with educational ideas." – Perhaps in the slightly awkward change of subject there rested an acknowledgment that, in spite of his inability to accept the new College policy, he nevertheless appreciated the reach of friendship emerging from four decades of association.

Robert had written him a gracious letter under happier circumstances in 1980, on the occasion of Royce's receiving an honorary degree from the University of Vermont, his alma mater. The exchange appears in Part Two. Royce had received a number of honorary degrees from colleges and universities by that time. Most of them had not been noticed in the press. There was always a certain awkwardness about it, because as a matter of principle Tim had never allowed the granting of honorary degrees at Goddard for any reason whatsoever. He wished to make the point that an honorary degree was simply not the business of a college concerned in the first instance with discovering the nature of education. It only confused the issues. If the point were to express institutional appreciation for a gift or for financial support, it only confused that issue in its turn. When in his retirement it became a problem because certain colleges wanted to express their appreciation for his educational stands over the years he may have thought that it would be embarrassing, even discourteous, to decline. He might risk obscuring some of the other points he had tried all his life to make. So, when those chips were down, he did not decline the honors. In this case the Vermont press did take notice; it was as if it were at last aware of the appropriateness of what the University of Vermont was doing in the recognition of him and other honorees of that day.[36]

In this approach to the thought and work of Royce Pitkin a consequence

---

[36]So Robert Mattuck and Royce Pitkin glanced off each other from time to time in the service of the College. They did not always agree, but they came to respect each other, for good reason. They were the two longest serving staff colleagues at that time. The College did not sustain Royce's refusal to engage in the award of honorary degrees following his retirement. Indeed, the first one was presented to Royce himself at his last Commencement as President in 1969. This story is told in Benson & Adams, *To Know For Real: Royce S. Pitkin and Goddard College.* Adamant, 1987. Pp. 259-260. His own written account of it appears in his final President's Report, for June 30, 1969, run here at the chronologically proper point among his Selected Writings in Part Two of this study.

One might think this was the end of this story. It is not, quite. In the spring of 1995, it was the turn of Robert and Corinne Mattuck to receive honorary doctorates from Goddard. Corinne's was awarded posthumously. So here in a manner of speaking the exchange of letters between Tim and Robert in 1980 came full circle. The two letters being run in the Part Two section below have particular reference to the nature of Tim's response, his equally gracious acknowledgment to his colleagues of their implied participation in his honors.

has been that the focus has been led, perhaps inevitably, to cross pre-set lines whenever the search suggested points of interest. It has also led farther into Royce's retirement than we had originally intended to go. Somewhat naively, when we heard he had retired we thought he had really and seriously retired. Actually, he only changed what he did. It is unlikely that he changed what he thought, except in the normal sense of the continuation of learning. What suggests itself at this point is to see what emerges from an effort at interpretation, without particular references to sources. We will probably not get away with that in any strict sense, either.

VIII

INTERPRETATIONS AND
ENDURING QUESTIONS

R oyce is not to blame for anything that happens in this section.
Most of the time when we were most closely associated with him we
felt an underlying, tolerant amusement from him at our reflective sallies,
when we had any, and perhaps at comments of a reflective nature, when we
had any. It has of course occurred many times throughout these pages that
ventures have been made at various points into interpretive material. It was
never an intention to avoid this. Here at least an effort can be made to confine the comments to interpretation. If by chance lines are still crossed, we
will borrow from Emerson that elderly saw about consistency and hobgoblins.
Somehow we think that that would be most appropriate from the several
standpoints involved. It is not to be expected that the wafted fragrance of re-
strained amusement will disappear from the neighborhood anytime soon.

Systems of thought have always been a matter of great interest. To us, that
is, – not to Tim. The risk of system is that it may be or become static. That is
also the risk of structure. System and structure may partake of common elements. They may not be identical, necessarily, because system may by definition involve process. Probably structure is not a form of conceptualization al-
lied with process. The static nature of structure has been a point of disputation
in sociology.[37]

Tim was a problem-solver. He was only incidentally interested in theoretical aspects of questions with which he dealt. In a strictly philosophical

---

[37]Insofar as sociological theory is a form of metaphysics – a search for the really real – this becomes significant. In this connection, cf. Davis, Arthur K., *Farewell To Earth*, Vols. I & II, Adamant, 1991, 1993. The
author is here committed to the idea of sociology as process. For risks of the static in structuralism, see
comments on Talcott Parsons and related topics. Index refs.

sense he had a system like everybody else. People who deal with questions entailing theory necessarily end up with a system. People who take positions in theory can be compelled to acknowledge their systems; systems are entailed by theoretical positions. It would not have been any use suggesting this to Royce; he would have smiled that mischievous small smile of his and gone imperturbably about his business. We probably think that because we tried it from time to time.

At Goddard there was not much discussion of philosophy as such. One might say that on the strictly philosophical level there was nothing to discuss. Everybody fairly well knew what the educational philosophy of the College was. We were not going to discuss that because it was not up for decision. The enormous range of discussion, which went on constantly, centered on applications: how was such-and-such an existing problem to be solved? This was where the Roycean dialectic applied with all its force. One might say that – again in strictly philosophical terms – the focus of the dialectic was not in the realm of metaphysics where the issues would have been concerned with what was really real, but in the realm of ethics, where the issues were concerned with how situations were to be improved.

The probability is that if there had been discussion centering on strictly philosophical issues there would have been a great deal more disagreement and disputation in the faculty and perhaps the community than in fact there was. It is interesting about that sort of thing. The experience of the CHERS-CONRAD consortium in Dayton between 1967 and 1972 was disconcerting in that it appeared to show that the separation of church and state was a pragmatic matter, not a philosophical matter. There seemed to be no reason of a reflective nature why church and state should not become social allies and operate in concert with one another in the service of certain causes, certain studies, certain ends. One should enter the reservation that this potential alliance would work best if the personalities involved were mutually sympathetic and forward-looking, determined in short to make the articulation work effectively for reasons held in common.[38]

Certain social reservations could perhaps also be identified through a comparison of mediaeval conditions of church-state relations with those of modern times. The chances are that church-state relations could be expected to work best as positive process (the CHERS-CONRAD dimension) in a dem-

---

[38]The staff executive officer/coordinator/facilitator of CHERS-CONRAD in this period was Dr. Frederick Kirschenmann, a native of the Dakotas, to which country he eventually returned. We have always thought his mix of diplomacy, determination, support, imagination, and personal magic went a long way toward accounting for the remarkable achievements of the consortium in the period when we knew it best. To this one should add the broad sympathy and understanding of the academic administration at United Theological Seminary in Dayton, where the consortium was centered for administrative purposes. These factors working in concert with the college, university and theological school memberships precipitated a powerful learning situation. There was only one institution of learning from the public sector in CHERS-CONRAD at this time, – Wright State University. It held up its end steadily in those years, thanks to Prof. Nicholas Piedescalzi and associates who carried on numerous academic studies in religion, helping procedurally, apart from the study contents, to define the fundamentally social nature of the church-state relationship.

ocratic social context as distinct from a monolithic social context, that is, in a pluralistic society rather than in one dominated by a universal viewpoint. When a socio-intellectual process is in full swing in a particular social situation one has to be sure that all the factors involved – which may be working to help the process – are being taken into account if the situation is to be fully understood. The socio-intellectual process in the CHERS-CONRAD consortium between 1967 and 1972 was successful because the operational factors were all pointed in the same direction. The later history of CHERS-CONRAD may indicate limitations that applied after 1972; we did not see what happened in CHERS after 1972, and we do not speak here about it; it would need to be researched. A similar comment might be made with respect to the mediaeval configuration of church and state; it was a successful arrangement within its own time. In later centuries the slow emergence of individualism, first in the arts, then in government, economics and politics, superannuated the philosophic uniformity of preceding centuries. The eventual outcome of this would be the appearance of the pluralistic society. The process does not end, of course. We appear now to be in a period of adjustment in which the balance of individual freedom with individual assumption of social responsibility is being worked out in a variety of ways.

It may be that at Goddard an interpretation of a similar sort applies. The first and primary factor was the philosophy of education which Royce strove for thirty and more years to work out and to imprint in its essentials on the institution and its processes. It will be convenient for Tim to state these principles to the readers of 1995 in the words he used to the Goddard faculty in December 1965, and variously in other scattered references; these will appear in Part Two of this study, as best they can be sorted out at this time, some of their implications indicated in footnotes. The Goddard philosophy was an ethico-moral, educational set of principles, rather than a metaphysical set of principles. The ethico-moral principles could have been compelled by argumentation on an abstract level to reveal the metaphysical principles which of necessity they entailed. It would have been very time-consuming and probably divisive within the house to do this. Understandably, Royce chose not to pursue it. Depending on the make-up of the faculty and staff at the time of his retirement, and particularly on their reflective interests, it may prove out that there was a loose latch-string at his retirement door at the end of June, 1969.

A second factor of immense importance was the Roycean dialectic. This was his own particular contribution, bearing on the entire history of the College throughout his professional life. It is really quite impossible to overestimate the formative effect of this continuing impact on the groups of associates who formed the slowly changing faculties of those years at the College.[39] It created some restlessness, to be sure; Royce was aware of this, and allowed for it. It would have been simply a human thing; in reaction to the condition of constant force applied in their professional environments activist individuals would periodically seek outlets for excess energies not otherwise finding expression. From time to time faculty motifs would appear in the interest of "making academic decisions" as conventional faculties were wont to do; another way of saying this was that people thought too much reflective discussion dominated faculty meetings leaving too little time for "voting" on decisional things in manners that would allow members to feel as supposedly normal faculties felt. In effect, he got together as teachers a potentially powerful group of personalities and then denied them the freedom to do as they pleased, except in that place of magic aura, the classroom, where of necessity what they did was their own particular self-expression. Here they would either survive or not survive, in their own ways. Both they and he accepted this in agreeing to the periodic performance evaluation.[40]

A third factor might be considered a principle of educational operation and so belonging to the first area of definition. In pragmatic terms it occupied a prime place in the developing thought of the College, and so should stand by itself. This was the definition of education in broad terms. It had perhaps two areas of fundamental expression, something of an achievement considering that ordinarily a system is built upon only one. The first might have been seen most readily in the experimental programs which developed within the Col-

---

[39]Bear in mind that "faculty" included those administrative staffers who attended faculty meetings. There were a number of these. Some moved back and forth over the borders according to current assignments. Some occupied dual roles. Movement was in both directions. Speaking precisely, administrators sometimes took up teaching; teachers sometimes showed up with administrative responsibilities. Not infrequently, they did both things. What Tim did in this dimension was create an atmosphere in which the prized occupation was teaching. When people took him literally it could make problems for him. People might come on staff to do things ordinarily classified as administrative, and soon they would show up in his office wanting to teach. This happened so often it became something of a bore. He was judicious in working out the problems involved in these situations; often enough, in time, people in this category would get a chance to teach, at least part time. The configurations were commonly interesting. Complications arising were by-products of certain of his positive vectors. Handling them was just part of the demands of the circumstance.

[40]Was Royce himself subject to performance evaluations? By all means, but realistically at unexpected and informal intervals. The presidential term was seven years. There would have been search committees, unless the trustees forestalled the event by re-electing Tim before the time for a search arrived. In the interest of survival, this would have happened occasionally. The trustees (and the faculty) were not fools; they knew who kept Goddard running; they would have wanted to keep it running. In later years, particularly on Greatwood Campus, there was talk of whom else to get as president. Mostly the people put forward as possible candidates never heard that there was such a discussion, unless perhaps years later. It was, so to speak, political pillow-talk.

The informal evaluation motif showed itself once, probably in the early 1950s, when Royce was invited to consider the presidency of one of the then New York State Teachers Colleges. He went over to talk to the place. Word got out in the Goddard offices that he had gone, we forget how; a mild panic spread itself around. When he got back a day or so later, jaunty and unimpressed as ever, and said nothing at all about it, the smoke of curiosity began to show around the floor. We decided the issue had better be faced. We nailed him in a corridor on his way somewhere, and said we had heard he might be leaving, and just what about it? He was amused. Oh, he said, passing it off, "they just wanted a fund-raiser. I wasn't interested in that." Things around the floor returned forthwith to normal.

In the various presidential search and evaluation situations which arose after his retirement, informal modes of assessment would again be operative. The details should be researched in the interest of understanding. It is also worth remarking that a good many times out of a hundred certain highly significant problems were clearly resolved in Royce's administrations the solutions to which may have been ignored following his retirement. The place of fundraising among presidential responsibilities was only one such problem. We will need to return to this category shortly.

lege operations from the beginning and in its outreach dimensions from the end of its first dozen to 15 years. The second was the inclusive nature of education such that all ages were in effect considered of equal importance in designing educational programs. The enormous outgrowth of this concern has been in the adult education programs which have become so much a part of college and university programs everywhere. The adult education movement can be said to have begun in America in the 1920s in the immediate vicinity of where Tim was carrying on his graduate studies. He emerged to take various secondary school posts and then the leadership of a college-level institution just in time to make major contributions to its expressions in colleges and universities. We have seen N.F.S. Grundtvig's role in the 19th century Scandinavian folk high schools and Tim's interest in these and in the educational values which they represented.

If one is after Royce's thematic contributions to education in America, these four or five categories provide ample grounds and points of reference in terms of which to understand what happened at the College and to review accomplishments at the College itself in the years following Royce's retirement in 1969, and at other institutions and in other educational situations as the spirit moves. Notice that the early survival elements in what he did, beginning in 1935 or 1938, depending on one's interest and approach, exist at any institution and in any context: these were communicational elements, financial support, and admissions or the development of a college population (within the context of a particular institution). In the first ten to a dozen years of the College, Tim would have been learning his job. The survival factors had to be developed and kept under control. This is so at any college or university. Every college president has to learn them. If that is so, to judge what happened at the College following Royce's retirement one of the things to be done is to see to what extent his successors mastered the three survival elements. That would be the preliminary requirement. First: Were they able to speak competently and effectively in behalf of the institution? Were they in command of the ideas of education and especially of progressive education? If not, what were they doing there? Second: Did they grasp the significances of financial support? Could they raise funds when they needed to? And did they understand one of Royce's absolutely cardinal principles of college operation as applied to Goddard – which was that fundraising was only in second place in the range of needs which the College had? The first demand on the president's time was *educational leadership*. Did they understand that? If not, what were they doing there? Still in the second category, did they grasp the elementals of managing resources and living within a budget? One of the most important things Royce learned in his early years was how to say no to people who wanted to do things at the College – things which in themselves were probably interesting, and often potentially useful. This had to be done in the interest of holding the College to a central task. Funds were always limited: choices had to be made. Did they understand this, and could they do it when it was necessary? If not, what were they doing there?

These were only the first three of the fundamental demands which Royce learned how to manage. They were survival demands, specific to Goddard only in their applications to its individual requirements and expectations. Royce learned them – as the saying goes – cold. They were the normal expectations placed upon any primary administrator. Then follow the special requirements placed upon Goddard as Goddard – a progressive educational institution committed to experimentation. If Goddard in thinking about itself intended to remain in the realm of progressive education, and if it intended to remain experimental, it was and is indispensable to figure out how Royce made an effective institution of it in these dimensions.

An awkward problem interposes at this point, – that of institutional momentum in a particular mode. This characteristic has been addressed before. On the whole, the College may have shown over the years a fair endurance of its distinctive patterns. Without careful study of the periods since Royce's retirement, not our present responsibility, it would be unsafe to make detailed assumptions about this, but there are at least encouraging indications of it. It might be helpful to catalogue the experiments which have been carried out over the years, in some compact and comparable forms, to provide fingertip judgments as to their general outcomes, in, let us say, a few pages of material. Certain instances of the trials of new forms and procedures might be assumed to have lasted well, others to have slowed or vanished. Why is this? Do they grow old, and show the marks of aging? If so, what are they? This could be significant in choices of experiments and of operational forms in which to pursue them, perhaps also as to objectives. It is probably not an adequate conclusion to a project to discontinue it when funding from an outside source runs out. Surely the College has had enough experience to perceive that the underlying experiential foundations of projects and procedures can be and have been to some degrees absorbed and built into institutional learning and teaching processes. Their results need not be lost or discarded, providing their results show effective outcomes.

There may be a problem of aging in a variety of social processes. Institutions themselves may grow old and show the effects of age. Programs may age, as well. Probably not much is known about this. In the fields of philosophy, some of us are fond of saying, characteristics of aging are shown by the withdrawal of interest in certain questions in certain cultural periods. It does not seem to be a result of answering the questions posed in a certain reflective position. They seem rarely to be answered; they come merely to be ignored. People are no longer interested in them. Perhaps no philosophical questions are ever really and thoroughly answered to the satisfactions of participants. People seem rather to work with them for a while and then get tired of them and move to address different questions. It may be something as simple as boredom. The learning of new things may have a built-in threat in its nature such that it comes to demand the excitement of constantly addressing the new and the different. We may see something of this in the modern devotion to research, that bete noir of the smaller educational institutions which often cannot find funds for pure research (so-called). It would be interesting to know whether the kinds of learning the College has talked about over the years really partake of the nature of pure research.

If the College were to study past educational experiments some of these questions might be addressed with benefit. Consider some cases. The Vermont Youth Study of the 1950s may have left some residues, or it may not. Which? And why? What happened to it? What became of its results? What studies does the College carry on now in this field? Are there resonances visibly remaining? Do faculty members and students 35 years later know all about this Study? About its forms and procedures? Its results? Comparative Cultures: the studies of languages in socio-cultural settings.... Languages are surely studied today in many institutions. What are the residues and resonances? What questions of a social nature were addressed in this mode of study? Were they all addressed as long as interest lasted, and did they then lapse – perhaps of a type of old age? Neither of these programs were flash-in-the-pan affairs; each lasted a good number of years. There was time for learning residues and resonances to accumulate. Similar queries could be posed to numbers of other Goddard programs from various periods, even from its present, in time from its future. Perspectives of this order might well be kept in mind as we turn to the major distinctive characteristics of the Roycean educational architecture.

With reference to these questions it is necessary to return to the educational philosophy of the College and to the Roycean dialectic, the two principal factors in what Royce did that were strikingly original. Which stands first? Ah. There's the rub.

We do not recall that Tim ever spoke with us specifically on this matter until his little thunderbolt in his Marshfield living room on March 1st, 1984. There he was very clear; there was no doubt that he considered the principles of educational philosophy expressed in and through Goddard College as being fundamental. In the first instance we were nonplussed, because of the frequency with which he had used the shorthand term 'innovation' as representing what he was talking about in education that was supremely worth doing. He had done this for years, and probably most of us were used to it. The difficulty with all this was that in the years we remembered best the term innovation was always applicable. It served in the context of those times quite accurately, because the proposals under consideration at and for Goddard were always innovative with respect to the ways in which education had worked up till then. There was just that much new work to be done among the colleges and universities of that period. The terminology worked well enough. Later on, the context changed.

In short, there had been some perceptual and intellective slippage. Royce had realized it in the years following his retirement, when confusion over this had become all too common at the College. The College, in its continuing efforts to find new expressions of what it considered its genius, had commonly shot off to the sides looking for more and more "innovative" programs. What was implied in the thunderbolt was that it should first have studied the long-established principles of educational thought and practice worked out at the College in a generation and a half of constant striving. That was where the hammer should have first come down. If one looks back at Tim's active professional life one would have said this was always so, always clearly the case, and not subject to modification. After all, most of us would have said we understood well enough the educational principles in terms of which the College worked.

But there were no issues in the metaphysical arena in those days on which the faculties of the period could readily have cut their teeth. In effect, bizarre though it seems to say it, the faculties were inexperienced in dealing with philosophical issues as such. There were not many situations in which those topics came up. What they were experienced in was the application of philosophic principles to practical situations. If issues arose in which the fundamental principles were at issue, Tim was there to set the boundaries of the discussion. After he was suddenly no longer there to do this, the situation changed radically. Bear in mind that he had attracted to the faculty a set of adventurous minds most of whom were ready to try anything, and still more of whom were well able to rationalize what they wanted to do in the approved Goddard tradition. They thought they were being experimental; they were proposing to do what Royce had always done. Before long the time was ripe for everybody to run off in all directions. The natural choice for them to make was the road to innovation. If they made this choice without the counterpoise of study of the principles of educational thought and practice, the risk would be that the road to innovation would become the road to craziness.

Where was Royce all this time? He was at home in Marshfield, or at meetings of boards or committees, or travelling, or doing the numerous things he did in retirement, and theoretically minding his own business. When he retired we heard he made a point of staying away from campus in order to give his successors a free hand.[41]

The contextual change in the educational environment following Royce's retirement may also be a significant factor at Goddard itself in the period following 1969. It is more difficult to assess, but it may be useful to refer to it. The difference lay in the rapid adoption of adult education programs for de-

---

[41]This sounded like a good idea to us at the time. We thought we should try it. We mostly did, with the exceptions of brief visits to campus in summer vacations from 1968 to 1970, during which we – so to speak – cased the joint. After doing this we would write up the experiences and impressions and circulate the sheets to a few acquaintances who might be interested. We had forgotten about having done it until we ran onto a copy of one of the summaries of the impressions, that for 1970, in a file somewhere. The details were gone from mind, but one generalization we did remember quite clearly. It was that the College in those first years after Tim's retirement was not at all an unknown or foreign place, but that it was striving to be, in whatever it was doing then, the same kind of institution it had always been. This experience contributed to a feeling we have had ever since, and to which we have often referred, that institutions are characterized by a strong tendency to continue in established courses, that they have as a major trait a momentum which tends to keep them on general lines of thought which have already been established. This is of course not evidence for anything; it is just an impression of the way institutions work.

gree purposes which appeared in numerous college and university programs. Realization spread that the so-called market among the public was relatively large, so that if low-residency programs could be designed for adult students in family and work situations a useful educational offering could be achieved. A good many institutions did this; the hypothesis in general proved correct: there was such an adult education market on the higher education level, and most of the programs were probably successful. When contexts change, changes in the central concerns often occur as well. Competition develops; programs exert themselves to do better and reach farther than other programs. Goddard had been on the ground early, and could be expected to work hard to stay ahead. Tim himself continued to work in this field, and to maintain his numerous interests in it. A few of his student advisees and thesis reading projects were from the Goddard graduate programs, though likely not a majority.

To do justice to a proposal for innovative educational effort one of the things to be done would be to consider reasons for not doing it. It is a difficult thing to consider in the midst of the excitement of wanting to invent and try something new. This is of course one of the things a responsible chief executive must do in an educational situation. In the years after 1969, who was going to do it? If the presidents were not going to do it, what were they doing there?

Now we come again to the last and in many respects the greatest of Royce's contributions to the reality that was Goddard: the Roycean dialectic. If the first of the fundaments, and Royce's own choice as the primary criterion for judging what was worth doing, was the educational philosophy of the College and the principles which went into its construction, how can this be? How can the dialectic be his greatest contribution to the College? Well, of course this is debatable and hypothetical and hardly subject to any sort of proof. It is just one opinion. Review for a moment what was involved in his educational philosophy: a set of principles, to be sure; a method of referral to the set, if anyone were going to make such a referral; and a determination to sustain this as the reference frame within which the College operation was to be defined. Philosophies are systems in the abstract, as a rule; they can be designed to include and encompass whatever factors the designer considers important. Traffics of a philosophic kind are mostly cast in the abstract dimension. One can deal with systemic histories, their interrelationships with other systems, their resonances with and their inheritances from other systems and their designers – all in the abstract. Royce was not really interested in doing this. Philosophy for him was quite different. It was an articulated system of idea-and-action, of idea-and-implementation. If one had inquired of him what an idea was, he would probably not have come up with anything close to a traditional view of the term: it would probably not have had a being of its own apart from a neurological event which he would have had as much trouble defining as anyone else. Somewhere in these pages we have suggested that the metaphor of the bridge which hangs over space, has no abutments, derives from no-thing and goes no-where, is perhaps the most useful metaphor one can put forward to describe his notion of a system of thought in terms of which to define and order and improve – that is, to educate – human life.

One could put it in an inelegant way, which might not be literally true, but might convey what is implied:– Royce rarely thought anything without doing something about it within the next ten minutes. If something were not done about it he might maintain that in a sense it had not been really thought at all. What this means is simply that for him the articulation between thought and action was marvelously close, – much closer than it is for most of the rest of us, who may think we know a bit about ideas. Tim was quite ready, always ready, to take the consequences for maintaining any notion that sounded as if it had pragmatic possibilities but might be unorthodox in relation to traditional notions, ideas, or philosophies. He would simply slough off whatever did not add up in his view and proceed with what did have a place in his view of human operations.

The Roycean dialectic was a methodology of communicational interaction. It too has a metaphor; indeed, we think it was an image, because we think we saw it nearly every week for 17 years. But it may have been a metaphor – a mental picture which stands for something other than its literal self. It is of Royce sitting half on the edge of his chair in faculty meeting, elbow bent, hand braced, the other in a partial gesture, facing intently into the faculty circle, exchanging the ideas, images, metaphors, pragmatic descriptions, notions, processes, which went to make up the discussion. The intensity of it was monumental; its substance, earthrooted; its outreach, limited only by practical considerations which were always in his mind.

Royce could come into a faculty meeting and center on a process or procedure which had been a familiar part of College operations for 25 years, and raise the following question: – here we have this process or procedure, representing such-and-such, which has been in effect for all these years; we know quite a bit about it; it has been tested and found reliable and helpful, and it is clearly something we ought to continue. There is simply no excuse for not doing it better than we have been doing it. *How exactly can we do it better?* We need ideas about this from everyone, and we can stay with this as long as we have to, to find out how we can do it better. – He could run a discussion for hours on such a theme or question. He would not let go of the question until it had been shaken till its teeth rattled; all sorts of new ideas about how to do things better would be sure to emerge. Faculty meetings could consist of these questions about familiar matters, or they could be made up of topics no one had ever thought about before. The issues, new or familiar, were always shot through with the strain of originality, framed in a compelling force.

The College was repeatedly involved in experimental programs – by which is meant programs which broke new ground – which lasted for years at a time, two, three, four to six, depending on conditions of the programs, and their grants if they had them, and during these the progress being made on the projects would repeatedly come up for report and consideration. These would occur in pre- or post-semester faculty meetings, or at periodic intervals. The project heads would report and discussions of issues would follow. What happened in these discussions was that members would be constantly reminded of the contexts in which the College worked with respect to the major programs. Fresh viewpoints might be developed. People understood in better part what the College was doing. It was a type of discussion that was equally intense with other types, and differed only in that it focused the institution on particular new ways of achieving and understanding educational ends. It was expected that as a result of these new projects the faculty's understandings of educational methods, objectives and contexts would be and would remain different from what they had been before.

As a type of group discussion, probably there was not much variation in the intensity levels of what went on week after week, semester after semester, year after year. They were highly and intensely educational; they were a remarkable series of learning experiences. One looked forward to them week by week; they were enormously interesting. It was not that all of us understood equally well all the matters advanced for consideration. Theoreticians like Will Hamlin and George Beecher could take off and leave the rest of the faculty in the dust. It might take an hour to catch up, or one might never catch up; one might be forever lost. But it was all very friendly; one could stop the discussion if one had the nerve, and back up, requesting further explanations. Some of it was simply necessary process; one learned to recognize that necessity and to allow it gracefully to take place.

The Roycean dialectic was the moving matrix in terms of which all of this intellective process worked itself out. Do not suppose that all of it was simple question and answer. The faculty was learning how to take part; it could challenge and respond with nearly the best of them; it could and did raise questions; it could and did express opinions; it could and did make judgments. It was all part of the process, which spread itself around like a contagion among the members. The faculties were made up of individuals in themselves far too powerful and too original not to have recognized a great learning experience when they saw one. It was a creative process of interaction which replicated and filled itself out. It carried discussants along with the discussions. As a process it turned corners, looked back upon itself, criticized itself, passed controls around from person to person, picked up and studied the points and questions, for all the world as might have been done with a design of lights sparkling as it turned. In some part the faculties became able to do what Royce did; group discussions all over campus benefited by resonance. It was a sustained and superb learning experience.

It is nearly impossible to believe, even now, that this process could go on for more than 30 years. It did not stay the same as a process, of course; it changed; people became more skillful at it. Probably Tim became more skillful at it. Gradually the faculties became better at whatever they did. It is interesting to reflect that the students, too, became better at what they did, student generation after student generation. We have always thought that when the independent study mode was introduced into the Goddard situation, it was primarily the older students, more than the faculty, who taught younger students how to carry on such studies, and often in the first instance to want to carry them on. This may not be the only way to pass new modes around a campus; one would need to check out situations like that at Wilmington College in Ohio to see what other possibilities there might have been. At Goddard, this appeared to be how it worked. It did work, apparently quite well for the most part. As a mode, among other modes which the College has pursued, it has seemed to endure. Think back to the early years of the new College in Plainfield, to what must have gone on there. It may all have started with the Roycean dialectic.[42]

There is a still a puzzle to work out in the operations of the dialectic with respect to educational philosophy, which in Tim's context meant educational thought-and-practice. Because there was never intended to be general discussion of problems of the really real in the faculty and associated groups on the Goddard campuses, we hypothesize that what happened was that when Tim retired and the setting of boundaries began to be more or less taken for granted, people fell back on their individual views of the really real, again without specifically discussing them, so that there was little or no interaction on that level of abstraction, and certainly no amalgamation, among the major group of persons who would be continuing in the situation. Heretofore the boundaries had been set by Royce's definition of the principal topics. The faculty had not had to bother their heads about boundaries and definitions. They felt no burdens to add this new dimension to other responsibilities they carried. What happened may all have been innocent enough. Some of the programmatic results of that period need study for purposes of clarification.

It was a time when disasters lurked around many a corner. Some potential catastrophes may never have developed. Those that did were sufficient unto the day. For a time – perhaps three or so years – institutional momentum was ballasted by existing customs. Visitors on campus who came looking for major threads and themes found them reasonably similar to what had gone before. Beginning with the obvious problems in budgetary control and extending gradually into areas of philosophic control, the buffeting windstorms of the 1970s were building off-stage. They would appear all too soon, sweeping up the major players into the maelstroms. These aspects of the later history of the College do not put in any extended appearance here.

Bear in mind that there would have been severe limitations to the reflective process had there been conscious considerations of intrinsic problems

---

[42]For a treatment of the classic sociological concept of the dialectic, cf. Davis, Arthur K., *Farewell to Earth*, Vols. I & II, Adamant, 1991, 1993. Index refs.

It would also be useful to review, with respect to the experience of the College in its early years, Veblen's idea of "the penalty of going first", treated in the same source. There can be little doubt that that idea applies to this local institutional instance. Even after 45 years, we remember the hostility toward Goddard among some Vermont colleges and universities in the early 1950s. Cf. Index refs.

A. K. Davis retired in the 1980s as Professor of Sociology at the University of Alberta, Edmonton, Canada.

in philosophy. Bear in mind that the Roycean dialectic was in effect absent from the developing situation on the Goddard campuses beginning in mid-1969. Its influence may have lingered, expressed mainly in residual custom. No controlling definition of dialectical topics was brought on campus by any incoming administrator. No one understood what it was that Royce had really done. No one would have questioned candidates for the succession as to whether they were prepared to fill Tim's numerous roles. If they had, the candidates might not have known what the questions were about. One heard wild stories about internal and external politicization at the College. This is a highly complex topic which may need separate and careful study in years to come. Politicization is essentially what happens in a reflective vacuum; if there is no reliable philosophy there is always politics.

Consider also that Tim himself might not have given much change to the idea of a Roycean dialectic. He was inside it, looking out; from his perspective, it was more a question of what William Heard Kilpatrick had done that counted. Kilpatrick came on campus several times in the early and middle years of Royce's administrations; the faculty would crowd around, in effect, to see and hear him. There was notable curiosity about him. After all, it was difficult to be around Tim for any length of time without knowing who Kilpatrick was and what his role might have been in the formation of the early Goddard.[43]

Through the transitions following 1969 one of the principal educational themes of the College endured, seemingly unaffected by all the changes. It had begun, as it seemed, full-blown, in the winter term of 1939 and had continued steadily since that time, first of course in the winter conferences, then in certain of the summer activities, then in the appearances of adult students in campus classes, then in separate adult groups, then in consortial conferences on and off-campus, then in the appearance of consortial umbrella groups with administrative structures of their own to manage off-campus conferences and related educational outreach programs. This was of course the College definition of education in broad terms, a foundation of the adult education movement.[44]

It is curious what the stabilizing capability of the adult education services was at Goddard and probably at other institutions. It began early, to be sure, and it never lessened its intensity or its originality. It constantly expanded its scope, slowly at first, gradually more steadily and rapidly. The move into the off-campus, consortial dimension could be seen later as a leap. If it was a leap, it was oddly surefooted in its landing and self-maintenance. There was an evenness about it, a reassuring self-reliance, which made it possible to regard it

---

[43]Kilpatrick was invited once to visit during a period of upset over campus behaviors. By that time he was quite frail; but he came, and sat and listened, for the most part silent, white hair flowing where there was no wind. We don't recall what he said; our impression was that he had come to learn something about this new social phenomenon where young people took the bit in their teeth and charged off into the sunrise. Older generations have commonly granted freedoms to younger people, not quite expecting what uses they might make of them. Kilpatrick would have been aware of this, more so, perhaps, than his hosts who had invited him to come.

as a steadying force among the multitudinous currents of the time. This may have resulted in part from its relative remoteness and lack of localized problems. Those of us who were preoccupied with on-campus responsibilities may not have been closely enough in touch with it to be aware of its promise and its characteristics. It would become one of the major factors in the continuance of the College and of some considerable number of other institutions. Looking back now, the current of its steady development is no doubt clearer than it was at that time. It is a little as if an external foundation were even then being poured around the earlier, internal (perhaps the residential) foundations of the College. In spite of the controversial sale of certain program formats to other institutions under the financial pressures of the early 1980s, it appears to have continued to serve as a ballasting weight in the spectrum of College programs.

By now it seems that the data-elements of this account have been joined by such of the interpretive elements as we can presently muster. From a reading of Tim's documentary source-materials one becomes aware that he continued in his retirement a good deal as he had prior to retirement. One should not imagine that he was uninformed on or unaware of developments at the College. Person after person can tell how informal consultations with him took place periodically, into and through the 1970s, perhaps into the 1980s. It is doubtful if much of it surprised him. A good deal of the confusion he referred to he would have regarded as part of an extended institutional learning experience.

He was consistent enough in his educational-thought-and-action patterns to have regarded it judiciously even in the controversial periods. We would hazard the guess that he was in general less disturbed and less anxious about the turbulent 1970s and 1980s than most others who contemplated the Goddard scene from farther off. All life is learning, he said, often enough. Humanly, it might have crossed his mind to wish the College could be spared some of the confusion. If indeed it had to go through the turbulence, he at least had left it in the mode of active learning.

We trust it is as clear as it can be at present what Royce did with educational philosophy in his time. It was surely different from what many people

---

[44]In this connection, particularly with respect to the period of the 1920s and ff., cf. David W. Stewart, *Adult Learning in America: Eduard Lindeman and His Agenda for Lifelong Education*. Malabar, Florida, Robert E. Krieger Co., 1987. It is curious that so far as we have been able to determine, there was no cross-hatching at all between the E. C. Lindeman strain of adult education activity and the more institutionally connected strains, at Goddard, at least. Lindeman did know Frederick Burkhardt at Bennington College, and did visit and speak or conduct discussions there, just as he interacted with Max Otto at the University of Wisconsin, and occasionally visited and joined in events there. Bennington at one time was after Lindeman as a possible staffer. Lindeman was by then too ill to respond. Cf. also, in these respects, Leonard, Elizabeth Lindeman, *Friendly Rebel: A Personal and Social History of Eduard C. Lindeman*, Adamant, 1991. It may be that Lindeman's age and context, as well as his declining health, displaced him just enough from institutional developments to negate possibly closer connections. Lindeman of course made himself into a prominent public lecturer with national audiences. This would not have been Royce's style. Lindeman spoke at innumerable colleges and universities, among other engagements, in the 1930s and 1940s.

do with ideas and with thought systems. His definition of philosophy was unusual in its close articulation – perhaps in its near-identity – of thought and
action. It was also intensely verbal. Speaking in the first person only, we
think it is practical to understand his view of the world and of human life
with particularly close attention to what may have been his most original
contribution, the dialectic, that discussional bridge, that force at once strange
and familiar, which marked so profoundly the individual lives and the collective life which went on in and around the College. Goddard was at once
his creation and his self-expression. The concept of Goddard may entail as
well its resonance in the wider community of higher education. What is to
come of that remains to be seen.

★★★★★★★★★★★★★★★★★

We like to end with questions.
Experiments, the modes of outreach into the unknown and the relatively
new, are predicated in their first stages upon questions, concerning things that
are not known and deserve to be known. In later stages they may become de-
clarative in form: the experiments will take such and such a shape, and order,
and procedure, be funded from certain sources, administered thus and so, involve certain persons as teachers and facilitators, and be evaluated in such and
such a way. Levels of social agreement may be involved in these later stages.
    Why should persons or institutions traffick in experiments? Perhaps be-
cause of interests which people have. What happens with interests over periods of time? Do they fade? If they fade, what is happening? In this dimension, what is change? Where does educational leadership apply?
    The situation with regard to experimentation at Goddard in Royce's day is
probably most usefully conceived of as gradually increasing. In the first decade and a half, perhaps, people might not have noticed. It was just an oddball
institution doing odd things. A series of discussions might help to decide how
to regard that early period. It was also a period when definition of educational forms within the College were achieved apparently by prior discussions
held in the first instance between Royce and selected citizens of Vermont.
Possibly when new faculty came on board after the move to Plainfield they
found the College forms fairly well set, at least in early years. Were these
forms experiments? Probably only in the sense that they gave rise to experiments in the course of time. Tim had the operating forms well in hand early
in the history of the College. He would not have expected to discuss them in
order to have them continue as the educational forms of the institution. He
probably conducted many discussions of them in order to see that faculty and
community members understood them, the reasons for them, and how to implement them. Yet with reference to other Vermont higher educational institutions they were certainly experimental. For the most part, in all honesty,
other Vermont colleges and universities had no enthusiasm for them, and

hoped only to see them and their upstart little host institution disappear as gracefully and with as much dispatch as might be managed. Goddard's chief function in those days must have seemed to be rocking the boat. Established institutions rarely think they need that.

By the mid-1950s experiments that were called experiments, and stood out in the College context as more clearly what they were, became more common. Some of them were pivotal in their roles as enablers of change and introduction of new ideas and programs on the Goddard campus. From then on, things were at once clearer and more distinctive. The institutional stance did not allow for disputation over experiments. Another way of saying this is that there wasn't any. The experiments were simply things we were going to do, things we were interested in, which everyone wanted to do. This is not to say that there was not resistance and reaction to the force which Royce exerted. It was a human thing. When force is exerted it is human to push back, to see what room there can be in which to introduce variation from the institutional positions. We have referred to this. Tim's response to it was more apt to be funny than annoyed. There were limits to freedom in the old Goddard, the limits imposed by common adherence to the central educational plan and its implementation, the institutional policy. Tim would convey the limits, most often by simply saying that such-and-such an issue involved the College educational philosophy, which was established and which was not up for discussion. He really did not have to do it very often. Goddard was known for its different ways of thinking about education and of expressing itself in educational programs. People came there and joined its staff and faculty because of it, not in spite of it. If there were occasional misfits they would have drifted away. It has been noticed that there would eventually be problems derived probably from the inexperience of the faculty in discussing the fundaments of the College philosophy. This is what would have given rise to Royce's little thunderbolt on March 1st, 1984. It was a thunderbolt not because of its restatement of the basic reliance on the educational philosophy of the College, a condition of life on the staff and faculty, but because in effect he was tacitly acknowledging a procedural mistake. The mistake lay not in the ethico-moral nature of the philosophical commitment of the College, but in the restraint with respect to periodic consideration of the metaphysical implications of the central philosophy. This might have been pursued; Royce did not pursue it, perhaps thinking it would raise unnecessary spectres of disagreement among the members, perhaps thinking it was unnecessary because everyone was effectively facing in the same philosophical direction. In time the inevitable divergence from the common philosophy occurred, after Tim's retirement; it happened because of a vacuum in primary leadership and a consequent lacuna in the dimension of adherence to the established educational principles.

The development of this condition of uncertainty with respect to metaphysical fundaments of the ethico-moral mainstem in the over-all College educational philosophy was quite unnecessary. A philosophical system can be begun anywhere, at any point in the range and scope of the system, and can take any position it likes as to the content of the metaphysical implications. The term metaphysics as used here has no implications of its own peculiar to itself. It simply refers to whatever is fundamental in the system. What is fundamental in a system is the responsibility of the system to define. There is no intrinsic danger of anything undesirable or inconsistent being dragged in by the feet.[45]

The point has been made earlier that if there had been discussion of the implied metaphysical substrates of the ethico-moral educational philosophy of the College, there might have been more disagreement and more time-consuming argumentation than there was. This is at least probable. It is also possible that discussants might have found that there was less to fear in facing those questions, minimally, than in leaving them to take care of themselves. As long as Tim was on campus and active in the discussions the metaphysical implications, the underlying assumptions, would have been contained – by the Roycean dialectic. That formidable mode of interchange could never have been surmounted in the group. It was when the dialectic was no longer operational that doubts and questions concerning the implied fundaments were loosed.

It may be of interest to suggest certain questions which could always be raised in these connections. Since the Goddard educational philosophy was fundamentally social, what are the social implications, the extended social reaches, of a topic at issue? If a program or a position is under discussion, what are its social implications? Just how extended is it, or ought it to be? If a person or staffer is at issue, what outreach factors are effectively present? If a definition is at issue, how inclusive is it, or should it be? What degree of breadth is in it? Structure and process are often at loggerheads, in pursuit of differing objectives: to what degrees are structures, present or assumed, interfering with desirable ends? If process is the preferred mode of understanding, what does process mean, here? If the fundaments are to be addressed effectively, in the interest of being able to move readily in and out of all of the levels of useful philosophic discourse, what is the nature of human nature implied in a socially based system? What are the ultimates in a social philosophy? Theories of human nature and theories of ultimates are both routinely required in reflective systems. It would be better to have the freedom to roam widely where interests fall, and to be at ease in doing so, than to risk a disability within the implied vectors.

---

[45]In the middle years of the College one of the programs on campus enabled Senior Division students to become assisting class leaders. Nicholas Howe of Jackson, N. H., who took a BA degree in 1960, was serving as assisting leader in a class in one of the reflective fields, we forget which one. For some reason, the definition of metaphysics came up as a question. We were reaching for the point that metaphysics was the study of the really real and that there was nothing odd or remote about it because each system defined metaphysics in its own terms. Quick as a flash, Nick reached for the consequence: – "That means," he said to the class, "the metaphysics of physics is physics!" – He was quite right. We have often remembered the moment.

On the side of institutional and professional practice the questions partake of down-to-earth practicality. Goddard is no place for presidential weakness. If there was anything Royce taught in everything he did, it was that the president leads; he does not follow. This was true in the budgetary realm: it was the president who allocated funds to various uses – nobody else. He could delegate what he liked and thought best to delegate, to whom he thought best. In the last analysis, the responsibility was his, and he approved or disapproved it. It was true with faculty and staff appointments: the president could and should consult around as he thought best; the actual authority to appoint – and, as Arthur Lyndes used to say, to disappoint – was never delegated. In the last analysis, those of us who watched him at close range for many years never felt we knew for certain what he was going to decide in this dimension. Staffers may have had a fair idea some of the time, following the customary consultations; we never knew for certain. If the faculty ever says it is the appointive authority with respect to faculty and staff, its trolley is off the line. Where funds are to be raised, in a small institution with a unique viewpoint to sustain, it is a presidential responsibility to raise them. There is no place at Goddard for a staffer to appear from the hinterlands dragging funds in his wake, much like the fisherman dragging dead codfish up the steps of Durgin Park in Boston. That would imply that the president could in theory be imprisoned within the institutional need for money. Goddard always needed money. It just needed what it needed for its purposes; by definition, it did not need more. Above all, the duty of the president was to lead in the educational realm; he did that first, first, first; everything else came second, especially fund-raising. The Roycean dialectic, which we assert was real and formative and fundamental, perhaps cannot be reproduced at will among others who may some day preside at Greatwood Farm. There are personality differences among individuals which apply anywhere. But be clear about this: the presidents of Goddard must always dialogue with the faculties and students, on issues that really matter, issues of prime importance, issues of educational significance. They *must* have the personal power to do this. For a presidential candidate to accept an invitation to preside at Goddard with restrictive provisos (that he is not a member of the faculty, or does not attend faculty meetings, or is defined as a fund-raiser), is a delusion and a snare. This will require that the president be clearly an educational leader who knows his way around in education and the reflective and interpersonal fields. The Goddard faculty and staff are where they are because of their original and adventurous force. There must be a presidential dialectic to balance the force. Institutional commitments must be encouraged with whatever resources there are. Let us see if this can say itself more gently.

A last bit of advice we leave before current players in the field: the Roycean dialectic need not have fulfilled its role at Goddard with only a limited application, that to a single lifetime. It was, in this perspective, the one most significant force in the formation and the continuing operation of the College from 1938 to 1969. It was Royce Pitkin's original creation, his modus operandi. Royce himself would have had reservations on this judgment concerning its immense effects. Nevertheless, we make it. The College has always drawn to itself adventurous minds of the first order to make up its faculties. It has expected them to be original and creative and adventurous in their turns. To match the sought-for originality and creativity, and to sustain the nature of the College as an adventurous institution, its educational leaders must in all instances dialogue continuously with the faculties and the communities, in the interest of institutional commitment and momentum. There have been dismal episodes since Royce retired from the College. They were quite needless. No doubt they resulted in useful learning about what does not work well. The times, however, need not have been wasted. The relevant knowledge was always in front of everyone. Royce would never have referred to it; in point of fact, he never mentioned it. When he was in the midst of doing it, he may not even have recognized it. Now that we make bold to address it, we more than suspect he might not have approved. It cannot be helped. We say what we must. But in doing so, we claim no special wisdom. In Royce's day, we did not think of it either. It is doubtful if anyone did. If they did, they did not say much about it. Royce retired a quarter century ago. It has taken us all the time since then, and a lot of evidence appearing since then, to figure this out.

It is a pity it took so long. There might have been chances to go over to Royce's Marshfield living room and discuss it. We might have incurred another thunderbolt or two. If so, we would have striven to remain impassive, in accordance with established procedure, pending further reflection. In the interest of the dialectic, and thunderbolts notwithstanding, it would have been well worth it.

The following historic photographs are presented here with the kind permission of Goddard College. Tim was no great hand to get his picture taken, and when he did, humanly, he often looked self-conscious like most of the rest of us. It has proved difficult to find instances in which the natural person shows through in all the familiar informality. If students and graduates from the 1960s have snapshots we may not have seen, copies would be gratefully received for the College Archives.

In the following group of photographs the early instances are the most formal, in keeping with the custom of those times. Later ones show the graceful self-disregard which we all came to know best as the years went by. It is these which are of greatest interest. In most cases there are no clues left to show who took the photographs. They were after all most successful when taken on the spur of the moment as circumstances and opportunity offered. Most of them have appeared in the past in a variety of College publications. One of the most attractive aspects of this study is the notion that in future we shall come to know more about Tim in many different ways, as more new things become known. The same pleasant anticipation applies to photographs. Some of the best ones may not yet have been seen in the College contexts, being hidden in private collections. We shall look forward to having numbers of them come newly to light as the years continue.

PART TWO

Selected Writings of Royce S. Pitkin

The following selections from the President's Reports and related sources are chosen for their bearing on topics of special interest in Part One. They are at once illustrative and substantive. Better than commentary they convey the history of the College with which Royce and others have been concerned. There is an obvious book waiting to be made, from a full presentation of the descriptive portions of all the Reports, taken as an unbroken series. The selection presented in Part Two as an expansion of the themes in Part One is not that full undertaking. It is conditioned by the choices already made of themes and topics in the first section of the study.

For present purposes, notice also that certain selections of the President's Reports contained here in Part Two are also defined in the first instance by Tim himself. This begins in and derives from the Faculty Conference discussion outline in the second item: he notes the seven selections he regards at the time as being most significant as statements of College educational philosophy. The seven selections referred to follow in the order he gave, in a first group of four and a second group of three. If we are after what Tim thought about the philosophy of the College this is as close as we are likely to get to his forms of thought and discussion at this stage. The opportunity to present them as central among his own writings on this theme is simply not to be missed.

It remains to place in perspective aspects of this study at this stage. There are obvious dangers in making selections from anyone's writings, on the assumption that they subsume major elements of his thought and intent. Can this be done without comprehensive inclusions? We think so. Call it an experiment: –there is a certain appropriateness in the term. It is even helpful, with respect to selections made, to address practical matters, to see how the selections ride on the page, whether in the amount of material there lingers a weight which obscures the purpose, even omitting the financial and statistical sections of the Reports as has been done here in most of these instances. We may also see whether the making of selections omits aspects of Tim's thought which can only be redressed in a full presentation.

There will be a few items in Part Two, most by Royce, from sources other than the President's Reports, and a small number of letters and other pieces, all included with permission of the writers if other than Royce. Footnotes apply perspectives coming to mind.

In a project such as this there is an inevitable temptation to include more and more material. Deciding what to include is not difficult; deciding what to omit is what is awkward. In the last analysis we have striven to remember our own perception – that sooner or later there will be a full volume of Royce's President's Reports. It will not be a serious matter if the many sections of Royce's writings which one would like to present are not as yet included here.

There is room for many histories of Goddard, by many different persons; they are to be encouraged as way stations on the road toward a true account. So is Royce's own history to be encouraged. He knew that he was writing a central history of the College even as he wended his way through its highways and byways. He took great pains with it, over his entire professional life. This is where his best educational thought and writing are to be found. This is also where a good deal of his best reflective (philosophical) writings are. There will be other histories of Goddard, certainly, as there should be. In making the selections for this volume we but prepare for more complete presentations to come.

This entire affair is more of an experiment than was anticipated at its beginning. In keeping with such of Tim's interests as we may have been able to catch, we shall see what there is to be learned from the doing of it. If it has defects – as it surely may – there will perhaps be opportunities to benefit from the mistakes, if not in our time then in later studies, and so eventually to "improve" upon inevitably unfinished ends.

- FKD
August, 1995

THE GODDARD COLLEGE PHILOSOPHY

A Talk at the Mid-Semester Conference on
Goals and Practices of College Education[46]

October 26, 1961
by Royce S. Pitkin

I have been asked to talk about the philosophy of Goddard College. From time to time some students say, "Why don't you say something about what the philosophy of the College is, I don't know what it is." Then I ask, "Did you ever read the catalogue?" and the reply is, "Yes, I've read the catalogue but it doesn't seem to say what the philosophy of the College is." And so they want somebody to put it in different words, apparently. Now this means really that I can say nothing new. Dean Forest Davis suggested that I might say something new, but I don't see how I can, because it wouldn't be quite prop-

---

[46]When speaking to an audience, Tim usually referred to his material as a talk, as he does here. He did not often call such pieces addresses or speeches. The invitation to give this talk would have come to him directly from members of the community. His mood here is relaxed and responsive, even peaceful. The talk does not appear to be in response to any sort of crisis. It suggests that he liked being asked to give a talk on College philosophy, particularly that the invitation to give it came from community members. The date here is 1961. The period may perhaps be thought of as an interlude, if Goddard ever had any interludes, before the campus expansion began to have its effects in the mid-1960s. But already Tim may have begun to seem somewhat more remote and to have fewer contacts with students than before. Community members might have felt the need to be reminded about what the College educational philosophy was all about. The level of writing here ranks with the President's Reports; it is clearly a talk to a present audience, with casual terminology and homely illustrations which the Reports would not have had. But it is also very carefully done as the Reports also were, leaving no slightest doubt as to meanings intended. Notice the references to dialogue and trialogue in the last third, and the accent suggested by the double subject a page or so earlier. This is not the earliest piece in this collection in point of date, but it may be among among the earliest direct discourses on College philosophy, and so stands first, the original document showing authorship as here, with his full name.

110

er to enunciate a change in philosophy in quite that off-hand fashion. Some of the things I say may be new to newer students, or to the present generation of college students, but it would not have been new to students who were here twenty years ago.

I think perhaps I ought to explain what I mean by philosophy. We had some discussion upstairs during and following the lunch hour about what philosophy might be, and I withheld my own definition of it because I was going to give it down here and I didn't want those people to have to listen to too much of the same thing. When I talk about philosophy, I am talking about a way of looking at life, or looking at some aspects of life, so when I talk about the philosophy of Goddard College, I am talking about the way I look at Goddard College, and the kind of institution I think it is. There is nothing very esoteric or mystical about this, and some people will say there is nothing very intellectual about it, but perhaps it has an intellectual appearance. A philosophy, if you take the view of it, is revealed, it seems to me, in at least three ways. It is revealed first by the way one behaves, so the philosophy of a college is revealed in the way the college functions on a day to day, week to week, and year to year basis. A philosophy is also revealed by one's aims, and sometimes one's aims do not exactly jibe with his practices. Nevertheless they are a part of the philosophy. And a third way in which one's philosophy is expressed, or the philosophy of an institution is expressed, is through the principles which guide behavior–speaking about a person, the principles which guide the behavior of that person. The principles which guide behavior are not necessarily the same as the aims, although it seems to me they ought to be very much in harmony.

The philosophy of Goddard College has been expressed in these three ways over the twenty-three years of its existence. In other words, we have had statements of aims, we have had statements of principles which guided our behavior, and then we have had our behavior.

The aims of the College, as they were stated in the first catalogue, which was issued in the spring of 1938 before the College opened, included the education of young men and women for real living through the actual facing of real life problems as an essential part of their educational program. We were trying to say that in making up the curriculum, we would give attention to the problems which seemed to the students to be real problems. And this led us into lots of places that we hadn't anticipated. One of the unanticipated things it led us into was a fairly extensive counselling system, and we discovered that although we had planned a counselling system, it developed in a way we had not foreseen. What we discovered was that students have a great many kinds of problems and that these are often the problems that they want and ought to work on but for which there has been no provision in the usual courses of study. And then of course we felt that many of the problems – and keep in mind that this was in 1938 when the American people were still pretty far down in the depression – seemed more insistent to students then than many current problems seem to us now. Students who came to college in the late thirties and early forties had on their minds problems which were not found in the usual courses of study, and so we said we'll start with these in building the curriculum.

The second aim was to test the idea that education is a process of securing a better understanding and enriching of life, rather than the teaching of subject matter in prescribed courses. Again, the meant that a college curriculum is not built simply in terms of courses that have been prescribed and worked out in advance, but rather that education is seen as the process, with the emphasis quite strongly on process, of attaining understanding of life and enriching life, whatever form the enrichment may take.

A third aim was the study of vocation as a part of living, rather than something distinct and an end in itself. We were trying to say that the liberal arts were a good thing to study, but that just because the liberal arts were a good thing to study did not mean that we should not include the study of vocation. As a matter of fact, a large part of the curriculum of the ordinary liberal arts college had originally been largely vocational. And this seemed to have been lost sight of. What had been discovered was that that kind of vocational curriculum had a liberalizing value. In other words, to train for the ministry one took a great many subjects such as Greek and Latin, and later English grammar, history, natural philosophy, and so on. These were found to have some value, so people came to think of them as being a part of a liberal arts curriculum, even though some of them had little relation to the original liberal arts. But we felt, even in 1938, that we ought to look upon vocation as having in itself liberalizing elements and we ought not keep the two things apart. Another way of putting this was that it is entirely proper that a student in a liberal arts college should have a vocational goal and should be permitted to work for that vocational goal.

A fourth aim was the integration of the life of the College with the life of the community, and the consequent breaking down of the barriers that separate the school from real life. This is one reason we instituted the non-resident term. We were not pioneers in that, but we thought it ought to be included in the Goddard program. To achieve this aim we thought we ought to develop courses and plans by means of which students could become involved in activities off the campus during the academic semesters. Curiously enough, we didn't do very much along this line until within the last four or five years, when we instituted the Educational Resources Program. But the idea was that a college ought not be cut off, it ought not to be an ivory tower, it ought to be very much involved with the life of the wider community.

A fifth aim was to use the community as a laboratory in which students may see life as a whole rather than as a collection of unrelated parts. The use of the word "laboratory" got us into some trouble. The people of the area around here took this to mean that we were to regard the residents of the community as guinea pigs and that we were going to watch their behavior in the community. But we did not mean that sort of thing at all. What we meant was that we would take a look at life as it really goes on in a community in order that we may understand what the wholeness of life is instead of just taking some small segment of it, which is the customary practice in schools.

A sixth aim was the participation of students in the formation of policies, in the management of the College and in the performance of work essential to the maintenance and operation of the College, and the inclusion of such work in the educational program. The idea was that the students who came to the College should be as deeply involved as possible in the total operation of the institution. We didn't know just what the limits were to be, we don't know now just what the limits are; they move in and out or up and down, whichever way you want to put it, so that in some years students have participated much more in the formation of policies than in other years. Looking over the entire period, one would have to say that they have actually participated a great deal in the formation of policy of the College. This does not mean that it ever was intended that students should decide upon the nature of the whole program of the College, but it did mean that lines of communication between students and teachers should be wide open so that the ideas of the students could be constantly presented to the members of the faculty. This has gone on consistently, and it has its effect. From the point of view of students the trouble is, I am sure, that the effect doesn't come soon enough. It may be after one has graduated and gone that the effect is felt. Nevertheless the effect is felt. Sometimes, however, it comes sooner. But this is what really gave rise to the institution of community government, a system that encourages faculty members and students to be constantly discussing policies of the College of one kind or another; and actually there is no subject that I can think of that the College has been concerned with, that has not been discussed in Community Meeting or other meetings that go on on the campus.

We felt too, for a variety of reasons, at that time, that it was very important for college students to have work experience – the kind of experience that you get in making any kind of institution go. From the outside it looks as though running an institution would be a lot of fun, that it would be very exciting. All you had to do was to sit in an office and dream up ideas and get them into operation. Or you could sit in an office and say "Let the students be fed" and presto, automatically they would be fed. Or say "Put up a building, and heat it" and it would be done. Well, to most of the students who grew up even in the late thirties this is really what happened in their homes; somebody heaved in some coal somewhere and some heat was produced, and the room was kept warm whether the windows were open or closed, whether it was winter or summer. A result of this kind of living, and it has been greatly extended since, of course, was a considerable alienation of the American college student from the cause and effect aspects of life, from those things that could be seen as producing results. Moreover, students who came to college in those days – and the number now is even smaller – who had had the responsibility of carrying out even small jobs was extremely limited, and therefore when they moved into a real job after they left college they had had a rather narrow experience. As the years have gone on, it has become quite obvious that this part of the program has become more rather than less important. A new development has taken place, which gives added significance to it, and that is the concern which America now has, but which it certainly did not have in 1938, for the rest of the world. We were pretty much an isolationist nation in 1938, in spite of the fact that we had been involved in one world war. But since the second world war, and all during the cold war and all its concomitants, we have become more and more aware of the existence of other peoples, and we have come to realize that the great mass of people in this world are very much tied to ordinary, simple, hand and foot operations, and we are now in the business of exporting young Americans and old Americans to other parts of the world to work with these peoples. This means it is all the more important for this generation to be familiar with the chores of life – to understand what it means to provide meals, serve meals, wash the dishes, clean up afterwards, build buildings, dig ditches, rake leaves, all the things that go into making an institution run, because these are things which people around the world have to do, and they're going to keep on doing them for many, many decades. We had reached the point a few years back when it seemed like the whole idea of work was not very important – I mean manual work – because it was said, "America has reached the pinnacle, we have all kinds of machinery, we even have automated machinery; consequently there is no need for people to work." And so the whole idea of work was out the window. But if we are going to understand the people of other cultures where the performance of arduous manual work is usual rather than unusual, we have to get some of the feeling which comes from doing ordinary jobs that require the use of hands as well as brains. I can in part illustrate my point from the unhappy experience of the Smith graduate who was in the Peace Corps. I am sure that this girl went through a very rigorous training, in spite of what the newspapers have had to say; I am sure she was told, not once but forty times, that life in Nigeria among the people with whom she was going to work was going to be very difficult, that there would be squalor, that there would be poverty, that there would be disease, that there would be discomfort. But my guess is that this girl had never experienced squalor and disease of that sort, and discomfort and poverty, and although she took it in intellectually, she never took it in emotionally. So what does she write home on this unfortunate post card? "We were not adequately prepared for the kind of life we found here." How could she be? It is my guess that if this girl had really been involved in some of the realities of ordinary work which can be found in Vermont, as well as in some other states, then she would have *felt*, she would have known what the words meant, and it would not simply have been an intellectual conception. So this is why we felt in 1938 and why I feel still very strongly, more so than I ever did before, that work, manual work, work necessary to make the institution operate, is an important part of the educational program. I think for some students it is perhaps one of the most important parts, for it enables them to develop aspects of their personalities that might otherwise be untouched.

A seventh aim was the development of a religious attitude that is free from sectarianism. And we went on to say that religion is here conceived in a broad sense as a way of unifying personality by getting a unified grasp on life's problems. This definition of religion wouldn't satisfy everybody, but we did want to make it clear that we were launching what was in essence a religious institution. And I still feel it is a religious institution. I think it is about the most religious institution in the country, although I am sure that many others think it is about the most irreligious one in the country. But it is because of this idea, that we look upon religion as a way of unifying personality through a unified grasp of life's problems.

Now, let me be quite frank, these were aims, they were not attainments, that I am talking about, you understand. I don't think we succeeded in helping every student or every one of us who were staff members in unifying personality. Some personalities left here as fractured as when they came, probably some were more fractured than when they came. But this was the aim, and as I said earlier, aims are one expression of philosophy.

The eighth aim was the provision of educational opportunities for adults, and this was felt to be an important part of the education of undergraduates. In other words, we felt that if the faculty came in contact with adults through an adult education program, the faculty would in turn become educated in what was going on in the world, what other people were thinking in the non-academic as well as the academic world, and therefore would be that much better able to work with undergraduates.

Well, those were the eight aims as they appeared in the Goddard College catalogue in the spring of 1938.

Now there were three principles which we used to say guided our practice, and from my point of view they still do. To get this material I looked back at the catalogue, and I also looked at some speeches I made in 1938, '39, '40, '41, and really what I am doing tonight is repeating some of these, so that you can see what the philosophy of the college is.

The first of these three principles, which we emphasized very strongly, was that *thought should be tested by action*. Because we felt, as I think most people would probably feel, that action without thought may be stupid, usually is stupid, whereas thought without action is futile. If you just sit and think and think and think and do nothing, your thinking results in futility; but if you think and think and think and then create an idea, something's happened, you see, something good has come out of it. Or if you think and think and get an idea and then act, a lot more comes out of it. So we believed that all through the college life we should insist upon the testing of thought by action. This is another reason why we instituted the work program. It's the best place in the

world to find out what the character of a person is. The best test of philosophy is the way one behaves, I think. A person studies Plato, and he studies
other somewhat more recent philosophers perhaps, and he thinks "this is a
great guide to action", but you really know whether he understands and believes it by the way he behaves. And this is the testing of thought in action.
People talk about charity, Christian and otherwise, but the way to find out
whether they have it is to watch the way they behave when they're on a work
program: whether they make it hard for their neighbor, or whether they don't
make it hard for their neighbor; whether they make a contribution to the
welfare of mankind.

A second principle that guided our action, and one we used to talk about a
great deal, was that *we learn what we inwardly accept.* This statement we owe
very clearly to William Heard Kilpatrick, for whom Kilpatrick House is
named and whom we will honor Saturday night. We learn what we inwardly
accept. In other words, you can be told a lot of things, I can tell you a lot of
things tonight – maybe some things you have never heard, maybe some you
have heard, but if you don't inwardly accept these and build them into your
own life, then you have not learned anything. And this is where I think most
college professors go wrong. They forget this, and so they talk and talk and
talk, and then they train the students to reproduce the talk without its ever
entering into the life of the student. Consequently the student hasn't really accepted it and made it his own. So one of the principles, I repeat, that guided
us was this notion that we learn what we inwardly accept, and unless we really accept it inwardly, it isn't learned. We can memorize it, to be sure, we can
repeat the words, but this doesn't mean that we accept the meaning of the
words and that it guides our behavior.

A third principle is that *one matures by carrying responsibilities suited to one's
capacities.* And this was the reason in a sense that we instituted Community
Government, the reason that we provided for free election, except that we
never used that term, of course – what we said was, the students are to select
programs of studies to meet their own needs as they saw those needs, and
then have to take the consequences of good or bad choices. If the choice happened to be bad, they learned presumably as much from it as if the choice
were good. We felt that college students had reached the point where they
could carry that responsibility. I might add that we knew they couldn't go
wrong, because they surely would know as much about what they ought to
study as somebody who had never seen them and didn't know anything about
their background, but who had already prescribed the course.

I'll repeat the three principles: *Thought should be tested by action. We learn
what we inwardly accept. One matures by carrying responsibilities suited to one's capacities.* Thus, you see, the whole idea of Community Government provided that
opportunity. The whole idea of Work Program provided that opportunity,
and so on.

What I want to do now, having recalled these things that we said some
twenty-odd years ago, is to make a restatement of our philosophy. We might

call this a restatement twenty-three years later; it's almost twenty-four as a matter of fact, because we began the formulation of this philosophy in 1937 in a series of meetings at Goddard Seminary and Junior College where we talked about educational philosophy and talked about philosophic and psychological assumptions. What I am trying to do now is to say how, by and large, the College as an institution regards its philosophy. We think of education as being growth. When we think this way, there are certain characteristics or certain conditions that exist, or certain meanings that follow. If education is growth, it means using one's inherent capacities for meeting life's problems. And this is what the small child does. The small child encounters problems. He uses his inherent capacities, he uses the capacities that are inside of him before his father and mother and all the rest of the adults have given him much. He has a voice, and he uses the voice early to make known his wants. This is a way of meeting problems. He's suffering from hunger, and so he lets out a yell. He's suffering from colic, or whatever other ailment affects modern children, and so he lets out a yell. Sometimes he gets results, sometimes he doesn't; more often he does get results among humane parents. But the point it, he's using his inherent capacities to meet a very important and insistent problem, and this enables the child to grow, it enables him to get command, to some degree, over his environment, and this keeps on all through life. This is, in part, what we mean when we speak of education as growth.

It means too discovering one's potential and then developing it. And one of the tasks of the school, if we view education as growth, is to help a student and to help the teachers discover his potential, the student's potential, and then to help the student develop that potential. And very often the potential is far greater than the student had believed it to be.

And then if we believe in education as growth, we see it as the process of selecting out of a great wealth of possibilities the experiences that promise most. If you stop to think of it, there are many kinds of experience one could have. You could go to the concert this evening that is to be held in Montpelier. This would undoubtedly promise more than staying here to hear me talk, but you have to make a choice, and it might be that concerts bore you and this would bore you less, in which case you might decide to stay here. But you do make a choice, and you make a choice every day, every hour probably, out of the many kinds of experiences, a vast number of experiences. The process of growth consists of selecting those that seem to promise most. In other words, we say, "I'll do this, not because it's the most pleasurable at the moment, but I'll do this because it will seem to me in the long run to yield the greatest satisfactions." I didn't say the greatest happiness, although I think the two are very closely related, but the greatest satisfactions.

And if we think of education as growth it means, I think, anticipating consequences and making our decisions accordingly. If one on impulse says, "Tonight I guess I'll go out on the town", he isn't really growing if he just automatically does it. But if he pauses and anticipates the consequences of going out on the town, if he asks, "What's it going to cost me, what's it going to do to my head, how am I going to feel in the morning if I don't get any sleep tonight?" he is growing. But the person who is not concerned about growth, is not concerned about developing his potential, he doesn't ask these questions; instead he goes out on the town, and the next day he looks like it. But this is the whole business of living, it seems to me. We have to anticipate the consequences of the courses of action we are going to take. This is the great problem, as I see it, that faces every nation of the world, and from our point of view, particularly the American nation. We have to weigh very carefully the consequences of a course of action, select the one which seems to us to promise most in terms of achieving the things which we believe in.

And if we regard the nature of education as being that of growth, we would say it would consist of confronting problems, of defining problems, of understanding the nature of the problems, and then of formulating proposals for solving those problems – the scientific term we use is formulating hypotheses, that sounds better, you know, than just saying you think up ideas, but it means the same – and then trying out these proposals. And it seems to me again that this is what the educational process in large part should consist of – identifying the problems that we really face, that we are really concerned about, not taking the surface appearance but really digging and seeing what they mean. Then, having some notion of what the problem is, we proceed to propose some ideas about dealing with that problem. And having done that, we try out the proposal. You see this is an application of the principle that thought should be tested by action.

Education as growth also means interacting with others and interacting with one's environment. In other words, you don't really get educated all by yourself. We talk a great deal about learning from experience, and of course we do, provided we do some of these things I have been mentioning. But we interact with others. This is the real way we learn – we interact with others through books, for when we read a book we react to it. The great word now being used is dialogue, but I think it's a little more than a dialogue, it may even be a trialogue or something of that sort, but you do interact with others and with your total environment – not only with people, but with things, with conditions, with your culture, with your history, with your traditions, with your aspirations and the aspirations of others. In other words, the process of growth is that of dealing with others. If the baby never got any response, if nobody showed up, you see, he would die. But somebody does show up, and this affects the way this child behaves the next time.

Well, those are some of the ways in which I conceive education when I think about it as growth. These principles, the aims that we had and still have for the College, and the philosophy of the College rest on certain assumptions or educational principles, and to understand the philosophy of the College one needs to understand the assumptions on which we proceed. If you don't accept the assumptions, you might not accept the aims, and you might not accept the principles, and you might not accept the description of education as growth. You might have other descriptions you would formulate. Most of these assumptions have come out of rather extensive studies that have been made in the last fifty to seventy-five years about the nature of learning. Some of them have been derived from studies in psychology, some have been derived from studies of culture, some have been derived from studies in psychotherapy, some have been derived from studies in psychoanalysis, but they have tended to emerge from a vast number of studies that have gone on for quite some time. I am quite sure that not every member of the faculty would accept all of these assumptions, but I think every member would accept some of them.

The first is that every normal person has within him the need, the desire, and the drive to learn. Learning, in other words, is almost as natural and just as essential as breathing. Probably I don't even need the qualifying adverb in there, for learning *is* as necessary and as essential and as natural as breathing. The infant begins learning probably before birth but certainly immediately after birth, and he goes on learning all the way through life. It just cannot be avoided. Every time you confront a situation, and you can't lift your head or open your eyes without confronting a situation, you have to do something about it, and you learn. You may not learn a lot, but you learn some. Learning is essential, in other words, to keeping alive and to moving and to developing.

Another basic assumption is that the purposes and the motives of an individual guide his learning. It is not the purposes and the motives of other persons that guide one's learning so much as the purposes and motives of the individual that guide one's learning. We try desperately as teachers to have our purposes and motives guide learning, but you know how often that goes astray. This is why teachers say – I have heard them say it a thousand times if I have heard them say it once – "But I *told* you that. Don't you remember, we had that in the fifth grade?" This is said by those who teach the sixth grade. Or "somebody else told you this" or "you ought to know this" – meaning that they have been told. In other words, the teacher, the school have tried to guide the learning, to provide the motives. But actually, it's the purposes and the motives of the individual that guide his learning. You can do a certain amount of influencing, but when you get around to the last analysis, it is what the learner himself decides he is going to do that determines.

A third assumption is that purpose and motive are internal; they're self-determined and, though affected by many factors, they cannot be imposed from the outside. Some people think this isn't so. They think you can impose motives, and they talk about external motivation. I am not quite sure what that means, except that it's a device and a method by which you attempt to get the learner to do something which you want him to do by so-called extrinsic means. But it seems to me that any attempt at motivation is successful to the degree that it relates or connects with the purposes of the learner. Let us suppose that you want your child to excel in geometry for some reason, so you think up various devices by which you can get him to excel in geometry,

and you think, well, if I offer him a chance to go on a trip on a jet plane –
that's kind of old-hat nowadays, but still a lot of children haven't gone on a jet
plane yet so it appeals to some of them – you say, well, if you'll only take
geometry this semester in high school and if you only do well in it, I'll give
you a ride in a jet plane. This is an attempt to use the purpose and the motive
of the parent to get the child to do something. Now the purpose and the motive of the child obviously are *not* to learn geometry. The purpose and the
motive of the child are to get the airplane ride, but for the sake of doing it, in
order to get there, he'll do the geometry. He may acquire an interest at this
point, and you can talk quite a lot about the conversion of an interest into a
real purpose, but this is what happens. And sometimes we're successful by
these extraneous means in getting a person to have the kind of interest that
we want him to have. But it's only because we can connect – this is the point
I am trying to establish – it is only because we can connect our own goals
with the internal motives and purposes of the individual.

A fourth assumption is that the stronger and more clearly defined one's
purposes, the more likely one is to learn rapidly and effectively. I think this is
the reason that adults very often learn a great deal more in a short period of
study than younger persons do; they may have a greater clarity of purpose, a
stronger purpose, and a greater drive. The younger person has been somewhat
satiated with the learning process as he knows it in school. He has learned lots
of things outside of school too, and he doesn't get satiated there, but he gets
satiated with the learning situation in school, and so he has no great drive and
no real purpose. Never a year goes by but what some college student comes
in and talks about how he doesn't have any purpose in being in college really–
oh, yes, he would like to get a degree, but he is not interested in education,
just interested in a degree, and he doesn't know what he wants to do, and so
on. But those persons who are pretty clear in their purposes are the ones who
can learn most easily and most effectively. And the more sharply they define
those purposes, the more they know about what they are going to do, and the
better they are able to judge whether they are doing what they set out to do.
And I submit it has far more meaning to one to work to carry out *his* purposes than it does to work in order to do something to get a degree. Getting
the degree may be a purpose, but it is a bit unrelated to a fruitful learning process as long as one can stack up credits or something of that sort to get one.

A fifth assumption is that as problems arise in the pursuit of purposes, one
inevitably becomes aware of new needs which one has. It works this way: you
have a purpose, you set out to achieve this purpose, you acquire some knowledge, you acquire some understanding, and then next thing you know you
have a whole new set of needs, and you can't meet these needs without new
knowledge and without new understanding. So this is a self-generating process. This is why you don't need to stand over a student with a whip and
compel him to go to class, you don't need to give an examination in order to
make him learn, you don't need to have the allurement of marks or even a

Phi Beta Kappa key to get him to work, because he has discovered his own needs, he has discovered he has to have new understanding and is interested in getting the understanding in order to meet those needs. And as the learner reaches out for resources to meet these needs, he undoubtedly develops new and more adequate purposes. As he acquires a new set of purposes, and they become more adequate purposes, so he lives more fully. And this is what goes on year after year if one really is given an opportunity to look inward and see what his capabilities are and is permitted to find his needs and ascertain the problems which are his problems, and then find solutions to them.

A sixth basic assumption is that the educational process–and this tends to follow from what I have been saying–consists in large measure of clarifying and trying to achieve one's purposes and objectives, or, to state it very differently and very simply, the educational process consists fundamentally of learning how to learn. So, if we really want to be effective as an educational institution, the thing to do is to get students to define their purposes clearly and then set about to achieve those purposes. This is easier said than done, as anyone here can testify, but nevertheless it seems to me to be the way we have to do it if we are going to be effective.

This leads me to the seventh and the last of my assumptions, namely that the content or the stuff of education is the experiences of the individual as he seeks to attain these objectives. These experiences are varied. What I'm saying is that the things that constitute the content of education are conversation, play, manual work, reading, expression, contemplation, guessing, creating, analyzing, comparing, dreaming, seeing, feeling, listening, and a vast amount of activity that goes on below the level of consciousness.

I could not have said this twenty years ago because I didn't know it, but I think we have to take account of the fact that a large part of the curriculum of an individual goes on below the level of consciousness. And there are those who say that what goes on below the level of consciousness is more determining than that which goes on above the level of consciousness. I am in no position to judge this, but I do think that a terrific amount goes on below the level of consciousness that determines the nature of what we learn and what we do. So we have to give more attention to that than we have before. This then, from my point of view, is what constitutes the stuff of education. This is the curriculum, the experiences that an individual has, to learn the things that he needs to learn to achieve his objectives.

Now then, this means, you see, that the function of the college and the teacher is simply that of facilitating the educational process, that is, to provide a setting in which these experiences can take place and can be evaluated. In short, the function of a college is to provide or to create the conditions for learning. It's as simple as that, to say, but extremely complex to do. The teacher or the educational institution has to know when to get out of the way. It has to learn when to be in the way, when to be an obstacle, when to raise a question, and when, on rare occasions, to provide an answer. But mostly it has to be concerned with watching individuals to see whether the conditions for learning exist.

Now the gist, I think, of Goddard's educational philosophy throughout the twenty-three years it has been operating and today is contained in the affirmation of William Heard Kilpatrick that "We learn what we live, we learn each item we live as we accept it, and we learn it in the degree we accept it."

GODDARD COLLEGE
FACULTY CONFERENCE

December 28, 1965[47]

College Aims and Philosophy

1. Introduction
   1.1 Quote from Gene Miller's senior study - ¶4-6, include his quotation from Robert A. Nisbet's *Community and Power.*
   1.2 How I came to suggest this meeting.
      1.21 Meeting with the Greatwood Educational Policies Committee and their comment on "Goddard is a place for study."
      1.22 Question by a new faculty. "Well, is it?"
   1.3 Review of semester's work by Senior Division Committee shows that there has been much study.

---

[47]This outline is presented here in typeset for obvious reasons; the original document is in Tim's hand. He would have prepared it ahead of time somewhere else. The use of the decimal numbering system suggests somewhat more tension in the situation. Considering the date this was to be expected. The second campus had been opened in September, 1965; these were All-College Faculty discussions occurring at the end of a turbulent first semester, during which Northwood students had been centered in Marshfield, their living space not yet having been finished on Northwood. There was probably some tautness on both campuses; part of the new Northwood population would need to camp on Greatwood through part of the spring term. If the All-College Faculty discussions scheduled on December 28th, 1965 were to be explained contextually, by conditions on the campuses and the suggestion of tension and the touch of urgency implied in the form, this may be a fair beginning at it. There is, however, one more aspect to consider.

2.   There are problems within the College. Not a new situation.

    2.1 Awareness of problems: starting point for learning.

    2.2 There is *suspicion* of others – their motives, their intentions.

    2.3 There is fear – that somebody is going to do something to somebody.

    2.4 There is competition for influence and power – ambition for leadership.

    2.5 There is bafflement and frustration for all of us because things don't come off as we had hoped and expected.

    2.6 There have been changes in society to which we are not yet accustomed. Hence changes in the outlook, interests and needs of students.

    2.7 Tendency in such situations is to revert to conventional solutions which more often than not make conditions worse.

3.   Given this multiplicity of problems and their effects on students.

    3.1 It seems wise to consider them in the light of the aims and philosophy of the College.

    3.2 This is our common ground.

    3.3 It is ground that was hard to win, but ground that we cannot afford to and will not relinquish.

4.   Let me illustrate.

    4.1 From my quarterly report of 17 years ago – December 31, 1948.

    4.2 From my quarterly report of 16 years ago – December 31, 1949.

    4.3 From my quarterly report of 8 years ago – December 31, 1957.

    4.4 From my quarterly report of 6 years ago – December 31, 1959.

    4.5 These reports have recalled some of the problems Goddard has encountered and have revealed some of its aims and philosophy.

(Note 47 continued):

    Notice the reference to Gene Miller's senior study, which Tim intended to quote, along with the Nisbet selection. Eugene K. Miller of Suffern, New York, had completed his study and turned it in on December 17th, 1965; Tim had presumably either just read it or had been Gene's advisor for it and was already acquainted with it. He evidently led off by quoting from it, #'s 4-6, including the Nisbet selection, all from Gene's Introduction. The section is locatable in the microfilm copy without difficulty. Copyright law today prohibits reprinting this selection without the author's consent. It is a very interesting section of a very interesting document, dealing with alienation from society as a widespread social phenomenon in America, which clearly Gene himself felt in an immediate and personal way. The title of the study is "Man Without A Worthwhile World." Efforts were made to locate the author in the interest of securing permission to reprint, thus far to no avail. He disappeared from the records following his graduation in 1966 and so far as is known had not communicated with the College since that time. The role of Gene's senior study in the initiation of Royce's discussion of "College Aims and Philosophy" on December 28th, 1965 remains tantalizing. That it had such a role seems at least possible. Tim had enormous respect for student ideas and positions. It was as if they foretold waves of the future, and he perceived it.

5.   But other reports refer more directly and explicitly to aims and
     philosophy.
     5.1 Annual report of June 30, 1954, – 11 years ago.
     5.2 Quarterly report of March 31, 1957 – nearly 9 years ago.
     5.3 Quarterly report of September 30, 1960 – 5 years ago
     5.4 These constitute what I understand to be the basic elements in
         the philosophy of Goddard College.

6.   Comments and questions from the group.

7.   Small group meetings will provide a better chance to discuss and
     prepare statements. Propose 7 groups – each is asked how can we
     best apply the Goddard philosophy of educational experimentation in
     a particular area.
     7.1 Planning and evaluating group courses.
     7.2 Encouraging academic achievement in group courses.
     7.3 Encouraging achievement through independent study.
     7.4 Utilizing off-campus resources.
     7.5 Carrying out work program.
     7.6 Dealing with personality problems.
     7.7 Administering community affairs.

     Groups are asked to return at 2.45 with statements on how we can
     best apply the philosophy in the areas indicated.

8   Schedule by Evalyn – rooms – groups.

REPORT OF THE PRESIDENT OF
GODDARD COLLEGE

For the Quarter Ending December 31, 1948[48]

Last October application was made for the admission of Goddard College to the New England Association of Colleges and Secondary Schools. This action was taken because of the interest of trustees, parents, students and staff in recognition by the regional accrediting association and in the belief that it would be helpful to be included in the list of senior colleges that are members of the Association. In making application it was the intent of the faculty that no modifications should be made in the practices of the College unless they were in harmony with its basic philosophy and principles even though it might mean failure to be admitted. Led by some of the parents and trustees a strong effort was made to bring the number of volumes in the library and other physical equipment up to the minimum requirements of the Association. These efforts were so successful that the minimum requirements were consid-

---

[48]Here begins the series of seven Reports referred to by Royce on p.2 of the preceding item, the topical outline. He would not have read all the material from any of them; notice that he refers to brackets as identifying what he planned to read. Brackets appear only once in this set of President's Reports. We do not know if he was working with a different set of Reports, or whether this was the only time he introduced brackets. Readers will have to select parts which he might have read, bearing on principles and their expressions already identified. Other materials included will serve other purposes. Each of the seven Reports is presented as it appears in the files, but without the statistical and budgetary sections. The Report for December 31,1948 is the first of the seven in the series. It deals entirely with the visit of the Committee from the New England Association of Colleges and Secondary Schools in 1948, on the occasion of Goddard's first request for admission to the Association, and Royce's detailed analysis and comparison of it with the contemporaneous President's Commission on Higher Education dated in December 1947; the "President" in this case would have been Harry S. Truman, and the Commission a national entity.

erably exceeded and the College was much better equipped to do its work. There are, however, still many improvements that need to be made.

The following statement of the Association seemed to suggest that the Goddard program would be judged in terms of the philosophy on which it is based and that, therefore, it would be proper to seek membership in the Association.

"An institution of higher education shall have clearly defined educational objectives. Its application for membership in the Association will be judged by:

A.   The effectiveness of its various curricula in realizing its objectives
B.   The preparation and experience of its faculty
C.   The administrative leadership it affords
D.   Its provisions for admitting students who are well qualified to benefit from its offerings
E.   The adequacy of its physical plant
F.   Its financial ability to carry out the purposes it has set"

In its application the College was asked for a statement of its aims and philosophy; a description of its plant; its requirements for admission and graduation; its catalog; a list of the staff members showing their educational background, experience, degrees and subjects taught during the current semester; provisions for social life and recreation among students; a description of the government of the College; a list of the colleges to which Goddard students have transferred with advanced standing within the last five years; a list of the graduate schools to which graduates have been admitted; and a copy of the financial statement.

Late in November an inspection committee of two representing the Committee on Institutions of Higher Learning visited the College. They arrived at about fifteen minutes after ten in the forenoon and left a little before four in the afternoon. Following a visit in the president's office, a tour of the main part of the campus was made. On the tour between fifteen and twenty minutes were given to visiting classes, the time being divided among three. The Committee lunched with four members of the college staff in the college dining room and conversed pleasantly about some of the aims, beliefs and procedures of the College. Following this session of approximately two hours, the Committee went to the library, apparently to compare notes and record observations. About a half hour before leaving one of the committee visited with the Goddard instructor in education concerning the work in that field, the other inspected some of the records of a few former students.

Early in December the action of the Committee on Institutions of Higher Learning was reported to me by a letter from its chairman, C. Scott Porter, Dean of Amherst College. Because of its revealing nature, it is reproduced here:

AMHERST COLLEGE
Amherst, Massachusetts

Office of the Dean

December 11, 1948

President Royce S. Pitkin
Goddard College
Plainfield, Vermont

Dear President Pitkin:

I am sending you this letter to supplement my earlier letter concerning the failure of your institution to be approved for membership in the New England Association of Colleges and Secondary Schools.

This year seven senior institutions and nine junior institutions applied for membership. Two senior institutions and two junior institutions were approved for membership. The application of the other twelve institutions were rejected.

Your institution was inspected by a committee composed of Vice President Freeman of Middlebury College and Professor Davidson of Dartmouth. They made a thorough and careful investigation of your institution and reported their conclusions to the Committee on Institutions of Higher Learning. Their problem was complicated by the fact that you are not a typical senior college and consequently it is much more difficult to determine whether or not your institution meets the requirements of the Association. The Executive Committee of the New England Association has told the standing committees on private secondary schools and public secondary schools, as well as the Committee on Institutions of Higher Learning, that only institutions that meet in full the Standards of the Association are to be approved for membership in the Association. The Committee on Institutions of Higher Learning did not feel that they could approve your institution at the present.

The curriculum in your school does not follow the pattern of the usual liberal arts college. Several fields that we consider essention (sic) in a liberal arts college are largely or totally omitted. We doubt that you meet the requirement that instruction must be given in eight major fields. We doubt that the curriculum as outlined in your institution would adequately prepare students for graduate work and we were not impressed with the transfer records for students who had transferred from your institution to other institutions of higher learning. We felt that the absence of examinations and the failure to record grades would make it difficult for a student to transfer to another institution at the collegiate level or to properly do his work in graduate school.

We were impressed with the personal qualities of your faculty, but felt that they had less graduate training than was desirable.

We also felt that the financial future of your school was uncertain. We could not be sure that your school would be able to exist in the future unless it had more adequate resources than it appears to have at the present time.

We regret that we cannot approve your institution, but we do approve the close personal contact that exists in your institution between students and members of your faculty.

Sincerely yours,

C. Scott Porter, Chairman
Committee on Institutions of Higher Learning
New England Association of Colleges
and Secondary Schools

csp/lcc

Apparently the Committee feels that the plant and equipment are adequate but that there are seven ways in which the College fails to meet the standards of the Association.

The Committee says that several fields which it considers essential in a liberal arts college are largely or totally omitted. Because it failed to specify any of these fields, one is forced to draw one's own conclusions as to what they may be. A comparison of the fields of study at Goddard with those of four typical New England institutions, namely, Amherst, Colby, Middlebury and Mount Holyoke, indicates that the one field in which instruction is offered at all four but not at Goddard is the classical languages. Each of them offers instruction in several modern foreign languages, whereas in 1948-49 Goddard has courses in German only although during the last three years it has had courses in French and Spanish.

The secondary deficiency cited by the Committee is expressed by its statement that it doubts that Goddard meets the requirement that instruction must be given in eight major fields. This requirement, as stated in a circular dated December 5, 1941, is that a "senior college should offer instruction in at least eight major fields of liberal arts and sciences, in each of which at least one teacher of professorial rank should devote his whole time to instruction in that field". Since there are no professorial ranks at Goddard, the question would be whether there was at least one full-time teacher in each of eight major fields. In the application the fields were listed so as to show the number of instructors devoting the major part of their time to each. The distribution is as follows: Languages and Literature, 3; Economics, 1; Sociology, 1; History and Government, 1; Philosophy and Psychology, 1; Science, 1, (usually 2); Education, 1; Visual Art, 1; Drama, 1; Music, 2. The instructor in sociology also teaches a course in Oriental culture or Oriental history each semester and the instructor in education teaches courses in the social studies or linguistics each semester, so it may be assumed that the Committee would feel that their standard was not met there. However, there are left eight fields in each of which at least one instructor devotes full time. One is forced to the conclusion, therefore, that visual art, drama, and music are not regarded as major fields since the others are common to liberal arts college. Probably it should not seem strange that the arts are not regarded as major fields because they occupy a relatively unimportant place at many colleges. For example, the reports published in the 1948 edition of *American Universities and Colleges* show that less than one tenth of the Mount Holyoke faculty, one eleventh of the Amherst faculty, less than one fourteenth of the Middlebury faculty, and about one thirty-fourth of the Colby faculty teach the arts. This compares with nearly one half at Bennington, slightly over a third at Bard, nearly a third at Sarah Lawrence, and over a fourth at Goddard.

The opinion of the Committee should be contrasted with the views expressed in the Report of the President's Commission on Higher Education published in December, 1947 and to which I referred in my quarterly report a year ago. Unfortunately for higher learning in New England, none of the Committee was a member of the Commission which included many distinguished educators and laymen.

The program recommended by the Commission for the colleges would involve a marked departure from their traditional practices and the application of principles that have been under test at Goddard since it was established as a college more than ten years ago.

The Commission said that education "will achieve its ends more successfully if its programs and policies grow out of and are relevant to the characteristics of contemporary society. Effective democratic education will deal directly with current problems." It spoke out for diversity in this way; "In the future as in the past, American higher education will embody the principle of diversity in unity; each institution, State, or other agency will continue to make its own contribution in its own way. But educational leaders should try to agree on certain common objectives that can serve as a stimulus and guide to individual decision and action."

It selected as the principal goals of higher education which should come first in our time: "Education for a fuller realization of democracy in every phase of living. Education directly and explicitly for international understanding and cooperation. Education for the application of creative imagination and trained intelligence to the solution of social problems and to the administration of public affairs."

In view of the apparent conviction of the New England Committee that Oriental cultures and history lie outside the field of sociology, it is interesting to read these words by the President's Commission: "In the past the liberal arts college has stressed the history, arts, and institutions of Western culture, without giving much time or attention to the kinds of civilization that exist in other parts of the globe. In the new world it is not enough to know and understand our own heritage. Modern man needs to sense the sweep of world history in order to see his own civilization in the context of other cultures." And these are even more relevant: "It is especially important that we acquaint ourselves with the oriental world. Asiatics constitute the largest single segment of the human race. . . . We must study the Orient – not as a remote and static display of artifacts in a museum, but as a *living* and d*ynamic factor* in *our own society*. The East is shaking off its traditional passive attitude toward the West and more than ever *we shall feel the impact of its cultures*." (underlining mine.)

Since the New England Committee seems reluctant to encourage departure from the typical liberal arts college, it doubtless could not accept the judgment of the President's Commission when it says, "It is imperative that we find not only the will but the ways and means to reorder our lives and our institutions so as to make science and technology contribute to man's well-being rather than to his destruction. We need to experiment boldly in the whole area of human relations, seeking to modify existing institutions and to discover new workable patterns of association. We must bring our social skills quickly abreast of our skills in natural science."

Later in its report the President's Commission advocates a reorganization of the colleges along the lines of Goddard in these words: "To teach the meaning and the processes of democracy, the college campus itself should be employed as a laboratory of the democratic way of life. Ideas and ideals become dynamic as they are lived, and the habit of cooperation in a common enterprise can be gained most surely in practice. But this learning cannot take place in institutions of higher education that are operated on authoritarian principles.

"The varied activities of the campus provide many avenues through which students could participate in making decisions and share in carrying forward their joint undertaking. If the college were conducted as a community rather than as a hotel, it would afford much greater opportunity for students to acquire the practical experiences so essential to the life of democracy outside the college.

"Nor should the college neglect the educational resources in that life 'outside'. Including 'field experience' – work, travel, research, and study projects in the community off-campus – as part of the program of general education can do much to break down the present tendency toward isolation of the college from the wider community in which the student is to live after college."

The concern of the New England Committee over the absence of examinations lends ironic emphasis to these comments of the President's Commission; "As a rule, however, a man's happiness and his achievement will depend in considerable measure upon his capacity for association with others. And this turns more upon personality traits than upon intellectual powers. It is all too often the case that a man in unable to make the most of his abilities because he cannot get on well with people or cannot find his way around easily in the maze of social custom and organization.

"American schools and colleges have hitherto paid little attention to the educational implications of this fact. They have been so preoccupied with the training of the intellect, with making sure students could pass examinations in sizable bodies of knowledge of this or that, that they have given little consideration to the problems of personality. General education should correct this deficiency. It should make growth in emotional and social adjustment one of its major aims."

Another area in which the President's Commission seems to diverge sharply from the New England Committee is in the arts. It declared that one of the aims of general education in the colleges should be "to understand and enjoy literature, art, music, and other cultural activities as expressions of personal and social experience, and to participate to some extent in some form of creative activity." Then it asserts that "a signal defect in much of American education, and in American culture, is its failure to recognize that music, painting, sculpture, the dance, the drama, and others of the arts are authentic statements of experience." That it would give the arts a prominent place in the college program is evidenced in these sentences; "The study of the arts in general education should not be directed toward the development of creative artists of exceptional gifts, though it may in some instances lead to this. It should aim at appreciation of the arts as forms of human expression, at awakening or intensifying the student's sensitivity to beauty and his desire to create beauty in his everyday surroundings, at developing bases for discrimination and interpretation, at inducing sympathy with arts and artists and active concern for their welfare . . . . Before completing his general education, the student should acquire a measure of skill in at least one of the arts or crafts, in some form of musical expression or in dramatics."

The Commission recommends that to achieve the aim of acquiring knowledge and attitudes basic to a satisfying family life colleges should organize for the general student a course very similar to the Goddard course called "The Family." With reference to the selection of a vocation, it insists that "general education should acquaint the student with the interdependence among jobs that characterizes the world at work. It should also make clear the close relationship that exists between one's abilities and interests and his satisfaction in a given line of work. The student should be helped to choose his vocation on a more objective and sensible basis than the ambitions of his parents, his own wishful thinking, or incomplete occupational information.

"It is experience on the job that best permits the student to measure theory against practice and to learn what abilities and skills his chosen work will require of him."

Although we are forced to infer that the New England Committee feels that the classical languages are essential in a well run liberal arts college, the only reference to foreign languages made by the President's Commission is to be found in this paragraph on critical and constructive thinking: "Ability to think and to reason, within the limits set by one's mental capacity, should be the distinguishing mark of an educated person. The conception long prevailed in our Western tradition that Latin and Greek, mathematics, and formal logic were the most effective instruments for developing the power to think. These disciplines can be made to contribute richly to that end, but so can many others. Development of the reasoning faculty, of the habit of critical appraisal, should be the constant and pervasive aim of all education, in every field and at every level."

If a college takes seriously the recommendations of the President's Commission, it would appear to be virtually impossible to meet the requirements of the New England Committee for approval because if the new courses which the former advocates are to be actually taken by live students, there would be practically no demand for those insisted upon by the latter. The Commission says, ". . . existing courses, however restyled, will not alone serve the ends of general education. New courses of a different kind are needed – courses that draw their material from wider division of knowledge, courses embodying unusual combinations of subject matter not closely related within the systematic, logical development of the subject, but intimately related to the psychological processes which human beings use in dealing with everyday matters. Examples would be courses in 'Problems of American Life' or in 'Science and Civilization'. Such courses call for an integration of content and an attitude toward the student that are lacking both in existing elementary courses and in survey courses."

This is an area in which Goddard has had considerable experience. Old materials have been reorganized, new materials have been added, traditional subject divisions have been eliminated and more vital problems have been studied in such courses as "The School and Society", "The Uses of Language", "American Literary Scene", "Literature and The Democratic Idea", "Religion and Philosophy in Modern Society", "Science and Living", "Biological Basis of Human Behavior", "Growth of American Democracy", "Basic Economic Problems", "Conservation of Natural Resources", "The Community", "Individual and Society", "The Family", "Communications and Social Policy", and "Oriental Cultures". For ten years Goddard students have been free to choose such courses and they have done so to such an extent that there have been very few who would enroll in the fields regarded by the New England Committee as essential in a liberal arts college. The Goddard experience is an effective demonstration that if new and vital courses are actually made available, the ineffective old ones are displaced. There simply is not time for a student to carry the old courses and the new.

The President's Commission goes beyond recommending new courses and suggests a different approach in the senior college (here it uses the term as it is used at Goddard to mean the last two years) that will permit broader fields of concentration. It describes a procedure which it calls the functional major but which is substantially the plan of study in the Senior College at Goddard. It is 'a sequence of courses and other educational activities leading to the attain-

ment of a clearly defined educational or vocational goal'. The student, with
faculty advice and approval, draws up his own plan of study, selecting subjects
that are related to each other and to a well-defined objective and arranging
them in a systematic program.

"This kind of major is perhaps the most far-reaching of the attempts to re-
vitalize the senior college curriculum. Not only does it permit greater flexibility than the conventional departmental major, but it emphasizes purpose
and unity in the individual's educational experience. It provides the integration that the modern college has so often failed to achieve and the purpose that liberal arts programs have so often lacked."

Returning to the specific comments of the New England Committee, its
third point was that it doubted that the Goddard curriculum would prepare
for graduate work. The existence of such a doubt must rest on the assumption
that preparation for graduate work consists of the study of a particular group
of studies rather than the development of the capacity for independent study,
reasoning and critical thinking. When one considers the broad scope of the
graduate schools, it borders on the ridiculous to suggest that there is only one
kind of a curriculum that will enable a student to prepare for graduate study.
Moreover, if the recommendations of the President's Commission, as well as
those of a host of eminent educators, are ever taken seriously, the New England Committee would be forced to say that the graduates of the reorganized
colleges would not be prepared to do graduate work.

The fourth point made by the Committee was that it was not impressed by
the records prepared for students who have transferred to other institutions.
This should be considered with its fifth point, which is that the absence of examinations and failure to record grades would make it difficult for a student
(1) to transfer at the collegiate level or (2) to properly do graduate work.
These observations indicate a remarkable pre-occupation with the externals or
crutches of the conventional school – marks and examinations. They disclose
a fundamental lack of faith in the seriousness of purpose of the American college student and a discouraging lack of understanding of the learning process.
Moreover, they indicate with pathetic clarity that the Committee finds it impossible to follow its professed policy of judging an institution with relation to
its educational objectives. Instead of trying to ascertain whether, in the absence of marks and examinations, students can really learn and can actually
equip themselves for graduate study and other kinds of work, the Committee
proceeds on an unproved assumption. In view of the fact that the record of a
single graduate of the Senior College at Goddard tends to run to more than a
hundred pages, it is obvious that no thorough examination of the records was
possible in the twenty or thirty minutes used by a member of the inspection
committee.

Furthermore, the Committee seems to have ignored the fact that despite
the absence of examinations and marks Goddard students have transferred to
more than fifteen collegiate institutions without loss of credit or time and
have made satisfactory and often excellent records according to the standards

of those institutions. Among the places to which these transfers have been made are Antioch College, City College of New York, Columbia University, Middlebury College, New York University, Ohio State University, University of California, University of Chicago, University of Minnesota, University of Missouri, University of New Mexico, University of North Carolina, University of Vermont, Western Reserve University, Wheelock College.

Within the last year three of our graduates have entered graduate schools at Boston University and Springfield College. One of these hade been accepted at New York University but decided to study at Springfield. Preliminary reports indicate that they are not finding the work beyond their abilities and that they do not seem to be handicapped because of the absence of examinations and marks at Goddard. These are the first of the Senior College graduates to undertake full time graduate work but within the next few years there will undoubtedly be several more. Actually, of course, the methods of work in the Senior College at Goddard are much more nearly like those in the graduate school than are those of the conventional college. With his extensive reading, organization of materials for long papers, participation in seminars, research and independent study the student develops his ability to do the kind of concentrated and sustained work that ought to characterize the graduate school.

Since a relatively small part of the graduates of the liberal arts colleges go on to graduate study, one feels impelled to question the soundness of the Committee's position in basing approval of an institution on the likelihood of success of its graduates in a graduate school.

The sixth point made by the Committee is that the Goddard faculty has less graduate training than is desirable. I think there is no doubt that more study would be useful to every member of the staff, but that observation may be applied with equal force to practically every college staff. Actually, however, all but one of the teachers in the academic fields have had at least one year of graduate study and that one has had six years of undergraduate work with a superior record plus several years of experience that is as valuable as graduate work. Most of them have had at least two years and some three years of such study. But there are only four members of the entire staff who have doctor's degrees and only two are doctors of philosophy. This then, appears to be the deficiency which concerns the committee. There have been so many comments about the lack of teaching ability among Ph.D.'s that one might be pardoned for smiling at the comment of the Committee and wonder if it wouldn't have been more scientific and reasonable to have judged the teaching staff by the way it taught rather than by the degrees it had accumulated.

While the Committee was engaged in rendering its judgments in accordance with its highly questionable assumptions and on scant evidence, the Association of American Universities announced the abandonment of its thirty-five year old practice of accrediting colleges and universities. In an interview reported by Benjamin Fine, education editor of the *New York Times,* the president of the Association, Dr. Henry M. Wriston of Brown University, "declared that the time is ripe to reform if not abolish altogether the present system of listing institutions on the basis of 'good' or 'bad'.

"For some time critical educators and harried college administrators have resented the growing influence of the accrediting agencies. These agencies have sprung up on the local, state, regional and national levels. Some professional accrediting bodies dictate to the colleges the amount of space that a chemistry laboratory should have, or the number of volumes that must be kept in a college library. Colleges and universities frequently find themselves bound rigidly to standards that actually harm rather than improve their educational offerings. . . .

"I'm not sure we know how to accredit a school at present," Dr. Wriston remarked. "Educational aims are getting more and more diverse. We have liberal arts and vocational schools; one is no more legitimate than the other – it is just different. If we are going to diversify in education as much as the President's Report on Higher Education suggests, any approved list is liable to bring about a rigid pattern.". . .

"Colleges and universities, in the opinion of Dr. Wriston, should have a great deal of freedom without being dominated by the graduate schools. That is not possible when the standards are iron-bound and the institutions are forced to follow a hard-and-fast line dictated from above . . . .

"The difficulty with establishing an adequate system of accrediting, many educators are convinced, is that such a system does not go to the roots of the educational problem, but touches upon the externals. For example, a college may be required to employ a certain number of men with Ph.D.'s, but there is no way of knowing whether the possession of a Ph.D. by itself will make a person a better teacher.

"It's the enthusiasm, the drive, the sincerity and the reality of purpose that makes a university great," Dr. Wriston asserted. "These are the things that you cannot measure."

The seventh and last point made by the Committee is that the financial future of the college is uncertain. Here the Committee is entirely correct, but again the same comment can be made of many colleges, especially as the relative amount of support from endowments tends to get smaller every decade. Besides, the Committee appears to give no weight to the facts that there has been a Goddard for nearly eighty years and that its career as a college has been confined to ten extremely difficult years for society. One is also inclined to wonder if the Committee approves an institution for the known present or the speculative future.

The experience of applying for membership in the New England Association of Colleges and Secondary Schools and of being rejected has been salutary for the Goddard Community. It caused us to examine ourselves more critically and it stimulated us to make much-needed improvements in our physical plant. It resulted in a re-thinking of the aims of the College. It has given us a new confidence and self-assurance and it has forced us to realize that the vital features of the College are not readily recognized nor easily measured by those who are committed to the ways of the conventional school.

The experience has made it clear that the task of reorganizing higher education along the lines proposed by the President's Commission is stupendous and that one of Goddard's great functions may be to serve as a pilot in the performance of that task. It indicates, I think, that the significance of the College for the future of American education can be truly great.

But it means that Goddard must win acceptance and be recognized by what it does, by how its students live and work and how well its staff teaches and administers rather than on the extent to which it conforms to traditional patterns. The experience seems to indicate that until it has increased greatly in size or unless it is willing to abandon its basic philosophy, Goddard is not likely to become a member of the New England Association. More than ever before, it is clear that the whole Goddard family — trustees, parents, students, alumni, staff — must strive vigorously to build the enrollment and the financial support that will enable the College to demonstrate to the nation that it can educate for living.

Respectfully submitted,

(Signed)   Royce S. Pitkin
President

Report of the President of
Goddard College

For the Quarter Ending December 31, 1949[49]

People are beginning the second half of the twentieth century with fear. Strangely enough, even Americans, whose nation is strongest among those of the earth, are afraid. They are afraid that the people will cast off democracy and take on communism or some other alien form of government. Obviously, this is not a healthy condition. Moreover, it is a condition that defies logic. It adds up to this: Americans who believe in democracy think it is the best kind of society. They believe it to be a society whose controls reside in the people who, in turn, believe democracy to be the best kind of society. But some of these people seem to think that others will lose their belief in democracy and adopt another set of beliefs. At the same time, the second lot are afraid that the first lot will give up democracy with all its advantages for communism with all its disadvantages. In other words, some Americans are afraid not only of the Russians and Chinese, but of other Americans who, in turn, are afraid of them.

This all-pervading fear tends to destroy the things in our world that are good. Confidence gives way to suspicion. Laughter changes to tears. Optimism loses out to pessimism. Freedom is exchanged for restrictions. Love surrenders to hate. Neighbors become informers. Exchange of information is

---

[49]This is the second of the group of seven Reports chosen by Tim in his list on p. 2 of his topical outline. The style will strike readers at once as something new and different. The ideas are familiar, and certain of the phrases. The reference to Kilpatrick is standard. The selection does not include a signature. Characteristics of the Reports are not invariable in details.

succeeded by secrecy. Reason succumbs to prejudice until faith in democracy itself is threatened.

With our society in such a condition something needs to be done and done at once. In fact, many things need to be done and wherever constructive work is discovered in this world of fear, it should be encouraged.

This is the kind of problem with which our colleges should be concerned. It is a part of the American tradition to rely on education for the solution of persistent social problems. It is a good tradition and with good schools it would be justified by works. If half of the energy and money that are put into organizations, prizes, contests, pamphlets, letters, foundations and campaigns were invested in the improvement of educational institutions, we could reap some very great social benefits.

The situation calls for colleges that are dedicated to education for democratic living. It calls for colleges that do more than preach or lecture about democracy, it calls for colleges in which democracy is actually lived by the students and the staff. Colleges that cling to the authoritarian system in which rules and orders are issued by trustees, presidents and faculties to be obeyed by students are not equipped to educate for democratic living.

If this all-pervasive fear that is making people unhappy and unreasonable is to be dispelled, there must be mutual trust by students and teachers. Yet what could be better calculated to stir fear and distrust than the mass production lecture-test-mark-credit system that is so common in the schools of the mid century? If teachers are afraid they may lose their jobs if they entertain liberal or radical thoughts, or if they express belief in the unfettered search for truth, how can they avoid fostering fears in their students?

America needs colleges that teach the democratic way of living by providing the conditions under which students and staff live democratically. It needs colleges that really mean it when they say there is no discrimination because of color, race or creed in the admission of students or employment of staff. It needs colleges that are small enough to give real recognition to the existence of individuals. How much longer will people give their wealth to perpetuate and enlarge the already overgrown, ineffective, ponderous degree mills that are called universities?

America needs colleges that recognize the difference between talk and learning. It needs colleges that encourage students to recognize problems, to seek solutions to those problems, and to think for themselves. It is high time that colleges recognized that learning involves activity on the part of the learner and that learning proceeds most effectively when the whole person is involved. If colleges are to justify themselves as educational institutions in a democratic society, they will have to provide young people opportunities for learning to make decisions, to carry responsibility, to select persons for positions of trust, how to live with others, and how to study. Lecturers and class rooms, quizzes and marks, credits and diplomas are not the hallmarks of educational opportunity; in fact, they may be impediments to learning. The provision of educational opportunity is as much a matter of the spirit as of materials. Given a staff truly dedicated to education for a democratic society and a college organized as a democratic community, learning situations will be rapidly created. They will develop in the classroom because the problems studied will be pertinent to the needs of the students and the students will actually participate in the running of the class. Moreover, the class will be small enough (not more than twenty-five persons) to permit consistent and frequent oral participation by every student in the group.

Learning situations will arise in the formulation and administration of the standards and rules of college life because students and teachers will work together in a community government. Practical and profound issues will be raised frequently as individuals and groups try to work out the problems of community living. In such situations the ability to teach will be severely tested because the declarations of the teacher will be examined and questioned and compared with those of other authorities and students.

Inherent in the democratic idea is freedom of thought. Every self-respecting college in the land expresses allegiance to this principle. But how far practice diverges from profession, and what means are used to discourage bold and creative thinking! This in itself is, of course, a manifestation of fear, an evidence of distrust in the basic principles of democracy. To surmount such obstructions, the colleges need to create a genuine understanding and enthusiasm for democracy and the use of creative intelligence. The real believer in the democratic idea does not stand in fear of new ideas or the revival of old ones. He encourages their examination and he favors digging up all of the available evidence in order that their soundness may be determined by reason rather than prejudice. If a generation of college students could live and study in institutions that were democratic in practice and spirit, there would be little cause for fearing the collapse of democracy in America. Three million informed, alert, enthusiastic young adults who had had four years of experience in democratic living would be a powerful force for dispelling fear and suspicion.

The advocates of the great books and the prescribed curriculum maintain that such schemes are essential to provide unity and a basis for common understanding. What a silly notion! Why not let democracy be the basis for common understanding, the meeting ground for the artist, the scientist, and the businessman? Is it not possible for the mechanic, the clerk, the teacher, the doctor, the farmer and the housewife to build and operate a democratic community? And will they not find plenty of common ground in working out the problems of living together? As they seek the solutions to their common problems, will not the chances for good solutions be increased by the diversity of interests of the people and the sources of their ideas?

By its very nature democracy rests on people. One of its great virtues is that it recognizes the importance and worth of the individual and provides the conditions under which his unique qualities can be developed without the restrictive effects of rank and station. Individuals differ in their native equipment and in their experiences. They differ from one another in the skills they possess and in their command of skills. Because of different backgrounds and aptitudes the extent and range of their knowledge varies. Because learning and growth are functions of the individual the materials of learning have to be suited to the individual learner. The good college takes account of this need by insisting that the program of studies for each student be built by careful selection of courses by the student concerned rather than by a general prescription of required courses. It also insists that classes be small enough to enable the student and the teacher to really know one another. It goes further and makes provision for regular and frequent individual counseling for each student.

The elimination of fear and insecurity is as much a job for education as for doctors, social workers or legislators. It extends, however, beyond the walls of the school buildings into every city, town, village and community. The college can work at this phase of education in two ways. First, it can incorporate work experience in industry and elsewhere in the school year through the device of the non-resident work term so that students see and know work life through actual experience. Second, it can arrange a program of adult education by which citizens can get stimulation and help in studying their individual and group problems. Such a program demands the same kind of dedication and creative intelligence as the teaching of young people and it has the virtue of helping the college staff to be better teachers of youth.

There are a few colleges in America whose trustees and staffs are trying to provide the kind of educational opportunities so urgently needed in building a democratic society reasonably free from fear. There are many colleges that are doing some things in this direction and there are many, many teachers who would like to do something but who do not see how within the limitations of their situation. The real promise lies, however, with the handful of progressive colleges. This is unfortunate, but it is merely being accurate to say that they alone have put into practice the philosophy and developed the techniques and organization that are essential.

William Heard Kilpatrick, dean of American educators, says that Goddard College is doing the most thoroughgoing job of all. It ought to. It was designed for such purposes. It has tried to improve its methods and its materials. It has made many changes in practice, but it has stuck to its basic purposes. Its chief concern has been education. It has stood for good teaching, academic freedom, sound scholarship, student participation in a democratic community. It has encouraged the application of the scientific method to the study of social issues. It has no quotas governing student admissions. Its students come from many states and a few foreign countries. They vary in wealth, in social position in their homes, and they have widely differing educational backgrounds. Some come from private schools and some from public schools, some from progressive schools, others from traditional schools. They hail from farms and from cities. They are a good cross section of college youth. At

Goddard they all work at maintaining and operating the college and take part in the government of the community.

Goddard students are attracted to it not because of its football teams or its debating squads but because they believe it to be a good place to work and study to educate themselves.

The Goddard staff is chosen, without regard to race or creed, for its ability to teach. Some are immigrants from other lands. Some have studied abroad, others only in America. Because Goddard is a place for learning, the ability to stimulate the search for truth and to counsel with young people outweighs degrees and prominence as a writer or researcher.

Goddard College was established in part to render educational service to the adults of the community, state and nation. Through this service it has been instrumental in breaking down prejudice, dispelling unwarranted fears and widening horizons. It has come to be regarded as a center for adult education, community leadership and freedom of thought to which citizens come to get from one another better ways of looking at life.

People who believe in democracy ought to be enthusiastic about Goddard College. Those who want to live in a free society should stand with it. Those who think there is still a place for individual initiative should lend it strength. Those who believe that the findings of psychiatry, psychology and other branches of modern science should be applied to educational methods should give it support. Those who want coming generations to get out from under the burden of fear that now rests on men should work for it. Those who cherish the Vermont traditions of freedom, integrity and progress should identify themselves with it.

Let's be clear about it. There is a place for the large university where the costly facilities for research and advanced study can be assembled. But there is also a critical need for small colleges whose chief function is the education of young men and women. Unfortunately for America, public funds and private philanthropy are directed mainly to those large institutions whose chief contribution is not teaching. Contrary to the opinion of many, large gifts to colleges and universities have not been discontinued. Private donors are still very generous but because of lack of information about the policies and needs of colleges their gifts are often misdirected.

It is almost twelve years since Goddard College was organized on the foundations of Goddard Seminary by a group of Vermonters who believed that the twentieth century needed a new kind of college. The soundness of the policies of that group has been tested. Its worth has been proven.

REPORT OF THE PRESIDENT OF
GODDARD COLLEGE

For the Quarter Ending December 31, 1957[50]

SIMPLY A MATTER OF DOLLARS AND STUDENTS

The second section of this report presents a record of the major activities of the quarter. This section is concerned with issues related to regional accreditation.

Nine years ago this fall Goddard applied to the New England Association of Colleges and Secondary Schools for admission to membership as a four-year liberal arts college. Although the Association did not then admit that it was an accrediting agency it in effect functioned as such, as one of its recent publications points out. I refer to the 1957 pamphlet entitled *Introducing The New England Association*. The application apparently was not approved largely because Goddard did not seem to the Visiting and Standing Committees to be a "typical liberal arts college". My quarterly report for December 1948 discussed rather fully the points made by the Association at that time and my reaction to them.

A good deal of water has gone over the dam in the past nine years. The

---

[50]This third Report of the seven is again concerned with accreditation, this having been attempted for a second time in 1957, nine years after the first application. Comparison of the two sets of correspondence shows inevitable differences in both Goddard and the Association. Some interesting materials appear here on the College divisions, the experimental and outreach programs, and Royce's plans for areas of and ideas for development of the College. His outline for Trustee involvement in financial and related development shows most formidably. Taking his start from the strictures of the Association he was turning them into a general institutional challenge. The next application in 1959 would be different in outcome, but would still give evidence of a close corner.

New England Association has frankly assumed the role of an accrediting agency, the Ford Foundation has made its large gifts to "accredited" colleges for the improvement of teachers' salaries, and the colleges have been hit by a dearth of students, inflation, competition with industry for manpower, and the prospect of greatly increased numbers of student applications. Accreditation has become a more important factor in the college world. There has developed a significant interest in educational experimentation at the college level, probably due in large part to the interest and support of the Fund for the Advancement of Education and the anticipation of teacher shortage coupled with larger enrollments. Goddard has undergone changes, too. It has a somewhat smaller number of students in the four-year college than it had in 1948. Its teaching has improved as its faculty has been strengthened. It has received some foundation support for educational experimentation and has thereby become a stronger and better place for learning. Its costs have risen astronomically, largely because it increased salaries greatly even before the Ford grant stimulated other colleges to do likewise. There has been a tremendous increase in the amount of money received in gifts. The Council for The Advancement of Small Colleges has been organized and has done a great deal to make the public aware of the special problems of the non-regionally accredited colleges. There has been something of a change in the climate of opinion regarding unconventional colleges.

The fall of 1957 seemed like a good time to make a second application to The New England Association, especially after a reading of the Minimum Requirements for An Acceptable Senior College. These read in part as follows:

"An institution of higher education shall have clearly defined educational objectives which include as an important element training in those subjects of cultural value commonly known as the liberal arts or General Education. Its application for membership in the Association will be judged by:

A. The effectiveness of its various curricula in realizing its objectives
B. The preparation and experience of its faculty
C. The administrative leadership it affords
D. Its provisions for admitting students who are well qualified to benefit from its offerings
E. The adequacy of its physical plant
F. Its financial ability to carry out the purposes it has set

"The minimum requirements outlined below are meant to serve as a guide to the institution applying for membership in the Association and as an aid to the committee of the Association in determining the adequacy of the total arrangements within the given institution to realize its avowed purposes. The decision will be influenced more by evidence that the institution is functioning as a whole in fulfilling its objectives than by its ability to meet each specific standard."

In late November a Visiting Committee from the Association, comprising Dean Harry W. Rowe of Bates College, Chairman, Dean Albert Dickerson of Dartmouth, and Professor Paul Hazelton of Bowdoin, made a twenty-four hour visit to the college. The members of the committee were alert, as thorough as the time allotted them permitted, interested in the activities of the college, friendly, and sympathetic to the needs and interests of Goddard. The committee did suffer the handicap of having no member from a college at all similar to Goddard either in size, student composition or educational philosophy. Nevertheless, they were conscious of this handicap and proceeded to do an intelligent job of inspection and study.

The report of the Visiting Committee to the Standing Committee on Institutions of Higher Education was discussed and acted upon at the time of the annual meeting of the Association in Boston in December. Both committees recommended against acceptance of the Goddard application. The findings of the Visiting Committee as reported to me by members of the committee are indeed interesting. In explaining the action of the committee to me, one of the members said, "Tim, it is simply a matter of dollars and students, and we recognize that it is hard to get both without accreditation. It took us only a very short time to decide that the quality of the educational work that Goddard is doing is as good as that of at least fifty percent of the colleges belonging to the Association."

In his oral report to me, Dean Rowe made these points: (1) the educational program at Goddard is effective, the students demonstrate this in their interest and enthusiasm and understanding of the program; (2) Goddard has a fine faculty, experienced, and enthusiastic about their work; (3) the salary scale is very good, especially for a college the size of Goddard; (4) the committee has confidence in the administrative leadership, though it wonders if too much depends on one person; (5) the library is good and seems to be very well administered; (6) excellent use is being made of physical resources and, though modest, they seem adequate for the program of the college; (7) of course the program is much different from those of the colleges belonging to the New England Association but it is good to have institutions with fresh ideas; (8) the Senior College seems overshadowed by the Junior College (in numbers); (9) the number of students seems to the committee to be too small; (10) the amount of scholarship aid (tuition reduction) seems large for the total income of the college; (11) the cost of admissions per student admitted seems very large and probably seems very large to the college; (12) the committee was torn between its desire to recommend Goddard for admission to the Association and its duty to be objective; (13) the smallness of the college and its lack of money are factors that ought to be corrected before being admitted to the Association.

A few days later Dean Nathaniel C. Kendrick of Bowdoin, Chairman of the Standing Committee, wrote me as follows:

"Dear President Pitkin:

"I greatly regret to give you the formal information that the Standing Committee at their recent meeting did not recommend Goddard College for admission at this time to the New England Association. A little later I expect to send you the report of the Visiting Committee or fuller comments based upon it.

"It is proper for me to inform you that both committees found much that was admirable and interesting about the activity going on at Goddard and there was a very lively discussion. It was clear to both committees that you have an alert faculty and a program which undoubtedly stimulates student interest. I should also add that great confidence was expressed in the administrative head, though there was some anxiety as to whether the whole enterprise was not perhaps particularly dependent upon him.

"The committees did not feel that the situation at Goddard was clearly sufficiently stable, particularly financially, to meet the association standards right now. They were also troubled by the smallness of the student body in spite of apparently rather expensive efforts to recruit students. The necessity of reducing tuition charges for so many seemed to emphasize the financial precariousness without necessarily securing a student body meeting uniformly high standards though on this latter point there was some vagueness.

"They also felt that the program gave only slight emphasis to some of the major aspects of a liberal arts program, notably in the field of science. On the other hand, they recognized the fresh and original approach in other fields and greatly admired the courage and enterprise shown in the utilization of rather limited facilities.

"I realize that this does not solve the dilemma confronting you. Without admission I know it is in some ways more difficult to raise funds. The committees I know join with me in hoping that you can find a solution to this problem and that the attraction of a larger number of well-qualified students may prove to be a partial answer. Mr. Frederick C. Copeland, Director of Admissions at Williams College will be Chairman of the Standing Committee for the following year and I know he like myself will be anxious to be helpful and I will send you more material shortly."

It is my impression that the Visiting Committee liked what they saw of Goddard so far as the effectiveness of its educational program is concerned and would have liked to recommend its admission to The New England Association. To have done so, however, would have been to run counter to the prevailing sentiment within the Association as I have heard it expressed on other occasions. It is instructive to compare the points made by Dean Rowe and

Dean Kendrick with the bases of judgment quoted above from the requirements of the Association.

It is pertinent, too, to refer to the paragraph in the Goddard application relating to the performance of Goddard students on the Graduate Record Examination:

"Reports are available for three classes of Goddard students on the Graduate Record Examination Area Tests, those entering in 1955 and 1956, tested as sophomores, and those graduating in 1957, tested as seniors. Percentile scores for the three groups (sophomores rated against sophomores, seniors against seniors) are markedly similar. In the 1957 testing program, sophomores averaged at approximately the 73rd percentile (national norms of the Institutional Testing Program, Graduate Record Examinations) in Social Science, at the 60th percentile in the Humanities, and at the 45th percentile in Natural Science. Seniors averaged at the 62nd percentile in Social Science, at the 78th percentile in Humanities, and at the 59th percentile in Natural Science. The sophomore group tested earlier followed a similar pattern: the average score in Social Science and Humanities was above about 2/3 of the sophomores in the normative group, and the mean in Natural Science was close to the national median . . . From these results it is evident that the performance of Goddard students compares favorably with that of students from regionally accredited colleges as represented in the Graduate Record Examination norms."

IMPLICATIONS

It would appear from the experiences which Goddard has had with relation to regional accreditation that *quality of education* is not the determining factor in gaining acceptance. Though this is unfortunate and from our point of view quite unsound, it is a fact with which we have to live for at least a while longer. Until and unless the climate of opinion within the accrediting associations undergoes further change, Goddard is not likely to be accepted as a member unless it enrolls more students and collects more dollars. Meeting these conditions is in nowise inconsistent with our aims and does not contravene our philosophy. This is a change from the situation nine years ago when to meet the objections raised by the Association it would have been necessary to change or depart from the principles on which the educational plan of the college was built. It is somewhat ironical, however, that attracting students and dollars is much more difficult for the college that is not regionally accredited than it would otherwise be. This is particularly true, I think, for the college that has fairly high academic standards and tends like Goddard to draw its students from the same strata as the long established New England colleges do.

One thing is clear. For the immediate future Goddard cannot enjoy whatever benefits derive from regional accreditation. It will have to make its own way on the merits of its program. Its continuation and growth must be assured. This should be accomplished in such a way that dependence on the leadership of any one person, whether on the Board of Trustees or in the administration, is not so great as to be the cause of anxiety.

If our imaginations are lively enough, if our organizational skills are good enough, and if our determination is firm enough, we should be able to turn this bit of adversity into glorious gains for Goddard. But first we have to do some stock taking.

THE SIZE OF GODDARD

As George Beecher recently pointed out, we say that Goddard is a very small college when it is really a big enterprise. Its purpose is to create favorable conditions for learning for those who want to take advantage of the opportunities it offers. Each year approximately 500 individuals come to the college to learn. In addition a great many persons who never visit the campus are influenced by the teaching of the college. There are approximately sixty persons employed as members of the staff on a full or part time basis. Their combined salary payments amount to $190,000, and the total budget for the year is now $360,000.

As Mr. Beecher also pointed out, there are three major divisions at Goddard. There is the four-year college with an enrollment for this academic year of about 100. There is the program of educational experimentation, which includes the Program for the Improvement of Teaching through Application of Findings from the Behavioral Sciences, initiated with a grant from the Pratt Foundation, the Educational Resources Project, the Comparative Cultures Project, both supported by grants from the Fund for the Advancement of Education, and the Nursery School. Thirdly, there is the division of adult education and community services, which includes the winter schools and conferences, one of which is aided by a grant from the Fund for Adult Education, the evening courses, the Music and Art center, Camp Winooski, the community theater program, the community music program, the Haybarn Theater concerts, the Family Life Education project, financed by the American Social Hygiene Association, and the new Community Development and Organization project, to be financed by a grant from the Emil Schwarthaupt Foundation. In addition there is the series of Great Ideas meetings which have been held in ten or more cities from Boston to Milwaukee. This winter people will fly from Puerto Rico, Oregon, California and many other places throughout the west, south and east to attend professional conferences at Goddard. The only proper justification for them to do this is the quality of the learning they expect to experience while they are here. This is indeed big enterprise for a small rural community in Vermont.

Although the work of the college may be placed in three divisions, there is a great deal of interaction among the parts and to a remarkable extent each tends to support and lend value to the others.

It is probably accurate to say that Goddard exercises considerable influence in a quiet way among many institutions of higher education. Three illustrations may be cited. When the Visiting Committee was at the college, Dean Dickerson of Dartmouth reported that beginning next September Dartmouth will inaugurate the three course plan which Goddard has tested through more than fifteen years of use. Dean Rowe of Bates went home from the visit to tell his colleagues of Goddard's experience with evaluation of classroom teaching by members of the faculty as well as by students and suggested that Bates might well do something similar. A member of the Bowdoin faculty reported that Professor Hazelton brought back an enthusiastic recommendation that they look into some of the things Goddard was doing. And recently I had a request from another staff member at Bowdoin for information about our School of Liberal Studies for Leaders in Industry as they are considering setting up a similar program.

After a year of demonstration at Goddard that college students can gain for themselves and help others by working as assistants in public schools, two other Vermont colleges were ready to try the plan. Now several other colleges in Vermont and New Hampshire are planning to send representatives to a meeting in Plainfield this winter to talk about an extension of the project to include their students.

The third illustration relates to the use made of Goddard experience in the Council for the Advancement of Small Colleges. Much of the planning for the workshops and conferences of the Council for the development of its program for Advancing Quality Education has stemmed from the years of experience Goddard has had with the study of education and the conduct of educational conferences. It has been said by several members of the Executive Board of the Council that Goddard has been the strongest influence in keeping the emphasis on educational improvement as a major goal of the Council.

AREAS FOR IMMEDIATE DEVELOPMENT

Goddard's opportunities and needs are greatly in excess of its resources. It ought to have a stronger program in the natural sciences, not because of sputniks but for the reasons set forth in my commencement talk last June. It ought also to be working with the small high schools in the area covered by the Educational Resources Project to improve the opportunities of their boys and girls for studying mathematics and science. We ought to extend our offerings in music and we ought to cooperate with the local radio stations and the public schools of the area to bring the values of classical music to the children and incidentally to some of the adults in north central Vermont. Ways should be found for utilizing the exceptional abilities of Thomas Yahkub as an interpreter of Non-western Cultures so that students at several Vermont colleges may be better equipped to deal with the issues of our times. We ought to make greater efforts to discover and release the intellectual talents of our students by making use of the understandings and insights of such men as Lawrence Kubie, Carl Rogers and Lewis Wolberg. And we ought to extend our adult education and community services until our physical facilities are fully utilized, summer and winter.

There is much to do but not too much to do with. But the need is urgent. Goddard must enroll more students in the four-year college and it must get more financial support and get it quickly. The big question is how do we do it.

IDEAS ON DEVELOPMENT

Ideas have come to me from several sources, including members of the Goddard staff and Board of Trustees. Some of them have undergone modification so I must accept responsibility for them as they appear here. They are presented in this report as a starting point for the immediate formulation and implementation of making plans for some glorious gains for Goddard. It is expected that they will be examined critically, some rejected, and some modified and accepted as useful and workable.

I propose that the administrative staff of the college be reorganized to take account of the growth in its activities and the division of functions to which reference has already been made. The reorganization would provide for the appointment of a director of the four-year college whose chief responsibility would be the development and administration of this division, a director of a division of educational experimentation, a director of adult education and community services, and a director of development which would include fund raising, public relations and enrollment. Insofar as possible these appointments should be made from present members of the staff but it is anticipated that some new members would have to be added. I think it likely that a full time director of adult education and a director of development could each increase the income of the college enough to more than pay for his salary and expenses.

Even though present costs for the admissions office are large, it is imperative that greater efforts be made to interest more students in Goddard. A recent article on Yale's program of admissions make the need for this kind of work abundantly clear, for even with its prestige that venerable institution finds it necessary to be constantly recruiting better students. As a preliminary to working out recruitment plans, members of the Goddard staff concerned with admissions have reviewed the situation and agreed that certain problems require attention and that certain obstacles have to be overcome. Will Hamlin is working on a series of letters to be sent to several thousand high school counselors, alumni, and ministers. These letters are designed to inform their readers of the truly remarkable opportunities for study at Goddard, qualifications for admission, the competencies and size of the faculty with relation to number of students, the achievements of graduates, and the high level of academic performance. It is expected that in many schools they will be supplemented by visits from representatives of the college. Some consideration was given to the role which alumni might play in interesting high school students in the college but no proposals have yet been made.

When a non-regionally accredited college undertakes to increase its enrollment it faces a dilemma: whether to admit students with low scholastic and personal qualifications in order to gain numbers or to insist upon reasonably good standards and sharply reduce the number of prospects for admission. Goddard has chosen to follow the latter course and so is not regard by many high school counselors as what is sometimes called an "insurance" college, whereas many other non-regionally accredited colleges have low admissions standards and receive quite large numbers of applications.

ACHIEVING GREATER FINANCIAL STABILITY

There can be no doubt that the achievement of financial stability and an increase in enrollment in all divisions of the college are closely related. Greater numbers give greater financial stability, more money helps bring more students. Yet achievement in one sector cannot wait upon achievement in the other. We have to push ahead in both, keeping in mind the concern already expressed that there should not be undue dependence on any one person.

Since securing financial support is regarded as one of the most important functions of a Board of Trustees of a college, perhaps we should try to see how the Goddard Board can work more effectively. During the last two years considerable progress has been made toward reorganization so as to release from membership all inactive members and provide for their replacement by interested, enthusiastic workers. If at all possible this reorganization should be completed this winter. Goddard still has too few Trustees who are full participants in the work of their Board. The vacancies must be filled. This is a first order of business.

Important as the Board of Trustees is in raising money, it is unlikely that it can do the job alone. The circle needs to be widened, many hands make light work. I suggest that the Board create a national committee with a title that will inspire its members to achieve the impossible. Members of the committee should be enlisted not because of their prominence (though that would not be disadvantageous) but because they agree to do at least *one* thing – give money, get money, write letters or stories or get people who will do these things. A systematic plan should be devised and worked for filling places on the committee. This would probably mean that each Trustee would be responsible for enlisting at least one committee member.

While the Board is being reorganized and the committee created, we should determine the yearly minimum financial needs of the college for the next three years or perhaps five to meet reasonable accreditation requirements. To establish a modest fund of working capital, make substantial reductions in our indebtedness and cover operating losses would probably require about $160,000 a year for three years. It would doubtless be helpful to allocate the requirements among the three major divisions of the college's work. Foundation support can probably be obtained in some measure for the division of educational experimentation and for adult education and community services when it would not be available for general operations of the four-year college. On the other hand individual contributions seem more likely to be made for such purposes as teachers' salaries, scholarships, library needs, science equipment, and the provision of more and better facilities to care for the impending increase in college enrollments.

Included in the funds to be raised should be money for completion of the Haybarn Theatre and William Heard Kilpatrick House so that rooms will be available for more students as rapidly as they appear. In addition the entire plant should be made to look more attractive by making some repairs, applying paint and varnish, and purchasing new furniture and other equipment. Through improved administration of the community work program the additional expenditure of $5,000 would yield impressive results.

After minimum needs have been established I suggest that each Trustee be given the responsibility for securing a definite number of contributions of a certain amount either directly or with the help of others whom he enlists. No person should be asked to raise more than he feels he can get. Assuming that the amount to be raised during the next year is $200,000, of which $70,000 might be for educational experimentation and adult education and community services, assignments might be made as follows: the president of the college – $70,000 for educational experimentation and adult education; the chairman of the Board – gifts of $25,000 from each of two persons; a second Trustee – five gifts of $5,000 each; a third Trustee – five gifts of $5,000 each; a fourth Trustee – ten gifts of $1,000 each; a fifth Trustee – ten gifts of $1,000 each; five more Trustees – twenty gifts each of $100 each.

Under such a plan each Trustee would know just how much progress he was making and just how much farther he had to go to get his share of the job done. Reports would be made monthly and circulated among all members of the Board. There would of course be a good deal of team work and the services of the national committee with the inspiring name would be used. The president of the college should be prepared to help a particular Trustee whenever requested. If a director in charge of development is employed, he would be expected to devote most of his time to assisting the Trustees to meet their quotas.

These are not world shaking ideas but they may serve to start the production of better ones when the Trustees assemble for the next meeting. The important thing is for us to move forward on our own steam. It is simply a matter of dollars and students.

Respectfully submitted,

(signed) Royce S. Pitkin
President

REPORT OF THE PRESIDENT OF
GODDARD COLLEGE

For the Quarter Ending December 31, 1959[51]

THE CHALLENGE OF ACCREDITATION

On December fourth the New England Association of Colleges and Secondary Schools admitted Goddard to full membership as a liberal arts college. To put it differently, the College was given regional accreditation. This action on the part of the Association deserves strong approbation because it was a difficult and a courageous decision on the part of a body whose membership consists almost without exception of conventional institutions fashioned in the conservative academic traditions of New England. The Standing Committee on Institutions of Higher Education made its recommendation for admission of Goddard fully aware of the experimental nature and the limited resources of the College. Thus the Committee said in effect that it was judging the College on its effectiveness as an educational institution rather than on the extent to which it conformed to a prescribed pattern.

---

[51]This fourth in the series of President's Reports chosen for the December 1965 discussion concluded the sub-group of four (of the seven) noted in Tim's topical outline already presented above. In it he reacts once more to the decision, favorable this time, of the New England Association, and does so, gracefully. He presents the correspondence for the record, and then appends a Supplement by George Beecher on the Goddard Program for the Improvement of High School Science and Mathematics. This having been a recurrent area of stricture from the Association, he would show what Goddard was doing with it. It might not be what the Association expected to see, but this was what Goddard thought was most significant to do. When Royce rolled out George Beecher for demonstration purposes, listeners and readers could register the thunder of the heavy artillery. This, be it remembered, was where the hammer came down most times out of a hundred.

These are quite different words than those I wrote for my quarterly report eleven years ago following the denial of admission by the Association. At the conclusion of that eleven-page document entitled *Accreditation or Education* I said:

"The experience of applying for membership in the New England Association of Colleges and Secondary Schools and of being rejected has been salutary for the Goddard Community. It caused us to examine ourselves more critically and it stimulated us to make much-needed improvements in our physical plant. It resulted in a re-thinking of the aims of the College. It has given us a new confidence and self-assurance and it has forced us to realize that the vital features of the College are not readily recognized nor easily measured by those who are committed to the ways of the conventional school.

"The experience has made it clear that the task of reorganizing higher education along the lines proposed by the President's Commission is stupendous and that one of Goddard's great functions may be to serve as a pilot in the performance of that task. It indicates, I think, that the significance of the College for the future of American education can be truly great.

"But it means that Goddard must win acceptance and be recognized by what it does, by how its students live and work and how well its staff teaches and administers rather than on the extent to which it conforms to traditional patterns. The experience seems to indicate that until it has increased greatly in size or unless it is willing to abandon its basic philosophy, Goddard is not likely to become a member of the New England Association. More than ever before, it is clear that the whole Goddard family–trustees, parents, students, alumni, staff–must strive vigorously to build the enrollment and the financial support that will enable the College to demonstrate to the nation that it can educate for living."

The College has no more undergraduate students now than then, its financial resources are still too small and its basic philosophy has not been abandoned. Viewed in the light of these facts, the action of the Standing Committee is indeed significant. It is a challenge to Goddard to demonstrate that as an accredited college it can continue to experiment, to improve, to strengthen its financial structure, to grow, and to extend its influence. The challenge is gladly and enthusiastically accepted.

The full report of the Evaluation Committee which visited the College last October for the New England Association is appended.

SCIENCE AND MATHEMATICS PROGRAM

Included as a supplement to this President's Report is a report by the Director of Educational Experimentation on the Science and Mathematics Program.

Respectfully submitted,

Royce S. Pitkin
President

APPENDIX

NEW ENGLAND ASSOCIATION OF COLLEGES AND SECONDARY SCHOOLS

Standing Committee on Institutions of Higher Education

Evaluation Report

GODDARD COLLEGE
Plainfield, Vermont

October 19-20, 1959

EVALUATION COMMITTEE:
Vice President Stephen A. Freeman, Middlebury College
Professor Walter A. Lawrance, Bates College
President William C. Fels, Bennington College–Chairman

PART I

(1) Goddard is an independent four-year residential college of the liberal arts. Its 200-acre campus lies on the edge of the little village of Plainfield, Vermont, ten miles northeast of the capital, Montpelier. The present enrollment is 121, of whom 75 are men and 46 are women.

Royce S. Pitkin has been President since the College was chartered in 1938. The faculty numbers 33, of whom 23, including the President, teach; the balance are administrators.

The tenure system provides for two one-year appointments, followed by a three-year appointment, then successive five-year appointments. The faculty does not have ranks.

In these matters of tenure and rank, as in most other particulars of organization and philosophy, Goddard resembles Bennington College, or at least the Bennington College of 1938, on which it appears to have been modeled.

Goddard differs from traditional colleges in many ways, but for the purposes of this report most significantly in constructing individual programs of study for each student rather than having all students meet general requirements set by the faculty. The students' individual programs are shaped with the guidance of faculty counselors and reviewed by Junior Division and Senior Division Committees of the faculty.

The College has one or more teachers giving the major part of their time to the following fields: Anthropology and Sociology (3), Art (1), Drama (1), Economics (1), Education (3), French (1), History and Political Science (2), Literature (2), Music (2), Philosophy (1), Psychology (2), Science and Mathematics (4). Because Goddard does not use faculty ranks, and because some courses and independent-study projects are interdisciplinary, it is impossible to say how many of these areas are fields of specialization in the terms of the "Minimum Requirements" of the New England Association, but we believe that the requirement of at least eight adequately-staffed fields has been met.

(2) (a) *General Control* is under the supervision of a 17 member, self-perpetuating Board of Trustees. The Trustees serve for five-year terms. The Board is unusual only in that the by-laws provide that one third of the members elected annually shall be from nominations made by the faculty. The faculty maintains two of its members on the Board at all times.

The administration of the College appears to be well organized and orderly. The various officers are competent to handle their duties. The Administration includes two officers who devote their attention to special features of the College, the Adult Education and Community Services programs, and the extensive program of educational experimentation.

(b) *Faculty.* With neither ranks nor department heads the faculty cannot be measured in the terms of the "Minimum Requirements." There are seventeen who have two or more years of graduate study. Among these are two Ph.D.'s (one of the President) from Columbia University, a third from Teachers College of Columbia University, and one from the University of Michigan. There are also an Oxford Doctor of Philosophy and a Paris Doctorat d'Universite.

The Committee would question whether the members of the natural science faculty were adequately trained to offer upper-division work, but this doubt is based on credentials rather than interviews. The faculty is strongest in the social sciences. The social science faculty of 12 is larger than the rest of the faculty combined (4 science and mathematics, 3 language and literature, 4 art, drama and music).

The student-faculty ratio, faculty load and number of students in laboratory classes are all well within the standards of the Association.

(c) *Program of Studies.* Goddard, as we have noted, does not have prescribed curricula. Instead courses of study are shaped for the individual students in relation to their interests and their needs by the students and their faculty counselors under the supervision of faculty committees. The "Minimum Requirements" provide that "each curriculum in the program of studies of each undergraduate college . . . should include a sufficient number of courses to provide an adequate cultural or general background and a degree of concentration and continuity of subject matter to fulfill the avowed purposes of the curriculum." In Goddard's case, then, the questions are whether the College as a whole has sufficient courses to provide adequately for distribution, concentration and continuity, and whether the counseling and committee supervision is strong enough to insure the carrying out of the purposes of the individually shaped and supervised "curricula."

In answer to the first question, we would reply that the College, through its regular courses and provisions for independent study, has more than enough courses. (Indeed the previous visiting committee felt the College had too many courses, since so many classes were very small. We did not agree with this. In a small college there is a minimum number of courses, different for each college, which is necessary to achieve range. Goddard's number is not excessive.) Though the *number* of courses is sufficient there is weakness in language and science.

The only foreign language offered is French. Its study begins as part of a Comparative Cultures Program which avails itself of the advantages of nearby French Canada. Goddard has had difficulty interesting its students in foreign languages. The Comparative Cultures Program has had some success in doing this. The visiting committee had serious doubts, though, whether the College is offering *advanced* work in French literature or any other aspect of French culture which requires the student to be conversant with French. The library has fewer than 250 books in foreign languages. Many French classics and modern works, for example, appear to be available only in translation. Whether or not the Committee was correct in its observations concerning French, the College's language offering, particularly at the advanced level and as an adjunct to other studies, is meager.

We have already alluded to what appeared to us to be the inadequacy of the faculty in science to offer the customary advanced courses. It should be said in praise of the College's high sense of responsibility that it is aware of its limitations in science and counsels students to go elsewhere—or, if they have already entered, to transfer—who cannot receive the proper scientific preparation at Goddard for, say, medical school.

Now it remains to answer the second question: whether the counseling is strong enough to carry out the purposes of the College through the individual curricula. Here we wish to be very clear. We grant the College its philosophy. We do not ask that each student be an equilateral triangle of humanities, social studies and sciences, or that every student should have studied a natural science or a foreign language without regard to his abilities, interests or needs. What we do ask is that when a student is permitted to choose an advanced project he be obliged to acquire the knowledge and techniques necessary to complete it creditably, and that when a student has a definite professional goal he be pressed into timely pursuit of its necessary prerequisites, however unpleasant they may seem to him—or be counseled to change his goal. That is, we agree with the statement in the Goddard Bulletin, ". . . that any experience is related to what has happened before, to what happens at the same time, and to what will happen later . . ." The College very probably does both these things in the majority of cases, but in reading personnel records and in listening to students we gained the impression that the faculty in a noticeable number of cases could be expected to yield to the students' desires when these did not coincide with faculty opinion (or ours) about the students' best educational interests.

(d) *Requirements for Admission.* Goddard's admissions standards exceed the "Minimum Requirements." The College ordinarily requires "graduation from high school with college-recommended status [and] satisfactory performance on the Scholastic Aptitude Test of the College Entrance Examination Board." The SAT scores made available to the Committee were:

| | 1957–58 | | 1958–59 | | 1959–60 | |
	V	M	V	M	V	M
Median	408	477	511	460	465	456
High	648	563	692	629	703	681
Low	334	293	316	304	341	271

The number of applicants in these three years increased from 64 to 97 to 99. The entering class increased from 27 to 47 to 51. As the size of the entering class increased the admissions cost per student declined from $432 to $256 to $207. The College discourages paid applications from students it considers to be unqualified. It rejects only 5 or 6 paid applications a year.

In admissions Goddard has an impressive problem. While suffering the disability of being an unaccredited college it is faced with the need to expand and to to improve its student body at the same time. While desirable, this is impossible. Faced with the dilemma of numbers or quality it has increased its numbers while holding its quality about steady. It is apparent from the SAT scores that perhaps one half of the admitted students are not capable of senior-division advanced work at a college of standing (but note that Goddard does not present the case one sometimes sees of a student body of uniformly low aptitude). The low aptitude of a part of the student body must be an important factor in withdrawals, which total about 65% over a four-year period. Of 30 students (or 27 as listed on another tabulation) admitted in 1957–58, 11 remain; of 40 (or 39) admitted in 1956–57, 14 remain; of 38 admitted in 1955–56, 7 graduated and 5 remain; of the previous two classes, 8 and 9 graduated. As of now, there are 12 students in the third year and 15 in the fourth. The prospect for next year's junior class is somewhat better.

Since it is Goddard's aim—indeed it is its financial necessity—to expand from 121 to 300, it is hard to see how, as long as it remains unaccredited, it can improve its student body and reduce withdrawals except slowly over many years.

An impressive proportion, some 45%, of the students who do graduate go on to graduate schools, where, according to the College, they are reported to do well. Seniors scored above average in the Social Sciences and Humanities and about average in the Natural Sciences Area Tests of the Graduate Record Examination. (Quaere: Percentage based on 25 students over four years, but 37 or more graduated in these four years. Was a selective factor operating?)

These achievements should be taken into account by the Standing Committee in evaluating our judgments on the preparation of students for senior-division projects and on the strength of counseling. They may indicate that we have been too severe.

(e) *Requirements for Graduation.* These, like the students' programs, are constructed for each individual, though all students are required to complete the equivalent of 120 semester hours. Quality control, as it were, is the responsibility of counselors and the Junior and Senior Division Committees. Ultimately, the faculty as a whole must approve the award of the degree upon recommendation of the counselor. A senior project, satisfactory completion of non-resident terms, participation in a campus work program and good behavior are other requirements for graduation.

(f) *Student Activities.* Community government, the student work program, planned recreational and cultural activities, and informal athletics are integral parts of the Goddard program.

(g) *Guidance.* Student guidance, on which a former committee commended the College, remains excellent (though we have quarreled with one aspect of it under "Programs of Study.") The counseling system is the core of it. Many and detailed records are kept for each student. There is sufficient standardized testing to relate Goddard to wider populations.

(h) *Library.* The "Minimum Requirements" call for at least 8,000 volumes. Goddard has over 13,000. The collection appears to be well selected under the supervision of a trained librarian. It is weak, as we have noted, in foreign language books and appeared also to be weak in science. About half the collection is in the social studies and a quarter in literature, reflecting the interests of the faculty and of the College. The Goddard library draws on nearby public and college libraries for assistance, which they give gladly. The students we spoke to did not appear to be hampered by the size of the library, and they appeared to be making good use of it.

(i) *Student Health.* Physical-health services are adequate. There appeared to be no provision for mental-health services.

(j) *Physical Plant.* The Visiting Committee agreed that the facilities of the College were rough but adequate. The College is housed in a former estate. The buildings are mostly of brown-shingled, frame construction. The library is an exception. Originally designed to be a science building, it is part brick, part greenhouse. In the present science building the laboratories are minimal, but adequate for lower-division work. While there are few amenities at the College, the students suffer no hardships.

(k) *Finances.* In viewing Goddard's finances, one must be aware that the College carries on a constant program of experimentation. Its experiments are financed by foundation grants based on proposals which the College has had the imagination to conceive and the energy to obtain. These grants relieve the College's budget of considerable instructional and other expenses. For instance, this year half of Goddard's instructional expense of $142,000 and more than one-third of its whole educational and general expenses of $342,000 will be met by foundation grants.

The College has a relatively large long-term debt which it is reducing only slightly. The short-term indebtedness is larger than it was in 1957. The interest charges are a significant item of expense. The College has no endowment.

Scholarships and tuition reductions amount to just over 20% of total tuitions.

From the viewpoint of the traditional college, Goddard's financial position is unsound, but the College argues and the Committee would agree, that the College's finances should not be looked at from the viewpoint of the traditional college. It does not finance itself primarily from fees, gifts and endowment income, but from fees, gifts and grants. Its scholarship and reduced-tuition budget is not excessive in view of its high tuition and its financial-aid plan, which adjusts tuition to need, using the College Scholarship Service. Goddard has succeeded in obtaining gifts from alumni and friends and in obtaining grants from foundations whose confidence it has inspired. The College claims it has the dynamic stability of motion, and indeed it seems to have. The Committee notes that there is an element of the ridiculous in visiting a college periodically for twenty years and telling it each time that it is unstable.

The question arises whether the stability of motion could be maintained if the bicycle rider, presumably President Pitkin, stopped pedaling (and peddling!). We are not sure it is fair to raise this question, but if it is we see no reason why the Trustees who chose President Pitkin could not be expected to choose a successor who would pedal as furiously, or who would adapt the College to a more traditional mode of financing. In this matter of financing, as in admissions, accreditation may be the key. If accreditation would bring more students, the College could sustain itself on student-fee income and gifts without such a large proportion of grant income as it now requires.

(3) One of the members of the Committee, who visited Goddard ten or eleven years ago for the Association, felt that the College had made substantial progress. He commented on improvements in the physical plant, particularly the library, which is now in a fireproof building, on better (and better kept) student records including those of senior projects, on improvements in the faculty and in faculty salaries. Another member of the Committee noted evidence of recent improvements in science laboratories and equipment, evidence that the College is correcting its deficiencies in this respect.

The College embarked this year on an extensive experiment in the use of learning aids and independent study under a grant from the Fund for the Advancement of Education. The College is banking on the success of this experiment to make it possible to handle a larger student body with its present faculty.

PART II

(1) The strengths of the College appear to be a fine site, a dedicated Board of Trustees, an extraordinarily able and versatile President, an explicit philosophy of education which permeates faculty and student thinking and action, an atmosphere favorable to education and experiment, and a dogged de-

termination to be a fine college that will make important contributions to education.

(2) The weaknesses of Goddard appear to be its inability to attract a sufficiently large and able student body and to hold a reasonable portion of it until graduation; a mildness of faculty pressure on students to meet requirements consistent with students' aims; questionable adequacy of the upper-division offering in foreign language and science; a faculty and library rather too heavily weighted toward the social sciences (really too lightly weighted toward other subjects); a financial situation which is not, by ordinary standards, sound; and a plant which though adequate is not attractive in the true sense of the word—one would not be attracted to Goddard by its plant.

How significant are these weaknesses in the overall effectiveness of the institution in the discharge of its functions? This is as difficult to answer as how serious is a persistent low fever. It is annoying to the patient and prevents him from operating at full efficiency. It may go away, but then again complications may develop and kill him. Let us say that the weaknesses are sufficiently serious to hamper Goddard in the fulfillment of its promise and to hamper some of its students in the fulfillment of their own promise.

(3) *Recommendations.* The Committee therefore feels constrained to recommend that the College not be accredited.

Three assumptions underlie this recommendation: (1) That the Committee is to make its recommendation in accordance with the "Minimum Standards," (2) that no middle ground is possible between a recommendation to accredit and a recommendation not to accredit, and (3) that accreditation is not the authorized method of breaking the "vicious cycle" of circumstances affecting unaccredited colleges.

If the Committee had not felt obligated to make these assumptions it would have looked for a middle ground, suggesting, for example, that Goddard be granted accreditation now with the understanding that it speedily correct its deficiencies under periodic observation by representatives of the Standing Committee.

The Committee feels that Goddard, more than most unaccredited colleges, is the victim of the inexorable disabilities of unaccreditation.

It has moreover, few deficiencies it is not aware of, and its administration has integrity and restraint.

The Committee notes that the previous Committee said it would not feel put upon if its recommendation was not accepted. We would go further and say that if the Standing Committee is disposed to test whether accreditation will break a vicious cycle, Goddard would be the institution to use for the test.

> By The Committee: Stephen A. Freeman
> Walter A. Lawrance
> William C. Fels

Supplement to the President's Report, December 31, 1959

PROGRAM FOR THE IMPROVEMENT OF
HIGH SCHOOL SCIENCE AND MATHEMATICS

George Beecher
Director of Educational Experimentation

The Science and Mathematics Program which Goddard carries on with fifteen high schools may be reported for the past semester under the following headings:

1. The distribution, care and repair of the Physics films.
2. The work of the college staff in assisting the high school teachers in Physics, Chemistry, and Mathematics.
3. Use of the Goddard laboratory and shop for laboratory work and preparation or repair of high school equipment.
4. Meetings of science and mathematic teachers at Goddard.
5. Student assistants working in the schools.
6. Future plans, including evaluating the films and the project as a whole with the schools and their communities, a special Saturday class at the college for any specially able physics students, consideration of possible purchase of the chemistry films, editing the physics films to a shorter length and for more varied uses, foreseeing possible uses of the college laboratory if Plainfield and Marshfield consolidate high schools next year, working further with the schools to see the curriculum implications of better programs in science and mathematics from the elementary grades up through high school.

Physics Eight of the fifteen schools are offering physics this year. Edward Powell records that besides using the physics films on a weekly rotation, the schools were visited or contacted over sixty times during the fall. Main activities on the initial calls in September were for:

Renewing contacts.
Meeting new teachers and acquainting them with the program.
Securing school schedules, names, telephone numbers.
Distributing and discussing film schedules.
Encouraging double periods for physics.
Discussing labmobile calls and field trips to the Goddard laboratory.
Determining textbook situation with emphasis on using the newly published White Physics text to accompany the films.
Clearing date for a meeting of teachers at the college.

The later visits to schools during the fall were for such varied purposes as helping secure the White textbooks, giving laboratory demonstrations, showing apparatus built in the Goddard lab-shop, furnishing films on special request, arranging Goddard student help for a general science class each week during the latter half of the semester, loaning equipment and assisting in laboratory periods, arranging field trips for classes to the college laboratory, helping on solutions of physics problems, helping repair school apparatus, preparing a looseleaf collection of physics materials for each school. During each visit or contact there were occasions to talk about physics teaching and the aims of the program indirectly. Edward Powell suggests that one of the best services the college can offer to the schools is to increase the distribution of laboratory equipment and the constructing or helping students to construct apparatus for physics experiments. Reconditioning of school equipment also would be of help. These activities draw the schools and the college together in determining ways of teaching and sharing information.

Chemistry The Chief work in this area was again to visit the schools to get to know the teachers and something of their problems. There has been less request for help in chemistry than in physics because of the nature of the films and the laboratory equipment used in physics. However, there are a few schools which have used much help and others that will do so next year when they offer chemistry again. Ralph Cullman has been going regularly to South Royalton to do special work in the chemistry class there, where the teacher has not had much experience. The Plainfield class of from fifteen to seventeen students has been using the laboratory regularly each week. In addition a few schools have used some of the appropriate physics films for their teaching of chemistry. A few schools have also been helped with a little material or with mimeographed sheets showing better ways of performing certain experiments.

Mathematics More effort was put into this area of work this year with a special college staff member investigating the needs and possibilities. Besides visiting the schools he has collected much new material on mathematics teaching which he has distributed to teachers who are interested in the new programs. He has also helped a little in one high school where some students were taking mathematics by correspondence. One idea that he is working on is that the college could serve as a center for some work in mathematics by correspondence or extension where courses are missing in the high schools. There are possibilities too for working with teachers in the elementary grades. Robert Schweiker who is doing this work has been reaching out in a number of ways to find where the schools will use help in considering their mathematics curriculum. He met with the Vermont Education Association planning committee to start more activity in mathematics and science at the annual state meeting.

The other items in the program need little comment now except for the teachers meetings. Besides meeting at the beginning of the fall to discuss the enlarged college staff to bring assistance there was one dinner meeting in November with good attendance from ten schools. The Goddard staff members presented new ideas in the field of science and mathematics teaching and involved some of the high school teachers in making presentations also or raising questions for discussion. Further meetings will be planned for the spring.

SIXTEENTH ANNUAL REPORT
OF THE PRESIDENT OF
GODDARD COLLEGE

Year Ending June 30, 1954[52]

As one listens to the comments made on the Goddard campus at the commencement season by alumni, students and their parents, he comes to feel that there is a unique quality about the College, a quality that is much needed in American life, yet one that is hard to define. During the course of the academic year, those who are intimately associated with the College are inevitably involved in ascertaining, discussing and analyzing its weaknesses. This involvement, which occurs in counselling, community meetings, committees, Board meetings, conferences, faculty discussions and incidental conversations, is so continuous and so engrossing one in sometimes unmindful of the significant contribution Goddard makes to higher education. The purpose of the first part of this report is to take a closer look at the elements that constitute Goddard's unique quality. It should be obvious that such a venture is not free from bias.

---

[52]With this Report begins the second sub-group (of three, in the total of seven) noted in the topical outline above. It focuses around the individual as center of the Goddard educational concern. It would have been an appropriate principle for emphasis at this point. Notice in the topical outline that Tim regarded this and the following two reports, the sub-group of three, as ,centering more directly and explicitly on the Goddard educational philosophy than had the first sub-group of four. Also, in this Report there appears a vertical line in the left margin of the file copy opposite the first and fourth paragraphs on the first page, not exactly brackets, but possible notes to himself about which paragraphs to use or where to begin and end in his readings. We do not of course know that these were his marks. They are no more than probabilities. No signature appears for this section.

The starting point at Goddard is respect for the individual. During a period in which a premium has been placed on conformity, when the ultra-conservative and timid have tried to control the thoughts and expressions of men by restrictive legislation, when it has been asserted that people exist to serve the state rather than the other way around, the College has stood firmly for the sacredness of personality. It has insisted that individual differences should be recognized, that each student be encouraged to think his own thoughts, act in accordance with his conscience and develop to the fullest his own potentialities.

At the same time, there has been a concern that each individual should become socially conscious and responsible. The daily work program, community government, student participation in the determination of policy and in classroom discussions are some of the means by which Goddard students educate themselves for responsible living by carrying responsibility.

From the beginning the College has operated on the principle that the best way to learn how to live in a democratic society is to live in a democratic institution. Because of its devotion to the democratic ideal, Goddard has avoided the evils of ranking its teaching and administrative staffs, it has accepted its students according to their individual merits and without regard to color, creed, family position or wealth. No false and superficial barriers have been erected between students and teachers. The relations have been friendly and informal with respect being shown to teachers by their students not because of their title but because of their character and their worth as men and women.

The democratic idea at Goddard has been interpreted to mean that responsibility for the welfare of the community, in this situation the College, should be shared by young and old, by staff and students. Working on this basis there has been no sharp line marking off the responsibilities of students from those of staff, there has been community government rather than student government. Under this plan the faculty is continually informed of the ideas, problems, interests of students while the latter have had the experience of working with older persons on issues and situation of real importance to them. In an important sense the College has adapted a valuable feature of the small community of our grandfathers by which the young obtained most of their education as workers and citizens by working with their elders. The absence of destructive horseplay among Goddard students is good evidence that it is a practice worthy of wider use in our colleges. The community in which people live is in itself a powerful educative force and the way they live determines their learning. Living in a democratic community demands responsibility, and so one learns responsible living.

Goddard has tested thoroughly the idea that a liberal college is a place for living. It has demonstrated the soundness of the idea. Its program is rooted in the lives of its students. It is a community in which students and teachers study and seek to understand the problems and issues of their lives and their times. To do this they use the great resources of literature, art, science, psychology, philosophy, history. As they discover old truths and new facts they put them to work and make them a functioning part of their lives. They make plans and they execute them. Experiments are proposed, criticized and tried. They create. There are failures and there are successes. There is action.

The curriculum at Goddard is actually the life of our times, including all the resources that extend to all lands and back through all ages of man. It consists of the ideas, situations, processes, problems, ideals that condition the lives of those who make up the college community. Though it is never wholly the same for any two students, there are many common elements. It is the aim of the College to create a situation in which the student will learn how to use the resources in books, people and nature as he strives to understand himself and the world around him. Courses are pursued and subjects studied, not to pass examinations and to earn marks, for such devices are impediments to learning, but rather to affect present living, to extend present understanding and to enable one to act more wisely as he goes about his daily affairs.

Because the lives of Goddard students are now so strongly affected by events and ideas in other countries, there are courses on Africa, Latin America, India, China, the French and Russian Revolutions, and Scandinavia. Modern man is a cosmopolitan, a citizen of the world, yet he lives in a community where there are face to face relationships. For studies in the latter area, the College draws on the rich resources of Vermont and especially the Upper Winooski Valley. Many Goddard graduates have found the inspiration for their choice of careers by actually working among the people and in the small communities of the state.

At the same time that Goddard undergraduates have found excellent learning situations in the life among Vermont's hills and valleys, the College has made its facilities available to the wider community. It has encouraged people to participate in and to enjoy art, music, drama, folk dancing. It has fostered area and neighborhood groups concerned with the study of such matters as public schools, community development and recreation. During the winter and summer months, it has made it possible for adults to experience the satisfactions that can be derived only from living and learning in a residential school.

Inherent in the whole educational program of the College is the idea that learning is an active process in which the purpose of the learner is of supreme importance. It is recognized that unless the student develops and directs his energy toward desirable goals, there is likely to be little growth. The Goddard student has to accept the responsibility for his own education, he has to develop his own ideas, he acquires his own stock of facts, and he has to find his own set of answers. The Goddard teacher is not engaged to disseminate knowledge but to encourage learning. His task is not to provide the right answers but to assist in the search for answers. His work is not to tell students what to think but to insist that they learn how to think. And so the Goddard classroom is a place where students are active, where they talk, present ideas and receive criticism, where the teacher raises questions, stimulates thought and facilitates growth.

Only in a small college can all the conditions essential for the fullest educational development of young adults be found. Goddard is deliberately small, and in the light of our present understanding of the requisites for growth, learning and character development, it ought to remain small. But it need not limit itself to a hundred students. A community of 300 of which 250 are students will still allow the necessary face-to-face, informal, direct and informed relationships so important in the educational process.

However, the small college has its limitations. Though the experiences provided its students can be more vital and stirring than those of our large factory-type institutions, there are certain types of experience which neither group of institutions can provide. It is for this reason that during January and February Goddard extends its campus to include shops, laboratories, factories, offices, boats and farms, in cities, towns and waterways throughout the country. In these places the students meet new faces, become acquainted with other ways of living and different kinds of persons. In a very real sense they test how fully they have learned some of the things they have tried to learn in library, classroom and student residences. Perhaps more than anything else they are called upon to live the traits they are building into character.

In its concern for the individual Goddard has, from its beginning as a college, given a prominent place to counselling. It has insisted that each student be allotted not less than an hour every week for meeting alone with the staff member assigned as his counsellor. In these meetings there is opportunity for the student to seek the unifying elements in all his experiences. He can use them to see more clearly the pattern he is making of his life, and as his counsellor raises questions concerning his studies and his other activities, he may have reason to seek new and perhaps better standards for living.

As the Goddard faculty has become better informed concerning the nature of the individual and more skilled in the educational process, it has attached more importance to self-understanding. It has always been concerned with helping individuals to change, but like teachers everywhere, it has not understood well the factors that stand in the way of change and growth. Though there has been tremendous progress in the behavioral sciences in recent years, our educational institutions have been laggard in helping their students to know and to free themselves from the restraints of which they are unconscious victims.

Dr. Lawrence Kubie said at the Goddard commencement a year ago, "Without self-knowledge it is possible to be erudite, but never wise.

" . . . just as the battle for political freedom must be won over and over again, so too in every life the battle for internal psychological freedom must be fought and won again and again, if men are to achieve and retain freedom from the tyranny of their own unconscious process, the freedom to understand the forces which determine their thoughts, feelings, purposes, goals and behavior."

In this vital realm, according to Dr. Kubie, Goddard is one of a few pioneering institutions.

To those who are concerned about preserving the finer elements in our culture the work done at Goddard during the last sixteen years is of more than ordinary significance.

In an age when the independence of the individual is being seriously diminished by the massive power of government and corporate business, Goddard College encourages individuality and the development of each student's potentialities.

At a time when the great traditions of America are threatened with extinction in the drive for conformity, Goddard stands for diversity of opinion, freedom of thought and expression, and creative enterprise.

To meet the challenge of civic indifference and lack of concern for the public weal in democratic America, Goddard plans its educational program so that living at the College requires learning social consciousness and moral responsibility.

To develop the capacity for independent judgement and self-criticism, Goddard students are required to establish their own goals and to evaluate their own academic progress rather than having to rely upon the marks and tests of instructors.

Democratic societies are dependent on the abilities of their members to think critically in group situations. Classes at Goddard are designed to achieve this purpose by use of discussions to which every student is expected to contribute in an informed and constructive way.

The educative values of living and working in a community have long been recognized by students of society, but Goddard is one of the few colleges that is organized as a community and has been successful in making these values available to its students.

The increasing complexity of modern life and the reduction in hours of remunerative work have given new significance to the education of adults. Through its conferences, workshops and residential schools, Goddard has for sixteen years been contributing to the growing interest in and understanding of adult education.

While hundreds of thousands of Americans suffer from and are rendered almost impotent by insecurity and fear, Goddard works at the task of helping each individual to know himself in order that he may be free from irrational fears and attain real serenity of spirit.

With or without the United Nations, Americans are citizens of the world. It is in recognition of this status that at Goddard many courses dealing with other cultures and other nations occupy a much larger place than in most liberal arts colleges.

These are some of the elements that make Goddard unique among American colleges. It is small, it is dynamic, it is dedicated to teaching, that is, to creating an environment in which people can educate themselves. It breathes the spirit of freedom. It stands for moral responsibility. It is experimental and pioneering. It places a high value on sincerity and integrity. Its material resources are meager, and the conditions of living are simple, but its spiritual resource passeth all understanding.

REPORT OF THE PRESIDENT OF
GODDARD COLLEGE

For the Quarter Ending March 31, 1957[53]

Goddard is an aspiration, an ideal. It is something better and greater than what now exists. Yet it is a reality. It is a living, growing human institution. It is a place where ideas are created and tested. It is a college with a unique record of achievement in the face of adversity. It is a college of unusual promise and potential. Still less than twenty years old, it is young and small, very small. But it is flexible and sensitive to the needs of a rapidly changing civilization.

Small though it is, Goddard has become widely known as a pioneer in several aspects of higher education. Some educational leaders regard it as the only truly experimental college in America. It developed and tested the plan for limiting to three the number of courses carried by undergraduates which Dartmouth College is inaugurating in the fall of 1957. When it was organized, it adopted as one of its basic principles the idea that college students should include work with people in off-campus communities as a part of their program of studies. A few years later Earlham College built its famous Community Dynamics Program on this Goddard-tested idea. Fifteen years ago Goddard began experimenting with a very modest program of residential

---

[53]This is one of the sharper statements to the Trustees of the need for additional funds to develop the College to its potential. Tim starts with its obvious advantages and in the course of his arguments refers to certain of its experimental teaching programs; these would have been what he was reaching for in including this report among his proposed readings. A pair of corner-brackets appears in this Report, one at the very beginning and one on p. 2 at the end of the last full paragraph, after "demands". There is a single half-bracket on p. 2, above, where the sentence begins "The times cry out...." – which does not close anywhere obvious. This section of the Report is signed in full in the original.

adult education, a radical innovation for a liberal arts college. Now the residential idea in adult education has been seized upon by such liberal arts colleges as Wabash and Pomona and such universities as Michigan State and Syracuse.

Many a college teacher has longed to be freed from the necessity of administering course examinations and giving marks; Goddard has operated in a highly successful manner for years without these encumbrances and inhibitors. Educational philosophers have decried the absence of opportunities for college students to assume adult responsibilities. Through its daily work program, its non-resident work term and its faculty-student community government, Goddard has provided these opportunities. With some colleges revising the curriculum is a major operation, as a result of which the number of courses is likely to be increased with no fundamental adjustment being made to meet the needs of a new generation of students. At Goddard it is a continuous process in which courses are added and dropped every year.

Goddard is an experimental liberal arts college in which teaching is regarded as the major function of the faculty, though in recent months attention has been given to writing for professional journals. As an experimental college, it is constantly searching for better ways of teaching and learning. This search is now carried on mainly through the Program for Improvement of Teaching through Application of Findings from the Behavioral Sciences which was inaugurated with a grant from the Eliot Pratt Foundation. As nearly as can be ascertained, no other college faculty has undertaken to examine its instructional practices in an endeavor to determine its weak and strong points and then gone to the behavioral sciences for knowledge that would help in correcting weaknesses and building on the strengths. As the program advances, its ramifications increase and its possibilities for wide application become more apparent. One of the interesting and promising incidental results has to do with the development of entirely new methods for determining the effectiveness of classroom teaching.

The Educational Resources Project on which senior college students (juniors and seniors) work as assistants in rural schools in the central Vermont area is another experimental approach to the improvement of higher education. This project, which is being financed by the Ford Fund for the Advancement of Education, also serves to correct the teacher shortage in public schools and brings new opportunities to children in science, art, music, and physical education. This work has had the effect of intensifying the appeal of college studies, in giving students a more responsible role for their age and abilities, and in interesting them in the process of education, perhaps in becoming teachers.

These are only two projects. There are many more ideas that need to be examined, developed and tested if higher education is going to come anywhere near keeping up with the demands being made on it. The times cry out for thoughtful experimentation and careful evaluation. The cultural lag in the colleges is astounding and deplorable. The need for creativity in higher education is overwhelming as millions of young Americans line up outside the colleges ready to crash the gates as soon as they receive their high school diplomas. There is a bright future ahead for the liberal arts college that will build its program to meet the needs of our times, but it is especially bright for a truly experimental college that can lead the way.

The capacity to lead the way is, however, dependent on the attitudes, outlook and experience of the college staff and the material resources available.

Goddard's small staff of dedicated and alert persons has had the kind of experience that is essential for building a great experimental institution. It takes years to assemble and train a group that is capable of doing the sort of work required in a thoroughgoing study of learning, counselling, and teaching at the college level. It is because the Goddard staff has been through these years of rigorous training that it is distinctive and unique. It would be hard, if not impossible, to find such a highly qualified group of teachers in any other liberal arts college in the country. This faculty provides a superior nucleus around which to build the much larger staff that the best kind of experimental college demands.

The setting of the College is superb. No better place for serious study and creative activity could be found that the Upper Winooski Valley in which the beautiful Goddard campus is situated. Though the setting is rural and somewhat detached, it is only a few minutes from two of Vermont's small cities and a few hours from Boston, Montreal and New York. The present plant serves its present purposes well though extensive additions will be required for greater numbers; but the campus is spacious and there will be no occasion for crowding building against building or floor on floor.

The only serious obstacle to making Goddard the great experimental college it could and ought to be is lack of funds. With adequate financial support it could soon increase its enrollment, enlarge its staff, become more widely known, extend its influence in higher and adult education, improve its equipment, construct new buildings, and meet the requirements of the New England Association of Colleges and Secondary Schools for accreditation. Until and unless money is raised the College cannot develop further.

To build the kind of institution that Goddard deserves a sum of three or four million dollars is required and in wealthy America this is certainly possible. There must be enough men and women in this country who have the means and who believe in the promise of Goddard to secure the money that is needed. With a little time and with further strengthening of the partially reconstituted Board of Trustees I believe our aspirations can be realized. But this is a job that, even with the most diligent effort, takes time. And unless we can find $90,000 almost immediately there is no time. Surely a way can be found to borrow less than $100,000 to save the "only truly experimental college" in America.

Respectfully submitted,

(signed) Royce S. Pitkin
President

REPORT OF THE PRESIDENT OF
GODDARD COLLEGE

For the Quarter Ending September 30, 1960[54]

THE EVOLUTION OF A COLLEGE

As Goddard moves into the second year of its Experiment in Curriculum Organization, the shape of the college of the future becomes a little clearer and the undeveloped potential looms a little larger. Viewed against the background of twenty-one years of searching for and testing better ways of teaching and learning, the experience of last year and of the quarter just ended encourages me to believe that a new and a much better college is evolving at Goddard.

Our students more than ever before are demonstrating that young people

---

[54]In this last of the series of seven Reports, parts of which Tim intended to read as a source of College educational philosophy, he weaves an intricate tapestry showing how the institution worked with respect to individual students and their studies, in classes, off-campus, in other activities, all in the interest of learning to live responsibly in a democracy. He reflects on how the Experiment in Curriculum Organization had provided incentives and opportunities for students to learn to work as responsible adults. He speaks of the added counselling burdens borne by Senior Counsellor Robert Mattuck and of the partial work program solution for some of it; of Arthur Babick and the Learning Aids Center, which could not keep up with demands made on it; of the growth of student interest in other cultures deriving from faculty member Tom Yahkub's leadership on campus in those fields; of the Labor & Farm Conference, of the Canadian-American Seminar for Management, of William Heard Kilpatrick and H. Harry Giles, -- of how all these forces and personalities wove together a living institutional design for a new kind of College evolving on the Goddard campus. The style here is again something noticeably different. We begin to see what will reappear also later, that when Royce speaks of principles of educational philosophy he is not merely listing points and statements: he is demonstrating how people behave, what they do, and thus showing what it means. He tells a story, as when in olden times points were to be made in mythic forms, they were often cast as tales; the difference here is that these tales are rooted in behaviors of persons, open to being seen and heard. Royce undoubtedly liked that and reached for it. Notice that his diction peaks as he describes the College. Passages like this are among the best he ever wrote.

in their first year of college are ready and eager to make study a serious but exciting adventure. As Dean Forest K. Davis puts it, they know they are coming into an atmosphere of work and responsibility and they respond to it. There are, of course, a few who are not prepared to accept the challenge of living productively in a complex and demanding community, and for whom good counselling and increasing self-knowledge are imperative, and there is for some the apparently irresistible urge to celebrate the cutting of apron strings by immoderate indulgence in liquor, personal dishevelment and aimless expenditure of time and energy. Given the handicaps imposed on most middle and upper class adolescents, the wonder is that there are so few who are unable, at least temporarily, to cope with the demands of an academic institution. In fact, one of the reasons change is so urgently needed in the American college is that the out-of-school life of the high school and college student makes very few adult demands on him and offers him little opportunity for assuming responsibilities in and contributing significantly to his neighborhood or community. Yet the American residential college was established and took its form when the home and the community provided most of one's real education by requiring children and youth to perform tasks having economic and social value and by the constant association of young and old. The college and the school were truly peripheral institutions whose chief function was to maintain a reasonable level of literacy. Learning to recognize and to solve problems, learning citizenship, developing character, carrying responsibilities that affected the welfare of family and neighbors were a large and regular part of the young person's family and community life, and there was little need for schools to concern themselves with this aspect of education.

Perhaps the typical college student of an agrarian America needed and welcomed relief from his life of serious responsibilities and early adulthood and found it in the somewhat carefree and light-hearted atmosphere of the college campus. Now the tables are reversed, and the college has to be central rather than peripheral if the student is to have a chance at attaining the status that he wants and deserves as a contributing rather than parasitic member of society.

Although this need was apparent when Goddard College opened in Plainfield in 1938, the astonishing and rapid changes in industry and technology and the accompanying changes in community and family living since then have accentuated and increased it. In trying to build a college where young men and women can assume the responsibilities of intelligent adults, Goddard has not relied on making things tough, nor has it indulged in the fallacy of prescribing particular subjects for its students on the theory that "father knows best". Instead we have said that knowledge accumulates faster than individuals can master it, that much of this knowledge becomes obsolete as new knowledge is acquired, and that no student can be expected to learn during the college years what he will need to know after he graduates. He must therefore learn how to learn and how to live intelligently and rewardingly while he is in college.

The maintenance and operation of a college community are complex and require the performance of many tasks. The costs of running colleges are almost always greater than the fees that students and their parents are able or willing to pay; to make up the difference between these amounts, Goddard seeks gifts and provides tuition reduction to those unable to pay the regular fees. If every student does some job that is needed to operate the college, he reduces the disparities in social opportunities between the wealthy and the poor. He also makes a significant contribution to the tuition reduction fund, thereby reducing the amount that must be asked from donors. And he assumes a measure of responsibility for the welfare of the college.

It may be that sometimes the job seems to the student to be tough; this is not because anyone is trying to make it that way but because it is the nature of the job that somebody has to do or because of the nature of the individual. Regardless of the type of job or its apparent difficulty, the Goddard student becomes a contributing person just as soon as he receives his work program assignment. This investment of self in the college seems to give him a feeling of proprietorship that he does not get when his parents simply pay the tuition bill. It becomes his college and he feels entitled to say what he wants to about how it should be run. To a degree the acceptance of the responsibility of a work program job gives him status, though this is sometimes offset by the feeling that has been instilled in him earlier in his life that it is inappropriate and demeaning for an intellectual to engage in manual or simple repetitive jobs. At the least he becomes aware that he has come to a place where work and responsibility are expected of every student. I think too the work program reinforces the idea that Goddard is a place where the student has to help himself and has to so manage his talents and time that he can achieve the goals he has set for himself.

The daily work program, however, does not satisfy the need and desire for all students to take on important responsibilities. There are many who want to work with men and women who are doing things in the off-campus community. They want to be identified more fully with the adult world and they want to tackle the problems they have read and talked about. They want to add another dimension to their education.

The non-resident work term was incorporated in the college program from the beginning to meet this need, and to a considerable extent it has succeeded. But frequently the necessity for earning money, the brevity of the work term, the types of jobs available or other factors make it difficult to relate the job to study. And so during the last few years we have developed a third type of work experience for those who have demonstrated through their campus jobs readiness for greater responsibilities. The Educational Resources Project, through which Goddard students work as assistants in public schools two days a week as a third or more of their study program, the Community Development Program, by which other students assist on special projects in small communities, and the Vermont Youth Study, through which students work on research in juvenile delinquency in the field and at the college, represent plans by which students can improve the quality and the quantity of their learning at the same time that they set aside the role of school boys and girls for that of semi-professional workers.

The incorporation of this type of work experience into the academic or study program of the student tends to modify the nature of the college. It becomes much more a place of serious and purposeful endeavor and reduces sharply the need on the part of students to acquire prestige and status by performance in such side shows as football, basketball and debating teams, cheering squads, and fraternity politics and social life. By his participation in the work of the off-campus community, the student is confronted with real and urgent problems, which require him to use the knowledge already at his command and to look for more. A superb learning situation is created--a situation in which the student has a clearly defined purpose, a lively interest, a sense of urgency, and a feeling of responsibility for acquiring knowledge that will enable him to do a better job as teacher or researcher.

At this point the college teacher is a real resource to the student--as consultant, expert, adviser, co-worker. There is no need for the teacher to set tasks, prescribe reading, devise tests; the student has done these things for himself and is now ready to use the teacher as teachers should be used rather than as task masters and reservoirs of knowledge. The involvement of only a few students in this kind of work has a noticeable effect on the college community. During the next few years the opportunities for off-campus work and the number of students participating will probably increase greatly as we try out the idea in new fields. One of the most promising is conservation, an area in which students can focus their learnings from many of the conventional subjects, such as biology, physics, chemistry, economics, mathematics, geology, sociology, history, political science and philosophy on issues of importance to the state and nation, which they would encounter as they worked with cooperating state and private agencies.

The Experiment in Curriculum Organization has provided other incentives for giving Goddard students more opportunities to work as responsible adults. As equipment has been added to the learning aids center and as teachers and students have been learned how and when to use it, Director Arthur Babick has not been able to do all the things needed to keep the center properly functioning. The need is not only for technical assistance but for liaison with the several classes. By arrangements with the work program committee, these needs have been met through job assignments on the work program to students with appropriate skills and interests. With the increase in demands on the time of Senior Counsellor Robert Mattuck resulting from larger enrollment, it became necessary for him to share certain of his responsibilities with someone. Again a new job assignment was made by the work program committee, and an able fourth year student now assists the Senior Counsellor by making a preliminary investigation of requests for special counselling. Planning and conducting the all-college mid-semester conferences that are a part of the Experiment make a demanding and responsible job which could be done entirely by members of the staff but which offers a splendid way for students to carry a part of the burden of running the college. The Executive Committee of Community Government took advantage of this opportunity last spring by appointing a faculty member, Evalyn Bates, as director and senior division students Sandra Hosmer and Hugh Glover as assistant directors of the 1960 fall conference. In all of these cases, as in others, of which there are many in Community Government, Goddard students and staff members work together, sharing their knowledge and understanding as they deal with the manifold problems of a college community. One of the effects is that the college atmosphere becomes more and more conducive to the development of maturity.

The Goddard College student has always been expected to assume a large share of the responsibility for his education and he has done much more of his study independently than his contemporaries at most colleges, but even so we have assumed that the approach to independence should be gradual from the first till the final semester. For about twenty years first year classes have met three times a week, second year classes twice, and senior division classes once a week, for one and half hour sessions. Usually every student enrolled for three courses, and no major independent study was undertaken till the senior year. Our experience last year in encouraging more independent study as a part of the Experiment in Curriculum Organization and reports from the experiments at Antioch College led us to believe that perhaps independent study ought to start in a student's first year, when he is looking for and eagerly expecting a study experience quite different from that of his high school years and before he has become habituated to the teacher-dominated lecture or discussion class routine. Moreover, we were trying to find a way by which students could establish what Director of Educational Experimentation George Beecher has called an apprentice relationship with teachers, a relationship which would require the student to give more attention to his purposes and plans for study in a given field and allow the teacher an opportunity to operate more as a consultant and guide than as a person who gives directions and provides the answers. To accomplish these aims, as well as that of breaking down the categorization of subject matter, we decided to offer our new students a chance to enroll for courses that would constitute two-thirds of their academic program, meet once a week with a full half day available for group purposes, and allow for independent study with a faculty member other than the teacher of the course in which the student enrolled. It was understood that the content of the course would not be determined in advance by the teacher but only after each student had stated his purposes in taking the course and had presented the problems that seemed to him most pertinent and important. The emphasis throughout was to be upon the identification and solution of problems, with each student evaluating from time to time the extent to which he was achieving his purposes. Five of these workshop courses were offered, but only four enrolled enough students to justify continuing them. The four include two bearing the title *Human Behavior,* one called *Language, Literature and Communication,* and one called *American Society.*

Though it is too early to judge the outcome and value of these experimental courses, they have already shown that first-year students can handle large blocks of time, can do large amounts of study without frequent teacher direction, and can assume a very large share of responsibility for planning and carrying on a program of study. I think these first-year students are encouraged to undertake this kind of rigorous academic program and to keep at it by the environment in which they find themselves and by the expectations of which they, as Goddard students, become aware. Prominent in the environment are older students who are engaged in independent study, students who are working on the Educational Resources and other projects, and students who are doing the kind of jobs mentioned above. This kind of work, of course, puts demands on a library and learning aids center to grow with the needs of students.

Another change in the evolution of the College that has received impetus from the Experiment is in the direction of more association with and understanding of other cultures. The Comparative Cultures program, which was introduced three years ago with a grant from the Fund for the Advancement of Education and which has concentrated on French Canada, has not attracted as large a number of students as we had expected, but it has stimulated interest in foreign languages and in study abroad. It has demonstrated that living and working in another country help immeasurably in understanding and appreciating another culture. The influence of Thomas Yahkub, through his courses in Non-Western Cultures and through his informal relationships during the fourteen years he has been on the faculty, is another potent factor in the growth of interest in other cultures. This has been augmented by the influence and example of newer teachers who, though native Americans, have lived and studied for extended periods in other countries, by the contributions of two visiting teachers from Denmark, Hans Rohr in 1954-55 and Helge Severinsen this year, and by visits to the College within the last two years of individuals and delegations from such widely separated areas as Canada, Guinea, India, Norway, Indonesia, Pakistan, Holland and Kenya.

This year three students who have participated in the Comparative Cultures program are studying abroad--one in Denmark and two in France. A fourth student is enrolled at University College in Ghana, and at least two are hoping to study in India next year. It seems likely that this movement to extend the Goddard campus to other lands will continue and that the typical undergraduate will have acquired a considerable knowledge and appreciation of other peoples and cultures by the time he leaves college.

Goddard College was established with the idea that one of its major concerns was to be the education of adults and that the staff was to use the facilities of the college during the non-resident term and the summer months for that purpose. Although no well defined plans had been drawn for the adult education program, it was assumed that it would consist chiefly of short residential courses for Vermonters that would be designed to stimulate interest in the humanities, the arts and the social sciences, with some attention to the problems of making a living. The original intention has persisted and has guided the planning of programs that have been offered to adults, but other influences have been felt, and factors that had not been anticipated have appeared which have resulted in the development of other emphases and the evolution of an unusual adult education program.

The adult schools, like the College, operate on the principle that teaching is the creation of conditions for learning. The first conference on current educational issues (it didn't go by that name) was held under the chairmanship of William Heard Kilpatrick during the College's first non-resident term in the winter of 1939. In addition to Dr. Kilpatrick other educators, including Hans Froelicher, headmaster of the Park School of Baltimore and later a trustee of the College, were invited to meet with the Goddard staff to assess the progress that had been made and to get some help in dealing with the problems that had arisen during the first semester.

Apparently the conditions for learning were good. Most and perhaps all of us felt that the conference had contributed to our education and that it ought to be held every year. Thus the College became involved in the education of educators simply by seeking the help of others in the solution of its own problems. Comments made by persons who have attended the Conference on Current Educational Issues have confirmed my own belief that the small residential conference (in reality an adult school) is a highly effective instrument for the education of adults. The skill, knowledge and unique personal qualities of Dr. Kilpatrick and of his successor as chairman, Dr. H. Harry Giles, gave the conference its special character of warmth and enthusiasm for learning.

The continued concern of the College with the solution of educational problems resulted in many conferences over the years on several aspects of education for laymen and professional educators, for people in the Upper Winooski Valley, and for those from other parts of Vermont and other states. With the addition of the conferences on Psychoanalytic Concepts and Education, and on Education and the Behavioral Sciences. the College found itself involved in a rather far-reaching program of education for educators. In these conferences we are exploring virgin territory as Laurence Kubie, Carl Rogers, and others lead us in our efforts to find out how each individual can develop his potential most fully and how the school can provide the conditions for that development.

The effects of all these conferences are to be seen in the modifications that are made from time to time in the college curriculum and int he ways that Goddard teachers work with their students. We are told, too, that the conferences serve similar purposes for the educational leaders who come from other institutions to participate in them.

The Labor and Farm Conference and the conferences on community development, adult education, and juvenile delinquency have likewise brought together leaders in a variety of fields to work with members of the Goddard staff in advancing their understanding of the problems with which they have to deal.

The Management Seminar on Canadian-United States Studies brings to the College a group of persons with quite different backgrounds and interests but leaders in their fields. The Seminar was designed primarily to provide an educational opportunity for representatives from the upper but not the top levels of management of large business corporations from both sides of the international boundary. We observed, however, during the first one, which was held at the beginning of this quarter, that it was also an excellent learning situation for the Goddard staff, for economists, historians and sociologists from other colleges, and for the writers, journalists and artists who came.

The interaction of the adult educational activities of the College with the undergraduate program is continuous as the staff translates its new ideas and understandings into their relations with students. On the other hand the Educational Resources Project, which was conceived as a means of extending the educational opportunities for liberal arts undergraduates, has become to a considerable degree an adult education program for teachers, principals and superintendents of the cooperating schools and to a lesser extent for the teachers and administrators of the seven colleges in the project. The whole problem of better utilization of our educational resources is raised by the students who are working as assistants in the schools, by the teachers and the principals, and again by the colleges, thereby creating an interchange of questions, information and ideas.

Out of all these activities and programs a pattern of adult education and a special role for the college have emerged. The role is continuing education for adult leaders, especially those concerned directly with the growth and development of children and youth and with those who determine policy at high levels. Because corporate business influences so profoundly the course of American life, it is just as important that its leaders continue their education as it is that leaders in other fields continue theirs. We have made a beginning with the Canadian-American Seminar, but I believe that Goddard and its sister colleges have an obligation to do for top business executives something similar to what our winter conferences do for educators.

Business enterprise, like all other sectors of American life, is in grave danger of destruction. Even now the fear of war forces us to divert the products of our mighty industrial machine from constructive social purposes to preparation for war. The nature of the problem of making a transition from cold war to peace is not well understood even though it is one of vast importance to all of us, and it is not likely to be solved until our business leaders devote their talents and energy to its solution.

Perhaps Goddard can make a start by inaugurating at the College a series of three or four day conferences for the heads of large corporations and other leaders on how to achieve and maintain a stable peace.

The developments of the last few years indicate to me that a new kind of college is evolving on the Goddard campus, a college fashioned to meet the needs of our times. It is a college that recognizes the rapidity of social, political and economic change. It recognizes also the need for constant and continuing educational research and experimentation. It is a college which expects its students to assume the responsibilities of adults. It believes that students are eager and able to study independently and productively if given the opportunity. It is a community for learning, a place from which teachers and students go to the wider community to perform certain tasks and to which they return for study, counselling, consultation, and creative endeavor. It is a college that looks upon the world as its campus. It believes that a college should find constant invigoration and enlightenment through a lively and well conceived program of adult education. It is a place which relies more on vital teach-student relations than on formal class sessions for stimulation and encouragement of learning.

It is a college which regards books, films, records, television, and teaching machines not as ends but as resources for learning, to be used whenever there is need for the kind of information or experience they can supply. It believes that intellectual growth and character development are inseparable and that a proper concern of the college is to assist its students in the acquisition of self-knowledge and the consequent release of their creative and productive abilities for the attainment of their highest goals. Goddard is not a college that has arrived but rather a college that is in evolution.

Respectfully submitted,

Royce S. Pitkin
President

Report of the President of
Goddard College

For the Quarter Ending December 31, 1965[55]

A Multi-Campus Experimental College

One of the first questions asked by observers of Goddard College when it opened in 1938 and one that continued to be asked over and over was, "But how could you apply the Goddard idea to a large institution?" It was and still is a challenging question. An obvious answer is to break the large institution up into several small units and then put the idea into effect in each unit. Although many persons talked about this possibility, no one, so far as I know, ever tried it. The obstacles seemed too great and the determination and interest too little. Nevertheless, the question deserves an answer, and to be convincing the answer has to be in the form of a demonstration.

The thought of making such a demonstration intrigued some of us for a long time, but it could not be tested by action simply because it took Goddard twenty-five years to reach what was regarded as the optimum size of two hundred and fifty students in residence. And how can you juggle two apples if you don't have even one whole apple?

With the completion of the Village of Learning in the fall of 1963 the

---

[55]For several reasons we here present his entire Report for this date instead of an excerpt. The statistical and financial sections are minor; the three sub-reports following show how Tim included divisional perspectives along with his own overview. This report is dated only three days after the All-College Faculty discussions immediately preceding. It would have been actually written during January and February, as the ensuing Winter Conferences allowed him time; he would surely have been reviewing in his mind those earlier discussions and the uses he had made of them. One would expect to find the retrospective approach we do seem to see in his first and principal section. One might say that here again appears the philosophy of the College, told as a tale is told, except that this was not mythic; it was history as he had watched it happen. At the end of his main passage he invites us to "see" it. We almost do.

outlook changed rapidly, and the prospects for testing the Goddard idea on a larger scale seemed so promising that the Faculty and then the Board of Trustees said, "Let us build a three-campus college during the next few years." And so we committed ourselves to an enlargement of the temple! Since then there have been occasions when it has seemed more like the building of the tower of Babel.

THE IDEA

Before discussing what is involved in the physical transformation of Goddard into a multi-campus college, a restatement of the idea of the college–of its philosophy–is in order, because the proposal was not simply to make an ordinary college larger by the addition of two units, nor to create a Vermont version of Cambridge or Oxford, nor to build a group of colleges on the Claremont plan, nor even to build a cluster of small colleges as the University of the Pacific had proposed. Instead the proposal was in effect to continue the evolution of an experimental college that is based on a well-defined philosophy of education while adding to its size.

The Goddard philosophy starts with the individual. It holds that each person is truly unique, has his own needs, has to contend with a special set of problems, possesses talents peculiar to him, and is worthy of the respect and love of his fellow men. It assumes that learning is inherent, natural, individual, active, and the means to self-fulfillment. It says that education is the reconstruction of experience of the individual by himself for himself, but that it is also a transactional process through which the learner is constantly taking something from his environment and giving something to it. It is a social as well as an individual process and it involves all of the personality, that which we call intellectual as well as the emotional and physical.

The aim of education is growth, growth as one develops his abilities toward their potential, growth as one seeks and tries to live a good life, growth

(Note 55, continued)

The closeness in dates of this Report and the All-College Faculty discussions represented in the preceding series of seven Reports on College philosophy, and in the discussional outline preceding, suggests the possibility of overlap in content. If it is present, so be it. It is a position of Adamant Press that it is better to include most of what is at issue in a design of writings than to risk the hazards of editing; the editorial judgment occurs as part of the decisional process; the decision, however, is to restrain the editorial presumption, while reaching for the author's original meanings. This situation has arisen once before. In a study of the writings of Sylvia Bliss (1870-1963) we were once confronted by two versions of the same essay (Cf. Bliss, Sylvia H., *Uncut Leaves*, Vol. II. Adamant, 1990. XXVI, "The Warring Hosts of Life", 153-158). The solution appeared to be to run both. The same choice is made here. This Report from late 1965 (actually, very early 1966) may be Tim's last attempt to focus attention on the educational principles of the College, except as he might have thought he was always doing that, in the most general of terms, in whatever he did. Hereafter, the focus will appear to shift. These were the years of the invasion of the drug culture, that strange phenomenon which in 1995, thirty years later, is with us still as a general condition in American society. A stupendous struggle ensued on campus, in, so to speak, slow-motion; the College repeatedly challenged the students to meet and work out ways of managing it, as had always been its pattern. They made efforts to do so, and then in effect resigned, without having done it.

We will run a series of divisional reports, from various of the President's Reports in 1966, to set the lines of the contest. A single President's Report for each of the years from 1967 to 1969, the year of Royce's retirement, will follow, to keep in touch with what Tim was thinking in this period.

as one builds his character, growth as one lives intelligently in a present that anticipates the future, growth as one solves the personal and the social problems that he encounters, and growth in self-understanding.

To enable each student to achieve the aims of education, the function of the college is to create an environment that is most conducive to learning. This means providing for a variety of experiences, including association and communication with teachers, usually individuals older than the student, in the identification and consideration of community problems, academic problems and personal problems; it includes working with others at tasks that are essential to the operation and maintenance of the college, hence the daily work program; it includes individual counselling; involvement and commitment to group courses, the initiation and pursuit of independent studies; periodic off-campus work as in the non-resident work term, and inclusion of off-campus experiences in one's study program during an academic semester.

For the student the Goddard philosophy requires a continuing search for and clarification of purposes; the assumption of responsibility for his own education; the exercise of freedom and self-control within the limits imposed by membership in a college community and world citizenship; a continuing effort to identify, define and solve problems on his own initiative; acceptance of responsibility for the welfare of the college community; the desire to learn for the intrinsic value in the learning rather than for a mark or credit; and the willingness and capacity to make and meet commitments.

For the teacher—and this includes all of the college staff though most clearly those called faculty—the Goddard philosophy requires interest in and dedication to continuing study of the educational process; a desire and determination to engage whole-heartedly in advancing one's understanding of the nature of learning; an eagerness to engage in educational experimentation based on carefully formulated hypotheses regarding the conditions of learning; continuing effort to improve his teaching; interest in and readiness to engage in adult education; investment of a large amount of time and energy working with students on community problems; counselling and study of counselling of individual students; imagination and ingenuity in helping students find opportunities for learning through off-campus experience; recognition that mastery of subject matter is only a means, not the end of education; high intelligence; knowledge of a wide academic area; and commitment to the aims and philosophy of the college.

Goddard was established as a particular kind of college. It was to be experimental, it was to be a liberal arts college. A major part of its program was to provide for the continuing education of adults; it was to operate twelve months of every year; it was to be small enough (and large enough) to permit and to encourage frequent association and communication between student and teacher; every student was to perform work essential to the operation and maintenance of the college through a daily work program; the barriers that separate a college from the wider community were to be removed through incorporation of off-campus work in the study program of students, through a non-resident work term, and through adult education and community programs.

There were to be no extra-curricular activities, for every aspect of a student's life at the college was to be regarded as his curriculum. The cost of education was to be covered by tuition charges, but insofar as possible these were to be adjusted to the financial needs and resources of the individual student. The college was to make no use of marks, grades, credits, or similar devices for stimulating learning, evaluating progress or determining readiness for promotion or graduation; instead students were to learn because they see value in the learning and they were to evaluate their own progress as an essential part of the learning process.

Students and teachers were to share responsibility for the direction and management of campus life by joint effort of the older and younger, the more experienced and the less experienced members of the college community, through staff-student government rather than the more common student government. Because his experience and needs were regarded as unique, each student's own program of studies was to be planned and built for him.

EXPERIMENTS AND PROJECTS

This is the experimental college in which for a quarter of a century many educational ideas have been tested and projects developed. Among them were the limitation of a program of studies to three courses (later adopted by Dartmouth), inclusion of non-Western studies in the curriculum (now practiced by many liberal arts colleges), elimination of required courses, elimination of academic departments and divisions, inclusion of all administrative officers in the faculty, participation by the faculty in the selection of College Trustees, a program for the application of findings from the behavioral sciences to education, the use of psychoanalytic concepts in education, the creation of a series of conferences each winter designed to provide in-service education for Goddard and other teachers, the assignment of large blocks of time in a single day for work (group and individual) in a single course rather than several small bits of time distributed over several days, extensive use of independent study, building and testing an experimental learning-aids center, creation of an Educational Resources Project that eventually included seven colleges and more than fifty public schools, a project in the teaching of foreign languages that combines study of the culture and the language simultaneously and includes a work and residence for two months or more in French Canada or Puerto Rico, a six-year study of Vermont Rural Youth involving as researchers Goddard sociology students, introduction of conservation as part of a liberal arts curriculum, a six-year Experiment in Curriculum Organization, an experimental cooperative nursery school-kindergarten, a mental health project involving the college, public school and families of the Upper Winooski Valley, a flexible calendar for individual students, a widely-acclaimed Adult Degree Program, a Canadian-American Seminar for Management, many conferences (really short schools) for adults, a Community Development Program, a training program for Head Start teachers, a summer-long Arts Center for adults, initiation by members of the college staff of the creation of the Vermont Foundation of Independent Colleges, the Union for Research and Experimentation in Higher Education, the annual workshops of the Council for the Advancement of Small Colleges, the Project on Student Development in Small Colleges, the Vermont Cooperative Council, the Vermont Labor and Farm Council, and the Upper Winooski Community School Association, and participation in founding the Council for the Advancement of Small Colleges, the Vermont Higher Education Council, the Section on Residential Adult Education, and the Society for the Study of Residential Adult Education.

These ideas and these activities are representative of the proper functions of Goddard as an experimental college and are expressive of its philosophy of education. It is to develop and test new ideas and projects on a larger scale but within the framework of this philosophy that the new campuses are being planned and constructed.

FROM IDEA TO ACTUALITY

Once the idea of building the new campuses had been accepted, its economic feasibility had to be determined. Former Business Manager Jack Elliott did this by making thirteen-year budget projections for a one-campus college of 350 students, a two-campus college of 550 students, and a three-campus college of 800 students. The gains in economy of operation for the three-campus plan were so great that the question of economic feasibility was answered with a strong affirmative. But economic feasibility or justification is not the same as financial feasibility. We had to find the money with which to build. Preliminary inquiries seemed to indicate that private corporations could and would furnish capital at a reasonable cost, but after several weeks of negotiation it was found that satisfactory terms could not be reached with private lenders. We then turned to our old friend, the College Housing Program of the United States Government.

Meantime the college acquired through purchase of the Cate farm in the spring of 1964 an additional 225 acres adjoining the existing campus property. Fortunately gifts received that year were sufficient to enable us to pay the full purchase price of $25,000 in cash. Having been assured that we had the land on which to build, we engaged the firm of Hill and Associates to develop a master plan and Robert Martin Engelbrecht to design the first new campus. Working closely with Coordinator of Campus Planning Ronald Pitkin and Coordinator of Land Use Belmont Pitkin, the architects worked diligently and imaginatively to solve the problems imposed by the terrain, the aims of the college, the limitation of financial resources, and the suggestions that were volunteered and solicited from students and staff. The aim was to have the first half of the first new campus ready for use by September 1965, and acting on the assumption that the aim would be realized, the Admissions Office sought and admitted students and the President's Office sought and engaged new staff members.

At the same time Provost John Hall, in cooperation with the Board of Trustees, started a Development Fund campaign while College Editor Wilfrid Hamlin and Director of Information Frank Adams designed and issued a series of publications calculated to enlist the interest and support of potential donors.

It became evident at the outset that the college water supply system, which had been constructed when the Village for Learning was built, would not be adequate to serve a new campus, let alone two new ones. Inasmuch as neither the college nor Plainfield had a sewage disposal system worthy of the name, the construction of such a system to serve the new as well as the existing campus had become a necessity.

Both of these projects required prolonged negotiations with the Plainfield Village Trustees, consultation with state sanitation officials, and consideration of proper land use, in addition to involved and complicated engineering and surveying. The water supply problem was resolved by drilling three new wells, building a 250,000-gallon reservoir and installing water softening plants for the new and old systems. The sewage problem is being met by installing a pumping station at the Northwood Campus and laying a long expensive sewer line from there to the Greatwood Campus and then to the river. However, if and when Plainfield Village builds its sewage system, the Goddard line will be connected with it at the Greatwood Campus and the line from Greatwood to the river converted to use as part of the fire protection system.

Inasmuch as the master plan includes provision for a new Library-Learning Aids Center as the first of the Core buildings to serve all campuses, it had to be designed. Hill and Associates were given this assignment. With the advice and assistance of Librarian William Osgood and Learning Aids Center Director Robert Sekerak, they produced the plan in time for its acceptance at the Board of Trustees meeting in January of 1965.

To finance this building, applications were prepared for submission to the United States Office of Education for a grant and a loan under the provisions of the Higher Education Facilities Act of 1963. This operation demanded the participation of all of the planning staff as well as that of several attorneys and Business Manager Richard Holbrook. As this quarter closed, funds for a grant of $281,803 had been tentatively allocated to the college, pending further study and collection of more information, and the loan application was yet to be completed.

With the assistance of Senator George D. Aiken's office, the application for the loan to construct six two-unit student residences and a community center was approved in May 1965 for $1,415,000. Having cleared all the hurdles arising from coordination of the new campus plan with the master plan and meeting the requirements of the Housing and Home Finance Agency, the contracts were advertised for bid, with the expectation that the first three buildings would be ready for occupancy by November 1. Alas, the lowest bid was too high. This necessitated a long period of replanning and negotiating with the low bidder, J. Slotnik Company of Boston, and the acceptance of a new time schedule that called for completion of the first buildings in February 1966.

COMPLEXITY AND DIVERSITY

Finally—on September 13, 1965—the contractors moved in and proceeded to convert pasture and woodland to a college campus. However, they were not the first arrivals, for they had been preceded by surveyors, conservationists, and earth movers. Under the direction of Tom Maclay of the Winooski Soil Conservation Service, two dams were built during the summer to convert a sluggish little stream and a swamp into two ponds which should add to the beauty and charm of the new campus. For several weeks the most apparent activity at the site was that of bulldozers, back hoes and power shovels digging, and moving earth, stone and trees, but at last foundations were poured and the outlines of buildings appeared. Even so the earth movers stayed on, digging and refilling trenches for power lines, water pipes, sewer pipes, oil lines, telephone systems, as skilled workmen plied their trades to install the underground systems that have become essential to the modern community. It is a fascinating operation—the creation of a whole new campus in an area so varied in its contours, its soil types, its exposure, its forest cover and its water distribution. Grades had to be established to meet the exacting requirements of hydraulic and sanitation engineers, and lines laid through muck so deep that no bulldozer or back hoe could operate—in fact on several occasions machines seemed hopelessly mired—and so had to be replaced by ponderous but reliable drag lines. New roads had to be constructed through swamp and woodland, power lines had to be strung, and woodsmen with axe and chain saw are still cutting a thirty-foot swath through the cedar, pine and fir forest for the laying of the sewer line and to provide the base for a foot and bicycle path between the campuses. All of these and other activities have extended from the site of the new reservoir in the highest corner of that part of the college property known as the Taylor pasture to the termination of the sewer line at the edge of the college athletic field—a distance of more than a mile.

The variety of skills that is required is impressive—architects, engineers, surveyors, electricians, welders, plumbers, machine operators, choppers, carpenters, masons, roofers, pipe fitters, and all around artisans—and for none of these is automation or the computer a substitute. Surely the day of the manual worker has not passed.

The coordination involved is equally impressive, as the services of the surveyors, engineers, architects, lawyers, bankers, government officials, college personnel, contractors and suppliers are dovetailed. While the power company is setting its poles and stringing its wires for the building contractor, the college has another contractor pushing the sewer line through the woods, another building the water softening plants, still another constructing the new reservoir, two score carpenters are hammering and sawing, the plumbers and electricians and roofers are all on the job, the masons are building an underground silo, negotiations are continuously going on with H.H.F.A., the U.S. Office of Education, and the Vermont Commission on Higher Education Facilities, and of course bills have to be checked, approved and paid.

It is truly a great adventure, but to be fully appreciated it has to be seen.

THE FALL SEMESTER

Enrollment at Goddard is not a static thing–late arrivals, withdrawals, flexible calendar, extended and suspended cycles in the Adult Degree Program make it difficult to give a figure that one can stand behind for even so short a period as a semester. To the best of our knowledge, the following figures represent an accurate accounting of the students enrolled during the fall:

	On-Campus	Off-Campus	Sub-Total	Non-Resident	Adult	Total
Greatwood Campus	282	19	301	10	15	326
Northwood Campus	113	5	118	–	1	119
	395	24	419	10	16	445
Adult Degree Program						109
					Grand Total	554

When one considers the fact that in 1962 the college enrollment for the fall semester was 220, it is not surprising that faculty and students find themselves a little breathless from the speed of change, involving a more than doubled enrollment, two campuses, and a new adult program in the three year span.

The attached reports from the Deans indicate the major concerns of the two campuses during the fall. The opening of Northwood Campus was deferred until November 8, so at the end of this quarter they are completing the first half of their fall semester. The second half will be spent on the Greatwood Campus while Greatwood students are on their Non-Resident Term.

George Beecher, Director of Educational Experimentation, finds that with two campuses and the Adult Degree Program, the questions for his consideration increase, as each campus moves towards its own solutions to experimentation in curriculum and community living. His report is attached.

On November 19 and 20 a conference on China was conducted at the college under joint planning by Thomas Yahkub's class in CHINA, REVOLUTIONS AND CONTINUITIES, and George Benello, Director of Adult Education. The sessions were open to both campuses, to faculty and students from nearby colleges, and to interested adults from the Vermont community.

We are indebted to one of the participants, Alan D. Sophrin, for his reactions, which were published on November 22 and December 13 in the *Bennington Banner*, from which the following excerpts are taken:

"At a three-day Goddard College Conference this weekend, conducted as a study of 'Revolutions and Continuities', an audience which varied from 150 to 400 persons listened to speakers from Canada, Pakistan, India and the United States whose views ranged from frank approval to complete censure of the Mao Tse Tung government in Peking.

"The high point of the conference and the portion which attracted a peak crowd of 400, about half students, was a sound film shown Friday evening, 'The 700 Million', presented with comment by Pat Watson, Canadian Broadcasting Company newsman and telecaster who, with a CBC crew, made the 90-minute film in China during a two-month visit from April to June, 1964 . . . ."

"The conference was well run and well balanced. Those who came with an unshaken conviction against China heard their positions supported. So did those who came with sympathy.

"But what is a better measure of the value of the conference is the fact that those who came with an open mind and in search of knowledge did not go away disappointed. I came away with the strong impression that the most pleased of all were those who came to the conference with a sense of history and a desire to understand what it is in China's past that made it possible for the China of today to come into being.

"The conference had another important value, one which had immediate meaning to Vermont. It was an excellent example of a small college sharing an educational experience with its local community. It has been a Goddard trade-mark to welcome everybody to the campus. The college has built a mailing list of non–campus Vermont citizens who have attended college programs and for this conference, besides making it clear in the publicity that the public was welcome, the conference committee sent invitations to all on the mailing list.

"As a result, for two days, Goddard faculty and students shared their campus (including their dining hall) with representatives of organizations such as the League of Women Voters and the American Association of University Women and with many others who can be identified as people who came to learn . . . .

"I came away convinced of three things: Goddard College deserves high praise for conducting an excellent conference; there can be no better investment than the money the state has spent and will spend to study and encourage the founding of small colleges in Vermont; and one of the small college's most important contributions to Vermont can be involvement of its surrounding community in the learning process."

Among the speakers were Jonathan Mirsky of the Department of Oriental Studies of the University of Pennsylvania; Irtiza Husain, Consul-General of

Pakistan; Prakash Shah from the Indian Embassy in Washington; and David Dean, deputy director of the Office of Asian Communist Affairs of the U.S. Department of State. Weather conditions unfortunately prevented Sunday's speakers from coming, so the events of that day had to be cancelled. The high quality of the events which did take place, however gave those who attended a real sense of satisfaction. Attendance from the college community was disappointingly small,. a condition somewhat hard to account for. Perhaps it is as Tom Yahkub said, "A prophet in his own country . . ."; if the conference had been held elsewhere the Goddard community might have counted it more of a privilege to attend.

On December 3 the New England Association of Colleges and Secondary Schools formally confirmed Goddard's continued membership as an accredited college, subject only to the conditions applicable to all fully accredited situations, one of which is a re-examination every ten years. The event was such an anti-climax that it passed with scarcely a ripple within the Goddard community. Thus the seventeen-year struggle to win unqualified acceptance as an experimental college came to an end in a very low key accompanied by no fanfare and no hallelujahs.

The School-College-Community Counselling Project was included on December 20 in a series on mental health which is being shown on Boston's educational television channel. Films for the show were taken in early June by Harold Mayer Productions. The college has been able to procure a print of the film which Harold Boris believes will be very helpful to him in developing the group consultation process.

During the fall the Project has concentrated on counselling groups in the eight communities in which we are now working. Preliminary visits were made to homes by the Project Associate, Barbara Davis. Those who expressed interest in joining a group were invited to an initial interview with the Project Director. They were then assigned to groups made up of persons from several communities. According to the director, the inter-community groups offer several advantages: they provide contrasts in schools, churches, social institutions, which seem to demonstrate more effectively than hearsay impressions the important role of these institutions in communal life; they provide a sense of wider horizons and diminished isolation; they provide some degree of anonymity and increased freedom to express things boldly.

Other activities of the Division of Adult Education and Community Services which continue are the Vermont Youth Study under the direction of Jerome Himelhoch, and the winter conferences and programs. A second series of Adult Degree Program has been set up, with resident periods in January and July. This will allow expansion of the Program while keeping resident groups at about 125 persons.

On December 29 the Liberal Religious Youth of New England, 249 strong, arrived in buses and cars for a three-day conference on the campus. This is the third year the college has served as host for this event.

An All-College Faculty Meeting was held on December 28, the first since the pre-semester conference in September. The meeting was devoted to consideration of the educational philosophy of the college.

FINANCES FOR THE FISCAL YEAR ENDING JUNE 30, 1965

Because of a protracted delay in the preparation of the annual audit, some of the information relating to the financial condition of the college that is usually included in the June President's Report was not available until December and is therefore made a part of this report.

The balance sheet and the statements of income and expense reflect a substantial easing of the financial strain that the college has been operating under throughout its life. This happily improved condition derives from the increase in enrollment over previous years, including the growth of the Adult Degree Program which has effected a fuller utilization of college facilities throughout the year. Even so, the demands for funds to provide new and better facilities and to improve existing plant appear more rapidly than the money to meet them.

The campaign for funds for the Development Program did not attain a full head of steam during the year but the college did receive $125,750.35 in gifts and grants, distributed as shown in the attached summary.

Respectfully submitted,

Royce S. Pitkin
President

APPENDIX
SUMMARY OF GIFTS AND GRANTS, 1964-65

	Number of gifts	Amount
Alumni	45	$ 2,782.94
Parents of students and alumni	37	14,552.43
Trustees and former Trustees	15	19,112.04
Friends	34	35,145.53
(including Houghton Hail property, $32,655.03)		
Businesses	6	4,530.41
Foundations		42,450.00
Goddard Community:		
Adult Degree Program students	9	1,031.00
Staff and former staff	4	910.00
Goddard College Community Government		3,680.00
(for Library)		
Gifts of books to Library, 1556 volumes at $1.00		1,556.00

Total $125,750.35★

*It will be noted that this total does not agree with the total of gifts and grants in Exhibit D of the Auditor's Report (129,786.40). The discrepancy is due to inclusion by the Auditor of four items which he has marked "disbursed but not collected" and one item (locks for residences, $50) which is not actually a gift.

REPORT OF GREATWOOD CAMPUS FOR QUARTER ENDING DECEMBER 31, 1965

This semester the Greatwood faculty undertook to become accustomed to operating as a separate group. It established several committees to do certain things, such as a Research and Planning Committee to study major faculty concerns, and one or two others. A number of faculty interests began to come to the surface, such as conditions of employment, curriculum and study offerings, staff composition, and the like. Some of these were referred to the Research and Planning Committee for study. The faculty spent a great deal of time on community problems, particularly conditions in the houses resulting from the reluctance of students to observe the limits of intervisitation hours and the implications of this problem. Organized discussions with the community involving small groups of students and faculty went on for some time but concluded in disagreement. The faculty decided to make a decision on this problem and related problems after the close of semester and to notify students of the conditions within the community to which they would be subscribing if and when they return to college in March 1966. With this arrangement a truce was put into effect and the semester concluded on a somewhat low-pressure key. At the time of writing this report the academic committees are still reviewing the semester's work, but we think that study conditions were about normal this fall. This means that a good deal of rather good work was done in studies, and that there were probably not an unusual number of persons who did not complete studies or who performed less well than usual.

Some variations in scheduling were introduced this fall, or more properly, re-introduced. Some faculty members preferred different lengths of class time for different types of studies, and therefore a considerable range of class times were programmed, from 1 1/2 hours to half-days according to the preference of the instructor. The time of Community Meeting was moved from the evening hour back into the afternoon on Monday in an effort to make this an expected function for all community members, students and faculty alike. It would appear that variations in class time may have worked well for the moment, in that faculty members are testing out the uses of different class times for various purposes. The removal of Community Meeting from Monday evening to Monday afternoon did not affect the decline of community interest in this function. The meetings became smaller and smaller as the semester went on, faculty and students alike tending to do other things in this period. As a consequence of community problems in general and this phenomenon in particular the organization of the community was made the major item on the agenda for the post-semester faculty conference on December 29, 1965.

A plan of community operation was devised centering on a considerable number of vertical faculty and student committees on major community themes, interests, and problems, the Community Meetings becoming a Community Forum without legislative concern, establishing a continuing Community Business Office, and reaffirming the two-pronged requirement of the College for the development of faculty and student individualism and originality on one hand and faculty and student involvement in community affairs on the other. It was specified again that ten to twenty percent of faculty and student time are expected to be put into community affairs, and therefore that membership on functional committees is to be expected in addition to work program as part of the conditions of membership in the college community.

After considering the advisability of having a Social Standards Committee as part of the new community structure the faculty undertook to have such a committee, Ray McIntyre and Jack Thomas agreeing to function for the faculty with provision for students to be added later. A Coordinating Committee to operate the new community plan and to be responsible for the Community Business Office was established with John Hall as chairman and Richard Hathaway, Jerry Richard, and Thomas Yahkub as members. Both committees undertook to meet immediately to formulate plans which would be communicated to the students again as part of the conditions of their return in March 1966.

It is intended through all these moves to reestablish a structure through which the sense of community can develop again on Greatwood Campus. It is our purpose to involve faculty and students in these developments, and to specify to students early in January 1966 what the conditions of membership in the community will be. Return of students in March or from flexible semesters will constitute acceptance of these conditions.

The problem of enforcement of intervisitation hours remains a difficult issue. The faculty divides evenly on whether or not additional staff should be taken on to provide closure in the matter. Inasmuch as additional night staff will be required anyway with the opening of Northwood Campus it is probable that a compromise arrangement will be worked out for at least long enough to see whether Greatwood students can be encouraged once again to take part in responsible operations of these aspects of the community as they used to do. We wonder whether we are living in a time in which the polarization of student-age young people against faculty-age older people is such as to provide a permanent or semi-permanent state the consequences of which we may have to live with for some time. This issue will remain open perhaps until we can see what the new policies in the community can contribute toward either information or solution.

Forest K. Davis, Dean

REPORT OF NORTHWOOD CAMPUS
FOR QUARTER ENDING DECEMBER 31, 1965

The Northwood Campus completed the first half of its initial semester in temporary quarters in Marshfield during the quarter. Ninety students lived in community homes in the vicinity of Marshfield and Plainfield, fifteen in commercial cabins, and eight in the Plainfield Inn. Ten continued their studies in French Canada. A bus leased from a local dealer transported the students each morning, noon, and evening to Marshfield, where meals were served in the Marshfield Youth Center building. Classes were held in the Youth Center, a converted store, a basement apartment, and a rented house. In addition, the village library and a faculty home studio served as additional facilities for the six-week period. Students also made extensive use of the Greatwood library and of private transportation.

Work program consisted of cleaning and maintenance of the physical facilities, food service, and library assistance. Since the bulk of the food was prepared in the Greatwood kitchen and delivered ready to serve to Marshfield, the major duties of the kitchen assistants were servings and hand dishwashing.

Course work followed a new pattern of a single area of study for the six-week period. Three of the area courses were, in addition, taught by teams of three teachers. The response to a single unit of study was by and large favorable. Well-motivated students found it helpful to be able to concentrate on a single area, and faculty members enjoyed the flexibility of scheduling inherent in the plan, although no radical departures in the way of extended field trips or lengthy sessions were tried. The effort to teach in groups was used differently by different teams. Some had regular meetings of the total group only, while others scheduled a combination of large meetings with small group meetings under individual faculty members. Although the joint teaching was stimulating, it also led to certain frustrations over teaching styles, group directions, etc. For the second half of the semester, some variations on the group teaching plan will be tried. Also, although the unit study plan will again be the basis of class programming, students will be offered the option of a second, limited course which may allow the opportunity for a change of pace or an introduction to another field.

Many students found that they enjoyed the opportunity to get acquainted with Vermont families, in spite of the difficulties of travel involved in the Marshfield location. Perhaps because of the separation at other times, a certain closeness and group feeling developed among the members of the new campus, and morale was on the whole quite high.

A community government was established, which dealt with problems of taxation and recreation and length of semester, and which also devised a proposal for intervisitation plans on return to the Greatwood campus in January. The faculty reviewed the latter plan and accepted it in part, at the same time preparing a policy statement of its own to guide further policy in this area.

The coming two months on the Greatwood campus will test whether the group cohesion and strong morale from the period in Marshfield can continue under the pressures of a faculty policy on intervisitation which will probably be viewed as restrictive, of being on the old campus again, and of sharing the campus with many members of the adult program. We will also be testing, from a faculty point of view, whether it is possible to teach both ADP and the undergraduate program concurrently. Our final major area of concern is whether we will be able to move into the new buildings the first of March and thus avoid further temporary arrangements.

Alan M. Walker, Dean

EDUCATIONAL EXPERIMENTATION

Educational Experimentation seemed to reach a new stage at the end of the six-year Experiment in Curriculum Organization. The Director had to take stock of the situation to see how much of a vacuum was left.

Some distinction has to be made, I suppose, between new developments in the college and strictly experimental purposes. This is sometimes hard to do at Goddard. Is the ADP a new program or an experiment in college education for adults? Is the two-campus program a normal development or an experiment? Probably nothing should be called an experiment unless it is definitely set up to prove, demonstrate, or find out some new facts about education. Yet most of our developments have some of these aims.

The Northwood six-week curriculum plan in Marshfield is experimental in the sense of trying a single-course team-teaching approach which many of us have long wanted to see attempted. Certainly some evaluation of the results will be helpful even though the Marshfield experience is something special
. Survivals from the six-year experiment in curriculum such as use of off-campus resources, independent study, and flexible semesters are still in operation though perhaps beyond the experimental stage. The problem now is to bring new life and control into practices that were previously found good.

What new opportunities do we have for experiment or development of new ideas? Goddard is part of the Antioch study of the future of Liberal Arts Colleges. Being one of the colleges under investigation we find ourselves taking new looks at what we are doing. Outsiders have ways of asking questions that surprise us. One question, for example, about the number of transfer students at Goddard revealed that more of our graduating class this year will be transfer students than students enrolled here four years ago. What does this dropout and transfer question mean?

Raising the question about the future of liberal arts colleges stimulated thinking about Goddard's interpretation of the liberal arts or the so-called disciplines. An opportunity to submit a proposal on this question to the Braitmayer Foundation seemed worth seizing on.

Another proposal to deal with our problem of off-campus resources has been revised for submission to the Esso Foundation. Since there is an opportunity to submit more than one plan for development of college resources, we have been looking at some of our other needs. The question of communication in the college is a possible problem to work on. We have thought of the college as a community but have not experimented with the nature of our communications and the improvement of quality rather than quantity. Developments in the library-learning aids center and in the multi-campus program make this question important now.

The opportunities for federal aid to education are now being rather carefully studied at the college. We still see the need for work on college teaching, on cooperation of colleges on broader problems, such as curriculum, teacher education, attraction of able high school dropouts to college, or strengthening experimental school and community programs. We have had some part in state planning for use of the federal funds for schools and a regional educational laboratory. Federal funds will probably go to statewide or cooperative programs except where they are focused specially at individual college needs. The opportunity for research in education is something open to us if we have the research ideas and people to handle the programs.

There is no lack of ideas for experiment but there are costs in taking on experiments. A lot of staff time has to go into drawing up plans and making applications. Then a lot of faculty time is needed to see where the experiments meet college needs and fit in with previous faculty commitments. Then there are costs in perhaps matching funds or continuing programs when the support ends. The chief value to the college is probably in getting people to think about education and how our flexibility is suited to trying out new ideas. There is a danger in having so many ideas under test that integration of them into a unified faculty approach to teaching may suffer. A faculty that is increasing in size and splitting along campus lines has disintegrating forces already. It is important to show how past experiments or developments have contributed to college stability and wisdom and how new investigations can answer new questions about teaching and student interest in learning.

George Beecher
Director of Educational Experimentation

REPORT OF THE PRESIDENT OF
GODDARD COLLEGE

For the Year Ending June 30, 1966
(Supplement)

Educational Experimentation, 1965-66[56]

For some years I have been saying that educational experimentation must be carefully examined as a name for something going on at the college. The name by itself is ambiguous. The experimental school or college has generally meant an effort to question some traditional or common educational assumption and to set up a program to demonstrate different and presumably better results from different procedures. The demonstrations often have widespread effects regardless of the measures used. The schools that experimented in making school a friendly rather than threatening place accomplished for schools everywhere what no amount of coercion could. The procedure of inviting a child or student to converse in determining his own education stimulated learning simply through bringing about a greater willingness to try for oneself.

One solution however may open the way to new problems. If students volunteer for a certain kind of cooperative learning, how can you keep faith with them when they vacillate in their purposes. This is the worry-question of teachers who still have preconceptions about what and how much a student should learn. With a broad range of abilities among incoming students

---

[56]George Beecher's perspectives were always interesting, always fresh and original. He was interested in the nature of experimentation (among many other things), and here examines it in the midst of the two-campus condition of "swimming in experiment". He focused attention on this matter on a number of occasions. This is just one of them.

and different levels of purposeful energy the college is a continually ambivalent pendulum swinging toward the experiment with friendly conversational climate and then toward greater rigorous and vigorous attention to standards.

The experimental college, if one may speak loosely, is difficult to comprehend because of the many complicating factors involved. There is an admissions job and policy, there is a social life responsibility and policy, there is a teaching responsibility and role, there is an evaluating and recording job and procedure, there is a public image and role as an experimental college, and worst of all there is an expansion and growth potential with the problem of absorbing new workers, teachers and students, into an intellectual vortex. To make sense of experiment under these circumstances requires an act of faith in the past and a hope for future clarity.

Perhaps the present difficulty has quite naturally produced more studies than new projects. There is great need to take stock of the experiments that have been done, of the present opportunity for experiment, and of the strength of our aim to continue under the experimental banner. This strength should be measured more by manpower and will power than by acquisition of grants. It may be that we can get no grants without first mastering greater man and will powers.

The studies we need to have completed and made known include the write-up of the Six-Year Experiment in Curriculum Organization. The writing is promised for this summer. Though we know and use some of the results of that curriculum organization pattern, we need to look at it more carefully and to know the quality and quantity of our effort. The story may help us know what we can do and what we might do better if we tackle another big task. This is important for our faculty who were present during those six years as well as for new members who were not and who have no notion what the attempt was nor what it proved.

A second study that is presently useful is a product of the Student Development Project. This study of Institutional Differences and Student Characteristics describes Goddard among thirteen colleges regarding curriculum organization, faculty or institutional objectives, and student characteristics. The study presents us with a question of the relationships between curriculum organization and mental health. Mental health is here defined as the range of situations with which an individual can cope productively and from which he can gain satisfaction. The study focuses attention on our flexible curriculum and self-evaluation process, on our minimal regulation and supervision of behavior but energetic discussion of it, on friendly and informal relations which seem to create a strong sense of community, and on our values placed on personal development, responsible citizenship, and intellectual concern. Likewise we have to look at our students' characteristics under the heading of intellectual altruists: artistic interests and activities, thinking relatively free from domination by objective conditions and generally accepted ideas, interest in critical approach to problems, and both sensitivity and emotionality.

These students are generally ready to express impulses and to seek gratification either in conscious thought or in overt action. They have an active imagination and value sensual reactions. They are experimentally oriented and fond of novel situations and ideas. They are tolerant of ambiguities and prefer to deal with diversity and complexity as opposed to simplicity and structure. They exhibit concern for the feelings and welfare of others and are trusting in relationships with them. They are skeptical of conventional religious beliefs and practices and especially reject those that are orthodox or fundamentalistic in nature.

Do we know what that paragraph means? Do we produce these characteristics by our ambiguities or simply attract students to novel situations and ideas in our community? The study does not pretend to answer but makes it necessary for us to reconsider what an experimental program means or might mean in student development.

Other studies that affect us this year include three or four other ones. Their very number reinforce the inference that concluding one experiment opens the door to new questions. The study of the future of liberal arts colleges by Antioch throws us into the same bed with another group of about twelve colleges. This study has meant exposure to a visiting team of experts and student observers and to discussion groups of the teams from all the colleges. The thesis of the study will be that these colleges demonstrate the health of diversity in liberal arts programs. The future will do better to maintain diversity of ideas rather than to jell a new mold to replace the ivy or other league models. This thesis is encouraging for us whatever the inspection team thinks of our practices. And it thinks of them quite critically. We will have to try to see ourselves as others see us, however sensitive we may feel to criticism of our loose organization which tries to invite students to taste responsibility of their own free will, of our openness to artistic and individual expression, and of our inability to hold larger proportions of beginning students to the full four-year achievement of self-fulfillment.

The study of the future of liberal arts brought out of me a rethinking of the liberal arts. A redefinition of liberal arts has been tried out with the Antioch study staff and with our faculty and with a four-day conference of experimental colleges. This rethinking simply asks us to look under the fancy dress of the college traditional disciplines to find what sorts of disciplines the students actually develop. The thesis is that students can be helped to be proficient in all the languages of expression – the liberal arts. The college curriculum can be the assorted experiences (with the aid of teachers) in developing disciplines of creativity, of problem solving, of decision making, of determining values, and of personal style. So far the study has only reached the stage of engaging people in thinking how to evaluate their own work as teachers. The Union of Experimental Colleges gave us a full four-day workshop to try the idea out on some very intelligent educators, teachers, deans, students. Our own team of three teachers and one Goddard student learned something in the process – that the first reactions are not enough – the four days were productive of good understanding and exchange – and that some form of experimenting with college teaching and learning could come from the study.

The next full scale study we need to look at is the Union Workshop itself. It was a great place to see what other experimental efforts were like and what the range of innovation in education might begin to produce for us. Further regional workshops next year will engage greater numbers of our faculty and may start new procedures in science teaching or other fields. We heed to have more of our faculty involved just to develop our experimental manpower.

Finally, what use can we make of these studies? Can we develop a communication within the college as well as without that will make clear what needs to be done better? One Senior Study suggests even Goddard is threatening. We should look at what the student means by communication, too. Tom Whitaker's commencement talk raised this latter question of communication more dramatically than long dry studies ever can. We do have the problem of structure – not to confine us, but to give us a home base from which to venture each time we define an experiment inviting the student to look and to question. The student, too, whether he comes tolerant of ambiguity or develops it here, deserves the greatest clarity regarding goal and achievement. The new teacher at our time of expansion wastes too much time and energy coming to Tom's conclusions and often doesn't achieve enough clarity of black and white to be able to speak it.

With two campuses we are swimming in experiment. With problems of living and of learning we are fully taxed. *Business Week* called already about the third campus. May the next experiment be very clearly directed toward a solution of any one of our problems and those of higher education elsewhere. One big problem I see is a kind of eternal one in every era I have read about – how to invite a student to see his opportunity. Only in our era we have given up any special content – we seem to really mean invite. We think of resources for promoting self-disciplines. But our time has produced greater numbers of affluent students with many means for deceptive action – dropout, string out, transfer, wait-for-deadlines. The factors change and we still haven't read the studies we make of our own experimental engagements. An experimental program at best is an education of teachers taking part in it. We have made some more applications for grants (one for a cooperative curriculum study among five New England colleges and one for a Head Start evaluation and research center) but have not heard any responses yet. My final hope is that we will be cleaned up and ready whatever the next may be.

George Beecher
Director of Educational Experimentation

REPORT OF THE PRESIDENT OF GODDARD COLLEGE

For the Quarter Ending December 31, 1966
(Supplement)

REPORT ON GREATWOOD CAMPUS

Forest K. Davis, Dean[57]

Community. College and Student Polarization.

The semester began on Greatwood with an extensive orientation period of nearly ten days in which a self-motivated group of students and two or three staff, notably Tom Yahkub, Bill Osgood and Frank Adams, put on a rather extensive orientation program designed to introduce new students into the College with the most benefit and the least anguish.

---

[57] In this item appear three Deans' reports and two Directors' reports, as part of Royce's December 31, 1966 Quarterly Report. In his own section, omitted here, he had referred back to his Report of December 31, 1965, "A Multi-Campus Experimental College", and then referred readers to a "kaleidoscopic" view of the College by way of staff reports. It is these reports which are presented here. They are diverse and can speak for themselves.

It was altogether a puzzling and difficult situation, relatively new in the experience of the College. One notices again, of course, that the Roycean dialectic was removed from immediate applications in the College community following the opening of the second campus in 1965. None of the staffers would have been able to apply it in the degree and intensity that Royce had done. It would not have occurred to Royce to think he should modify the new campus administrative arrangements in order to apply it – especially as he probably did not think there was any such thing, taken in quite those terms. In any case – for whatever it is worth – we think the point is moot. We think the origins of this cultural slide lay off-campus, in families and among the contemporaries of students of that generation. We think it was and still is a widespread cultural adventure into metaphysics and epistemology, whereby people of whatever age who use drugs which are mind- and experience-altering have ventured to expand, as they saw it, their relationships to the environment and to the substrates of the really real. No doubt many who did and still do this become the victims of the substances used; but whatever the forces driving people to do it, the predominant feelings appear to be that there are new things to be learned from participating in it, powerful enough in their attractions to overcome legal, parental and community strictures against it. Indeed, if reports are accurate in 1995, parents of today may by now be participants in the cultural movement in the direction of drug use as a "legitimate" if not legal element in their life experiences. On the face of it, in 1995,

202

This ten-day period seemed to work well. New students and old students alike, as well as staff, appeared to feel this. Yet the semester did not go well thereafter, and it is a question why. There appeared to be some evidence that student leaders of the orientation group were not really committed to standards of community operation, but merely performed their function of leadership as a kind of role which they played for its own satisfaction, being at the same time fairly clear that they did not propose themselves to do much with community operations or community standards for the remainder of the semester.

Narcotic use (psychedelic) and inter-house hours violations were heavily up this fall, and an elected Judiciary Committee of faculty members chosen by the faculty and student members chosen by the community struggled with these problems for several weeks. It concluded that it was too subject to internal contradictions to operate effectively, and resigned in toto toward the end of November. It handled a good many cases, and talked extensively about these problems. It did not complete work on the cases effectively from the standpoint of the community and the College, and it is difficult to know the extent to which it helped or hindered with community standards this fall. This was a pity, because the College has always been committed to the idea that common social problems would be handled commonly, by which is meant handled by the students and staff in concert, rather than separately by one official or another. Wilfrid Hamlin advances the idea that Goddard students are now simply refusing to handle their own social aberrations and that it cannot be expected to be otherwise while the college upholds social standards in the setting of which the student members of the community did not participate directly. My view is that, however reluctantly, we probably have to come around to Will's view in this matter. This means that we would not again, at least in the immediate future, expect to establish an effective operating Judiciary Committee from the community. Cases of violation will then have to be handled either in the Deanery or in a Faculty Judiciary Committee.

(Note 57 continued)

it is absurd for the law enforcement and legislative entities to align themselves against popular use of drugs while avoiding totally the market dimensions and attacking only the delivery and importation elements in drug traffic. The reason some people engage in drug trafficking is because other people continue to buy drugs on the illegal markets. Looking back upon thirty years, we think the College was basically helpless against this newly developing situation in the mid-1960s. Its strategies were fundamentally rational; the Roycean dialectic itself was a fundamentally rational methodology; discussion as a way of knowing was a rational epistemology. The students were saying that they knew better than the College what the proper avenues to truth were, and the movement in those directions was simply not going to be denied. To this day, thirty years later, people who purchase drugs and use them may still be saying this same thing. It has yet to be shown that the country is not relatively helpless against a movement of this size and pervasiveness. The only recourse remaining is education: it is essentially the same potential policy to which Royce devoted his enormous energy and so much of his time at Goddard for so many years, so long ago. People have to decide for themselves where reality is, what they think they can know about it, and how they can best learn it. Goddard was the victim of a social condition, looming on a grand scale, rather than the perpetrator which to some degree the surrounding community may have thought it was.

Alone among us, as we can see from other sources, the one person who figured it all out at the time, and wrote it down in plain English, was he of the flashing mind and brilliant intellect, Wilfrid G. Hamlin. The rest of us put in our varied numbers of years and slowly came to the same conclusion.

It appeared to be true this fall that polarization of students against adults had proceeded further than we have ever known it on this campus. Not only were individuals and groups involved in social problems refusing to talk to the faculty, but also students who in general favored order in the resolution of problems away from narcotics, house violations, and alcohol, also were refusing to talk with the faculty. The exceptions to this occurred with faculty persons whose absolute discretion could be relied upon; students would tell faculty members things in which they were engaged if those faculty members were committed ahead of time to not doing anything about these conditions, and were understood to be more or less supporters of students regardless of what they did.

The Deanery felt that this was a significant problem in the counseling program here. Faculty counselors apparently choose in effect between keeping the channels of communication open to students, at the price of not taking a stand on issues which come up, and therefore being understood to be in favor of what the students are doing regardless of its lawfulness or unlawfulness, and on the other hand making their positions clear on problems of narcotics, house hours, and alcohol, at the price of simply not hearing about things in those categories. Our best guess is that all counselors do make this choice in one way or another and operate accordingly.

Faculty

It was my impression after a customarily turbulent semester that at long last the various factions within the Greatwood faculty group might be beginning to talk with each other in a real way. Various members continued to be heavily preoccupied with how things get done, with procedural matters among committees, with practical problems like salaries, and with what appeared to be in general a reaction against their own perception of "being had." Most obviously, numbers of them wished to be included more than before in the early stages of faculty decision on matters such as appointments of new members, transfers among teaching fields, and the like. This will probably come down in the end to an issue of power: who makes the decision on staff appointments? Or, who decides where the College money goes? Or, who decides whether such and such a staff member gets to teach and in what field, and who adjusts his time? Decisions have to be made; but who is to make them, we or they? The faculty is moving hopefully in the direction of more faculty control of what it conceives to be faculty issues.

Study Programs

Studies offered this fall appeared to be fairly diverse and to provide a good spread. My guess is there may some tendency to offer self-study approaches to fields, as in literatures, social studies, philosophies, etc. A contradiction obtains in this. Students are clearly heavily involved in the throes of self-knowledge. Studies which articulate with these interests can therefore be expected to be successful, and usually are. Balance also suggests that straight, objective studies might well also be offered, but that these might be more nearly empty of students. This, too, appears to be the case. In short, we may not entirely like the self-centered student curriculum, its refusal to study the sciences, and its emphasis on mystical knowings in a variety of fields. But there it is; at least for the moment, we have to live with it.

In general this appears to have been a difficult semester, so heavily marked with social problems on campus that at times we were not really operating like a college. This fact does not obviate the other side of the picture, which is that numbers of students continued to do serious and intensive study just as students always have here. It does continue to raise for us all the question of what we are doing and how best to work in peculiar and difficult circumstances.

A brief exposure to the Committee on Research and Experimentation suggested that the old magic of the single Goddard faculty was somehow captured in that pent-house appendage of the two Goddard faculties in the present day. It might be worth thinking how this degree of interest, sense of movement and useful change can best be reintroduced into the separate faculties once again.

REPORT ON NORTHWOOD CAMPUS

Alan Walker, Dean

Northwood opened in the fall on the new campus with all six dormitory buildings available, and definite progress made on landscaping. It was a pleasure to have the buildings completed and room for every staff member to have office space on one campus. Due to lateness in receiving use of C building from the builders, the completion of temporary quarters in the basement for the kitchen and dining room was delayed. The postponement of building the new community center makes the temporary quarters for these uses more important, and the dining area in particular definitely needs to be improved, with installation of heat and ventilation as well as better decoration. A small dance studio was installed in the basement of E Building, and has proved quite functional there. Tom Yamamoto, the art instructor for Northwood, has capably fixed up an art studio in B Building basement, with an added section for work in graphics. D Building basement was used for meetings and film showings this semester, but next year will be assigned to the drama classes except for one weekly film night. In late October, a successful production of "Jack" was produced there, under the direction of faculty member Paul Vela.

One of the big problems of campus life at the beginning of the semester

was the lack of a campus community center. Although C Building functioned in this way in part, with a mail room, laundry room, work program
headquarters, community government office, classrooms, reading rooms, and
learning aids center, there was no center or gathering place, such as the Green
Room in Marshfield or the coffee shop on Greatwood, where students could
go to relax and meet other students. Various efforts were made to establish a
coffee shop, but it was not until November that recreation coordinator, Joe
McEntyre, and a senior year student, Irene McDermut, succeeded in getting a
recreation room and coffee shop functioning in the second half of C Building
basement. Irene has also installed a branch of the Goddard Bookstore upstairs
in the same building, and is carrying out the business end of the operation as
part of her senior year study, under the direction of Jack Elliott and Vernon
Dixon.

As previously reported, new students outnumbered old students this semester (and "new" faculty old faculty, if common service personnel and transfers from Greatwood are counted). The rapid assimilation of persons new to
the campus was difficult to achieve, and many of those who were on Northwood last spring were still finding the differences hard to accept at the end of
the semester. For their part, the new arrivals – perhaps because they were so
plentiful – found many of the old customs, patterns, and expectations con-
fusing or misguided. It is sincerely to be hoped that next spring will bring the
amalgamation of the old and new into a cooperating community.

One evidence of the difficulties in functioning harmoniously as a community appeared in community government. Our first community moderator, Jim Cowling, chosen last year to serve as head of the government, left
college for personal reasons after a month and a half on campus. At the same
time, as an outgrowth of efforts to deal with criticism of the form of government, a series of adjourned and postponed meetings to attempt to find a valid
substitute form, effectively delayed any other community business for more
than a month. The vice-moderator, Sheldon Kaye, is presently undecided
about returning to college next semester.

This year also witnessed a marked and dismaying increase in the use of
drugs on campus. Two older students, Kenneth Beck and Dan Rosenberg,
prepared an important statement called, "Academics and the New Student,"
which was distributed and discussed in a special meeting with a large proportion of faculty and students present, arguing that so many of the new students had gotten off to a bad start that a moratorium on all classes should be
called for a week during which an effort would be made to reduce guilt feelings and to build a basis for more effective work. Although the solution they
proposed was not accepted, the statement indicates the nature of the concern
felt by many.

The statement drafted by Ken and Dan actually began in a meeting of a significant new group on campus, a group of student counselors, which announced its willingness to counsel with any student in addition to the regular

counseling by the faculty. This group met regularly with Corinne Mattuck and occasionally with other staff members, including Dr. Donald Bloch, throughout the semester, and served an important function for the campus in providing a selected and knowledgeable group of older students to whom younger ones could turn for help and assistance.

Toward the end of the semester, a public re-statement by the president of college policy on the use of drugs on campus was widely circulated. Dr. Chris McAree, of UVM, talked to both the faculty and the community on drug abuse; a group of third and fourth year students met on their invitation with the faculty; and the faculty proposed the formation of a special committee to deal with this problem in some depth next semester. The best methods of handling this problem have still to be found, and deserve a high priority.

Among the unusual activities of Northwood students may be cited the anthropological field trip by Gerry Gamburd's class; a large enrollment in mathematics courses with new faculty member, Lou Irwin; the personally significant participation by some students in a production of "Waiting for Godot," which may be invited to travel to Expo '67; the activities of Genie Barry in a kindergarten program in Waterbury State Hospital, and of other students under the direction of Corinne Mattuck, Francis Fay and Kehnroth Schramm in the New School in Plainfield. Courses in art and in enameling were very popular this semester, along with continued interest in literature courses. Three instructors collaborated on a course in Revolutions with some success.

Faculty member Mark Ryder began a program of dance classes for local children on Saturday mornings, taught by his wife, Ann, and has plans for enlarging the program of cultural enrichment with participation by other faculty and students. Kehnroth Schramm is giving a paper on the anthropology of the irrational at the meeting of the AAAS in Washington in January.

Work program this semester was under the overall direction of Cary Smith, with Anson Hamel as his assistant on Northwood. Anson's full-time availability as a supervisor of work crews helped a great deal in keeping the work program running smoothly.

The office work on Northwood has been capably and efficiently handled by Lolita Sicely who takes care of most of the records functions as well, under the supervision of the Dean.

The chief public event on Northwood was the formal opening of the campus on October 7. National press representatives were flown up from Boston by courtesy of a member of the Goddard board ,and parents and friends of the college were invited to a brief ceremony held on the lawn in the quadrangle outside of E Building. After remarks by Forest Davis, Alan Walker, Harlan Logan, and a talk by Royce Pitkin, the buildings were opened to visitors and refreshments were served by house committees. In the evening, trustees and faculty enjoyed a social hour and dinner.

Report on Adult Degree Program

Wilfrid G. Hamlin, Dean

The Adult Degree Program has grown to the status of a third campus in terms of enrollment, faculty involvement, and administration; it still, however, draws on the faculties of the other two campuses. More accurately, its enrollment makes possible the presence of faculty members on both campuses; in a very real sense, then, there is an ADP faculty made up, as it were, of pieces of Greatwood and Northwood teachers.

In January 1966 a second series of ADP cycles was started, meeting for resident sessions in January and July (the original series meets in February and August). This was done to keep the resident groups present at the College at any one time reasonably small; the nominal top is 120, which I suspect may prove to be somewhat too large, but I think we do not yet have enough experience to know. (My aim is a group small enough so that its members can come to know each other at least by name over the two-week period they are in residence together; I should guess that this isn't practically possible for a group of over 75 to 100.)

The enrollment for the first January-July cycle was 25, working with three faculty members. In July the group increased to 55, working with six faculty, with a choice of two cycle topics. This January it will probably be between 80 and 85, of whom 6 will be graduating; the others will choose work in three cycle topics taught by a total of ten faculty members.

The February-August cycle in 1966 had 135 students in residence, of whom 11 graduated; those who remained in the program worked with 12 faculty members. In August 152 students were in residence, of whom 29 graduated; the remaining 123 have been working with 12 faculty members. This February we expect to have about 145 of whom 22 will be graduating; the others will choose from five cycle topics taught by 11 of the Goddard faculty and the first non-Goddard teacher to work with the ADP, Dr. Grace Smith of the New York University School of Education.

The average ADP load has been somewhat higher than it perhaps should be; the current winter will see it a little smaller in the January-July cycle. We don't yet know what an appropriate faculty load is for this program; I personally found it hard to keep in touch with more than five or six ADP students and carry on regular college work as well, but other faculty members have handled twice as many or more – with, it must be admitted, a necessary cutback in their work with the regular on-campus undergraduates. A few faculty members enjoy working with the adults enough to want to be involved in both series; in this way we have acquired three persons whose primary affiliation is to the Adult Degree Program though they also work on one or the other campus.

Interest in the program continues high; our ad in the Saturday Review continues to be our largest source of inquiries. During 1966 we had 2,666 inquiries, reasonably evenly distributed over the year (May was the high month was 356, July the low month with 135). Out of these we enrolled 34 new students in July, 45 in August, probably about 30 for January, and an unpredictable number for February, probably about 25.

The work these people do is enormously varied. I should not want it otherwise. There has, however, been something of a problem of standards having to do with the difficulty of making a satisfactory definition of what 'a full semester's work' is. I have put together some questions to be asked about a student's work at the end of a six-month cycle which may help in evaluation; roughly they have to do with eliciting such objective evidence as we may have about the student's use of his time and resources during the period just past.

The program has had little attrition. A few students have left to study elsewhere, with our blessing; one of the proper functions of the program, I should say, is to help an adult discover that he can do college work successfully, in spite of (or because of) his advancing years. If the discovery leads him to want to work in the structure of a nearby college or university, perhaps in subject-matters we are not prepared to teach, all to the good. A few people have dropped out temporarily, they say, because of finances or for some other reason; how many of them will re-enter the program at a later date I have no idea. We had to ask one person to withdraw because she was not working within our standards as we interpreted them; another person withdrew after we made those standards clear to him. Perhaps both of these persons should not have been admitted originally, but I think we rarely have the kind of information which would help us predict difficulties of this kind in advance.

I've indicated two of the unanswered questions about the program as I see it, what the faculty load should be and how large the resident groups should be. Let me list a few others.

1. Is the current cycle structure satisfactory and practical? Some faculty teams do what seems to me an excellent job of putting together a resident seminar program in which each teacher applies his own ideas to some central problem in such a way as to demonstrate intelligent scholarship at work. Others either find this more difficult or disagree with the concept, and we come out with several quite separate projects, loosely hung together at best. Some teachers have been able to help students generate independent study programs which are both personally important to the students and genuinely related to the seminar concerns. Others have either been unable to do this or have simply encouraged students to work at whatever they wanted to, as long as the teachers felt competent to guide or criticize. We may need to examine other possible uses for the resident seminars (which seem to me vital to the program) and other ways of planning independent study. I should like counsel on this matter.

2. To what degree should ADP teaching be a regular, usual part of every faculty member's duties? And how often? I found I welcomed a six-month

cycle off after one in which I taught, but another faculty member to whom I suggested some respite from the program took umbrage, fearful that he was being eased out. And there are persons on the faculty who don't want to work in the program at all and haven't. The question of hiring non-Goddard persons for the program naturally arises in this context; I wonder somewhat about how we could keep in touch with them (perhaps we don't need to), how we can identify persons who might prove useful, what we should pay them, what this does to the notion that the ADP is part of Goddard and that its degree is the Goddard degree.

3. There are some requests for a graduate program. Were we to go into this – and I think we might seriously consider it – I should want to limit it to the area of education, and limit enrollment in it to working teachers (or other educators) who would spend at least two years earning the MA. But this would raise some subsidiary questions of importance – how to screen applicants, how to get a faculty who could handle such work over long enough periods so that a student could work with the same advisor over the full two-year period, whether one could or should limit the program to a very small enrollment (two per year, perhaps), whether the resident sessions should be longer, etc. I do feel we should talk more about this over the coming year.

4. I think we don't yet know quite what to do with the orientation period for new members of the program (at least I don't). Would it help to get people to work on subject-matter of some kind very early on? Should the testing be postponed until the last few days of the two-week resident period? What needs to be done to help students use the program as effectively as possible?

5. What should our curriculum be? My inclination is to make it problem-centered, but I think the faculty are not in essential agreement on this. I would like to see each cycle planned about a contemporary problem to which various disciplines might be applied (including information from the past); I should like to see independent studies centered also about problems. We are experimenting with something this winter we've not tried before, work in the performing arts; I think the basic question raised here is how to make the work truly an educational experience (cf. Dewey, *Experience and Education*) and how to make six months of independent work in a performing art a valid 'full semester's work.' We face a major problem also in relation to the sciences – as we do in our regular undergraduate teaching. How can they be most appropriately approached in the Adult Degree Program as part of a liberal arts educational program?

6. Finally, I think we need a careful evaluation of persons who have entered the program with no previous college work, or very little. I should want to know whether we can bring about significant growth in knowledge (facts and vocabulary) in the three areas measured in the Graduate Record tests we give, and in other respects how ADP students who get all or almost all of their college education through the program compare with students in the regular college and with ADP students who enter with two years or so of previous study behind them;

I am not much of an administrator. I should like here to say a big thank you to Jane Zerby who is handling the administrative details I would make a botch of so completely.

REPORT ON COLLEGE – SCHOOL – RURAL COMMUNITY MENTAL HEALTH CONSULTATION PROJECT

Harold N. Boris, Director

With September of this year the Project entered into its last year of existence. This has meant two things. One, that we had this year our last opportunity to introduce modifications of our approach and procedure which have grown out of the findings of previous years. And two, that the time was at hand to write up and present the findings of the Project to the professional and other communities.

It has also meant formulating the plans to take the essential work of the Project forward so that it can become established and useful at other institutions and facilities.

These have comprised the agenda which has guided our efforts.

Considering first the Project as demonstration research, we have explored the feasibility of communicating the approach to previously inexperienced and untrained people to learn what it would take for such people to pick up its rationale and apply its methodology. Accordingly we have hired and trained two new people to see to the contact work of the Project.

We have introduced certain modifications in both the overture and group phases of our process and tested these with encouraging results.

By way of our obligation to publish or otherwise present the experiences and results of the process, we can report the following:

1. A small book dealing with the situation in which the mental health professional is experienced by others as an alien, even inimical figure – and far from a helpful recourse – has been outlined in detail preparatory to being written between January and June of 1967.

This book will include a report of the project but will also focus on the implications of the situation where the mental health professional is experienced as alien. For mental health methodology in general it will translate both the project's experience and the methodological considerations into a presentation of specific techniques and procedures for working under those conditions.

2. Two papers have been prepared, one presented to the Tri-State Psychological Association meeting, the other to MENTAL HYGIENE, a well-regarded journal in the field, and accepted for publication in a forthcoming issue.

3. A third major paper is in first draft form and is intended for submission to some other journal in the field.

Whereas the first two papers attempted to identify the factors in the mental health system or culture which have proved alienating to the population at large – outlining alternatives as represented by our project's experience – the third paper undertakes a more thoroughgoing analysis of what goes into the decisions people make, pro or con, in the issue of seeking psychological assistance or accepting it.

The presumable contribution of these papers derives from the fact that most psychologists and psychiatrists only see persons who have already made a 'yes' decision and have geared their technique to that condition, with the result that they have had relatively little success in treating the reluctant patient. It has been our thesis that if we can shed light in the areas of the profession's unfamiliarity, that is, by describing and analyzing the factors associated with reluctance to accept mental health treatment as a recourse, the scope of those to whom the profession can be useful may be considerably expanded.

Two further presentations on the subject of mental health methodology are scheduled for the winter and spring. One at the Dartmouth, the other at the Boston Beth Israel Departments of Psychiatry. Both of these institutions are concerned with the problem of effectively reaching and engaging the hard-to-reach, and have expressed a continuing interest in the developments of our work here in Vermont.

An earlier series of presentations at the Tufts New England Medical Center's Department of Psychiatry has led to a consulting relationship which, in turn, has produced intimate collaboration this fall toward developing a project for that group. Thus the basic approach of our own project is now central to a major program of work in a large mental health effort directed this time toward an urban population.

REPORT ON ADULT EDUCATION
Beverly B. Cassara, Director

List of Activities
1. Helped George Benello coordinate Labor Conference
2. Pre-semester mailing to adult students
3. Advertised three days in *Times-Argus* for adult students
4. Organized Coffee Hour Discussion at Bebe's Restaurant, "Getting Parents Ready for College"
5. Organized Canadian-American Seminar
6. Canadian-American mailing
   A. Sent publicity to major new sources
   B. Sent flyer to total mailing list (about 500)
   C. Final program to total mailing list
   D. Sent final program to new sources of interest
      1. Exhibitors at Expo '67
      2. Management consultants
      3. Chamber of Commerce (both National and Canadian) Committees on Canadian-American Relations
      4. Invited all alumni to attend two-day field trip in Montreal
7. Organized three Education Conferences
   A. Current Educational Issues
   B. Behavioral Science and Education
   C. Psychodynamics and Education
8. Sent out general flyer on three Education Conferences to total mailing list and individual flyers on each conference to special conference listings

REPORT OF THE PRESIDENT OF
GODDARD COLLEGE

For the Year Ending June 30, 1967[58]

COMMENCEMENT

This year Goddard exceeded, in the number of its graduates, its enrollment in any single year during its first eight years of existence and, discounting the veteran enrollment from 1946-1951, for the first 21 years. There were 57 graduates from Greatwood Campus, 9 from Northwood Campus, and 54 from the Adult Degree Program, for a total of 120. This exceeds any expectations we had until the development of the Adult Degree Program and the multiple campus idea.

As I pointed out in my remarks concerning the graduates, size compels the College to abandon some of its earlier traditions, thus demonstrating the rel-

---

[58]In this concluding Report for the 1966-67 College year Tim begins with routine events, mentions a number of interesting dimensions (as the entry on Eliot Pratt's pottery and Japanese artwork, and the section on Buildings and Grounds), and only reaches his major interests when he gets to Programs and Projects. He does not often discuss as much concerning consortial areas in these Reports as is the case here. We emerge from this section with a new grasp of the external reaches of College involvement, quite useful at this point when there might have been danger of over-emphasis on the social and personal problems of the College community.

His first six lines under Personnel Changes were a surprise to us when we first read them 28 years later. One did not often know what he thought about such things. On our last day in the Greatwood Deanery, packing the truck for the move to Ohio, he came over to call, and sat for a while, passing the time of day. It was a gracious moment, a shared courtesy, a pause to remember. Often we have thought of it.

He ends his Report with a return to "the perplexing problem" to which he had constantly to refer, that of finances and fund-raising. There were always more things to do with money, if he had it, than could be paid for with available resources. Nevertheless, the details of his account this time were very different from many of his reports on finances in the past. Things had gone better in the year that was ending. Typically, his advice to himself and the College was still "to find new sources of continuing support."

ative ineffectiveness of the large institution. Instead of being able to say something about the life and work of each candidate, I mentioned some of the accomplishments and attributes of the group, and then took a look at this group in comparison with the graduates of 1946, '47, '48 and '49.

This year's graduates consisted of 38 men and 29 women; of this number 13, or 20%, have been married (I am speaking here only of the Greatwood and Northwood graduates, excluding the Adult Degree Program graduates.) The range of interests, as expressed in their senior studies, was wide, including such diverse subjects as "An Analysis of the Modern Architectural Design Revolution," "Uses of the Winooski River," "T.S. Eliot on Poetry," "Play Activities with Disturbed Children," "The Concept of Mathematical Truth," "The Truman-MacArthur Controversy," and "Retailing Methods."

Some of the differences, and similarities of this year's graduates and the earlier group:

(1) The earlier group included 12 women and 11 men; 7 of the 23 were married; thus we see a slight shift in the ratio of men to women, and a sharp drop in the percent that were married – from 30% to 20%.

(2) In conducting their studies, 43% of the alumni group and 33% of this year's group engaged in off-campus activities.

(3) 4% of this year's studies were centered on Goddard whereas 10% of the alumni studies were. Both alumni studies dealt with community government, whereas the 1967 studies were directed toward an understanding of individual reactions and development.

(4) In 1948 a Negro girl made a study of The Negro as a Creative Artist, and this year a Negro girl made a study of Negro speech.

(5) 5% of the 1946-49 studies and 4% of this year's studies took the form of creative writing; the same holds for the natural sciences and mathematics, psychology, philosophy, and the social sciences (other than history, which went from 5% to 9%). There was a decline in painting and architecture from 13% to 6%, but this is offset by the appearance of studies in drama, music, and the film. Education holds about the same place, with 18%; interest in literature rose slightly, going from 5% to 9%.

(6) Some new interests have appeared: a strong concern for the economically disadvantaged of all ages; disturbed and handicapped children; an interest not clearly defined but related to communication, linguistics, cybernetics and prospects for a better society; exploration of the self or a search for identity; studies concerned with body movement or non-verbal communication.

(7) An arresting though not necessarily significant fact is that of the seven marriages in the alumni group all of them remain intact, while of the 11 marriages in the 1967 group, 3 have been dissolved.

The major difference, if there is one, is that the Class of 1967 has devoted much more attention to finding out who they are, why they are as they are, and how they can find a satisfying life than the 1946-49 graduates.

Adult Degree Program graduates, 54 in number during the year, represent even a wider range and diversity in their culminating studies, often bringing years of experience in the field to their work as students. Concern with education and social issues, as with the regular undergraduates, runs high with Adult Degree Program students.

A special feature of this year's Commencement was an exhibit of Chairman Eliot D. Pratt's pottery, together with some Japanese work which he brought back from a trip to Japan. The exhibit, in the Oak Room at Martin Manor, was arranged by Charlotte Clifford, ceramics teacher.

Another special feature was the Saturday morning discussion before an audience of parents, students, faculty and friends, during which sixteen of the graduates and I talked about their Senior Studies – what goes into the choice of topic, how one goes about collecting data, searching out references, writing, evaluating; the frustrations encountered (several told of "vacations" during which for several days they gave up even thinking about the study), and the satisfaction derived when at last they knew it had been read and the award of the degree was imminent.

BUILDINGS AND GROUNDS

Several improvements to the buildings and grounds of both campuses have added to the enjoyment of students and faculty. Tiling of the floors, installation of acoustical ceiling and ventilators, painting make the temporary dining room of "C" Building on the Northwood Campus a much more pleasant place in which to eat. The installation of a Coffee Shop in the left lounge of this building contributed greatly to its usefulness as a Community Center. It houses, in addition to these eating facilities, small branches of the community store, library and learning aids center, mail and laundry rooms, as well as faculty offices.

Another added dining facility is now available in the Red Birch Room (the original dining room – not used by us for this purpose since the first year of the College) in Martin Manor. Throughout the spring three faculty committees held regular weekly luncheon meetings there, special lunches for the Community Service Project and the Project on the Study of Older Americans were held, and, at the end of the year, Beverly Cassara arranged an evening dinner for adult students enrolled in the regular undergraduate program. Food is cooked in the Greatwood kitchen and served from the former butler's pantry.

Finally completed this spring is the latest addition to the buildings of the College – a silo-inspired greenhouse near the Science Building. Designed by Senior student Peter Saman, it has been under construction by Work Program over several semesters using materials garnered from an abandoned greenhouse in the vicinity.

Another addition which has long been in progress was also completed this spring – the addition to the Haybarn Theatre which also provides additional kitchen storage and office space. Two posts on the stage were also removed, giving free access to the total stage space. A projection booth was added to the balcony. Most of this work was done on Work Program under the supervision of Harold Townsend.

To provide more adequate fire protection for the College buildings a newer, larger and better fire truck was acquired this spring through the Surplus Commodities Division of the state. This acquisition was facilitated by the efforts of former Trustee, Senator George D. Aiken. The old truck which was purchased from the Waterbury (Vermont) Fire Department by the Community Government several years ago has been honorably retired. A three-way mutual assistance arrangement is in effect with the Marshfield, Plainfield, and Goddard Fire Departments. When the Plainfield Department is called out, the Goddard fire crew serves as stand-by for Plainfield.

The ravages of Dutch Elm disease can be seen on the Greatwood Campus, causing the loss this spring of the beautiful old elm by Greatwood Cottage (over 150 years old, by Dean Forest Davis' count of its growth rings, after he had watched it being skillfully brought to the ground by hired tree men from the Deanery window) and the impending loss of the young elm which has shielded the President's Office in the South Silo from the hot summer sun. Such trees are literally irreplaceable and one has pangs of regret as they succumb to the ravages of disease long before their natural span of life.

The Greatwood parking lot was re-surfaced this spring, with gravel. There is need for more work to be done on the walks of both campuses. The need for lighting on the path between Northwood and Greatwood was discussed at the President's Council and with Superintendent of Buildings and Grounds Bill Lyndes, Coordinator of Campus Planning Ronald Pitkin and Provost John Hall. The problem is not one with an apparent simple solution.

Progress on landscaping the Village for Learning on the Greatwood Campus has been slow, due to erosion problems, and shortage of Work Program crews for outdoor work. The flowering crabs did blossom in early June, and the tiny Scotch pines begin to show above the clipped grass of the lawns. Despite continuing erosion the Northwood landscaping of last summer resulted in quite well established lawns and the survival of several trees that had been transplanted.

PROGRAMS AND PROJECTS

The five colleges engaged in the Developing Colleges Project under Title III of the Higher Education Act met in a conference on the needs of first-year students at New Ocean House, Swampscott, Massachusetts on May 5, 6, and 7. Students were included in the conference membership, and according to those from the State Colleges it was a rare and remarkable opportunity for communication between students and faculty. It was proposed at the conference that each college follow this up with a conference of its own before the end of the academic year.

Only two colleges actually did this – Lyndon and Goddard. The Lyndon faculty met for several days at a nearby resort, and found it a very profitable experience to share educational views and ideas without the necessity to arrive at operational decisions. The Goddard Conference was held at Bonnie Oaks resort on Lake Morey at Fairlee. Faculty members and two students from each campus spent June 21, 22, 23 and 24 together, the first day in full session, the second and third by campus, working out a program for first-year students, and the fourth day informing the other group of the plans developed. It is interesting to note that the plans, while embodying some new approaches, had many similarities.

On the same weekend as the Swampscott Conference there was a conference on "The New Breed of College Student" at Goddard, organized by Ernest Cassara's and Corinne Mattuck's classes on student problems, and attended by students from some sixteen other colleges.

Since the 1st of January a Cooperative Community Service Agency, under the direction of Mrs. Rosemary Rexford with funds from Title II of the Higher Education Act, has been operating from the Goddard Campus. With two part-time assistants, Mrs. Ellen Pitkin and Mrs. Clotilde Pitkin, the agency undertook to get some idea of the thinking of persons living in the rural towns of Marshfield, Cabot, and Calais. Town officials, organization officers, school teachers, individuals were interviewed with the special purpose in mind of trying to find out how the Community Service Agency might function as connector between individuals, town problem areas, and the agencies established to deal with those problems. In addition to this survey many meetings were attended by the three agents, individuals were referred to helping agencies which might assist them with problems; a workshop was held for rural high school students on opportunities for summer jobs and employment beyond high school; assisted various groups and organizations in special projects such as planning a winter conference, a fall foliage festival, a transportation pool for kindergarten, getting volunteers for an aide-training course for ambulance service, assisting in getting out information on alternatives for a union school. In all the activities the emphasis has been on involving low-income members of the community, helping them find ways of participating in community life.

During the spring, with a small grant from Vermont's Interdepartmental Council on Aging, a study of the needs of Older Americans in the Upper Winooski Valley was carried on by a staff consisting of Mrs. Janet Morse of Calais, Duane Wells, a Goddard senior student from the area who based his Senior Study on the Project, and nine Older Americans engaged as interviewers. It was decided, in consultation with the Project's volunteer consultants (Alan Walker, Jane Yamamoto of the Central Planning Office of the State, and myself) that the most satisfactory method of obtaining the desired information would be the personal interview, with the interviewer writing down his findings after concluding the informal conversation of the interview. Names and places of residence of Older Americans were obtained from town clerks, ministers and neighbors. It was estimated that there were 500 persons over 60 living in the five towns; the actual number interviewed was 472, of whom 14 were in the 55-59 age bracket.

Conclusions of the study were (1) that the ability of many Older Americans in the area to live satisfying lives is seriously hampered by their wide dispersion and isolation, and by the lack of transportation facilities, (2) that with few exceptions, the Older Americans of the area have very low incomes, (3) that there is great need for employment opportunities and sales outlets for crafts, (4) that there is a great deal of loneliness among older rural folks, (5) that there is a clear need for physical help for some of them.

During the summer we expect to develop a proposal for funds with which to establish centers in these towns to meet some of the needs indicated by the study.

A third community project carried on this spring was the Martin Manor Project, planned with James Roos of the Central Vermont Community Action Council, and Frank McFaun of the Neighborhood Youth Corps. Under the supervision of Mrs. Ernestine Pannes of the Goddard faculty seven Goddard students constituted the teaching faculty for two groups of Neighborhood Youth Corps enrollees, providing remedial instruction to functionally illiterate school dropouts with an intense aversion to school. Each of the Goddard students incorporated his work on this project in an independent study and one of them, Sykes Equine, made the Barre group in the project the subject of her Senior Study and, as a result, we have an excellent report on this experimental learning project involving college students and local disadvantaged adolescents. The project called for two three-hour sessions weekly from March to June in Martin Manor lounge for approximately twenty youths from Barre and Montpelier. An extensive paperback library of an astonishing array of subjects was gathered by the college students and set up in the Ash Room, adjacent to the lounge. Field trips to the St. Johnsbury Museum and the Cabot Cooperative Creamery were included. The student teachers planned and directed the group sessions. They found themselves unable to devise a comprehensive plan for the series, but met before and after each class to discuss the effectiveness of what had been done and to plan for the next meeting. The teaching staff attempted to devise a program of cultural enrichment, which would give the youth a better understanding of themselves and their world with the hope of preparing them for the eventual task of learning such necessary skills as reading, writing and arithmetic.

Sykes writes, in her chapter on the effectiveness of the program, "We boast no glaring achievements. We have not awakened any dormant genius or even equipped a single enrollee with the minimal 20th century survival kit. What we have done is to lighten some of the handicaps placed on these young people by a disadvantaged environment and inadequate educational experience. . . . The most obvious successes for the Youth Corps students are the increase in general experience and improvement in their ability to communicate – both of which are prerequisites for their future development. The trips we took were of distinct value." For the Goddard students, she says, "This program has been an eye-opener for all of us as teachers. We have been face to face with one of the toughest educational problems in the country, and we have had to deal with it practically rather than, as is too often the case, theoretically. . . . The program has made us more tolerant and patient. . . . All of us have learned the difficulty and importance of good team-work. Over and beyond everything else we have gotten from this program the hard realization that it is incredibly tough to be a really good teacher."

After the semester ended the campuses were used for three programs. Mrs. Corinne Mattuck directed another one week Head Start Orientation Program from June 19 to 23. From June 23 to 25 a Conference on Teaching about War and Peace was held under the sponsorship of the American Friends Service Committee. Some twenty-five persons attended. Mrs. Beverly Cassara reports that there were some very inspired sessions where those involved really shared with the group their authentic concerns, while the atmosphere was always congenial it was not always calm. Beginning June 26, and running for three weeks, Mrs. Barbara Eniti, Director of the Learning Aids Center, directed a Media Workshop, with Robert Sekerak, formerly of the Goddard faculty and now at The University of Vermont. Although only five persons enrolled, it was decided to go ahead with the Workshop.

At the end of June the five-year School-College-Rural Community Counselling Project, funded by the National Institute of Mental Health and directed by Harold Boris and Evalyn Bates, came to an end. We are now awaiting copies of the 155 page report of the Project to which Hal has devoted most of his time this spring. His detailed description of group consultation as a preventive mental health approach should be an important contribution to the literature of psychotherapy as it pertains to rural communities.

We wish Hal well as he leaves Goddard to go on with somewhat similar work at the Tufts-New England Medical Center.

PERSONNEL CHANGES

It is with deep regret that I record here the resignation of Forest K. Davis, who came to Goddard in 1950 as director of admissions and leaves as first dean of Greatwood Campus. In those seventeen years Goddard has had a no more loyal and devoted teacher and administrator. He has given fully of himself to the College and its people – students, staff, faculty and trustees. He takes on his new job as Coordinator of Federal Programs at Wilberforce University in Ohio in July.`

Ernest Cassara, who joined the faculty this year as teacher of history, has been appointed the new Dean of Greatwood Campus.

On leave during the spring semester have been George Beecher, Director of Educational Experimentation, and Mrs. Beecher, Assistant to the Business Manager. They have spent several weeks travelling in Italy and Greece.

The resignation of Helen Johnson as Director of Food Services made it necessary for us to examine this area of operations carefully to determine an appropriate course of action. We have spent a considerable amount of time this spring weighing the advantages and disadvantages of employing a food services company to manage the kitchen-dining rooms. After extensive consideration, it was decided to employ the Prophet Company, and a contract has been signed for management services to begin July 1st.

Other resignations effective at the end of the academic year include Frank Adams, who returns to the South to work on Civil Rights issues; Charlotte Clifford, who plans to devote herself to her family responsibilities; Buryl Payne, returning to the West Coast and further study; Joshua Berrett, to undertake further graduate studies at the University of Michigan; Vernon Dixon, for graduate study at Princeton University; Erlend Jacobsen, who will be teaching at Mount Holyoke College.

New appointments to the faculty as of June 30th include: Jakob Amstutz of Bern, Switzerland, Secretary of the Swiss Philosophical Society and lecturer at the Albert Schweitzer College, to teach Philosophy and Religion; Olivier Chesaux of Sterling, New York, who has been teaching French and directing the language laboratories at State University College of New York at Oswego, for French Comparative Cultures Program; Mrs. Virginia Heffron of Davis, California who has just been awarded the Master of Arts degree in History from the University of California, where she also taught in the History Department last year, to teach Political Science; Philip Homes of Holland, Michigan, formerly Chairman of the Art Department at Hope College, to teach ceramics; Irwin Tuttie, who has his own studio in Waitsfield, Vermont and last year taught in the Art Department at the University of Vermont, for the Fall Semester while Joseph Fulop is on sabbatical leave; Mrs. Nancy Wagner of Los Altos, California, formerly instructor in Psychology, San Jose State College, to take over Kenneth Carter's work while he directs the Kauai Field Study Center next year. Mr. and Mrs. Peter Hart of the faculty of the folk high school at Orivesi, Finland, will come to Goddard next year as Visiting Lecturers. Mr. Hart will teach Literature on the Northwood Campus, Mrs. Hart will teach Finnish Life and Literature on Greatwood, and will work in the library.

FINANCES AND FUND RAISING

The Auditor's report of current operations for the year ended June 30, 1967 looks better than was forecast when the budget was adopted in the fall of 1966. Instead of an operating loss there was sufficient gain to cover the purchase of equipment, reduction of debt, and improvements to the amount of $117,800. Inasmuch as some of the equipment purchases and improvements tend to be recurring, they were included in the budget as estimated current expense but called by the auditor capital expense. A second reason for the apparent gain was that much needed repairs for which provision had been made in the budget were again deferred because we did not want to deplete our cash at a time when an operating loss was anticipated. Thirdly, initial payments on the U.S. College Housing Loan for Northwood were about $50,000 less than anticipated. However, they will be at full scale during

1967-68. Fourthly, because the 1967 Head Start Training Program occurred in June, its income was credited to 1966-67 along with the two programs held in the summer of 1966, thus the income from Head Start Programs was received in one fiscal year rather than two. Fifthly, there were also some increases in tuition income over the amounts that seemed justified by the actual enrollment in September 1966.

Gifts and grants received during the year amounted to $194,707.76 compared with $195,148.03 reported last year. The largest single gift was made by Chairman Eliot D. Pratt for $50,710 toward the Library-Learning Aids Center. An encouraging sign is the increase in number of contributions from Alumni from 55 in 1965-66 to 89 for this year. The total received from Alumni was about $300 less.

The total number of contributors (not counting individuals making group gifts) was 230. Mr. and Mrs. Harry Houghton did not make a transfer of a portion of their interest in the Houghton Hall property in Ontario in our fiscal year but had made two such transfers in the year 1965-66, but in two calendar years.

A notable development in the sources of support for the College is the rise in grant funds received from the federal government. For the first time the government provided the largest amount of grant or gift funds received to a total of $76,467.03. This does not include a grant of $32,000 made to Goddard as trustee for a Developing Colleges Program under Title III of the Higher Education Act of 1965. It seems likely that federal funds will become increasingly important in the operations of most colleges during the next few years.

Although the resources of the College did not increase as much this year as had been projected two years ago and although insufficient funds were accumulated to permit the construction of the Eliot D. Pratt Library-Learning Aids Center, it was a good year when viewed against the preceding 28 years.

The necessity for an increasing diversity in the College's educational programs was clearly demonstrated during the year. Whereas the total number of students taking college level courses at some time during the year 1966-67 was 778 or 116 more than in 1965-66, the number of regular undergraduates declined by one and was much smaller than was anticipated in June 1966. Fortunately, total enrollment in the Adult Degree Program rose from 162 to 252 and that of commuting adults from 27 to 54. The Head Start Training Programs, the adult conferences and the Arts Center also helped in carrying the continuing operational costs of the College and thereby eased the burden created by the unexpected drop in anticipated admissions among regular undergraduates for the year 1966-67.

A major task during the coming year is to fortify the financial resources of the College and to find new sources of continuing support.

Respectfully submitted,

Royce S. Pitkin
President of the College

REPORT OF THE PRESIDENT OF
GODDARD COLLEGE
TO THE BOARD OF TRUSTEES

For the Year Ending June 30, 1968[59]

COMMENCEMENT

Recognizing the growing separate identities of the two campuses, and in keeping with the tradition established in Adult Degree Program graduations, this year the Commencement Committee arranged for the President's Commentaries on Senior Studies to be made on each campus with the degrees being awarded at a joint meeting. On Friday morning, June 14, the Greatwood graduates, their friends and families, and faculty members gathered in the Haybarn Theatre at 9:30, and the Northwood group met at 10:45 on the

---

[59] A novel approach appears here in Royce's general main section. He reports on characteristics of the two campuses as shown in the Senior Studies he had just finished reading. Then he goes to the Deans' reports for the campuses, then to the Goddard Experimental Program in Further Education (GEPFE), of which Anita Landa was Director at the time, assisted by Joanne Chickering with James Roos and Diane Reeves; still another new and unfamiliar program then appears in the report by Rosemary Rexford, who had become Agent for the Cooperative Community Service Agency. Amid this welter of the new and unfamiliar then appears a program well known from earlier times, the Non-Resident Term, which now had its own Director (Priscilla Backman), who provides an account of its results in the 1968 year. We have spoken of this before in these pages. It serves to show that Royce never forgot, in the midst of swift-flowing new programmatic currents such as GEPFE noted above, the basic programs which had been fundamental in the College since its founding, and which in their early days had been new and experimental in their turn; he took just as much interest in their accomplishments in 1968 as he had in the earliest times in Plainfield thirty years previously. The NRT had always before been bracketed with other programs. Here once more he had appointed a graduate of the College to head it, a move he often made, with clear satisfaction. One can see other instances of this in the GEPFE section of this same Report.

223

lawn in front of E Building. Buffet lunch was served in the dining rooms on both campuses, and then the celebrants gathered in the Haybarn Theatre for the President's Address and the awarding of degrees. The crowd exceeded the Haybarn's capacity, indicating that in the future either a larger space must be available or separate ceremonies conducted. Fifty-two were graduated from Greatwood, twenty-one from Northwood. With the sixty-two graduated in 1967-68 from the Adult Degree Program, the total number of degrees award-ed in this, the twenty-fifth year in which the bachelor's degree has been giv-en, was 135. Except for the two-year period from 1946 to 1948, it was not until 1960-61 that we had that many students enrolled in the College in any one year.

The prefatory remarks in my Commentaries on Senior Studies may suggest something of the uniqueness of each campus:

For Greatwood –

"If these is any one characteristic that appears more often than any other in this year's Greatwood Senior Studies, it is the process of searching. Sometimes it is a searching for self, at other times for God, sometimes for a better way of life, sometimes to understand a philosophy or a religion, at other times it is a searching for the basis of a better educational system, and usually a searching for answers.

"The searching process begins in the here and now – in one's own school-room and community – and extends back through the ages to the myths and legends of pre-history, from the earth of the college campus to the heavens above, from the works of the poet to the behavior of animals, from the pot-ter's wheel to the novel, from the rural hamlet to the urban slum, from black America to Africa, and from the decisions of the Supreme Court to the trag-edy of Vietnam.

"There is little evidence of certainty, of having found the final answer. Occasionally the reader senses a little arrogance – strangely enough among those who intend to teach small children – but the overall impression is one of humility.

"The Greatwood Senior Studies – there are fifty-four of them – include works of art – paintings, sculpture, photography, choreography, poetry, a short story – architectural design, play production, historical inquiry, teaching,

---

(Note 59 continued)

Then came the heavy artillery again, George Beecher, of course, this time addressing himself to an "Outline for a Positive Environment" – no doubt to provide the staff with new ideas to apply to familiar problems. Following the Staff Changes section Tim enters on his own 5-page review of the history of the College, "Decade By Decade". He concludes this longer-than-usual Report with a tribute to retiring Board Chairman Eliot Pratt, who had supported the College for nearly two decades through every sort of crisis and every sort of need and challenge. Eliot was gravely ill that summer, no longer able to participate in his many interests and activities, and had been made Chairman Emeritus by the Goddard Board. His moving into the shadows would have been hard for Royce to take, knowing so well what Eliot's enabling role in the College had been.

service to public welfare agencies, sociological research, and literary criticism."

For Northwood —

"In reading the Northwood Senior Studies this month I became aware that my understanding of language was utterly and sadly inadequate and I was forced to recognize that though this year's graduates use a common tongue they speak many languages. At first I ascribed to the words I saw the meanings which I had hitherto associated with them but when, after several vain attempts, I discovered that that approach yielded little or no understanding of sentences, paragraphs or even entire pages, I turned to the dictionary for other definitions, only to find that what I really had to do was to learn a new language, that of the student writer. This, I found, was a slow and difficult process, but a rewarding one, for a new world seemed to be opening up to me. So I rejoiced and was exceeding glad that I had persevered and was able to enjoy the fruits of my labor and could look forward to reaping a rich harvest from the nineteen literary gems that lay unread before me.

"Alas, my joy and my presumptuous pride were short lived; a glance, followed by measured scrutiny, revealed that the second writer had invoked a language that bore little resemblance to that with which I had struggled so valiantly in my first effort to fathom the thoughts of a Northwood candidate for the degree, and I was left stranded as it were in a strange land completely without compass or guide. Knowing that this morning's occasion was moving nearer and nearer with unwonted speed, I decided to survey the situation, as my four year old daughter of some years ago phrased it. Should I try to master this second new language, or were there so many languages hidden in those deceptively slender volumes that to master them all would be far beyond my meager intellectual capacities?

"Your guess is correct; my survey disclosed that to really comprehend what the Northwood sages had written I would have to master at least ten new and thoroughly unfamiliar languages. So with the clock ticking loudly in my ears, I reverted to the practices of my boyhood years on the farm and slowly plowed the fields of erudition furrow by furrow, sliding as best I could around the boulders and the trees that were too big to move.

"Despite my limitations and inadequacies of comprehension, I was amply rewarded for my efforts."

THE SPRING SEMESTER

The searching of which I spoke in connection with Greatwood Senior Studies seems to have pervaded the atmosphere of the campuses this spring, judging from the reports received at the end of June from members of the faculty.

During the spring it became clear that we had to make a choice: be more restrictive about admissions to the Adult Degree Program, or enroll a larger number. We decided to set up a third group, with resident periods in early July and January. The enrollment expectation for the summer is 290 students, approximately 40 in early July, 120 in late July, and 130 in August. Because of the anticipated increase, we are adding five new persons to the Goddard faculty, above the normal replacement appointments.

Dean Ernest Cassara commented on the Greatwood Campus climate in this way:

> Midway through the spring semester of this academic year, the Greatwood faculty undertook a radical re-examination of the whole Greatwood program. In order that the spadework be accomplished for this re-examination, it appointed an "Ad Hoc Committee on the Quality of Life at Greatwood." It was felt by the faculty that a conscious effort should be made to create a greater variety in our program – variety, it was felt, which could only be made available by conscious effort to build it into the program of the campus. The faculty observed that it has seen, time and again, efforts such as the establishment of a newspaper come to naught because the individual student or students embarking on the venture failed to find the support which was necessary to sustain it. In other cases, activities of various kinds which would be available with some small measure of planning were lacking because of the failure of faculty and students to bring them about.

> Complicating the situation on the Greatwood campus was the most recent example of breakdown of community government. A small measure of comfort was gained by the Deans and other members of the faculty when they learned at the spring meeting of the Vermont Student Personnel Association that about a dozen of our sister-colleges in the State had undergone the same kind of disruption of student government activities. This added to the conviction of the "Ad Hoc Committee on the Quality of Life at Greatwood" that new forms must be found in order to facilitate conditions for a more pleasant, viable living situation. During the last part of the semester, the Ad Hoc Committee met a full evening weekly and brought its thinking to the faculty for examination, discussion, and refinement. Although the task is far from complete, already there is emerging from these discussions a pattern of re-organization which the Greatwood faculty hopes will sustain many new forms of activity on the campus and improve the morale of the students.

> . . . . It seems clear to me that the addition of Scott Ball as Dean of Residences was a step forward in our program. He was able to become very well acquainted with the students in their everyday living situations and was available to help them in various circumstances. I am convinced that the success or failure of many of the new forms Greatwood will be experimenting with in the months ahead will be due to the intimate knowledge which the Dean of Residences is in a position to share. During this semester, it was obvious that many students found him to be

a respected and trusted confidant and many faculty members and counsellors turned to him to help them in the solution of problems which arose in the various houses.

The second semester on Northwood was "not a tranquil one" in Dean Alan Walker's view. He reports that:

Early in April, a student group proposed a plan to boycott or otherwise refuse to cooperate with the procedures suggested by the faculty members of the presidential nominating committee to ensure student involvement in the selection process, unless they were given equal voting rights on the committee. The matter came to a head with a letter from an ad hoc student committee to members of the Board of Trustees which was responded to by the chairman of the presidential nominating committee suggesting a procedure for joint consultation. The suggestion was accepted and three students were selected in a meeting of students from both campuses to sit with the committee.

Regular meetings of the Educational Policies Committee attended by students and several faculty members, discussions prompted by the idea of initiating the third campus and by George Beecher's grouping of ideas for a positive environment, as well as the ferment of the presidential choice controversy, sparked a variety of proposals for greater student involvement in educational planning, involvement in decisionmaking, and modification of existing structures. Ideas for an off-campus group study and living experiment under Lou Irwin and proposals for starting a new college to test the ideas of self-directed study in a small community, communal setting culminated in a proposal from eighteen of the present Northwood students to rent a farm and run an experimental program for themselves. The faculty have agreed to consider evaluating the experience for equivalency to a semester in residence upon request.

The most engrossing project of the community was construction of a log cabin in the woods several hundred yards behind F building. Following a work day when logs were cut and hauled to the site, regular work program crews and other volunteer groups debarked logs, erected the frame and closed it in, raised the rafters, built the floor, set in windows, and sodded the roof. This was a project which engaged both faculty and students and absorbed many hours of manpower. Only a few details remain to be completed before the cabin is ready for use.

A large number of students have requested a chance to study abroad or work away from the college next fall. Approximately twenty besides the members of the non-resident group have asked to go overseas or to another institution in this country, but wish to return for the last year or two before the degree.

The chief production of the Goddard Players this semester was Twelfth Night, under the direction of Paul Vela. All but one of the members of the cast and stage crew were Northwood students. The play combined traditional and modern elements in an intriguing fashion and was well-received by the audiences.

Charles Zerby as Dean of Residences had a difficult, but useful, semester establishing a way of working with students toward better living conditions and more active participation in community affairs. In a parallel development, the Northwood community government was formally dissolved at the end of the semester and replaced with a bi-weekly business meeting, presided over by the moderator originally chosen as head of community government.

. . . . Spurred by the recognition of need for more understanding of the dynamics of small groups and of themselves, several faculty members took advantage of the opportunity to participate in encounter groups organized by the college during the month of June.

Northwood ended the semester, in my opinion, in a state of involvement but uncertainty as to future directions. One area of consensus among students opting out of "the system" in various ways and of others – both students and faculty – seeking to study and plan on campus for the future appears to be that change is inevitable. If new and feasible ways of operation can be found in the present situation, we will be justified in saying that we have discovered opportunity in the presence of danger, the Chinese definition of crisis.

One of the most exciting and rewarding programs which the College has undertaken is what we have called the Goddard Experimental Program in Further Education. This project, which was started last September under a contract with Educational Projects, Incorporated and funded by the Office of Economic Opportunity, was designed for persons working in a variety of jobs in Head Start Centers in New Hampshire and Vermont. Mrs. Anita Landa who directed it was assisted by Mrs. Joanne Chickering and Goddard graduates James Roos, formerly director of the Central Vermont Community Action Program, and Alumni Secretary Diane Reeves. Mrs. Landa says in her end-of-semester report:

(1) Thirty of the thirty-four students in the program have done satisfactory college work.

(2) Of the nine students in the program who had not finished high school, five took their High School Equivalency Exams and obtained their GED's. (Two more will be taking the exams during June and should score successfully.)

(3) Two students have been given more responsible (and better paying) jobs in Head Start. Two more are being considered for promotions. (Their participation in the Further Education Program has been at least a factor in these situations.)

(4) One of the Community Action Programs from which we have students has given employees in the Program time off during working

hours for both class attendance and independent study.

(5) Students agree overwhelmingly that residence at the College is a valuable learning experience and worth making personal sacrifices. (Their vote against on-site classes is 2 1/2 -1.)

(6) The program doubled in size the second semester, the attrition rate was about 20% both semesters, and we are serving only a third of the eligible Head Start staff. A little over half (55%) of the students plan to continue in the program, 12% definitely are not coming back and the rest are undecided.

(7) 100% of our students are women.

The special character of the program is to some extent revealed in these sections of her report:

The primary question for all of us involved in the Further Education Program was, Can our students do college work? Is this the appropriate place for them? The next question was, Under what conditions?

After a year, we have some answers. To begin with, highly motivated adults with limited academic backgrounds who are engaged in socially meaningful work can – and do – succeed at college work. The conditions necessary for success, however, are different from the conditions found in most colleges, and even somewhat different from the conditions under which other adult students operate at Goddard. Speaking to the conditions of physical, cultural, and intellectual isolation which exist in rural Vermont and New Hampshire, the college designed a program which combined residence at the college with independent study at home. However, the resident periods were closer together and shorter than the pattern established for Adult Degree Program students. Our program involved approximately a weekend of residence per month. We found that students needed financial and practical help with making arrangements to come for weekends. We found they needed support in getting their families to accept their going to college. Many husbands objected to their wives being away over night: "You expect me to feed breakfast to five children?" Husbands were also threatened in other ways. What would happen when their wives became more educated than they? What would their wives think of them after they'd been exposed to more cultivated and sophisticated people? Funds, counseling, inviting families to join in some activities at the college were solutions to these problems, but we found new problems.

Students needed to pass their High School Equivalency Exams before they could receive credit for college work and before they could feel they were *really* in college. We encouraged them to take their exams, helping them prepare in subjects which they felt were doubtful, but mostly offering support and boosting confidence. One by one, they took the exams and passed them satisfactorily. We have four students who have not yet taken their exams, but they are scheduled to do so before autumn and we feel sure they'll do well.

That was a fairly simple problem compared to the real academic difficulties which the students faced. They were largely unaccustomed to reading. Their reading speed was low, their vocabularies limited, they were unfamiliar with the kinds of books college students read, as they were with libraries. In response, we offered the reading machine (Craig Reader) in the LAC to pick up reading speed. We let, even encouraged, students to read difficult books, giving them a lot of time and a lot of help. They began to use dictionaries, dictionaries of technical terms, resource books and periodicals. They began developing research skills and technical vocabularies. The library staff was patient and helpful, the teaching staff was patient and hopeful. (It took one student 6 weeks to read Erikson's *Childhood and Society*, but she ultimately understood it, and the next book went a little faster.)

Writing was, and still is, a problem. If students were unaccustomed to reading, they were even more unused to writing. They were asked to keep working journals to help them get into the habit of writing something – anything – daily. Some students, who were terrified by the idea of writing a paper, found they could write letters to their study supervisors about their readings or could write down questions which certain readings had raised for them. We were careful not to ask students to write anything which didn't have meaning for them and we tried to be realistic about the quality of writing without being discouragingly critical. In response, students began to write more, the writing improved. During the second semester, we helped students organize their thoughts into more formal presentations, and papers, reports, case studies began to look at least like presentable beginning college work. There is still a good deal of distance between form and content. The students think and talk better than they write, and we will encourage them to write more, and more carefully, next year. But we feel this takes time: had we insisted immediately on the development of acceptable writing ability, we would probably have lost the interest of many students and the physical presence of others.

There were many more problems. Students kept feeling they weren't doing well enough, they would never do well enough, and they might as well quit right now. This usually happened when a student was doing particularly well, but beginning to realize what along way was left to travel (education lights up the darkness a little), and we had to offer a great deal of support to keep such students from dropping out. We also had to speak to extremely severe personal and financial problems. I hesitate to make generalizations, as I realize that all people at all socioeconomic levels have problems, but it seemed to me that our students have more chronic problems and fewer resources for dealing with them than those of us with more education and larger incomes. I mentioned earlier the resentments and uncertainties of husbands as problematic, but the lack of husbands was also a major problem. Many of our students were bringing up children alone, they suffered from too much responsibility, too little money, lack of support, loneliness, frustration. Any additional problem thrown into the context of these conditions was often enough to upset a student so that she could do neither her job nor her school work decently. These situations were chronic. Other problems were more dramatic – the sudden operation, the desertion, the close relative in jail. We tried to help students deal with these situations, again buy offering counseling and support, sometimes by finding agencies which could offer practical assistance. (We found that psychiatric services are particularly scanty in this part of the country.)

At first, we were baffled and a little resentful of having to deal with so many situations which were clearly outside our province as teachers. Then it became clear that we could not fulfill our function as teachers unless these situations were dealt with, so we had no choice. I think that as our participants become established in their roles as students, life problems will interfere less with their studies. It is also possible that the skills they learn here will help them solve some of these problems, avoid others.

What are the skills which have been learned this year? Reading and writing, as I have mentioned, and some research skills. Talking in groups, organizing activities. Most students have learned a lot about education, teaching and psychology. (A great many of the independent studies undertaken were in these areas and we were able to observe improvement in the students' actual teaching skills in their Head Start Centers. We were also impressed with the results of an exercise with which we closed the academic year. The problem, on which students worked in small groups, was to design, equip, staff, plan an ideal Head Start Center. The four centers which emerged were well worth implementing: the plans were sophisticated, thorough, imaginative, beautiful.) The students have gained enormously in their awareness of social problems, their feelings of competence to deal with these problems, their feelings of competence altogether.* Mostly, they have gained in confidence, in feeling that they can, in fact, influence their surroundings, determine at least some of the conditions of their lives. It is this last which is of greatest interest.

The residential weekends were designed as times during which students could meet with their supervisors to plan and evaluate independent studies; meet in groups to discuss common concerns and interests; participate in workshops; interact with outside speakers or watch films. All these things did, in fact, happen during residential weekends, plus many more activities which the students themselves requested and

*Some of these assertions are based on data collected from questionnaires designed to measure attitudinal change; others on evidence such as student papers, interviews and evaluations.

many of which they planned and carried out. But what *really* happened is that students began to plan and execute all aspects of their own education. The staff (four of us) found ourselves taking a less and less active role in the learning activities of students. As individuals and as a group, they began to identify their own needs and find ways to meet these.

The ability to determine the course – style and content – of their own education seems to have carried over to other aspects of the students' lives. They feel more secure about their ability to earn a living, less frightened of losing their jobs, more confident they could find new jobs. They feel less hopelessly poor themselves and more able to help others, whom they now perceive as poor. They feel less politically impotent and more able to influence affairs on a community level. They feel less helpless in relation to the education of their children, more able to face and reform the school systems in their towns. In short, for better or worse, they have taken on the attitudes, the stance, of the middle class.

Community Service Agent Rosemary Rexford, though seriously hampered by a tiny budget, says:

The Cooperative Community Service Agency, which is supported by a grant under Title I of the Higher Education act of 1965, continues its work with community problems on several levels.

The Agency has worked with the community aide employed by the University of Vermont Extension Service to work with low-income people, in setting up a family problem-solving group meeting at Goddard. A professional counselor was found who would donate his time, and while the group is very small, we anticipated that it will resume successfully in the fall.

As a result of an Environmental Planning Conference held for Title I project directors and other people engaged in promoting a quality environment, Beverly Cassara, Director of Adult Education, arranged a group meeting at Goddard of the Vermont persons interested in this subject. The importance of starting programs of environmental awareness among communities and trying to encourage schools to inculcate this awareness in elementary and secondary schools was strongly emphasized.

CCS has the support of the Central Vermont Regional Planning Council in a plan to start a Community Voice Institute, which would be a series of twelve meetings at which town planners, organization members, town officials and others would meet to discuss and receive factual information about problems in the orderly development of their communities.

The Director called on the Governor with the Director of one of the OEO programs involving the training of low-income people, in an effort to encourage the exploitation of State sources for funding these programs when Federal funds are not available.

Individual contact and group work, using the resources of the college whenever and wherever possible, is the main concern of this agency.

Priscilla Backman, Director of the Non-Resident Work Term, furnishes interesting information about students during the non-resident work term. Here are some items to be noted:

The number. . . 23 (11 Northwood and 12 Greatwood) who worked at other colleges; Brandeis, Yale, University of Mass., New York University, Friends World Institute, Harvard – as library assistants, office workers, bookstore employees, cafeteria workers, research assistants.

13% held a job they had previously held.

10% wanted to do their own thing: reading, writing, thinking, going to museums and theaters, preparing for their thesis, supporting themselves by making candles or jewelry, etc.

While 'friends' were still the prime source of jobs, by far, the w-t office moved up to more or less equal terms with 'family' and 'pavement pounding.'

New York, Boston, and Goddard are still sites for the main concentrations of w-t students. San Francisco fell off drastically. New Haven which drew six students this year may be a small but rising planet on the horizon.

Two groups of students went out of the country. One went to Mexico as part of the Spanish Comparative Cultures Class. This group was plagued by the lack of responsible preparations on the part of the man in Mexico supposedly doing this for the college. Once there, and past the first shock of finding that there were no jobs, no living arrangements awaiting them, most of the students set out to make their own way and to immerse themselves, as best they could in Mexican life. Most of them seemed to find it a very challenging and exciting and rewarding experience.

The other group went to Jamaica. Some previous arrangements were made by a Greatwood Jamaican student. Experiences and reactions and length of stay varied somewhat among this group. Some had a very fine and even beautiful experience. Others did not, and left very shortly. Probably one of the big lessons from this experience is the difficulty of experiencing a country and the people of the country through elements of what might be called the ruling class or through other outsiders.

It is interesting to note the small but steady number of students who find the NRT a chance to relate to their parents in a new, more independent and autonomous role. These students are going through an important experience, no doubt, of defining themselves more clearly, and so being more free to love and be loved.

So indeed does the NRT serve many important purposes.

SOME ROUGH STATISTICS –
BASED ON THE 320 REPORTS RECEIVED BY MID-SEMESTER

Job Sources

friends	33%	agency	5%
work term office	17%	Goddard	3%
family	14%	newspaper	3%
previous job	13%	pavement pounding	15%

Location   # Of Students:

NYC	68	N.Y.	15	N.J.	7
Boston	40	Mass.	27	Wisc.	2
Goddard	19	Vt.	18	Ore.	2
Philadelphia	11	Penn.	4	Missouri	2
San Francisco	8	Calif.	9	Hawaii	2
New Haven	6	Conn.	18	Canada	3
Washington, D.C.	3	Ohio	4	N.H.	3
Chicago	2	Fla.	11	Mich.	2
Baltimore	2	Md.	2	1 each – Del., Iowa, Idaho, N.M., Ariz., P.R., V. Is., Germany, Israel.	

Living at home – 118 students
Lived away from home – 174 students

Kinds of Jobs

office	60 – 18%	general sales	11 – 9%	Peace work	2
teaching	32 – 10%	bk. store sales	19 – 9%	architecture	1
hospital	26 – 8%	child care	9	psychological counselling	4
(incl. mental	19)	dance	2		
library	17 – 5%	personnel	2	maid	2
research	15 – 5%	P.B.X.	2	switch board	2
factory	13 – 4%	theatre	3	computer Prog.	1
laborer	11	photography	6	modeling	1
waiter/ess	13	T.V.	3	phone campaign	1
ed. &		clerical ass't.	2	house painting	2
M.R.	13			jewelry making	2
				art shop	2
				misc.	2

Student Objectives

job of particular kind	25%
primarily to earn money	20%
live in certain area	15%
"interesting, useful"	10%
be independent	10%
fulfill W-T obligation	8%
live at home	2%
do own thing, reading, writing, thinking,	
go to museums, theatre	10%

Achieved Objectives

yes 75%, no 14%
Partly 12, W-T was connected with career goals – 33%

Earnings

volunteer – 32 students – 10%
pay – average about $65-$70.

———————

From its beginning as a college Goddard has used the conference as an educational form or institution for adults, and this year was no exception. Nine conferences attended by a total of 295 non-Goddard persons were planned and conducted under the direction of Beverly Cassara, Director of Adult Education. In addition 5 conferences of an educational nature but not planned by Goddard staff were held on the campuses with total attendance of 451. An additional 36 non-Goddard persons attended the winter Fortnightly Evenings and 8 men took an 8 week course in Psychology for Supervision. In early June a sensitivity training (or basic encounter) group was conducted by psychologist Ruth Cohn with 11 non-Goddard participants. In the last half of the month Albert Lopez-Escobar had a Family Science Institute underway with 16 non-Goddard attendants. Thus there were at least 817 persons who came to the campus to take part in educational functions other than regular courses, Adult Degree Program and the Experiment in Further Education.

New Directions

There are now four persons who devote their major energies to directing adult activities throughout the year, in contrast with one person in 1948. These are Beverly Cassara, Director of Adult Education; Will Hamlin, Dean of the Adult Degree Program; Anita Landa, Director of the Experimental Program in Further Education; and Rosemary Rexford, Community Service Agent. The latter two programs are financed by federal funds, the former are supported by tuition charges and conference fees. Three full-time staff secretaries are engaged in this work. In addition, the Arts Center employs six Goddard faculty members and six non-Goddard persons on its faculty for the two summer months. We were recently invited to propose an educational program for the New Careers Program of the Champlain Valley Community Action Council, which would involve a year-round operation with a full-time director and two part-time instructors.

To encourage students to get involved in adult responsibilities off the campus as part of their study programs, a full-time Field Services Director – Adolf Unger – was employed this year. As a result, about eighty of our students found educational opportunities in voluntary jobs in nearby Vermont communities. This aspect of Goddard's program, which was emphasized in the launching of the Experiment in College Curriculum Organization in the fall of 1959, may be regarded as a move toward an adult college – one in which students assume that part of their college experience is to participated in the adult world around them.

Throughout the spring the faculty group known as the Committee on Research and Experimentation continued to meet weekly at lunch to discuss possible areas for experimentation. At the end of the semester George Beecher, Director of Educational Experimentation, drew up an Outline for a Positive Environment, proposing a new approach to the undergraduate program of the College. This was presented by him to the campus faculties for further discussion. His proposal which follows points in new directions for higher education and deserves serious consideration.

OUTLINE FOR A POSITIVE ENVIRONMENT

1) Start the first year student off with chance to find out what college can be a) apart from negative campus culture through rescheduling our various student and adult groups, and b) expecting internal selection and self-selection process to guide his decision at end of first year – toward a work-term year, toward a work-study year, toward a non-resident year, toward a continuing education plan over a number of years on ADP model, or in a minority of cases toward a second campus year in full knowledge of the commitment needed, c) using the short-term study as means of finding many concepts, skills, and problems which are not in the usual high school and college course categories, of working with many more of the faculty, and of knowing how to plan, carry out, and evaluate a clear contract over a visible 5 week period, and d) keeping a student record that shows the contracts completed – not the evaluations, doubts, or incompleteness.

2) The second year is mainly a non-resident plan with various options for study and work, possibly in social and educational agencies, volunteer corps, and apprenticeship jobs. The decision for a third year comes from finding out in action what a college education can mean and from evaluating the active experience.

3) The third and fourth years could have strongly self-selected students presumably of an age or maturity to value more intensive studies and in-

dependent work – possibly with shorter campus terms than now, but doubt-less with local off-campus responsibilities. (Much reduced 3rd and 4th year groups would presumably be balanced by much larger incoming 1st year groups.)

4) Commitment to a third year gives membership in the college as a "cor-poration." Members include 3rd-4th year students, adult students, ADP students, alumni, and faculty. An annual college meeting is held to review re-ports and studies of curriculum, experimental programs, and general policies.

5) Work program concept is enlarged for all the above membership to take responsibility for volunteer support of varied quotas of students unable to at-tend college without help. A clear social goal and accounting can generate positive feelings through work and economics at the college, inventive use of and discovery of new resources, fund raising, and other efforts.

A positive environment tends to have an impact on negative response de-riving from personal and social problems at college. It helps in distinguishing soluble problems from those that under present circumstances appear insoluble and perhaps are.

A proposal for a special educational program for low-income and educa-tionally disadvantaged black students and others was discussed and submitted to two foundations.

About the middle of the semester Assistant to the President Evalyn Bates suggested that members of the faculty be given an opportunity to participate in a sensitivity training group the week following Commencement. The fa-culty response was so good that she made arrangements with Goodwin Wat-son, a widely known and highly regarded psychologist, to conduct the ses-sions as a part of his duties as a staff member of the Union for Research and Experimentation in Higher Education. Reports from among the 15 par-ticipants indicate that it was a very effective and helpful affair.

Using the findings of the Study of Needs of Older Americans in Five Towns of the Upper Winooski Valley, which the College conducted in the spring of 1967, as supporting evidence, the Trustees of the very small Jaquith Public Library in Marshfield developed a proposal for a Center for Older Americans. The proposal was given to Vermont's Inter-Departmental Coun-cil on the Aging with a request for a grant to help support part-time centers in Marshfield and Plainfield. A grant of about $4,000 has been authorized, thus enabling the Marshfield Library and the Plainfield Grange to use their build-ings as social and information centers. Not all studies of this sort lead to ac-tion programs but this one did and thereby added to the value of Duane Wells' senior study which he completed last summer, after having invested over 500 hours and 1500 miles of travel as one of the interviewers in the Study.

Rosemary Rexford, Goddard's Community Service Agent, will assist in de-veloping and coordinating activities for the centers. It is hoped that some

Goddard students will participate in this new venture for the elderly which is apparently the first plan to be tried for a thinly populated rural area.

Staff Changes

Persons retiring from the College staff this year include: from food services, Mrs. Loretta Copping, who has served as cook since September 1959; from the maintenance staff, Joseph Bean and Herbert Neill, who came to Goddard in April and December 1947; from the Greatwood Faculty, Joseph Fulop, who came in 1957, and Thomas Yahkub, who joined the faculty in 1946.

Joe Fulop and Tom Yahkub continue their association with the College for another year on a part-time basis, the former on the Northwood Faculty, and the latter as the first faculty member to be employed solely for the Adult Degree Program. This happy arrangement makes it possible for the College to continue to benefit from the wisdom and skills of these able and dedicated teachers who have given generously of their lives and talents to Goddard.

Diane Reeves leaves her position as Alumni Secretary and part-time teacher in the Further Education Program to study at Claremont Graduate School.

Leaves of absence have been granted to Ernest Boaten, who will continue to teach in the Adult Degree Program but will study during the fall and spring semesters; Robert Mattuck, to devote full-time as consultant for the Committee on Research and Development, for the Council for the Advancement of Small Colleges; William Reeves, to undertake studies in Education at Claremont Graduate School; and Thomas Yamamoto, to travel and paint. Sabbatical leaves are being taken by Evelyn Bates and William Osgood. The latter plans to spend the year in Finland, the former to study at Claremont Graduate School and the Esalen Institute in California.

Peter and Marja-Liisa Hart who brought to the College sparkle and youthful enthusiasm as well as competence and special knowledge as teachers, complete this year as visiting teachers and return to their home in Finland in the summer. Jakob Amstutz, George Ball, Orus Barker, Francis Fay and Florence Ludy are leaving the faculty for other positions or further study.

New appointments to date include the following:

To the Greatwood Faculty:

  Thomas D. Absher, candidate for Ph.D. at University of Pennsylvania, in literature

  Carla Thomas, teaching assistant in philosophy at State University of New York at Buffalo, replacement for Jakob Amstutz

  John R. Turner, candidate for Ph.D. at University of Virginia, in history

  Irwin Tuttie, artist from Waitsfield, Vermont, replacement for Joseph Fulop

  Chin Sei Yu, candidate for Ph.D. from Temple University, in Asian

Studies, to replace Thomas Yahkub

To the Northwood Faculty:

Stuart P. Adler, candidate for Ed.D. at Boston University, in education, as replacement for Francis Fay

Robert Jervis, Emory and Henry University, Virginia, in the biological sciences

George Moseley, candidate for doctorate, St. Antony's College, Oxford University in Oriental studies

Paul S. Nelson, Jr., Franconia College, New Hampshire, in literature

Donald E. Polkinghorne, candidate for M.A., Hartford Seminary Foundation, Connecticut, as replacement for Orus Barker in philosophy and religion

Lin Webster, assistant professor of history, State University of New York at Cortland, as replacement for Ernest Boaten

DECADE BY DECADE

It seems incredible that thirty years have passed since that rainy July day when some of the furniture and equipment of Goddard Seminary and Junior College in Barre was transferred to Greatwood Farm in Plainfield. The administration, consisting of three persons, settled into the one-time creamery, now known as the Clock House. During the first year there were 49 students enrolled in the College, 257 persons attended winter conferences, and 54 young persons were on the campus in the summer of 1939, for a total of 350 persons served in an educational capacity by the College in its first year. Our new building program started that year, accompanied by considerable remodelling of farm buildings for college purposes, with the construction of the Flynn Building, the brick structure built to connect with the greenhouse to house an herbarium and to serve as a science building. A single contribution of $10,000 from John Flynn of Burlington as a memorial to his wife, Nellie Flynn, covered the construction cost.

In June 1948, I reported to the Board of Trustees that more than 550 persons had availed themselves of educational opportunities at Goddard during the year 1947-48, including regular students and attendants at winter construction and summer programs. In that year another major building reconstruction occurred when the haybarn and cowbarn were converted to a Community Center, providing a new dining room and kitchen, music rooms, and offices. The staff of 17 ten years earlier had grown to 38 in 1948. A Director of Adult Education was appointed in March 1948 to direct the rapidly expanding adult activities. From a deficit of $235.56 reported by the Treasurer at the first Annual Meeting, the College had moved to an operating gain of $15,723.71 at the end of its tenth year. Gifts in 1938-39 totalled $7,640; in 1947-48 the total was $14,226. By then we were using twelve buildings, compared with the four of the first year; and we had connected with the Plainfield Village water system at a cost of $406.99! In the fall of 1948 we applied for membership in the New England Association of College and Secondary Schools, but were not accepted primarily because of the experimental character of the College.

Ten years later, in June 1958, gifts and grants for the year totalled $202,929, but operating income and expense were out of balance to the extent of a deficit of $32,745. Total student enrollment for that year was 92, winter conference attendance totalled 216, and summer program enrollment was 107, making the total number of persons during the year 415. The College had developed several experimental programs, financed by foundation grants, including the Comparative Cultures Program, the Educational Resources Project, Vermont Community Development Program, the Program for the Improvement of Teaching through application of Research Findings in the Behavioral Sciences. In the fall of 1957, we made our second unsuccessful effort to join the New England Association. Despite financial difficulties and decreased enrollment after the veteran peak years of 1946-51, the College was actually in a much sounder and more promising, but not more hopeful, position than in earlier years, for hopefulness was a sustaining and persistent characteristic of the College.

The third decade, 1958 to 1968, has seen the fulfillment of many of our earlier hopes and expectations as well as the realization of some newer ideas and the evolution of new dreams. Plagued with limited financial resources throughout the three decades, we nevertheless have made considerable progress in the last ten years in the improvement of physical facilities and faculty and staff salaries. Meanwhile the cost to the regular undergraduate student has risen from $1000 in 1938-39 to $3600 in 1968-69. In 1957-58 the starting faculty salary for a person with no experience was $3,000, for one with a Bachelors degree, $3,300 for one with a Master's degree, and $3,900 for one with the doctorate. The annual increment was $200. For 1968-69 the comparable schedule is $5,800, $6,400, and $7,200 respectively; with an annual increment of $700.

By 1959 experimentation had attained considerable respectability even among conventional colleges and so Goddard was given accreditation that fall by the New England Association of Colleges and Secondary Schools. The Village for Learning was started in 1961 with the construction of Pratt House, a fourteen-student residence; this was followed by the building of eleven residences in 1962-63 with federal government loans to bring the Village's housing capacity to 196. In 1963 the Adult Degree Program was inaugurated; in 1965 the atom split and Goddard became a multi-campus college, with Northwood and Greatwood as the first two of three or more campus units of approximately 260 regular students. The "invisible third campus," the Adult Degree Program, in the summer of 1968 will have a larger enrollment than either Northwood or Greatwood, and the total number of adult students, enrolled for study in the regular program, the Experiment in Further Education, and the Arts Center will be greater than the total number of regular undergraduates on the two campuses. Recently it has been proposed that Goddard become an adult college – when actually we were moving in that direction with many members of the community being quite unaware of it.

This year has seen another major development in physical plant with an addition to the Studies Building on Greatwood Campus to provide badly needed space for maintenance and for housing the fire truck, the beginning of construction of a temporary community center containing a dining room and kitchen for Northwood Campus, and the signing of the contract for construction of the Eliot D. Pratt Library-Learning Aids Center. Under Harold Townsend's direction, who has given generously of his time, the Upper Garden House has undergone extensive repairs and will soon be ready for much more extensive use, especially by Bedrich Vaska's cellists in the Arts Center.

THE FOURTH DECADE

So much of our thinking about the College of the future is colored by the forms of the College of the past that it is extremely difficult to develop models that will meet the needs of the period of Goddard's fourth decade.

If we were to design an institution to provide suitable educational opportunities for young and old adults, it seems fairly certain that it would be quite unlike the conventional college because we would take into account the educational institutions that have come into existence since the liberal arts college was invented. These include the modern business corporation, the automobile, the jet airplane, television, radio, the movies, trade unions, nuclear warfare, the computer, paid vacations and the multiplicity of government and private programs for training in a wide variety of vocations.

Just what kind of an institution should the college of the 1970's be? I do not know but I believe it should provide educational opportunities not only for those who are now regarded as of the usual college age, that is from seventeen to twenty three, but also for those above those years. Moreover the students should include persons from all economic levels, those whose prior school experience was not satisfactory and those who have attended excellent schools, those who have been handicapped because of poverty, discrimination or neglect and those who have been highly favored by circumstance, those who come from the large cities and those who come from the suburbs and the rural communities, those who want a degree and those who already have or do not want one, and those whose planned period of study is four years and those who come for a few days or weeks.

Obviously no single program would be appropriate for such disparate groups and individuals and even students in their late teens and early twenties cannot be fitted into a single pattern of college life. The need for variety in approach, style and ethos seems likely to increase rather than decrease.

Goddard's present programs are suggestive of what is to come. The regular undergraduates are involved in group courses, independent studies, tutorials, participation in overseas studies of languages and cultures through established organizations such as the Experiment in International Living, the Scandinavian Seminar and universities, in the New German program and the Field

Study Centers of the Union for Research and Experimentation in Higher Education, individually planned travel and study plans, and our Comparative Cultures programs; in off-campus field work as part of an on-campus study, a daily work program and the non-resident work term. The two regular undergraduate campuses now operate somewhat differently but both within the basic Goddard philosophy and thus partially meet the criterion of variety.

Earlier sections of this report have indicated something of the scope of our adult programs: conferences, training groups, Adult Degree Program, Arts Center, part-time adult students, and the Experiment in Further Education. If the sole measure were the number of persons involved during the past year, we would have to say that Goddard was more an adult College than one for those of conventional college age by a score of 908 to 534.

It strikes me that one of the inhibitors of change in college programs is buildings. A visit to the campuses of our more venerable institutions reveals a massive conglomerate of stone, brick and concrete that is symbolic of the resistance to change that characterizes their educational programs and practices. Once one of these expensive monuments has been erected the uses to which it can be put are severely limited because they are designed for very specific purposes – lectures, laboratories, offices – and reconstruction is costly. Fortunately the Greatwood Farm buildings though expensive for farm purposes were inexpensive for college purposes and were so constructed as to be remodeled rather easily as our needs changed. The Village for Learning and Northwood were planned to allow for a variety of uses and relative ease of conversion. Even the Eliot D. Pratt Library-Learning Aids Center, by far the most elaborate and costly structure planned for the College, could be converted to other purposes. Wherever possible the original investment in College buildings should be kept small enough to eliminate it as a major factor in re-construction or removal. And always they should be designed to serve several purposes.

The development of different campus styles is undoubtedly best encouraged by the creation of several semi-autonomous campuses, each with its own faculty and students and so Goddard's Fourth Decade will probably see the building of at least two new campuses one of which might be primarily for adult programs.

If recent trends are reasonably accurate indicators, the next decade will see an increasing percentage of regular college students taking a semester or a year away from the campus for study. This year there were fifteen Greatwood and eleven Northwood students who were studying elsewhere for a semester or more. Two were enrolled in the Scandinavian Seminar; two were in the Experiment in International Living – one living in Spain, the other India; four studied at the San Francisco Art Institute, one each was enrolled at Universities of Copenhagen, Grenoble, Helsinki, New Mexico, Columbia University, and Harvard University; one each was working at Juilliard School of Music, Neighborhood Playhouse in New York City, and the Training School at Brandon, Vermont (the student at Brandon also took some courses at the

College of St. Joseph the Provider in Rutland); five students were at the Union's Field Study Center in Kauai, Hawaii and two at the Union's Field Study Center in Pike County, Kentucky; and two were in residence at a religious international community in New Milford, New York.

When the proposal for the Experiment in College Curriculum Organization was submitted to the Ford Foundation in the winter of 1959 it was anticipated that eventually twenty per cent of the students would be studying or working away from the College at any one time. To reach that level it was assumed that many students would take advantage of the flexible calendar and take their non-resident work term at times when there were unusual opportunities for a highly desirable job rather than always in the winter. A few students have done just that but it appears that the flexible calendar has sometimes been used for less laudable reasons than the exploitation of a particular kind of job or the enhancement of educational opportunity. Even so, fewer than six per cent were engaged in non-resident study in the year 1967-68.

Serious problems arise when flexibility characterizes a college program. It demands of faculty and students more careful planning, a better grasp of the nature of education, much greater self-discipline, more rigor and greater firmness than is called for when programs are prescribed and somewhat rigid, otherwise the college experience degenerates into time wasting and mis-education. Unfortunately the graduate schools provide very little help to those who aspire to teach in the kind of college that Goddard should be in its Fourth Decade, consequently the college has to maintain a continuous and continuing effort to improve its teaching, that is the conditions for learning.

To make possible the flexibility and variety in its educational program that are indicated it will probably be necessary to make further changes in the calendar. Goddard has always operated twelve months of the year with most of its adult activities taking place in January, February, July and August while the regular undergraduates were away on their non-resident work term and summer vacation. If some of the proposals for shorter study terms that have been under consideration for the last five years were adopted and if the number and types of adult students continue to increase, the "academic" year might consist of six terms of two months each. Such a scheme would require some re-adjustments in managing the residences and food services as well as in arranging vacations and periods of employment for all members of the staff. Moreover, to insure reasonably efficient use of the college's physical facilities, especially student residences, careful planning by students and staff would be essential. The problems are likely to be difficult but the possibilities are intriguing.

Goddard enters the Fourth Decade as a going concern financially, but strong emphasis must be placed on *going*. As we suggested several years ago and as the late President William C. Fels of Bennington College pointed out in his report as Chairman of the Visiting Committee of the New England Association of Colleges and Secondary Schools Goddard's financial stability is the stability of the bicycle rider who must always keep pedaling.

The size of the annual operating budget – two million dollars – seems to convey to the superficial observer the notion that the College is affluent when in reality the margin between breaking even each year and having a deficit is distressingly thin. Perhaps this is the way it should be. Without a long portfolio of investments Goddard does not feel impelled to follow a conservative course, instead it is forced to operate with economy, emphasize support for the essentials, eschew luxuries, and maintain an everlasting search for new programs and a broader base.

The Auditor's Annual Report for 1967-68 shows an operating gain of $160,000 all of which had to be applied to capital outlay, a continuing cost for every college which in any sound plan for financing should be regarded as a part of the current cost of education and incorporated in the yearly budget.

Gifts and grants received during the year amounted to $241,000 of which $86,000 was from the United States Government for special programs. Nineteen Trustees and former Trustees contributed $83,000; 270 alumni $9,000 (this represents a large increase in number of donors as about 140 alumni turned their old breakage deposits over to the College); 42 parents of alumni and students $11,000; 4 staff members $745, of which one long-time member gave $625; 2 ADP students $375; business corporations $5,000; and 51 other friends $19,000. The gifts also include the deeding of seven hundredths interest in the Houghton Hall property in Portland, Ontario (on the Rideau Lakes) to Goddard by Mr. and Mrs. William Harry Houghton, thereby bringing the total undivided interest of the College in this valuable property to 71 per cent.

A special tribute to our Chairman, Eliot D. Pratt, was made by six of his friends and relatives by contributing $12,000 to the Library-Learning Aids Center Fund. These gifts were especially appropriate as they came in the year in which Eliot having completed 18 years as a member of the Board of Trustees and 15 years as Chairman was chosen as Goddard's first Chairman Emeritus.

On the occasion of celebrating the Twenty-fifth Anniversary of the College and the One Hundredth Anniversary of the founding of Goddard Seminary I tried to express my feelings about our gallant and generous Chairman in these words which I now reaffirm.

> Few men in America have devoted their lives to as many great and good causes as Eliot Pratt. Civil liberties, industrial democracy, a free and enlightened press, rights for sharecroppers, the arts, education, politics, farm prosperity, better housing, integration, mechanical inventions, and many more benefited by his concern. Farmer and lover of rural life, designer and maker of beautiful pottery, magazine publisher, partner in many business enterprises, he manages to find time for a host of interests. His belief in the nature of experimental education has been demonstrated over and over by the time, energy, and support he has given to Goddard and other schools. Like Lawrence Doolin and Hans

Froelicher, he has served as Chairman of the Board of Trustees, in which capacity his modesty, his integrity, and his gentleness have been manifested in abundance.

Though the Eliot D. Pratt House is the seventh on our list tonight, it was, as it should have been, the experimental or pilot structure on which the others were modeled, and was actually tested by use before the others were designed. It is highly gratifying to dedicate it in the name of one who has given so freely of himself and for whom so many have a deep affection.

Respectfully submitted,

Royce S. Pitkin
President

REPORT OF THE PRESIDENT OF
GODDARD COLLEGE

For the Period Ending June 30, 1969[60]

COMMENCEMENT

The thirty-first Commencement of the College and the one hundredth in the entire Goddard series, which includes those of the Seminary and the Junior College, was held under a tent on the lawn of Martin Manor on June 13th. The Commencement Committee resorted to the erection of a tent because the attendance at last year's ceremonies exceeded the capacity of the Haybarn Theatre and the graduates had indicated their preference for a joint assembly for the awarding of the degrees. The arrangement worked very well,

---

[60] One would have needed to run the June 30, 1969 President's Report in its entirety simply because it was Royce's last, but there are also other substantive reasons for doing so. Here we see an enormously important emphasis coming through as Royce contemplated the very real efforts the faculty, students, indeed the entire College, were making to handle the problems of the College culture.

The Research and Experimentation Committee, made up of 15 or so staffers from both campuses and five or six students also from both campuses, had made its appearance several semesters before. It was a study committee, with open membership from both campuses on both faculty and student levels, a central purpose of which was to generate ideas for future experiments on either or both campuses. Notice what this meant. It meant that an effort was being made to generalize Royce's role as source of new ideas for things to do, an element in the life of the College since its beginning the importance of which could not be over-estimated, so that the need for new experiments could be met, their conditions and possibilities discussed in accordance with good and useful custom, and results and arrangements recommended to the faculty and administration. Whether or not this Committee, this collective force, on the campuses was successful in practice over a period of years is a proper topic for research and study in future. Its history and role do greatly need to be studied. For the moment, the mere fact of its existence was profoundly significant. It meant that at this point, hard upon Royce's actual retirement, an immensely important step had been taken to carry on one of the most crucial roles which he had filled more or less by himself for so many years. It had also been done far enough ahead of his retirement so that group members could have some experience getting used to what they were supposed to do. (cont. p. 247)

246

the attendance of nearly five hundred justified the innovation, and the weather was propitious even though showers began later in the afternoon.

Of the 106 degrees conferred on undergraduates, 72 were on the recommendation of the Greatwood Faculty and 34 of the Northwood Faculty. Earlier in the year 67 degrees had been granted to graduates in the Adult Degree Program to make a total of 173 for the year. An additional Bachelor of Arts degree was awarded to me by Lois Weinstein Sontag as Chairman of the Board of Trustees in recognition of the completion of my work at the College. That the vote of the Goddard Faculty authorizing this action was kept a secret from me until Lois made the award was indeed a mysterious and remarkable achievement which made it all the more gratifying.

The 106 senior studies dealt with a very wide range of subjects, including projects in the performing arts, short stories, poetry, education, historical research, philosophy, psychology, mental health, social work, science, living in other cultures, and many other areas. A reading of the studies is sufficient to convince one that the typical Goddard graduate has engaged in extensive and serious study for a considerable part of his college years and that as a group the sixteens have had a lot of experience in the wider community – a community that reaches from Vermont to Africa, Europe and Asia. A list of the studies is to be found in Appendix A of this report. (omitted here. – Ed.)

GROWTH AND LEADERSHIP

Helen and I returned from my first sabbatical, which was generously allowed by the Board of Trustees and which enabled us to use the three months for travel in New Zealand, Australia and India, on April 22nd or just about the midpoint of the spring semester. Everything was under way – faculty meetings had been going on as usual, community meetings had continued in one form or another on each campus, the President's Council and the Committee on Research and Experimentation had met regularly, and the search for a new president had become even more intense. And senior studies had begun to accumulate in my office. It was quite clear that Assistant to the Pres-

---

(Note 60, continued)

Observe particularly in this last Report the section on "Growth and Leadership", and the review in its last paragraph of his original ideas for the eventual "creation of two or three more campuses" beyond the first two. It seems clear that we should lay to rest the theory that Royce ever gave up the plan for a third campus; he did not give it up. He would have been willing to postpone it for practical reasons, such as not having enough funds. But he speaks here of as many as five campuses before the testing of the idea of the multi-campus institution could be complete. On the whole, this conclusion alone is consistent with the figure of the Royce S. Pitkin whom we knew.

Remembering themes and lines of development which may have had a bearing on the evolution of Goddard over its first thirty years, one possible approach to a study of the later history of the College would be to investigate developments with respect to each theme and line in the periods following Royce's retirement. We do not propose to do this now. It would be better done by historians acquainted at first hand with later periods. Suffice it to present themes and lines as we see them, extending the study into the 1970s and beyond only as aspects are suggested by Tim's activities as a retired professional. It is his thought and practice that we have been after, rather than second-generation impacts, granted that those do have great interest of their own. There will follow here certain documents appearing in the files which bear on earlier and later periods, as may be helpful in expanding acquaintance with Royce's educational ideas, their origins, and their formation of College and consortial realizations.

ident Evalyn Bates, who had returned from her own half year sabbatical in February, had handled the role of Acting President in a highly competent and effective manner and the thing for me to do was to devote most of my time and energies to reading and assessing the senior studies. Although this was a rewarding and enlightening experience, it meant that I was unable to become as involved in campus life as I usually had been and so felt that I was something of a stranger in my own land.

Actually, the process of withdrawal from many campus activities began several years ago and was a direct result of the growth of the College. By 1964 it had become evident that if students and staff were to participate intelligently and in an educationally productive way in conducting the affairs of the college community, the College would either have to limit its size to what it was then or become a multi-campus institution. It had been clearly demonstrated that a group of three hundred was too large to permit genuine participation in community meetings by any substantial portion of students or staff. Hence the decision by the faculty and the Board of Trustees to develop at least three campuses, each with its own community government. This decision carried with it the necessity for re-examining the role of the president. With three campuses he simply could not attend all community meetings and faculty meetings on each campus, and to attempt to meet students and staff from all campuses in one big session would not only be impossible physically – there being no room large enough to accommodate more than one campus, it would be an educational farce. The kind of exhaustive, and often exhausting, discussion of issues and problems that had occurred in community meetings when the College was smaller would not be possible.

Moreover, if each campus was to function effectively as an educational community, the leadership had to reside in that community and be familiar with the problems and possibilities as they emerged day by day. This meant that the campus dean would have to be the educational leader of his campus and assume many of the responsibilities that had hitherto been mine. It also meant that most of the matters that had been discussed by the faculty with the president presiding and participating in the discussions would have to be handled in meetings of the separate campus faculties. It further meant that the president would have to exercise his leadership as a coordinator through occasional all-College faculty meetings, a few all-College committees with student representation such as the President's Council, the Committee on Research and Experimentation, and the Agenda Committee, and through conferences with individual students and staff members. Although I found this removal from face-to-face meetings and the kind of active involvement that has been possible earlier hard to take, it seemed then and seems now to have been the only proper course to follow. To have done otherwise would have minimized the authority and impeded the leadership of the deans and severely limited the autonomy of each campus faculty and community.

Adoption of the multi-campus idea implied developing forms of representative government. If the enrollment on each campus was limited to approximately 250 students, a substantial fraction of each campus community could participate actively and in many ways that had meaning for each person in managing the affairs of his campus. But the management of the affairs of the entire college, which had become extensive, required that means be devised for having each campus choose representatives to one or more central bodies. Only tentative schemes have been tried; this part of the multi-campus experiment has not been adequately developed and probably cannot be until the polarity that is inherent in a two campus setting is displaced by a small constellation that will follow the creation of two or three more campuses.

THE SEMESTER

Some of the activities of the semester have been reported to me by the Deans and other staff members as the excerpts that follow indicate. Most of the writers mention problems that pertain to their fields of operation, thereby making it clear that Goddard continues to suffer from growing pains and that its staff is not content to let things stay as they are. Because of the length of the reports I have tried to select those portions that describe what has transpired during the last six months.

Northwood Dean Alan Walker's account of the semester at Northwood says, "Northwood slept fairly quietly over the winter work term, as ADP students gathered on Greatwood and the regular undergraduates worked elsewhere. The Committee on Nomination of a President pressed forward its investigation of nominees with the intention of presenting a candidate at the March meeting of the Board. One nominee was found in February to be the first choice of the six trustees and faculty members of the committee, but the student members either abstained or voted negatively on the grounds that the chosen individual had not been seen on campus by regular students nor by faculty who were away during his visit in February.

"The first large event of the spring semester, then, was a community meeting in the Northwood dining room, attended also by many people from Greatwood, to hear a report from members of the nominating committee. The strong sense of the meeting was that the trustees should be urged to delay a decision and to re-open the investigation with the assistance of an expanded committee. The Board accepted the general terms of the 'Nelson Report,' involving the addition of one more student and faculty member from each campus. Northwood selected its two members, Mark Ryder and Gary Sugarman, and settled into a marathon of meeting with and discussing eight candidates. In the end, as is known, the first candidate of the expanded committee removed himself from consideration but the second, Jerry Witherspoon, proved acceptable to the Board and was named Goddard's second president as of July 1, 1969.

"A second incident, early in the semester, involved a protest over the closing of the switchboard at night due to excessive unauthorized calls the preceding semester. A group of Northwood students 'liberated' the switchboard, operating it for several nights after hours until arrangements were made for around-the-clock manning by student operators and closer control and supervision. Finally, a few students, two of whom later left college, 'decorated' a wall in the dining room. Later, another student volunteer, in collaboration with the Work Program, painted the wainscotting of the dining room.

"Student and faculty participation in policy-making and discussion of the future of the college continued to grow. The Northwood members of the Agenda Committee for All-College Faculty Meetings were Stuart Adler, Don Polkinghorne, and Norman Unrau. Student Kim Cunningham and faculty members Bob Brandstetter, Dale Anderson and Alan Walker served on the President's Advisory Council. Corinne Mattuck, Stuart Adler, and Alan Walker regularly attended the Committee on Research and Experimentation meetings. Norman Unrau and Corinne Mattuck were representatives from Northwood to the Admissions Committee. Paul Vela, Mark Ryder, Belmont Pitkin, and Alan Walker comprised the Committee on Faculty Appointments which cooperated closely with the Educational Policies Committee chaired by student Gary Sugarman. Stuart Adler and Paul Nelson were elected to an All-College Committee on Policy Making. Student Livia Bowditch and Alan Walker represented the campus in discussions on exchanges with Sir George Williams University. Corinne Mattuck, Donald Polkinghorne, Jack Elliott, Stuart Adler, Dale Anderson, and Alan Walker formed a committee on counseling. The latter two also participated in the spring meeting of the Vermont Student Personnel Association, which will hold its Fall meeting at Goddard. Students Cassie Bagshaw and Joe Barth, and faculty members Alan Walker, Donald Polkinghorne, and Dale Anderson were chosen to consider long-range planning in a post-semester session. Lin Webster, Mark Ryder, Don Polkinghorne, and Dale Anderson formed a committee to work with a large number of students on plans for pre-semester orientation in the fall. Mid-term Donald Nathan, Northwood Community Moderator, left school, leaving community government in the hands of the Vice Moderator, Bob Arsenault.

"Among other issues which engaged attention of the faculty as a whole during the semester were: criteria for readiness to enter the Senior Year; procedures for change of courses; possible changes in the annual calendar; plans for a new educational facilities building; the concept and values of residential education; the quality of campus life; what to do when many faculty are unhappy over the apparent progress of a student over several semesters yet unwilling to recommend that he terminate his community membership; the appropriate expectation for a final report on a senior study by students in the creative arts; cooperation with the Afro-American Society proposal for a special program for entering black students; our relation to the Action Group Experiment, headed by Ken Carter; and cross-visitation with the Greatwood Faculty.

"Faculty vacancies caused by the departure of Norman Unrau for more graduate work and of Ken Carter to work with the Action Group Experiment were filled by the selection of Eleanor Forster and Anthony Mayhew respectively. In addition, Scott Nielsen was added to the faculty in the areas of economics and social change.

"Courses and independent studies as usual occupied the major attention of the campus, particularly of graduating students and their committees. It is difficult to capture in a brief statement the scope and intensity of these activities. Perhaps a few representative course titles will suffice: Thoughts of Mao Tse-Tung; Javanese Gamelan; Existential Philosophy and Psychotherapy; How Can New Politics be Organized? The Hippie Culture; Natural Habitats of New England; Working in Small Groups; Acting Workshop; James Joyce; American Decorative Arts. Sixteen Northwood students graduated on June 13, representing the first complete four-year cycle for this campus, as well as the thirtieth and final commencement for Tim Pitkin, whose vision and leadership have made Goddard possible. As he leaves us, I hope that the core of his philosophy and spirit will continue to live and grow at Goddard in each succeeding cycle of faculty, students, and staff."

Greatwood   Dean Ernest Cassara reports this way: "This has been a year of re-evaluation for the College as a whole, in regard to the search for a new President, but also for Greatwood in a different context. While the College has been re-examining its goals, and means to achieve them, and has considered the virtues and failings of various candidates for the presidency who have been brought to converse with us, the Greatwood faculty has been involved in a prolonged and often heated discussion of evaluation and records procedures. A rabbi told me once that when you get two Jews together to discuss a problem you soon find that there are three opinions. If anything, the Greatwood faculty has improved on that situation. But despite the fact that various and diverse points of view were discussed at great and heated length during the process of this re-evaluation of our procedures, we were delighted to find that members of the faculty felt much more rapport with each other than has been true in the past. As one of the members said, "faculty meetings are fun." Near the close of the semester the faculty voted to abandon the "total semester concept" which has been in operation at Greatwood for a number of years and to break the student semester into various component parts. In other words, the faculty would now look at the various courses and work program that a student has engaged in during the semester. Where a student did not live up to the commitments he had made in a particular course at the beginning of the semester, then that course only would be judged to have been inadequate. Many of the faculty and student body over the last few years have come to view the "gaining" of a total semester as the price of inadequacy in one area as unfair and unjust.

"Although the Greatwood faculty voted the new approach to evaluations, at the request of Tim the new plan was not put into effect this semester. Also at his request, Tim was invited to meet with the faculty and to discuss the old total semester approach and the new plan. What was feared as a potential jousting match turned into a pleasant discussion at the conclusion of which the faculty decided not to implement the new plan but to continue its discussions and explorations for better ways of doing things in the fall semester.

"Both the faculty and the student body at Greatwood was much engaged in discussions of the future of the College and in examination of the potential presidential candidates as they appeared periodically on campus. One wag suggested that we continue the presidential search and substitute it for the performances brought to campus by the Arts, Concerts and Lectures Committee. Obviously, people were having so much fun choosing a new president, it seemed a shame to bring the process to a conclusion. As everyone is aware, for a while it seemed this humorous suggestion might become our modus operandi into the indeterminate future.

"Our retiring Dean of Residence, Richard Wright, and others have observe a new stability in the living situation on the campus as the result of the introduction of the Senior Residents as his assistants. A responsible and relatively mature student from the Senior Division is now assigned to each of the residential houses and acts as a student counselor to 13 students as they enter the College, helping them to adjust to the very different situation they find at Goddard. He also helps cope with the continuing problems all students have during the course of the semester. Senior Residents have met periodically with the Dean of Residences and have shared their views with him on ways to improve the quality of living at Greatwood.

"All was not Utopian, however. It seemed for a while that Greatwood might very well reach the end of the semester without the usual invasion of the constabulary of police seeking to incarcerate members of our student body involved in the drug traffic. Actually, two drug arrests were made during the course of the semester. They were made off campus – if that is any consolation.

"Overall, I am happy to report that the morale at Greatwood during the spring semester of 1969 was high. Both students and faculty were intensely engaged in thought and discussion of the future of the College and the future of Greatwood. This genuine concern probably took our minds off the minor irritations which are always with us. I believe the new Faculty Lounge and the periodic social hours which are held there have proved to be a more valuable tool for bringing the faculty together in greater understanding than the newfangled idea of Basic Encounter groups."

Adult Degree Program   Among Dean Wilfrid Hamlin's comments on the Adult Degree Program are these statements: "All the evidence suggests that the Adult Degree Program works and works very well for a large majority of the students enrolled in it. Many graduates write to express their gratitude and to tell of academic or professional success: an advanced degree granted, a new and more responsible job. Often they use the words "my life has been changed" in talking about their experience in the program. Often they include small donations to the College. Current students write, too, of the help-fulness of the faculty. When they call teachers and the Dean by their first names, and sign their own first names to the letters, it appears to be a genuine expression of fellow-feeling, of sharing in a deep way in the educational ven-ture faculty and students are engaged in together. What follows, as it discusses problems and needs, must be taken within this warm and positive context.

"In early July of 1968 a third group of students was added to the Adult De-gree Program. The A group (August and February resident periods) and the B group – the second to be formed (late July and January resident periods), had grown beyond what seemed a functional group size for a two-week resident period. Since one of the aims of the resident period is to have students come to know each other, teach each other, and learn from each other, it has ap-peared to the Dean of the program that on-campus groups should be limited to not more than seventy students, a figure a number of social psychologists have suggested as the maximum for certain kinds of informal information and opinion sharing. (As group size increases much beyond this, a dialectical change – quantitative to qualitative – takes place, and interaction patterns must become far more formalized and/or the group tends to break up into subgroups or cliques.) On grounds not clear to the Dean, an optimum and maximum figure of 100 continuing students (that is, the group less those who graduate at the close of the resident period) has been stipulated by the Pres-ident. Total potential enrollment for the resident periods of the three groups was set at 375, allowing about 25 graduating students each semester in each group.

"The new C group (we do things backwards at Goddard; C comes first, in early July and early January, then B, then A) got off to a very good start. It was made up entirely of students new to the program, and almost all of its faculty were likewise in ADP – in some cases at Goddard – for the first time. The students included – as is usual in ADP – a number of persons with ex-periences of great interest they were ready to share with others. Much of the time, the thirty-or-so students and the five faculty members worked together as a single group, reminding the Dean of the early days of ADP. Group C added an almost equal number of new students in the January resident period; its projected size for the summer of 1969 is about 85. Faculty members have, of course, been added too.....

"Two persons are presently making studies of the Adult Degree Program, which should furnish some objective feedback on its strengths and weak-nesses. Mrs. Beverly Cassara, Director of Adult Education at Goddard, has just begun a doctoral study in which she will attempt to find out how different kinds of students use the program, and whether certain types of learners seem to use it more successfully than others. Ed Bunnell will visit the campus this summer to gather material for an MA thesis describing and evaluating the pro-gram. Mrs. Cassara is doing her graduate work at Boston University, Mr. Bunnell at Ohio State. Both studies will take some time, so the feedback won't be immediate."

Experiment In Further Education James Roos, Director of the Goddard Experimental Program in Further Education, writes: "The weekend of June 6 and 7 brought to a close the second full year of operation of the Experimental Program in Further Education. During the academic year we had forty-three students registered in the program, about half of whom had participated in the 1967-68 program. The program for this year included ten short residential weekends at the College starting with Friday evening and ending Saturday night. The program was financed by two separate grants from federal funds; one for $39,000 through Educational Projects, Inc. for members of the regular Year Round Head Start Program, and one of about $2,100 from the U.S. Office of Education to finance the cost of three staff members from the Head Start Follow Through Program. The purpose of the program is to increase the confidence and competence of Head Start staff, including teachers, social service workers, secretaries, bus drivers, cooks, and others. About half of the persons admitted as new students this year had not completed high school and have worked toward passing the high school equivalency test. Four or five students took the test during the school year and passed it. Another took it and failed by one point, but is more confident now that she will pass it in another try.

"As the program progresses the staff has become increasingly aware of the ineffectiveness or inability of the general educational establishment to meet the needs of society. As Anita Landa pointed out in her report to the President last June, we discovered through the operation of the program last year that the people involved, regardless of their education, or cultural backgrounds, could in fact do satisfactory college work. We continue to find this true and have become increasingly aware that growth and change, the ability of our students to develop their potential, to see themselves as whole persons, to make contributions to their families and their jobs, and to recognize and articulate these changes, are not only possible but probable, given a minimum opportunity.

"In reading through the evaluations of individual students, one gets a general feeling of excitement and a feeling of accomplishment on the part of the students, and a feeling that a growth process has started that could not easily be reversed. Many students express changes in attitude toward their jobs and toward the educational process itself. Many students expressed anxiety at the beginning of the program and traced the development of their interests through conference and association with staff members and other students toward effective participation. The evaluations indicate that the residential weekend, coupled with independent studies between weekends, is an effective structure in that it allows the student maximum freedom to develop his own ideas with his own points of reference and his own resources, and yet to bring these ideas to other students and co-workers for support and consolidation.

"An important and noteworthy aspect of the program this year has been the participation of three of our students in regular Goddard courses in addition to their participation in our program. These three students took courses with three instructors. We consider this to be an area to develop further and in our application for funds next year we will include more funds for tuition for such courses and will encourage more of our students to take advantage of this opportunity.

"There was more participation of the GEPFE staff in the field this year. Staff members became involved in Head Start parent meetings, in nutrition programs, in staff training programs, and in Head Start Center affairs. The result of this was to increase the degree of involvement of the students and to heighten the excitement of the overall experience.....

"An interesting sidelight and one perhaps of significance to the College is the participation of the director in the development of institutional change in other colleges and universities participating in the Head Start Supplementary Training Program around the country. There are over 80 such programs, involving over 170 colleges and universities. Goddard was the second such program funded in the nation, and I believe the first to go into operation, in the fall of 1967. Educational Projects, Inc. and Head Start National in Washington have looked on the Goddard program as somewhat of a model or an ideal and have called on me for several occasions to outline the possibilities, as I see them, in an effective educational program. I cannot say that this has been an easy or even a pleasant job, as many of the conferences have developed into confrontation situations, in many cases involving black power advocates and very conservative 'educators.' At times the simple, direct truisms that I have to offer in regard to education have within the framework of the listener seemed blatant, even condemning. In the words of Bill Barse, of Educational Projects, Inc. following a conference in Denver, the Goddard message came 'straight down the line.' And he adds, 'There was a turning point for them (the institutional representatives). It had to be your explanation of education and learning as opposed to conditioning.' He adds that action is already being taken in Idaho, Montana, and Utah, as well as in Kansas, which means that in a modest sense the Experiment at Goddard is having some outward effect."

Other Adult Education As Director of Adult Education, Beverly Cassara has continued to be responsible for adults taking work on the two campuses and the more informal type of adult education that occurs in Goddard conferences. She describes some aspects of her work in these terms: "The services rendered through the Office of Adult Education are somewhat varied, and as an example I would like to mention these matters among others which required my attention on the last day before I left for Boston. I was engaged in lining up a conference in connection with the appearance at Goddard of the Theatre of the Deaf for October 3 and 4. We had just received their acceptance of our contract and it was very important to get some things organized quickly in order to be ready for a conference so early in the Fall. However, this work was interrupted by the appearance in my office of a very attractive but very troubled woman. One does not turn such a person away without trying to be helpful. She thought she wanted a summer course, but it became obvious to me that she needed a psychiatrist much more, as she was indeed at the point of breaking up. Through an alumna of our program, I was able to get this woman an appointment at Waterbury. The psychiatrist confirmed my decision as the right one and I could leave town knowing that at least someone was helping her. She won't show up anywhere in the statistics of my program's work, but this was one of my most important functions.

"On that same day a woman called me who had been a Sister and was now returning to lay life. She had planned to finish her work for her B.A. at the University of Vermont, but the roadblocks that they were putting in her way financially and academically were finally too much for her after a semester and when she heard about Goddard she came to see what opportunities there might be for her here. She is a very bright attractive young woman and will be a credit to Goddard. She had signed up and was ready to start Summer School at UVM, but hating the thought. I took her over to see the adult-child team dance class which was in progress and told her about our other courses. We called Joe Rosenberg and talked with him about the theatre course. As a result, she signed up for two of our courses, feeling that Goddard was a friendly place where people tried to be helpful instead of throwing up roadblocks. She will finish with us on a part-time basis.

"The point of recounting these two episodes is to underline the fact that this program has integrity only as it serves the particular needs of the kinds of persons we serve. Its future must be based squarely on these needs and grow slowly if necessary in order that that integrity never be violated.

"Enrollments for Spring Semester

Adults and children enrolled	97 + 7
Classes serving adults	29
Adult independent studies	18
Adult senior studies	14
Faculty on Greatwood working with adults	18
Faculty on Northwood working with adults	18
Graduates: in 1967 – 2, in 1968 – 7, in 1969 – 18	
Degree candidates enrolled	69
Summer classes scheduled	4

"I spoke to a group of adult educators about Goddard's philosophy of adult education at the University of New Hampshire. Participants were from three groups: Association of University Evening Colleges, National University Extension Association, and Adult Education Association (New England States). I have been working all Spring with our Governor in the planning of a new State Commission on the Status of Women. He has asked me if I will be permanent chairman of same when it is finally established. Also in connection with this, I was elected as a regional representative to work for two days at the

Labor Department in Washington, D.C. helping to plan a U.S. Council of State Commissions. I worked with the Teacher Services Office of the Vermont Department of Education in planning projects for Educational Professions Development Act grant. I spoke to a group of local ministers at the request of Dolf Unger about adult education generally and our program in particular. I worked with the Vermont Department of Corrections to get federal tuition grants for four corrections officers to attend our regular program. At the request of Commissioner of Education Harvey Scribner, I took training to serve as a state consultant to the new required Elementary School Standards Committees.

"This list, however, could really be endless, as the nature of my work keeps me in contact with the public of Vermont, but also with the world beyond to a considerable extent. This is important to the development of the program, but it is also important that the best of Goddard's ideas get more exposure in the world outside the campus if they are to carry the impact they should in helping to create better educational opportunities for today's young people."

Non-Resident Work Term   In her report Priscilla Backman, Director of the Non-Resident Work Term, gives us glimpses of that part of the College's educational program: "This year, 1969, some 390 students had work terms during the regular January-February period. In addition, 3 had travel terms, 7 study terms, 31 were on non-resident years, 13 on flexible calendar, another 15 or so had completed their work term requirements....

"As always, there were many extremely interesting and worthwhile experiences and reports. It is an impressive array of attempts on the part of many students to explore new areas of experience, or geography, or self. For others, it was an attempt to pursue to greater depth an already familiar area. Here are some quotations:

A 13-1 who worked in a New York State Hospital in New York City: 'I met psychologists, psychiatrists, social workers, ward attendants, occupational therapists, etc. Not only could I discuss their work with them, but I would watch and occasionally participate. From meeting various members of the staff I found that the hospital is a paradoxical and frustrating place to work. There were great policy disagreements between departments.'

A 13-1 student who became a member of a fishing boat crew off Cape Cod: 'The capitalistic society of this county tends to become a subliminal reality in the protective and isolated community at Goddard. . . . a change in environment is an essential part of the Goddard program.'

A 14-2 who worked as an assistant stage manager: 'I learned to pace myself through the day, so I wouldn't burn out by six p.m. I had never worked long hours before. Having a job where (during rehearsals) I had to keep my mouth shut, never do anything without asking and keep my mind pinned down on lines and blocking, was difficult at first. . . .'

A 15-1 who taught in a Vermont elementary school: 'I was here to gain all the experience I could. I taught at every grade level almost every day. Because I wanted this experience, I agreed to this small amount of pay. I remember how I felt in Junior High and how I was so often bored and I feel that learning can be made interesting and it is this desire that makes me want to be a teacher. . . . '

A 15-2 who worked in an inner-city school: 'My objective was to find our for myself how an inner-city schoolsystem, specifically the one in the city in which I grew up, functions..... Never before have I encountered such an inefficient, hypocritical and self-defeating system..... Each teacher is required to cover a particular set of books each semester. There is little or no attention paid to whether or not the children can understand the material..... they must simply get through it.....'

A 13-1 who went to Puerto Rico with the Spanish Comparative Cultures class: 'I find it impossible to write everything I want to say – it would fill a book. I am still far from fluent in Spanish but I have learned a great deal more than I would have from a few years of study out of books, I am sure..... *I had* to learn Spanish in order to communicate..... I did very little work . . . as a work experience, it was not great and I wish I could have accomplished more. However, as a living and learning experience, I feel it was the greatest I have had so far.....'

"Of course there were many less positive reports from students who had endless difficulties in finding work and from many who felt that it was regrettably necessary to lie about the fact that they would be returning to school in seven or eight weeks. Some students could not find work in their field and felt that the two months was a stupid waste of time. Some wrote that they had already had much routine job experience and did not want to be forced to break off their academic term for more of the same kind of work.....

"During the work term, two social gatherings were held for work term students from Goddard, one in Boston and one in New York. Work term offices at Bennington, Bard, Wilberforce, Antioch, and Beloit were contacted and their students were also invited. Considering the shortness of notice students received, and the general lack of organizing help, these meetings were both quite successful and certainly well worth repeating.....

"During the spring semester, three or four meetings were held on each campus to provide for more discussion of work term problems and more feedback from students. Attendance was small, yet discussions were thoroughgoing and helpful. Students again expressed a wish for longer work terms, for more jobs related to their fields and/or tied in with a specific course.

"Obviously, the complex problem of changing the college calendar is not going to be resolved within the next few months. However, some expansion of the work term program can take place within the present calendar. Six-month work terms would fit in very well, running either from September-February or January-June (or August, if the student wished). Such a work term would not even raise the problems of the usual flexible semester: 'Which faculty will be available for me to study with?' The six month work-termer could begin his next academic semester with the main student body, at the usual time: either in March or in September.

"Hopefully, some Goddard work term students who wish to may be able to take part in an Urban Problems Seminar held in the area in which they are working. Such seminars may be available in Washington, D.C. and in New York City. This is being tried now by Wilberforce University very successfully with its co-op students. They have invited our participation. Discussion as to ways and means is underway. Goddard participation, if it materializes, comes about as a result of our attendance at the CEA Mid-Winter Conference in Flint, Michigan and subsequent attendance of Wilberforce students and faculty at the Goddard work term social gathering in New York City in February. More information on this program will be available by mid-July.....

"Increased funds are needed to implement these programs, chiefly or at least most immediately, by providing more and better office help. This would enable the director to spend more time on developing new programs and less on keeping the records and doing other very routine jobs. Funds are available for 'developing and expanding a Co-op Program' through the Office of Higher Education. Application for such funds is being explored. Some money must also be available if we are to participate in the Urban Seminars.

"As always, many students made excellent use of the two month work term. It is hoped that the attempt to build the three additional work term possibilities suggested above will increase the general value of the program."

Off-Campus Field Services Adolf Unger, Director of Off-Campus Field Services, gives an excellent account of the relationships Goddard students have built with Vermont communities: "Off-campus field services have been an integral part of Goddard College since its earliest years. Only the last two years has the program been coordinated under a single faculty member.

"The program combines several ideas; foremost among them is that through field services students are enabled to combine academic and experiential learning. But also while he is involved in study on campus, he is able to make a contribution to the larger community surrounding Goddard. As many students hail from suburban or urban areas they are offered an opportunity to be involved in rural America, share life with individual Vermonters, participate in the state's government structure, and come to know the poor of this part of the country. In doing so they have learned a great deal about an area of life with which they otherwise would never have come in contact.

"Vermonter from their side again have warmly welcomed one fifth of our students. Communities have opened homes, schools, institutions to our students, putting once more to rest the legend that Goddard is too far out a place to be really a part of Vermont's life. As a matter of fact, more schools (public and private) have asked for our students to assist in their work than we have been able to provide. This is true for other places of field work also.

"From evaluations (which are given at the end of the semester by both students and their supervisors in their particular field) it was again clear that many students put aside preconceived ideas about their work with youth, pre-school children, involvement with adults, etc. A number of students have already expressed the desire to continue in the same field for another semester; several fields have indicated that they would not only like to have the same students come back but also to have more participate.

"Students' field work extended from Barton, northeast Vermont to Vershire, southeast of Plainfield, and Waterbury, west of the College. Though we had some complaints from students about transport (they are transported free up to 50 miles a week), in general Marion Metcalf was able to provide a smooth transportation system.

"Instead of students coming to see me in my Greatwood or Northwood offices, I spent most of the semester visiting the fields and communicating with them at their place of work. We included first year students in some carefully chosen areas, such as Head Start, and almost every one of them did very well. As a matter of fact, we have very few complaints from fields this semester. By visiting their places of work regularly I was also able to stay in much closer contact with their field supervisors, thus preventing small tempests from becoming major storms. Some students (about five) withdrew from the program and some of them from the College. Their reasons for withdrawal did not concern the field service program itself.....

"Fields covered this semester were: public schools (kindergarten-elementary-high) in Plainfield, Marshfield, Hardwick, East Montpelier, Orange, North Calais, Barre City, Barre Town, Montpelier, and Northfield. Private schools (elementary, high, two for retarded children) in Plainfield, Vershire, Barre, and Montpelier. Head Start Centers in Barre, Montpelier, and Graniteville. Day Care Centers (under OEO program) in Montpelier and Barton. Other fields: Departments of the State of Vermont (Forests and Parks, Social Welfare and Mental Health); Vermont Historical Society. Winooski Mental Health Clinic (Big Brothers and Sisters, therapy groups); The Grange in Plainfield. Others were involved in working with youth in different churches. The Goddard-Plainfield Community Dialogue Group was continued. Students worked with Central Vermont Community Action Council (with low income families). Again we had students at the Vermont State Hospital in Waterbury.

"This being the third full semester in which I coordinated the program, I have now come to see how we have only begun to touch the surface of the possibilities of field services. We could have placed some 175 students instead of some 100 if they had been available. There is no doubt that the Vermont communities (including Plainfield and Marshfield) are extremely eager to have students come and do work which otherwise could not be done (e.g., in home economics, physical education, the arts [dancing, drawing, pottery]) or work in the Montpelier and North Calais museums. The major weakness in the program is not lack of cooperation but finding ways to reach students and get them involved in the program....

"The work is a challenge and I enjoy it immensely. It is education in action and has been taken note of by other colleges. One day this semester I spent visiting fields of service with a faculty member from Johnson State College, who invited me to speak to his faculty this September. I was also invited to write an article for Community Action Curriculum Project, United States National Student Association, and have filled several speaking engagements for PTA's, churches, service clubs, panel discussions, interpreting the uniqueness of the program."

EXPERIMENTATION AND RESEARCH

As George Beecher, Director of Educational Experimentation, says in his report, studies and discussion of the impact of the college experience continued throughout the year. "During the college year," he writes, "the Committee on Research and Experimentation of about 15 faculty members and 5 students met regularly each week to investigate the effectiveness of college programs and to consider proposals for new ones. The Action Group Experiment, which has been previously presented, was one proposal of the Fall which underwent scrutiny and emerged during the winter as a new program for 1969. It was an outgrowth of studies of student characteristics and reasons for dropout. The Action Group Experiment has as its aim to change the first year experience of the college student to enable him to find his need for college through deeper involvement and communication with others before concluding that higher learning is simply a continuation of lessons and book work in the high school pattern. College can have a personal meaning and holding power if the student finds personal relevance in his early college experience. This is an hypothesis that is being tested with a group of 30 first year students.

"Discussions during the spring semester focused on such topics as a new calendar on the quarter system and further studies of student characteristics and institutional functioning. A depth study of 2 samples of Goddard students labelled effective or ineffective students by the faculty was reported by Barry Goldensohn. This study seemed to show that the faculty is not wholly aware of the changed student role of today or the insufficiency of their demand on students. A related subject of investigation led by Robert Mattuck centered on what student concerns really are and what interaction there is between what students seek and what college offers.

"A student member of the committee presented a study of community at Goddard. In student eyes community here is the universe of trust, support, sharing, working together, and making judgments through knowing each other.

"Two proposals for the coming year included an experiment for 12 students living for a year on a farm, a kind of study and survival experience, and another for a course of study combined with encounter group experience. The farm experiment was approved but postponed for lack of commitment of students in the group. The other will operate in the fall as a two-teacher course offering on Northwood.

"Toward the end of the spring as time was running out Will Hamlin discussed some points on Richard Jones' book, *Fantasy and Feeling in Education*, and his own "Personal Perspective on the New Youth Culture" to close out our investigation of some problems of students and teachers in college today."

Kenneth Carter, who has been teaching at Northwood this year and continuing as Assistant Director of Educational Experimentation, began his work as Director of the Action Group Experiment in earnest during the winter by joining in a search for teachers to work with him in developing the program.

Another experimental program came out of more than a year of discussion in the Committee on Research and Experimentation, the President's Council, and groups of students on how Goddard could develop an educational program that would reach more black students. Very little of the grant of $10,000 that was made in the summer of 1968 by the Alfred P. Sloan Foundation for starting an ambitious program for low income young people whose school experience had not been satisfactory had been used because efforts to secure additional funds from other sources were unsuccessful. Inasmuch as a big project could not be financed, it was decided that the Sloan money should be used in a more modest plan.

Such a plan was proposed to the President's Council by members of the Goddard Afro-American Society and after much discussion and some modifications it was adopted. Its main features provide for active recruitment of black students during the summer by black students; independent studies for entering students, to be taught by black students already at Goddard; each student tutor would conduct his tutorial as an independent study with a faculty member as advisor; entering students would be allowed two academic years before a judgment is made concerning their educational qualifications for continuing in college, and financial aid in the form of tuition adjustment, educational opportunity grants, and work study funds (the latter two are federal programs) to be assured for four years for those who qualify in terms of financial need and personal development.

Undoubtedly the plan will undergo changes and may not become what the Goddard black students proposed and the President's Council approved, but it is an imaginative and constructive idea for which its student originators deserve hearty approval.

During the winter the editorial and publication offices of *Current* were moved to Plainfield. Editor Grant McClellan continued in his post but he was the only member of the magazine's staff to stay with it. The Board of Trustees of Goddard Publications, Inc. asked John Hall to serve as General Manager and to secure such assistance as was needed to handle the business affairs of the magazine. Ernest Cassara, Richard Hathaway, Carla Thomas and John Turner of the Greatwood Faculty and Lin Webster of the Northwood Faculty volunteered to join the Board of Editors, and Rosemary Rexford, who had been director of the Cooperative Community Services program, became Assistant

General Manager. Mary Ellen Spencer joined the staff as Circulation Manager. Before the principal hypotheses of this educational experiment could be tested the new staff had to demonstrate that it could produce a magazine equal in quality to that which *Current* had maintained since its founding by Chairman Emeritus Eliot Pratt in 1960. They have done this and done it well, as the issues that appeared during the spring have clearly and convincingly shown.

The next step was to devise ways for testing the hypotheses which were (1) that the educational opportunities of some Goddard students could be greatly enhanced by active and responsible participation in the editing of a magazine that dealt with the frontier problems of their times, (2) that the selection and editing of articles and excerpts from books for *Current* would be an interdisciplinary activity of great educational value to the student and faculty participants, (3) that faculty editors could offer group courses related directly to the magazine and thereby add pertinence and meaning to their instructional efforts.

During the semester at least two of the editors were working on plans for courses and procedures for the fall that would test the hypotheses. Little has been said on the campuses about *Current* as part of Goddard's educational program, but it is a truly unique experiment among colleges and universities and one with tremendous potential. The generosity of the Pratt family has made it possible for the College to pioneer another advance in higher education.

ENROLLMENT

Total enrollment at the College reached 1021 during the year, the largest in its history. This figure represents the number of persons who were students some time during the year and not the number enrolled in a single semester. Details of enrollment are to be found in the Appendix. (Omitted here. – Ed.)

Director of Admissions Charles Zerby reports that in the twelve months ending June 30 his office had received 8028 inquiries about admissions, this compares with 5860 for the preceding year, 5361 afor 1967, and 4685 for 1966. Applications for admission for the coming September began to show a sharp rise over earlier years in the fall of 1968. By the end of December they were 37.5 per cent ahead of the year preceding, by the end of January they were 46.3 per cent ahead, at the end of February the gain was 47.3, at the end of March 53.6 per cent, end of April 64 per cent, end of May 54 per cent, and on June 30, 51 per cent. At that time 1738 applications for admission in September had been received, the corresponding figure for 1968 was 1129.

One might get the impression from these figures that Goddard could pick and choose its entering students almost at will, but that would be far from actuality. The important point they make is that the admissions office, with a smaller staff than last year, had to handle a monumental amount of work to come up with 654 completed applications by June 30 out of which 461 applicants were accepted and 245 actually enrolled. The corresponding numbers for 1968 were 516 completed applications, 330 applicants accepted, and 151 actually enrolled.

For the first time it looked as if Goddard would be able to close its applications in July with reasonable assurance of having a full house in September.

PERSONNEL CHANGES

In anticipation of an increase in enrollment in the coming year and because of a few resignations, several appointments to the faculty were made this spring.

Charles Zerby resigned as Director of Admissions to do graduate work at the Claremont Graduate School. Robert Mattuck, who has been on leave this year to serve as consultant for the Committee on Experimentation and Research of the Council for the Advancement of Small Colleges, returns this summer to fill the new position of Coordinator of Admissions and Counseling. The position was created with the hope that the transition from applicants to full-fledged Goddard students would be fraught with less trauma and more education. To assist Robert, David McConnell has been appointed Director of Admissions and David Sartwell, a Goddard graduate in 1968, as Assistant Director of Admissions. These changes should make it possible for Provost John Hall to be relieved of the responsibilities he has carried for the many years in the oversight of admissions which began with his appointment as Director of Admissions and Records in 1956. In that post John became one of the best informed and most competent admissions officers in the country.

Current Editor, Grant McClellan, was appointed to the Greatwood Faculty with the expectation that he would teach a course in the social sciences that related to the editing of the magazine.

Other appointments included Eleanor Forster as literature instructor on the Northwood Faculty, as replacement for Norman Unrau. Miss Forster recently taught at Community College of Philadelphia, and earlier at Sparta, Pennsylvania High School. She graduated from Wilson College, earned the Master's degree at Harvard, and her Ph.D. from the University of Pennsylvania. Her special interest is in British Literature and Folklore.

To replace Ken Carter on the Northwood Faculty, Anthony J. Mayhew was appointed to teach Psychology. He has been teaching at the University of Vermont since 1966 and held a post-doctoral research fellowship at the University of California at Berkeley following the award of the M.A. and Ph.D. from the University of Colorado. His undergraduate work was done at Princeton.

An addition to the Northwood Faculty is Scott Nielsen, in the field of Economics and Social Change. For the past four years he has been director of the Farm Labor Program for the American Friends Service Committee in southeastern Pennsylvania, after several years as Director of Research for the Travelers Insurance Company in Hartford, Connecticut. He has a B.A. and M.B.A. from the University of Chicago, is a C.P.A. in Illinois, and earned the Ph.D. from the Massachusetts Institute of Technology in Economics. He taught for several years at the MIT School of Industrial Management.

To replace Richard Wright, Assistant to the Greatwood Dean, Edward C. Smith was appointed. He comes to Goddard from several years of teaching at the secondary level, at Cherry Lawn School and Cheshire Academy in Connecticut. During the past three summers he served as supervisor of the Connecticut Valley Hospital Service Corps in Middletown. He graduated from Wesleyan University's Experimental Program, and undertook advanced study at Brandeis and Wesleyan in Literature and Psychology.

Erich Walka, instructor at Royalton College last year, was appointed to the vacancy in Literature on the Greatwood Faculty caused by Robert Mattuck's acceptance of his new post. Mr. Walka attended the Teacher Training Institute and University of Vienna in Austria, held a Rotary Scholarship at Bates College in Maine, and is a candidate for the Ph.D. from the University of Innsbruck. He will begin his teaching at Goddard in the spring semester. Prior to teaching at Royalton, he was a ski instructor at Stowe, Vermont, St. Michael's College, and Perisher Valley, Australia.

J. Victor Laderoute joins the Greatwood Faculty for a year as sabbatical replacement for Ray McIntyre. He was artist-in-residence at such institutions as Laurentian University, Conservatory of Music at the University of Kansas City, Peabody Conservatory of Music, Jordan College of Music at Butler University, and has been tenor soloist with leading orchestras in this country and Canada. He attended Sault Ste. Marie Collegiate Institute, Royal Conservatory of Music in Toronto, College of Music at Cincinnati, New England Conservatory of Music, Berkshire Music Center.

New medical services will be available next year through the appointment of Dr. J. Paul Michlin of Los Angeles as College Health Director and Dr. Victor Chase of Burlington as Consulting Psychiatrist. Dr. Michlin recently completed a year of advanced training at the Albany, New York Medical Center Hospital, following medical training at the Washington University Medical School at St. Louis, from which he received his M.D. He will also serve the Plainfield community as a general practitioner. Dr. Chase is affiliated with the Washington County Medical Health Service at Montpelier and was formerly on the staff of the University of Vermont.

Other appointments, mentioned in the March report, include Robert Tarule and Stephen Zeigfinger to the Action Group Faculty, and Dr. M. T. Merrill and Miss Joan McKibbin to the Greatwood Faculty.

SABBATICALS

By action of the Board of Trustees last January a member of the Goddard Faculty becomes eligible for a sabbatical on July 1, 1969 after nine years of service and on July 1, 1970 after eight years. Previously the required term of service was ten years. Those who will be eligible this year are Provost John Hall, Ray McIntyre of Greatwood, and Paul Vela of Northwood.

INSTITUTIONAL ORGANIZATIONS

Like individuals, the modern college is a joiner and Goddard is no exception. It is a member of the American Association of Admissions Counsellors, American Association of Collegiate Registrars, Association of American Colleges, American Council on Education, College Entrance Examination Board, Council for the Advancement of Small Colleges, New England Association of Colleges and Secondary Schools, New England Association of Collegiate Registrars, Union for Research and Experimentation in Higher Education, Vermont Foundation of Independent Colleges, and Vermont Higher Education Council.

Much of the recognition that Goddard has received in recent years has resulted from participation of its staff members in the activities of these and other educational organizations. By reason of its representation on the Committee on Experimentation and Research of the Council for the Advancement of Small Colleges, Goddard became a participant in the Project on Student Development which is directed by Arthur W. Chickering, who resigned in 1965 as Coordinator of Evaluation at Goddard to take on that job. The Project has carried on what is probably the most thorough study of what happens to students during their four years of college that has been made of a group of colleges (the study covers 13 institutions) on the American continent. Data derived from the study have been used at Goddard throughout the four years of the Project to shed light on the effectiveness and ineffectiveness of our teaching, the areas where change was needed, and the factors affecting the high dropout rate at the Colleges.

Drawing on his experience with the Project and with the Six Year Experiment in Curriculum Organization at Goddard, Arthur Chickering has written a book – *Education and Identity* – which has been named the outstanding education book of the year for which he will receive the American Council on Education Book Award of $1,000 at the October meeting of the Council.

The Union for Research and Experimentation in Higher Education, which had its inception at Goddard, continued its Field Study Centers this year, making it possible for two Goddard girls – one from each campus – to work and learn on the island of Kauai in Hawaii and two boys – one from each campus – to study the German language and culture in Germany and Switzerland. Although the Union set out to study the progress through college of students who entered the Union colleges in the fall of 1966 through an arrangement with the Center for Research and Development in Higher Education at the University of California at Berkeley, unfortunately the study has not been pursued in a way at all comparable to that of the Project on Student Development and consequently the benefits have not been nearly as great.

Under the chairmanship of President John Elmendorf of New College in Sarasota, Florida a committee of the Union has been studying the possibility of creating a Union Graduate School which would offer a doctoral program for persons already in or wishing to enter the education profession. Assistant to the President Evalyn Bates, who had been working on a possible Master's degree program at Goddard while on her sabbatical at Claremont, was a member of the committee. There is a strong possibility that the Union program will get underway in 1970 and that one of its four or five proposed centers may be at Goddard.

BUILDINGS AND LAND

The major construction of the year has been, of course, the Eliot D. Pratt Library-Learning Aids Center, the only sizeable non-residential structure the College has built. Progress on the building has been on schedule and the prospects for completion early in the fall semester are good. The construction company, H. P. Cummings Construction Company, which built the Flynn Building in 1939 which has been used as the library for many years, has done excellent work and cooperated nicely with architects Hill and Associates, who in turn have again demonstrated their interest in and devotion to the educational aims of Goddard. Coordinator of Campus Planning Ronald Pitkin has had general oversight of the entire project.

During the year the temporary (perhaps semi-permanent is a better adjective) dining hall and community center at Northwood has been thoroughly tested by use. Its acoustical problems remain to be solved, otherwise it is satisfactory pending the erection of a more permanent Community Center at Northwood and the conversion of this one to a maintenance building.

In accordance with the authorization of the Board of Trustees, an architect was engaged to work with the Coordinator of Campus Planning and the Northwood Community to develop plans for a badly needed laboratory and studio building at Northwood. Several conferences were held during the spring but no wholly acceptable plan has been produced.

Again Harold and Marjorie Townsend have shown their long-continued concern for Goddard by contributing money and talent during the year for rehabilitation of the Garden House. Members of the Arts Center have honored Bedrich Vaska, master cellist and teacher on the Center staff, by contributing funds for the Garden House as a tribute to him.

The Plainfield Inn, which was purchased in 1946 as a stop-gap dormitory for veterans of World War II and which has been used to meet a variety of housing needs since, will justify its retention as a college property once more, this time as the residence and headquarters for the Action Group Experiment. Although it is not ideal as a third campus, it should suffice for the first year.

As the year reached its end, arrangements were being made for the installation of a sprinkler system in Kilpatrick House, thereby fulfilling a long-standing need. This will reduce greatly the fire hazard on the Greatwood Quadrangle but the Studies Building still poses a real threat.

Coordinator of Land Use Belmont Pitkin reports that the College Nursery, started last year by graduating student Charles Woodward, has been carried on by a few students this year and that young trees are being grown for use in completing the landscaping of the Village for Learning at Greatwood as well as for other areas.

In June an option was secured from Marjorie and Harold Townsend for the purchase for six hundred dollars of four small parcels of land adjacent to

Goddard property. The option extends till October 20, 1969. These parcels are important for the protection of the campuses from possible undesirable developments.

LIBRARY

Acquisitions to the library made during the year brought the total number of volumes to about 38,360. The periodical list numbers 300. In addition, extensive use was made of other libraries through the inter-library loan system and by visits to them by students and staff. The College started in 1938 with about 4,000 books, which were placed in what is now Martin Manor Lounge. When that area became too small, the collection was moved to what is now the Greatwood science building and later to the Flynn Building, which in turn it outgrew.

FINANCES

Financially, it has been a good year. As the Auditor's Report shows, total combined income applicable to current operations amounted to $2,429,000 and total current expense to $2,170,000, making it possible for $259,000 to be applied to debt reduction and capital expense such as buildings, equipment and improvements. Actually, debt reduction was greater than appears at first glance as the $108,000 that was transferred to the bond sinking fund account for the Village for Learning and Northwood residences went to interest and debt reduction but appears as current expense.

Gifts actually received during the fiscal year were $56,880.89, a somewhat smaller amount than in the last few years, mainly because Mr. and Mrs. Eliot Pratt made a contribution to be used for *Current* his year and one for the Library-Learning Aids Center near the end of June 1968. The only substantial foundation grant received during the year was the Sloan grant.

Mr. and Mrs. Harry Houghton conveyed to the College another part of their remaining interest in the Houghton Hall property on the Rideau Lakes in Ontario during the year, bringing the book value of Goddard's share in the property to $248,393.

The list of other contributors to the College is included in the Appendix to this report. (omitted here. – Ed.).

Although the outlook for next year is not quite as favorable as last year, the prospects are good. The tentative budget of June 14 shows an excess of current income over current expense of $72,660. To this should be added the assured government grants for Educational Opportunity, Work Study, and Library-Learning Aids of $52,501 to yield a total estimated excess of current income over current expense of $125,161 which can be applied to new construction, including the Library-Learning Aids Center, debt reduction and other capital costs in 1969-70 as compared with $248,393 this year. Of course, a modest increase in enrollment above the 963 we have forecast should yield a somewhat greater margin. Even so, it is quite clear that the increase in tuition that was authorized by the Board of Trustees at its annual meeting will be sorely needed for the year 1970-71.

A CONCLUDING NOTE

The thirty-four years that I have worked for Goddard, three at the Junior College in Barre and the remainder in Plainfield, have been absorbing, interesting, exciting and rewarding, despite the despair and discouragement that marked periods in the first twenty-five years. Goddard has been extremely fortunate in having a superb Board of Trustees throughout its collegiate career. The faculty and other members of the staff have been a truly fine group with which to work. As I have said many times, the Goddard Faculty is probably the best college faculty in the country. From the splendid group of young women that constituted the first class at Goddard Junior College through those who entered this year, the Goddard students have been stimulating, creative, critical, lovable, and intelligent persons with whom it has been a joy, sometimes tinged with sorrow, to work.

I am grateful to all members of the Goddard Community for allowing me the privilege of working and living with them over the years that in retrospect seem so brief.

It is with pleasure that I welcome Gerald Witherspoon to the Goddard presidency.

Respectfully submitted,

Royce S. Pitkin,
President

A PROGRAM FOR THE LIBERALS
OF VERMONT AND QUEBEC

Report of the President
October 3, 1941[61]

Events that have transpired since our last Convention cannot have been wholly reassuring to liberals. Many of the tendencies cited in my report a year ago have continued. The need for vigorous defense of democracy on the home front is still acute. And as we feel the increasingly bitter effects of a terrible war, the need of the spirit of liberal religion becomes greater and greater. These are truly "times that try men's souls." How shall we as liberals meet them?

I propose a simple program.

First, let each church and each society devote the year to a consideration of how to improve human relations. Let that be the goal of every church organization. Let us candidly examine our relations with other parts of our church and endeavor to remove any cause for unhappy living that may be attributable to us. Let us give thought to the operation of our homes to the

---

[61]The presidency referred to here is that of the Vt. and Quebec Universalist Unitarian Convention, a volunteer elective post Tim held during his early terms as President of Goddard. Some of the themes as well as the main broadside itself are of interest. Improvement of human relations, social service, young people on Trustee Boards, and the support of civil liberties are all familiar points in Royce's later positions. Notice also his idea of cooperation with the Quakers. In the more general sense, he sees a lacuna in the Convention program area, and fills it. A later instance of this pattern which does not appear here occurred in the summer of 1969 when he wrote a draft of a plan for Vermont public schools and handed it to Education Commissioner Harvey Scribner. There would have been the usual resistance from organizations which had their own ideas of appropriate programs they should follow. Royce would of course have been prepared for this. He simply believed in doing it anyway.

end that they may be harmonious and democratic institutions. Let us cooperatively seek to remove some of the tensions of modern life by study and discussion.

Second, let each church and local group render a needed social service in its community. This might be using the church building for a day nursery for working mothers, it might be providing medical care for some family, it might be giving radios to persons without sight, it might be building a better playground, it might be one of many such projects.

Third, let the Convention organize summer play schools and community betterment work camps.

Fourth, let every church and local group send at least two alert high school juniors or seniors to the Institute of Civic and Social Affairs.

Fifth, let every church place at least two persons under twenty-four on its Board of Trustees.

Sixth, let every liberal parish be represented at the Older Young People's Conference in January.

Seventh, let us join forces with the Vermont Church Council in such enterprises as we can properly endorse.

Eighth, let us as individuals, as societies, and as a Convention oppose any and all attempts at the suppression of freedom of thought and expression and the restriction of civil liberties.

Ninth, let us join forces with the Quakers in making the United States and particularly our own communities places of refuge for the oppressed of every land.

It is within our power to achieve such a program. I urge its adoption.

An Adventure in Adult Education

(1933)[62]

by Royce S. Pitkin
Headmaster, New London School, New London, N.H.

Are the adults of rural America interested in studying modern economic and social problems? If they are, what can be done about it? The results of an undertaking in New London have convinced me that the answer to the first question is an unqualified "Yes" and to the second, "A great deal."

Located in the lake region of New Hampshire, New London is a beautiful hill town eight miles from the nearest railroad station. The permanent population of about 850 is supported by the summer tourist and residence business and by general farming, although an increasing number of persons are depending on occupations arising from the growth of Colby Junior College.

Rural New England Is Setting

Studies made of the public school pupils indicate that the distribution of intelligence is about normal. The range of ability is from that of morons to superior minds. Like most small rural communities of New England, New

---

[62]This item turned up unidentified as to source. Probably it was a flyer used as a handout rather than a reprint from a publication. Three photographs appearing in the original are omitted here as unrelated to the content of the piece. It is of interest as the earliest known example of some of Royce's first work with citizen groups in discussions of topics of pressing concern. This type of activity would have been the ancestor of the Labor and Farm Conferences at Goddard in the first twenty years in Plainfield, and of Royce's lifelong belief that citizens from communities around the College would willingly join in discussions of problems of significance to them. The Roycean dialectic may have begun here. From internal evidence the date of this piece is 1933.

272

London has been conservative in education, politics, religion and social theory for decades. For more than ninety years its intellectual life centered about Colby Academy, a traditional coeducational institution that had as its chief aim preparation for college. Five years ago the school was reorganized as a junior college for women with Dr. H. Leslie Sawyer as president, and since then has been enjoying a steady growth in enrollment and usefulness.

To provide educational opportunity for the boys and girls of New London of high school age, the school district voted two years ago to establish a high school in connection with the central elementary school already in operation.

Though conservative in social theory, in actual practice the community has been progressive and has moved steadily toward collectivism. It has installed an adequate and efficient water and fire protection system, it has built a modern sewage disposal plant, it has an excellent system of country roads, many of which hare hard surfaced, it employs a school nurse, it maintains a public hospital, and it supports with the aid of private benefactions an excellent library employing two full-time librarians. Except for its public school facilities, which are quite inadequate, its community equipment is much better than is ordinarily found in small New England towns.

Contrary to the opinions of some of the summer visitors, there is a great deal of activity in New London after the tourist season has closed. As a matter of fact the real community life is most active and varied in the cooler seasons. The grange, the lodges, the church organizations, the hospital aid association, the dramatic club, the garden club, the women's club, the junior college and the high school all provide opportunities for people to use their talents and time. It is not uncommon for two or three major events to be taking place the same night. Hence it cannot be said that there is nothing for the townsfolk to do. In spite of this extensive program of community activities there has been no forum for the planned discussion of social-economic problems and no adult organization that was primarily educational in nature.

Believing that a few of the adults might welcome an opportunity to study and discuss some aspects of contemporary life, Dr. J. Duane Squires, instructor in history at Colby Junior College, and I announced through the little weekly paper that we would offer an evening course in the problems of modern society to adults who might be interested. Upon hearing of the proposal the librarians at the Tracy Memorial Library announced their desire to join the class and volunteered the use of the conference room in the library for the meetings.

The First Night Audience

With some fear and trembling lest there should be no further response to the call and that we would be found all dressed up with no place to go, Doctor Squires and I went to the library for the first meeting in the latter part of November. Imagine our surprise at finding more than thirty persons who wanted to enroll for the course! The response was almost disconcerting but the plan for the winter was outlined and the first talk given. As the winter progressed additions were made to the group until it included more than forty persons. The occupational distribution is interesting. There were housewives, teachers from the public school and the junior college, laborers, librarians, farmers, a doctor, a minister, bookkeepers, business men, a contractor, a retired business man and a surveyor. Of this number two were members of the local school board.

The course was called "An Introduction to American Civilization Today." Among the topics discussed were the characteristics of modern economic society, the influences that mold our opinions, the influence and development of machines, economic influences in American history, the place of the modern corporation, the growth of the constitution, the relation of government to the common man, the influence of the frontier and the results of its passing, and the possibilities of a planned society. At the opening of each meeting either leader would present his views on the subject under consideration and this would be followed by animated and sometimes heated discussion by the members of the group.

With this method there was actual participation by the group and not mere listening. Naturally the discussions would turn to such timely matters as the Tugwell bill, the cancellation of the air mail contracts, the NRA, Hitlerism and the investigations of the Senate committee on banking. Time after time in one form or another this question would be asked "How can the glaring defects in our social order be corrected"? Of course, the proposed remedies would call for collective action.

A general reading list was prepared and mimeographed at the beginning of the course and smaller lists were distributed for each subject studied. The libraries of the junior college and the high school cooperated with the public library in making up a special shelf of magazines and books for the use of the group. Books not found in any of the local libraries were obtained from the state library through the efforts of the town librarians. The enterprise was, therefore, cooperative in spirit and practice. It seemed to be a happy and profitable experience for all concerned and it demonstrated the possibility of extending the services and facilities of private and public educational institutions to the adult members of the small town.

This spirit of cooperation was carried into the program of the community church when the minister began a series of sermons dealing with the social problems of the nation.

Reports that have come to me from rural communities in which adult courses in contemporary history or economics have been given this winter through the agency of the FERA indicate that there is genuine desire on the part of country people to become familiar with the social problems that are now pressing for solution in America.

One cannot refrain from speculating on what the results would be if every state department of education were to organize a group of skilled teachers trained in the social sciences and acquainted with rural life to go to the rural sections to lead adult study groups; if every county and district superintendent of schools were to stimulate the organization of such groups, and if every small high school faculty were to join forces with other agencies in its community for the planned study of the social order.

Would it be too much to expect to see the disappearance of apathy toward government? Would people continue to endure a condition of poverty in the midst of plenty? Would farmers and laborers remain destitute while the managers of business enjoyed princely incomes? Would schools stay closed while billions of government money were poured into private industry?

When discussing the possibilities of achieving a planned society, I stated that one of the difficulties that stood in the way was lack of information on the part of most people. Immediately one of the older members of the class said, "But if there were more groups like this people would get the information." Doesn't that statement constitute a challenge to the educators of the nation?

It seems inconceivable that the forces of reaction could withstand the demand for improvement in our American life that such a mass movement in social education would surely bring to pass.

AN EXCHANGE OF LETTERS:
ROBERT MATTUCK AND ROYCE PITKIN

Robert M. Mattuck . Plainfield . Vermont
30 May 80[63]

Dear Tim,

Living way up here in the hills, we seem not to hear the news. We'd picked up a rumor that you were to get an Honorary Doctorate, watched the paper, saw nothing – until this morning I read it, (of all places!), in the free "Washington World"!

So, belatedly, our very best congratulations. At that, we're not as "beloved" at UVM, who ought long ago to have recognized what you have meant to Education and to the State of Vermont. So we're glad that, finally, they did so, and proud of you. Not bad, as that lady once said, "for a Marshfield boy"!!

Best love,

R & C

P. S. Remember what I've always said? That any ordinary intelligence could get a Ph.D., but that it takes real significance to "earn" an Honorary one!

June 2, 1980

Dear Robert,

Your letter of congratulation was and continues to be very much appreciated.

Actually, the doctor of laws which UVM bestowed on me was a recognition of the achievements of Goddard College and these achievements resulted from the efforts and dedication of a group of creative individuals who led and sustained the faculty for at least two decades. So by the laws of justice, equity and honesty the degree should be shared by Evalyn Bates, George Beecher, Forest Davis, Wilfrid Hamlin, Corinne Mattuck, Robert Mattuck, Helen McKelvey Pitkin, Harold Townsend, Marjorie Townsend, and Thomas Yahkub.

Recognition should also go to a group of generous, able, and imaginative trustees among whom were Hans Froelicher, Mike Giles, Clara Littledale, Monica Owen, Eliot Pratt, Larry Doolin, Joe Weinstein and Sylvia Wright.

We really were very lucky to have had the opportunity of working and worrying with such a distinguished bunch of folks. It was a great day for all of us when you and Corinne descended on the Goddard campus more than forty years ago!

Love to both of you,

---

[63]Here is the exchange between Robert Mattuck and Tim to which reference is made in Part One above. Tim was always generous when there was an honor to pass around. He refers in his third paragraph to certain early trustees who had disappeared from the Goddard scene some time previously. He retained warm memories of all of them, speaking about them by name occasionally when something reminded him. Larry Doolin was an old friend from early times who had helped rescue the College financially in the days when its needs were not as large as they became later. Hans Froelicher, Jr. was Headmaster of The Park School of Baltimore, from which numerous students had come, over the years. Hans knew all about progressive schools and educational methods. Goddard Admissions staffers invariably visited schools in Baltimore, appointments for which had been set up by him and his circle. In doing so they were exposed to a glimpse of old Baltimore society as it still existed in those days. George Beecher spent time as Hans' assistant at The Park School during the early to mid-1950s. Clara Savage Littledale was Editor of *Parents' Magazine* and a Goddard parent, and for years took a great interest in Corinne Mattuck's work and writing in early childhood education and related areas represented in Goddard educational programs.

In the preceding paragraph Royce includes among the persons who should share the degree with him the name of his wife, Helen McKelvey Pitkin. This may be the only place in the Goddard literature where this occurred. It was a delicate matter. For the College President to name his family members as persons outstanding in his perception of contributions made to the College over many years would have risked raising undercurrents of reservation over implied conflicts of interest. The truth was that Helen Pitkin worked endlessly and hard at many educational tasks at the College, often without compensation, and she was better at them than she ever received credit for being. Under the circumstances the matter simply could not be open for discussion or recognition while Royce was President of the College. At this very late date, toward the conclusion of this study of her husband's special genius, and in the years of her advancing age, surely the bonds of silence can be loosed. Goddard had no greater friend.

Reply to Reed College

(on the Goddard Work Program, 1970)

UNION FOR EXPERIMENTING
COLLEGES AND UNIVERSITIES

Field Study Center Office
The Inn
Plainfield, Vermont 05667
February 13, 1970[64]

Mr. Ross B. Thompson
Financial Vice President
Reed College
Portland, Oregon 97202

Dear Mr. Thompson,

Thank you for your letter of February 5th asking about the work program at Goddard College. Although I retired as President of the College last July, I am glad to comment on the work program.

It was incorporated in the educational program of the College when it was established in Plainfield in 1938 and has continued to be an important part of the life of the College. Although some minor modifications have been made in the program from time to time, it remains about the same as it was thirty

---

[64]Tim writes in reply to this inquiry, from his new office at the Plainfield Inn in his first retirement year, when he was Coordinator for the Field Study Centers of UECU (formerly UREHE). This was his first job after leaving the presidency of Goddard. It is another of his comments on an early and fundamental Goddard program for which he was always willing to go to the mat when opportunity offered.

years ago.

It was instituted (1) because we believed that most college students had had very little experience in working on jobs with others and that there is a great deal to be learned about what it means to work on ordinary unexciting jobs with others, accepting and carrying responsibilities, and exercising leadership in getting necessary work done; (2) we wanted to avoid the situation in which the students of low income had to work a great many hours a week in order to get through colleges while well-to-do students better situated financially had a lot of time available for out-of-class activities; (3) we wanted to make it possible to maintain a truly democratic atmosphere on the campus. To achieve these ends, every student was expected to work about eight hours a week on a job essential to the operation and maintenance of the College and the savings that come from that work are used to provide tuition adjustment for those who cannot afford to pay the full amount.

With an enrollment of about 550 regular undergraduates last year the contribution of the work program was estimated at about $200,000. Even though much of the work is not really well done, the savings are real and substantial.

In carrying out the program, the students work in the kitchen and dining room, assist in the library and learning aids center, manage the college switchboard at night, do a great deal of secretarial and clerical work, work on the grounds, help in the construction of buildings, care for the gardens and lawns, work in the community store, drive college cars, serve as assistants to members of the staff, and do many other things that need to be done on a college campus.

The program has always been administered by a Work Program Committee made up of students working with the Director of the Work Program, who is a member of the faculty. In fact, the Work Program Committee has been one of the most important arms of community government. Of course, it means that policies are changed nearly every time the committee changes. At the same time it means that there is a great deal of student involvement and commitment.

The performance of one's work program is required for promotion from one year to another. Although there is often grumbling among some students about their jobs, there has been relatively little difficulty in getting the work program requirements met.

I hope you will find the foregoing useful in your deliberations at Reed.

Sincerely yours,

Royce S. Pitkin
Coordinator

RSP/b

THE GREATWOOD RECORDS
DISCUSSION

(June 1969)[65]

June 4, 1969

Dear Ernest:

The Agenda Committee has referred to me the action taken by the Great-wood faculty on May 28, regarding evaluation and record procedures.

Unfortunately, a copy of this proposal did not reach me until a few minutes ago, although I had had a general impression of it from some members of the Greatwood faculty earlier as I indicated to you in the conversation we had about two weeks ago. To state it in the mildest terms possible, the action of the Greatwood faculty and the wording of the proposal distressed me greatly for the following reasons:

1. The proposal to break up a student's curriculum into parts is in clear violation of the basic principle of the College that the teaching of the Goddard student includes all of his activities and is to be regarded as a whole. Obviously, the proposal to base the progression of the student on the number of courses he "completes satisfactorily" is to fracture the life of the student.

2. The proposal of the Greatwood faculty is a move toward reversion to the credit system, the system which many colleges, consid-

---

[65]This letter is written by Royce to Dean Ernest Cassara of Greatwood Campus. It and the following pages bear on the year-long discussion of Records and record-keeping which went on in the 1968-69 academic year. They are included here as source materials for Tim's thought on this matter. They expand somewhat the discussion begun in Part One on this topic, and may modify the analysis reached there. Notice also, on pp. 251-252 above, Ernest's different view of this issue.

version to the credit system, the system which many colleges, considerably less experimental than Goddard, are now trying to escape from. It is instituting the notoriously unacceptable pass-fail system.

3. The proposal of the Greatwood faculty violates the basic philosophy of the college by placing the emphasis upon the completion of the work laid out by the teacher, rather than upon the process of education as it proceeds with the student. The effect inevitably would be to encourage the student to shift his attention from the pursuit of his own education to studying the teacher and working to meet the demands of the teacher.

4. The proposal, placing insistence upon "passing" a certain number of courses, will make it necessary for the student to invade his vacation period or his non-resident work term if he is to "make-up" the courses that he "failed."

5. The proposal overlooks completely the basic principle of the College that the real test of a student's progress has little relation to the extent to which he meets the demands of the teachers but rather to the way in which he handles his time and resources to meet the commitments that he makes. The effect of the proposal will be for teachers to substitute their aims and purposes for those of the student, and even less time will undoubtedly be given to working carefully with the student in helping him to identify, clarify and state his aims.

6. Unfortunately, the adoption of the proposal was far from being unanimous and has, therefore, exacerbated an already unfortunate schism within the Greatwood faculty.

It seems to me that the members of the Greatwood faculty who voted for this proposal have in effect said that they no longer wish to be part of an experimental college. Perhaps in the long run it would be a good idea to have one campus at Goddard which is not experimental but which constantly turns back to conventional practices. However desirable such an arrangement might be, it would be inappropriate to take such a step without a full discussion by the entire faculty of the College and such a discussion would be premature now. It strikes me that it would be quite unfair to a new president to create the kind of rift which the Greatwood faculty proposal would create within the Goddard Community.

I regret that I was not able to participate in the discussions of this proposal with the Greatwood faculty in order that I might present my views directly and that persons might react directly to them. Under the circumstances it would be inappropriate for me to say that this proposal is not to go into effect this semester, but I do strongly urge you to have a thorough reconsideration of the proposal before any move is made to put it into effect. If it is the wish of the Greatwood faculty, I would be very glad to meet with it for as many days as seem necessary after the 15th of June.

It is with great anguish of spirit that I write this.

Sincerely,

MINUTES OF THE GREATWOOD FACULTY MEETING 6/4/69

The meeting was called to order at 4:05 P.M. by E. Cassara.

R. Pitkin★ relayed a message from T. Yahkub to the effect that comments regarding presidential candidates should be submitted to him by 6/6/69.

P. Kuehn requested that RSVP's for Tim's dinner be returned promptly.

In closed session and with a request for absolute secrecy, the Dean initiated a discussion of appropriate ways of marking the President's retirement. He suggested that the award of a B.A. degree, which would make Tim Pitkin a member of the class of 1969, would be preferable to an honorary doctorate. The faculty received the proposal favorably, although there were some misgivings as to possible misinterpretation of the gesture. The Dean pointed out that the significance of the act would be understood by anyone who is connected with the College. June Edson moved that the proposal be accepted (seconded by John Turner), and it was voted unanimously.

The Dean introduced a letter from the President regarding the action of the Greatwood faculty on the matter of student progress through the College. The R&P proposal, which was accepted at the previous faculty meeting, was interpreted in this letter as contrary to Goddard's tradition of evaluating the student's total experience and growth during a semester. A number of objections were cited: that implementation of the proposal would be tantamount to a reversion to a credit system, that emphasis would shift from the student's development to teacher requirements, that stress on successfully completing a certain number of courses would tend to interfere with vacation and work-term periods, that the lack of unanimity in the vote has exacerbated ideological schisms within the faculty. The President urged reconsideration before implementation and offered to meet with faculty for further discussion after June 15. Discussion of the letter ensued.

A. Lopez-Escobar advised that the faculty not respond to in haste. He and B. Goldensohn suggested that the goals of the proposal had been misinterpreted. J. Rosenberg said that the President was essentially correct in reading the action as a reversion to conventional academic practices. G. Benello noted that awareness of a student's total progress is not dependent upon the whole-semester concept. J. Turner regretted the haste in implementing the new procedure, and pointed out that it would be difficult at this point to delay or rescind the implementation in view of the publicity the faculty action had already received among the student body. J. Rosenberg said that the seemingly

---

★Probably Ronald R., not RSP.

college policy. E. Cassara suggested that only the All-College Faculty has the power to overrule a Greatwood faculty action, and that further discussion might well be reserved till the fall.

T. Absher questioned the existence of firm college policy. R. Hathaway counseled moderation. E. Pannes and N. Wagner stressed the long and careful consideration given to the proposal before its adoption.

There followed an extended discussion of the relevance of student sentiment and of the college catalogue. D. York moved that Tim Pitkin's offer to participate in further discussion of the matter after June 15 be accepted (seconded). R. Levin suggested that such a discussion would not be appropriate in view of the advent of a new president (!). There was more discussion of the merits of the plan and of the philosophy (or philosophies) involved. G. Benello moved the question. The motion as made by D. York was passed.

A further discussion of implementation of the plan and of the jurisdiction of the All-College Faculty followed. E. Cassara suggested that a delay in implementation would allow resolution of various technical difficulties, such as the question of entry into Senior Division. G. Benello moved that the implementation of the plan be delayed until the fall. (Seconded by J. Rosenberg.) There was more discussion, followed by a vote on the motion: 13 in favor, 8 or 7 against.

The next item on the agenda was voting of degrees. According to a prior agreement, only problem cases were to be discussed. A member of the Northwood faculty, P. Homes, recommended two students who had worked under his supervision, for graduation. . . . B. Goldensohn moved that degrees be awarded as per custom (seconded). The motion was acted upon favorably by the faculty.

The Dean raised the question of additional Greatwood faculty meetings this semester, to act upon items still on the agenda. J. Thomas moved that there be a meeting next week (Wed.). Seconded and accepted.

A Deans' meeting to discuss policy and planning for the future growth of the college was proposed, to take place June 19-20. Such a meeting would include both faculty and student representatives. A motion to this effect was made by J. Rosenberg, seconded and passed. Recommendations for student and faculty representatives were made, and agreement was reached that ballots are to be sent out.

J. Edson suggested that problem candidates for graduation be resubmitted at the next faculty meeting. Accepted.

R. Wright moved that the mandatory community commitment be dropped next semester. It was voted to table this motion.

The meeting was adjourned at approximately 6:30 P.M.

Respectfully submitted,

Carla R. Thomas, secretary

Office of the President • Goddard College • Plainfield, Vermont

Greatwood Faculty Proposal for Student Evaluation
Meeting on June 18, 1969[66]

1. Requirements for promotion from one grade level to another

    1.1 Satisfactory completion of 2 courses and work program.

    1.2 Not accumulate more than 3 unsuccessful courses and 1 semester's work program to continue in the college.

    1.3 To enter the 16 year
18 courses must have been completed successfully semester work programs = to one less than the number of semesters enrolled at the college.

    1.4 To graduate one must have completed 21 courses, work programs = to one less than semesters in college, and senior study

2. Make up

    2.1 May be by taking 4 courses a semester

    2.2 2 regular work programs in a semester

    2.3 Or take courses elsewhere.

3. My assumptions as to what the Greatwood Faculty sought:

    1. Proposal is an attempt to improve the conditions for learning.

    2. To avoid requiring a student to take an extra semester.

    3. To improve student-teacher relations
Eliminate what students regard as the punitive aspect of evaluation and promotion procedures.

---

[66]These are Tim's notes for the Greatwood faculty discussion of June 18, 1969. Notice the outline and decimal numbers, (like previous instances, handwritten in the original), the resolved self-control and the careful definition of the problem by a series of determinedly optimistic interpretations. It all went off quietly, and participants emerged with a practical relaxation of the issue and of the potential tension. People described it afterward as an unexpectedly friendly conversation. Royce could do this very well. He would appear to wind his scimitar around his head until the swish was audible, and would then settle down for a friendly chat over tea and crackers. It would all work out peaceably.

The final page in this item appears to be taken from the Goddard catalogue of May, 1968. We don't know what it is doing in the file at this point. It is just there. Probably somebody thought it was relevant, and supplied it as a handout at the meeting. Will Hamlin had probably written it. He wrote most things like this.

Some weaknesses in the proposal.

1. Presumably those who do not live up to their commitments fail to because they haven't the strength.

2. To encourage such persons to take on a bigger load is hardly sound.

   Either the make up student will be doing 1/3 more than he would normally do – or he will do what is normal – so why not 3 courses?

3. It shifts the emphasis to accumulation of courses – rather than to how to make better use of one's time and resources.

EVALUATION

John Dewey defined learning as "the reconstruction of experience." The self that needs and plans and acts is not a learning self until needs are examined, plans checked, and actions evaluated. Only then can past experience furnish guidance for present behavior and future growth. Evaluation is thus a constant and necessary part of all education, and, like all of the activity of learning, something individual and personal, to be done by the learner, not to or for him.

Two kinds of standards are involved. One set is derived from the learner's own intentions. He must compare what he has done with what he intended to do; as he does so, it is important that he reconstruct his expectations of himself in the light of the evidence he has himself produced. Thus evaluation is a process not only of using standards but of creating them. The second set of standards has to do with the college's definition of an appropriate use of its resources for learning. The student is asked to evaluate himself against institutional expectations that he will become an increasingly independent learner who may be expected to continue self-education throughout his life; that he already has or will develop the ability to speak and write clearly and accurately; that he can work constructively with other persons on a variety of tasks from maintaining the college to dealing with intellectual problems; that he is constantly growing in his ability to appreciate and evaluate the consequences of his learning and assume responsibility for them. Such standards are at several levels of abstraction: in the reconstruction of experience they may be applied to specific instances or events as well as in the answering of more general questions.

The teacher's role in such evaluation is what it is in other aspects of learning: that of assistant, guide, facilitator, resource. Often he is the person best qualified to know and ask the important questions. Sometimes he can furnish or suggest a model of the behavior or skill the student wishes to learn. He can be useful in holding a mirror up to the student: objectively recording his behavior as a learner, so that he can alter or improve it. No letter or number grades can serve these purposes, and Goddard teachers make no use of them.

A basic evaluative tool for the Goddard student is his cumulative file. Each semester, he prepares a series of reports for his file, one on each study activity, written in conference with the instructor or including instructor notes and comments, one on his work program activities, including comments by faculty or staff job supervisors, and a general evaluation of the semester's work, prepared after a final counsellor conference.

The student's evaluation is primarily his own concern. While counsellors and other faculty members welcome inquiries about students from their parents, and attempt to answer them as completely as possible, it must be understood that material in a student's cumulative file is confidential, open only to him and to members of the college staff. No regular periodic reports of student progress are sent to the student or to his parents. When a specific decision is made about a student (to admit him to the Senior Division at Great-wood, to approve his final-year plan at Northwood, to ask him to leave the college for a period or to spend additional time at college before taking the next academic step, for instance) the student is informed by letter.

– Goddard catalogue, pp. 18-19 (May 1968)

EDUCATION AND HUMAN LIBERATION

(A Talk Prepared For A Seminar At Wilmington College)

April 10, 1975[67]

By Royce S. Pitkin

If we are to think about the relationship of education, to human liberation, it seems to me that we must ask from what is one to be liberated and for what is one to be liberated. Certainly it is essential for its survival that the small child be liberated from complete dependence on others. Obviously, the five-year-old cannot rely on getting its food from the mother's breast nor can ten-year-olds expect their parents to put on and take off their clothes every time a change is desired. And twenty-year-old college students cannot count on, and indeed do not want, their parents to decide whom they shall choose as friends or lovers.

Just as certainly, if one is to survive in any society, one must be liberated from ignorance of the essentials for survival. One simply has to learn how to find food, water, and shelter and, in a society such as ours, most persons must

---

[67]Tim typed this piece as an article or essay on his old ink-filled typewriter probably at home before going to Ohio. This is interesting in its own terms. He had made innumerable addresses everywhere he went, without any preparation at all. He did not do this piece in his customary off-hand way. He took pains with it, and signed it formally. Somehow, it mattered. He made a few editorial changes in it. We made more; there were typos and off-the-page omissions here and there. Of course he may have been invited to Wilmington College specifically to give this "talk" to the Seminar. In that case he might have behaved like any other academic, preparing carefully what he wanted to say. We really don't know the precise circumstances of this later visit, and we are not likely to find them out at this late date. There seems little question but that he was interested in Quaker thought and practice, and had been all his life (cf. the reference above, in the proposed "Program for Liberals of Vermont and Quebec", dating from 1941, more

be able to read. For Frederick Douglass the ability to read enabled him to be liberated from the chains of slavery.

To the extent that they exist one needs to be liberated from rigidity of thought, from narrow-mindedness and from the restrictions that derive from uncritical acceptance of the political opinions, moral codes, and social prejudice of the community in which one was nurtured.

The list could be extended indefinitely but it is more rewarding to dwell upon those things *for* which we want to be liberated. Probably most of us would be willing to say that we find it difficult to agree on just what the good life is. For my part I suggest that we seek liberation to become self-respecting, self-confident, and self-directing individuals who are capable of thinking clearly and independently about the issues that confront us as we make our way through life. At the same time we also seek liberation for participating effectively, helpfully, intelligently, and with love in our families, communities, nations, and world.

The attainment of these and other desired goals has long been regarded as the purpose and function of education. George Washington in his Farewell Address to the American people said, "Promote, then, as an object of primary importance, institutions for the general diffusion of knowledge." And Thomas Jefferson, in 1786, wrote to his friend George Wythe saying, "Preach, my dear Sir, a crusade against ignorance, establish and improve the law for educating the common people." On another occasion, referring to his proposals for an educational system for Virginia, Jefferson said, "The general objects of

---

(Note 67 continued)

than 30 years before.) For a person who made out that he did not know much about philosophy and religion, he was remarkably well informed. This article belongs with the group of pieces which he did occasionally, probably for special reasons, where he had something to say that meant a good deal to him and which he wanted to say with care. In general, we have not looked in this study to Royce's published pieces for his fundamental thought. No published version of this talk has so far turned up anywhere. There are still other lines of study to be followed out in the course of time. Wilfrid Hamlin has kindly offered us the use of his file of another series of Roycean papers, some printed, some not, which again do not appear here; these were his Commencement addresses at the College, the series he gave as President, and the occasions when he was invited back from retirement to talk to a group of graduates. These articles and graduation talks will need to be studied at some point to see what modifications they make in the conception of the work and thought of Royce Pitkin. We have always thought of them as centering on social ideas and social conditions rather than on the particular reaches of education and related areas of thought and practice.

Sufficient unto the day, as Tim so often said, with a touch of classic wit after the Roycean manner, is the evil thereof. (The accent goes on the "-of".) This part of the on-going study of Royce S. Pitkin can conclude here. As suggested above in various of these pages, other studies should surely follow, if possible by different hands. There are some difficult matters to address.

Among the topics which need explication is precisely how the decisions were made in the years following Tim's retirement to discontinue the central experiment with the Multi-Campus College. This clearly held a fundamental place in Tim's conceptualization of the College as he looked forward to what he regarded as its future. We have found enough references in his materials so that we can be certain he never gave up this idea. Aspects of the plan could be delayed for lack of funds at a particular time. In times to come, the prospect would have been that additional funds could have been found. This, and only this, is consistent with what he himself said and wrote, and did not say and write, about the future of the College as he saw it. There is a cloudy area in this matter which needs to be explicated as a basis for reconceptualizing the future of Goddard even at this late date.

—FKD

this law are to provide an education adapted to the years, to the capacity, and to the conditions of everyone, and directed to their freedom and happiness."

Thus from the very beginning of the Union, Americans have affirmed and re-affirmed their faith in education as the process by which the people were to attain liberation. Horace Mann, the great educational leader of the first half of the nineteenth century, even declared that the common school is the greatest discovery ever made by man.

As I struggled with the topic of this seminar: "Human Liberation and Problems in Education," I slowly became aware that what I see as the process of liberation is essentially what I see as the process of education. Both are concerned with the growth of the individual, both are ends and not simply means, both must continue throughout life for no one is ever fully liberated and no one is ever completely educated. So for me, the most promising way to think about human liberation is to think about the nature of education.

I see education and liberation as the process by which an individual develops his abilities and his potentials. Sometimes it is planned and sometimes it just happens, but at all times it involves learning by an individual. It starts with the needs and wants of the child as he first seeks to satisfy his hunger and to command the attention of his parents or those who stand in place of his parents. It continues as the child interacts with his environment – the people, the things, the situations – around him. He gives something from himself to the environment and receives something from it. Often the environment does something to him and he interacts with it. But rarely, if ever, do two children react the same way; each individual has his own motivations, acts on his own impulses, develops his own purposes and thus has his own unique experience within a given situation.

Education, or human liberation, is more than a series of events, an aggregation of activities or a set of experiences; in fact, some activities and experiences may be miseducative and non-liberating. To be educative a new experience must relate to and extend the meaning of previous experience. In a very real sense, education – the process of liberation – involves a reconstruction of experience, taking something out of the old and fitting it into the new and using the new with parts of the old to enable the individual to go on to newer and more meaningful and productive experiences.

Obviously, education is not limited to schools. Quite the contrary for the child learns something in almost every situation that he encounters and his education proceeds in many unplanned situations. For most persons the earliest and most influential educational institution is the home, for here attitudes are developed, interests encouraged and discouraged, beliefs are engendered, creativity is stimulated or repressed, love flourishes or withers, values are generated and personality is formed. With the presence of television and radio in the home powerful external forces affect the education of the chid before he can read or even move freely outside the home.

As soon as the youngster moves about in the community a multitude of forces, including traffic, stores, people, animals, playmates, travel, industries, farms, woods, streams, churches, museums, and theaters, contribute to his education and his liberation from complete dependence on the home. To every encounter with these forces he brings his own set of experiences, his own unique personality and his own motivations and purposes and, accordingly, takes from these encounters the learnings that fit into his experience and that he can inwardly accept.

Wherever one goes and whatever one does he finds himself meeting problems, becoming aware of a need, or feeling insecure or uncertain and facing the necessity of doing something to ease the situation. The degree to which the individual responds by utilizing his prior experience in determining a course of action is a measure of the extent to which the process of liberation is progressing. To put it differently, much of education and human liberation is engagement in the process of solving problems. And the more effectively one interacts with his environment in solving problems the better his liberation proceeds.

How is the process of human liberation to be facilitated? Are there any particular skills or disciplines that lead toward liberation? George Beecher has suggested that we think about personal development as the acquisition of disciplines. These would include valuing – that is, being able to attach values to one's acts (an essential in the liberating process), problem solving, critical thinking, decision making, and creativity. The person who possesses these disciplines in good measure is as ready to deal with events, new situations and the rapid changes that characterize the modern world as one can be expected to be, and is, accordingly, advancing in the liberation process.

Actually, each of these disciplines is a part of problem-solving. From the time one wakes up in the morning until one drops to sleep at night, there is an endless stream of decisions to make and problems to solve. Our success in solving problems, whether big or little, is dependent on our ability to identify them before they get beyond our control, locate the factors involved, think up some trial solutions (that is being creative), test these against our set of values, weigh the pros and cons of each possible course of action, try to anticipate possible consequences (this involves critical thinking), and make a decision. If the process proceeds haltingly and too slowly, life becomes unbearable as events move past us but if the process goes too rapidly, our attempted solutions may make more problems than we started with and we will feel anything but liberated. In any event, the more important the problem seems to us, the more thoughtfully we work at its solution.

Developing the ability to solve problems is most likely to occur when one engages in solving problems that seem important to him. The task of the educational institution is to create a situation in which students are encouraged to bring problems with which they are concerned for help in understanding them and developing techniques for thinking up solutions. These problems may range from the highly personal to those which are international in scope. They may fall within the domain of science or literature or history or they may touch many subjects. As the educator works with students, the aim should be – not to supply solutions and make judgments – but to ask questions, to insist that the student use his own values and draw from his own experience for possible solutions and to anticipate what is likely to follow from the available choices.

If the problems are of the type that directly affects the individual student, he should be allowed to make his own decisions even though the advisor thinks they are wrong. If the student is to develop as a person and is to become liberated, he must be free to make his own decisions and be required to accept responsibility for his decisions.

To achieve the aim of personal development and to further the process of liberation the situation must be such that the student is asked to exercise the traits, disciplines and characteristics that constitute the person he aspires to be. In other words, the situation should be one in which he lives what is to be learned.

If one is to be liberated for participation in the life of the wider community, some thought has to be given as to how that can be achieved. But to talk about education *for* something tends to divert our attention from the educational process itself to some future condition. An unfortunate outcome of such a diversion is that it separates ends and means to such an extent that education and the liberation process comes to be regarded as academic, removed from life and sterile, and the school or college as a place that dwells on the past to reach the future without living in the present.

To avoid this predicament we should talk about education *by* participation in civic and social life or education and liberation *through* citizenship rather than *for* citizenship. Participation in community life means doing things with others and so the educational institution becomes a place where students and teachers do things together, not as bosses and workers, but as citizens having different functions and working toward common goals arrived at by the participants. Participation in civic and social life requires that individuals assume responsibilities as free citizens. Thus the school or college has to be operated in a way that requires students to assume important responsibilities which may extend to actual care and maintenance of physical facilities.

While watching and listening to the educational television program known as Bill Moyer's Journal a few evenings ago I kept thinking about the subject of this seminar. The program dealt mainly with the problems of Jamaica since it became independent but one part told of the organization of an agricultural cooperative on the island of Dominica. One of the members of the cooperative told about the ways in which the members participated in the cooperative, saying, for example, that they had to make decisions as a group, that they were responsible for the care of the crops, and that they had to provide for irrigation of the crops even though they had almost no money with which to buy equipment. As he described each activity he would say with great feeling, "This is education", "This is education for us." To me it was a superb illustration of human liberation of desperately poor people who have been victims of a colonial system over which they had no control. And it was, of course, a moving demonstration of how adults were educating themselves by seeking and finding solutions to problems that are terribly real and pressing.

On visits over a period of years to the State of Gujerat in India I saw a similar process going on among members of a rural dairy cooperative as they worked together to control the sale and processing of their buffalo milk and thereby to liberate themselves to some extent from extreme poverty and domination by others. Here, too, human liberation and education seem to be one and the same.

THE FULOP PORTRAIT

The Fulop Portrait

At the 25th Anniversary Dinner marking a quarter century of Royce's presidency and of Goddard itself in its Plainfield dimension, held in the Fall of 1963, one of the surprises was a portrait of Royce S. Pitkin by Joseph Fulop, of the Goddard Art faculty, produced from the back of the room during the after-dinner program and brought forward to where the Pitkins were sitting at the head table. Joe told how he had done sketches for it in faculty meetings without anyone's noticing, over a considerable period of time, and had finished it at home working from the sketches. The portrait is signed and dated in 1959, so Joe had had it in storage for a while. He kept his collection of canvases in his garage at home, a place where we had once rented storage space for a 1929 air-cooled Franklin automobile. After a while he finished so many canvases that the Franklin simply had to go, to allow him space for his paintings. Even then he still had more canvases than he knew what to do with; he painted constantly. So did his wife, Mounia L. Andre. Over the years they gave away a large number of paintings.

One day in December, 1958 they both arrived unannounced at our house in Calais with a painting by Mounia Andre dated in 1955 which they briskly deposited amid seasonal cheer; it had a note on the back, in Joe's hand: – "Mounia thought, he will find shelter with you."– It was a pieta, an upright head of the dead Christ, bent slightly to one side, in colors sombre but illumined warmly from behind, not in agony but resting, serene, in repose. It has gone wherever we went, in the years since, and now is back again in the

Calais house where it came that day. It has always had a curious power to dominate its surrounding background. Joe and Mounia would have known this was a houseful of Unitarians. They were artists sensitive to the reaches of art beyond the canvases on which they worked. Joe Fulop painted mostly in the abstract in the years we knew him best. Portraits were not his usual mode. We never saw another that he did.

In all directness, Royce Pitkin did not look like this. He had no sternness in his gaze, no curl of lip, no black and brooding shoulders. Art has mystery in its perceptions; the artist seems to try what others may not see. The portrait has always been of great interest to us. Rather than a portrait, we think it may be a different type of painting, abstract in terms of its own. The question of the relation of art to truth also arises. Can artists make mistakes? It depends what the reference is. In the artist's frame of reference alone, there is no other standard by which to judge. It stands by itself, unjudgeable. In another, more realistic frame? Certainly; there are right and wrong delineations, no doubt socially determined. A third possibility is that of the artistic joke – perhaps of artistic mischief. We think this occurs oftener than one might expect. And why not? Is all art serious? Some artists have great senses of humor, and compelling tools at their command. They need only perform their art, and keep silent. Some viewers are sure to take it seriously, convinced that it opens new ways to the real. When this is the case, the artist can hug himself in delight. He has the better of his public. The question endures.

The Fulops retired eventually to North Carolina. The Pitkins used to call on them regularly on their ways to and from family reunions in Florida. They were all good friends. Joe discovered an extinct tree wood which he could carve in 3 dimensions; to obtain it he had to excavate in the Caribbean islands where pieces had been buried in house foundations for three hundred years. Mounia died in 1974, Joe some years later.

The portrait hangs now in the Eliot Pratt Library at Goddard, and is reproduced here with the kind permission of the College.

–FKD

Color photography by Andrew Kline, *AfterImage*,

26 State Street,

Montpelier, Vt. – August 1995.

INDEX